The Future of NATO Expansion

Four Case Studies

This extensively researched book offers a comparative analysis of four East European states – Bulgaria, Romania, Slovakia, and Slovenia – that were invited to become members of the North Atlantic Treaty Organization in 2002. Through a rigorous examination of their postcommunist domestic and foreign policies, economic performance, security situation, campaign for NATO membership, civil-military relations, and the state of their armed forces, Professor Barany demonstrates that in several respects they do not satisfy the Alliance's own admission criteria. He contends that, once it had begun, NATO should continue its expansion process but he argues that there is no pressing reason for NATO's haste. The Alliance should hold off further expansion until the invitees become *fully qualified* for membership. The alternative is to repeat and compound the mistakes of the first wave of enlargement the beneficiaries of which – Poland, Hungary, and the Czech Republic – have been liabilities rather than assets of the Alliance.

Zoltan Barany is the Frank C. Erwin, Jr., Centennial Professor of Government at the University of Texas. His recent books include *The East European Gypsies: Regime Change, Marginality, and Ethnopolitics* (2002) and *Russian Politics: Challenges of Democratization* (co-editor, 2001), both published by Cambridge University Press.

The Future of NATO Expansion

Four Case Studies

ZOLTAN BARANY
University of Texas at Austin

CAMBRIDGE
UNIVERSITY PRESS

CAMBRIDGE
UNIVERSITY PRESS

32 Avenue of the Americas, New York NY 10013-2473, USA

Cambridge University Press is part of the University of Cambridge.

It furthers the University's mission by disseminating knowledge in the pursuit of education, learning and research at the highest international levels of excellence.

www.cambridge.org
Information on this title: www.cambridge.org/9780521821698

© Zoltan Barany 2003

This publication is in copyright. Subject to statutory exception and to the provisions of relevant collective licensing agreements, no reproduction of any part may take place without the written permission of Cambridge University Press.

First published 2003
First paperback edition 2011

A catalogue record for this publication is available from the British Library

Library of Congress Cataloguing in Publication data

Barany, Zoltan D.
The future of NATO expansion : four case studies / Zoltan Barany.
p.   cm.
Includes bibliographical references and index.
ISBN 0-521-82169-X (HB)
1. North Atlantic Treaty Organization – Europe, Eastern.   2. North Atlantic Treaty Organization – Membership.   3. Europe, Eastern – Defenses.   I. Title.
UA646.8 .B37   2003
355'.031'091821–dc21   2002035086

ISBN 978-0-521-82169-8 Hardback
ISBN 978-1-107-40518-9 Paperback

Cambridge University Press has no responsibility for the persistence or accuracy of URLs for external or third-party internet websites referred to in this publication, and does not guarantee that any content on such websites is, or will remain, accurate or appropriate.

To Patti

Contents

Acknowledgments		*page* ix
	Introduction	1
1	The Pros and Cons of Further Enlargement	9
2	Slovakia: Catching Up to Its Neighbors	45
3	Slovenia: A Regional Leader	89
4	Romania: Twelve Years of Disappointments	124
5	Bulgaria: Progress After Seven Wasted Years	175
6	Conclusion	217
References		239
Index		259

Acknowledgments

I received assistance from many individuals who arranged meetings, responded to queries, and were willing to be interviewed. I am grateful to them all but I want to especially thank Anton Bebler, Col. Marian Božik, Col. Péter Deák (Ret.), Col. Anghel Filip (Ret.), Col. János Gömbös (Ret.), Brig. Gen. Mihail Ionescu, Lubomir Ivanov, Lt. Col. Mateusz K. Jastrzebski, Col. Jozef Kapcala, Capt. Ognian Kirilov, Lt. Col. Dušan Kulik, Col. Valeri Ratchev, Velizar Shalamanov, Larry Watts, and Stanislaw Zatorsky. I am also grateful to Major Joseph Derdzinski (USAF), Major Brad Gutierrez (USAF), Jacob Kipp, Matus Korba, Dan Oprescu, Michael Shafir, Jeffrey Simon, Thomas Szajna, Michal Vašečka, and Larry Watts for their assistance of various kinds, from providing source materials to commenting on individual chapters. I thank Joe Derdzinski, Christopher Jones, and James Wirtz for invitations to speak on the issues examined in this book at the U.S. Air Force Academy, the University of Washington, and the U.S. Naval Postgraduate School, respectively, and thus inducing me to rethink my arguments.

This is as good a place as any to pay my respects to my old teacher and friend, Iván Völgyes, who urged me to write this book. He helped generously at the launching of my career and was an indispensable source of contacts after he returned to his beloved Budapest for good in 1994. Iván died in a plane crash on 14 June 2001 in southwestern Hungary, at the age of sixty-four. He was a true character, more full of life than anyone I have ever met. I miss him and the conversations, the jokes, and the meals we will never share.

x   *Acknowledgments*

On an infinitely more cheerful note, this book is dedicated to my wife, Patricia Maclachlan, who tolerated my work schedule and did more than her fair share of caring for our delightful daughter, Catherine, who made her grand entry into the world while I was working on this volume.

I am grateful to the Ford Foundation for a major grant that, while earmarked to support my work on the East European Gypsies, provided the opportunity to do field research for this book as well.

My gratitude is extended to Deans Larry Carver and Richard Lariviere at the University of Texas at Austin. Thanks to their flexibility and support, I was able to devote the entire fall 2001 semester to the preparation of this manuscript.

I wish to thank the anonymous reviewers whose comments made this a better book. And I am grateful to Lewis Bateman and the entire staff at Cambridge University Press for shepherding the manuscript through the publication process.

Introduction

Michael Zantovsky, the chairman of the Czech Senate's Foreign Affairs, Defense, and Security Committee, announced in June 2001 that the planned modernization and professionalization of the Czech Army would take two election terms (i.e., eight years).[1] A month later his counterpart in the Chamber of Deputies (the legislature's lower house), Petr Necas, lamented that Prime Minister Miloš Zeman's cabinet had "done nothing" to promote military reform since the country's accession to the North Atlantic Treaty Organization (NATO).[2] In March 2001 General Lajos Fodor, Chief of the Hungarian Defense Forces' (HDF) General Staff, revealed that the country's air force would be unable to meet NATO's requirements for pilot training "again this year."[3] His views were corroborated by a recent NATO report which proclaimed that the HDF would not be able to fully participate in the Alliance until the end of 2003.[4] NATO leaders have repeatedly castigated not only the Czech Republic and Hungary, but also Poland for the relatively modest sums they spend on defense despite their earlier pledges to reform their militaries in accordance with NATO criteria. They have every right to do so: Since 1999 these countries have been full members of the Alliance.

---

[1] CTK (Czech News Agency, Prague), 14 June 2001.
[2] CTK (Prague), 11 July 2001.
[3] *Népszabadság* (Budapest), 19 March 2001.
[4] See Péter Matyuc, "NATO-jelentés a honvédség hiányosságairól," *Népszabadság*, 6 April 2000.

The enlargement of NATO has been one of the most important events in post-Cold War international affairs, American foreign policy, and East European politics. In 1997, NATO invited the three East-Central European states in which democratization and market-oriented transitions had progressed the farthest – Czech Republic, Hungary, and Poland – to join its ranks.[5] Two years later, the three states became members of the Alliance on the occasion of its fiftieth anniversary summit in Washington, D.C. As the quotations above imply, Czech and Hungarian membership (Poland has performed considerably better) has given NATO few reasons to celebrate the decision to expand.

Still, NATO leaders have maintained that expansion is an on-going process that entails the integration of additional East European states. At its Prague Summit in November 2002, NATO invited seven countries – Bulgaria, Estonia, Latvia, Lithuania, Romania, Slovakia, and Slovenia – that are expected to become full members after the legislatures of the member states and the candidate countries ratify the Alliance's enlargement. In order to avoid the problems resulting from the first round of enlargement, it is important to understand the benefits and drawbacks of subsequent rounds. NATO has set numerous membership criteria and has assisted aspiring members in satisfying them. We must gauge their preparedness to assess the impact they will have on NATO's cohesion, capabilities, and future role. My purpose in this study is to do just that, focusing on four East European states invited to membership: Bulgaria, Romania, Slovakia, and Slovenia.

MAIN ARGUMENTS

This study posits two basic arguments: first, that NATO's expansion to Eastern Europe should continue; and second, that states should fulfill the Alliance's membership criteria prior to becoming full members. Let me flesh out these arguments in a bit more detail.

---

[5] For an examination of the states in the first round of enlargement, see Andrew A. Michta, ed., *America's New Allies: Poland, Hungary, and the Czech Republic in NATO* (Seattle: University of Washington Press, 1999).

Introduction

I opposed the first round of enlargement on the grounds that it was unnecessary and expensive, not to mention potentially dangerous insofar as it threatened to provoke Russia. Nonetheless, once the process had started, I became a supporter of further enlargement. I argue that extending full NATO membership to the four states in my inquiry is desirable for four fundamental reasons. First, given its oft-repeated promises of an "open door policy" (meaning that qualified members would be allowed to join), NATO has a moral obligation to deliver on its pledge. Second, the status quo divides postcommunist states and could inadvertently serve to promote the cause of extremists who might create tensions between member and non-member states. Third, including these four states in NATO will create a security system that will increase the Alliance's deterrent potential and ensure rapid intervention capability in the traditional trouble spots of the Balkans. As such, it will be more useful in strategic terms than the first wave of enlargement in 1999. Finally, a second wave of enlargement that includes these four states will create a geographically contiguous NATO that links Hungary with members on its borders (Slovakia, Romania, and Slovenia) and Greece and Turkey with the rest of the Alliance through Bulgaria.

At the same time, I will argue that rushing the second wave of enlargement makes little sense. Admitting unprepared countries in 1999 was, on balance, a mistake. The experiences of the three new members have tempered much of the enthusiasm in NATO circles about the rapid expansion of the Alliance, and for good reasons. They, with the possible exception of Poland, have been free riders – consumers rather than providers of security. Both the Czech Republic and Hungary have been less than eager contributors to European security since becoming NATO members. Before joining, political elites in both states were quick to promise the kinds of military reforms that Brussels required. Once they had become members, however, their incentives to deliver on those promises had largely disappeared in large part because NATO does not have an expulsion mechanism in place. I believe that it is imperative that the states aspiring to NATO membership actually fulfill all stated requirements before being invited to join. Even more importantly, there is simply no need to rush the incorporation of Bulgaria, Romania, Slovakia, and Slovenia into NATO because they face no serious challenges to their security. A more judicious approach to enlargement will ease the integration of new members and will serve to safeguard alliance cohesion and capabilities.

The international organizations East European states want to join (European Union, NATO) or appease (World Bank, International Monetary Fund, Organization for Security and Cooperation in Europe) have contributed substantially to democratic consolidation in the region – after all, they have the leverage to admit or exclude them. Clearly, it would be useful to determine the extent to which prospective membership specifically in NATO influences policies in aspiring states. Unfortunately, however, this is difficult to do because NATO is seeking many of the same policy adjustments in these countries that are being sought by other international organizations – most importantly the EU. Nevertheless, especially since the first round of enlargement – precisely because of the relatively poor performance of the first three new members with respect to their military affairs – NATO has become more keenly interested in military effectiveness, civil-military relations, defense expenditures, and a host of other issues that other organizations are not concerned with. Therefore, in these instances, a causal link between NATO and domestic policy change may be identified with some measure of confidence.

CASE SELECTION AND RESEARCH METHODS

Why focus on these four countries and not others? After all, there were nine aspirants in NATO's Membership Action Plan (MAP): Albania, Bulgaria, Macedonia, Romania, Slovakia, and Slovenia and the three Baltic States (Estonia, Latvia, and Lithuania). The choice of the four countries is based only partly on the convenient fact that NATO turned them down in 1997. Romania, Slovakia, and especially Slovenia were already serious contenders at that time, though Bulgaria was not yet unambiguously committed to a policy in support of joining the Alliance. These four states also stand out as some of the least studied postcommunist countries. Bulgaria and Slovenia have been especially neglected in the last decade partly because they have not been perceived as pivotal states. Slovakia, on the other hand, has been the victim of diminishing scholarly attention after the 1993 break-up of federal Czechoslovakia. Of the four states in my project, only Romania can be said to have received adequate scholarly attention in the 1990s, due to its relatively

Introduction 5

large physical size and population as well as its dismal failure to live up to its potential.

An evaluation of the remaining five MAP countries' preparedness for NATO enlargement is beyond the scope of this book. The three Baltic states are geographically contiguous with Russia which, in turn, has repeatedly expressed its resolute opposition to, and since 2001, reservations about their NATO membership. The Baltics shared much of their recent history with the Soviet Union – having been part of the USSR for fifty years (1941–1991) – and all of them are home to large ethnic Russian populations which further complicates their relationship with Moscow. These factors set the Baltic states apart from the other six MAP countries which neither share a border with Russia nor have any ethnic Russian minorities.

Albania and Macedonia, on the other hand, are handicapped by different factors. Political, economic, and military reforms have proceeded at a much slower pace in these two states than elsewhere in Eastern Europe – with the exception of Serbia and some of the former Soviet republics. Moreover, Albania and particularly Macedonia are integral parts of a fluid security puzzle. In 2001 Macedonia was involved in a serious armed conflict between government troops and ethnic Albanian rebels who, at the very least, demanded substantial changes in the institutional arrangements of the state. It is clear, however, that the ultimate wish of many Albanians in both northwestern Macedonia and Kosovo is secession and the possible unification with Albania proper even if it is rarely voiced publicly. NATO troops are deployed in both locations to maintain a fragile peace. The uncertain outcome of these conflicts makes it difficult to predict with any measure of confidence Albanian and Macedonian political and military-security trajectories – even in the near future. In sum, Bulgaria, Romania, Slovakia, and Slovenia have not only advanced considerably farther in terms of postcommunist reform processes than Albania and Macedonia, but they have also not had to face the type of security problems confronting those two states.

This book draws on several years of field research in Eastern Europe and dozens of in-depth interviews with Bulgarian, Romanian, Slovak, and Slovene defense officials, military officers, academics, and politicians. I have also interviewed NATO officials and numerous representatives of NATO member states' governments. Furthermore, the book

6 *The Future of NATO Expansion*

benefits from a comprehensive reading of official documents, newspapers, and the scholarly literature published in the four states, Western Europe, and the United States.

OUTLINE AND ANALYTICAL FRAMEWORK

This book is divided into five chapters. Chapter 1 weighs the strengths and weaknesses of the numerous arguments advancing and opposing the first and second rounds of NATO enlargement. It briefly examines the evolution of Russia's position toward NATO expansion and outlines the criteria the Alliance has set for prospective members.

In order to ensure an optimal level of comparability, Chapters 2, 3, 4, and 5 examine the four cases (Slovakia, Slovenia, Romania, and Bulgaria, respectively) according to an identical analytical framework. All of these chapters are divided into four parts. Part I of each chapter analyzes postcommunist domestic politics, including the main political institutions and personalities, electoral results, and governmental changes, particularly those with a bearing on NATO enlargement. The focus then shifts to a brief discussion of economic performance, with particular attention to the European Union accession process. The mechanisms of EU integration are important because they provide yet another measure of the progress of the individual states. Finally, I examine the various challenges to the country's security and the evolution of its military doctrine.

Part II of the empirical chapters evaluates the state's relations with its neighbors, NATO members, and Russia. It also explores campaigns for NATO membership, including levels of public and elite support for NATO operations, the various political forces' views on joining the Alliance, and participation in regional organizations and NATO programs.

Part III concentrates on civil–military relations. It begins by scrutinizing the depoliticization of the armed forces and proceeds to analyze the institutional arrangements of civilian control of the military. Here I am concerned with the role of and the relations between the president, the government, the defense minister, the chief of the general staff, and the legislature and its committees in ensuring balanced civilian oversight of the armed forces. I then identify the deficiencies in civil–military relations – in particular, shortcomings pertaining to the

Introduction

balanced and democratic civilian control of the armed forces – that need to be remedied prior to joining NATO.

Part IV is divided into three sections. The first examines military reform processes, the strengths and weaknesses of their design and implementation, and the degree to which they fulfill NATO criteria. The second focuses on the conditions of armed forces personnel, concentrating on the prestige of the profession; the training, morale, and living standards of the officer corps; and changes in the conscription system. The last section briefly analyzes the state of the armed forces as indicated by changes in its manpower, equipment maintenance and acquisition, and the condition of the country's defense industry.

WHAT THIS BOOK IS AND IS NOT ABOUT

In order to prevent undue expectations I want to lay out clearly what this book is and is not about. The focus of this study is the second round of NATO's enlargement involving four newly invited states: Bulgaria, Romania, Slovakia, and Slovenia. I will summarize the arguments opposing and supporting the first round and prospective second round of NATO expansion. I am interested in arguments germane to the first round only insofar as they form the intellectual and political background for the second round.

My objective here is to ascertain the extent to which the second-round invitees are prepared for membership in the Alliance, using NATO's membership criteria as a guide. The book evaluates the four states' readiness for NATO membership from a comparative perspective and using the case study method. In concert with the widely recognized notion that the decision to enlarge NATO – in the first round, at any rate – was based on political rather than military-security criteria, this book is as much if not more concerned with the four states' domestic and foreign policies, economic performance, and civil–military relations as it is with their military reform processes and weapon acquisition programs.

This study does not provide a detailed analysis of how NATO member states reach the decision to enlarge or not to enlarge the Alliance; nor does it present an in-depth analysis of NATO's internal policies or duplicate the studies already published about how the U.S. government arrived at its decision to expand in 1997.[6] I will, however, summarize the polemics concerning initial NATO enlargement because they remain germane for the subsequent expansion process. This book has also little to say about the wars in the former Yugoslavia and NATO's role therein. This, too, is a topic that has received ample scholarly and journalistic attention and I will discuss it only to the extent that it bears directly on the issues I do want to examine closely.

Finally, this book makes no pretention of building or testing theory.[7] My ambition here is no more and no less than to examine the competing arguments favoring and opposing NATO's enlargement and to assess the credentials of the four invitees for membership in the Alliance. This study, then, is first and foremost a comparative analysis of the postcommunist records of four East European states from the perspective of NATO expansion.

---

[6] See, for instance, Gerald B. Solomon, *The NATO Enlargement Debate, 1990–1997: Blessings of Liberty* (Westport, CT: Praeger, 1998); James M. Goldgeier, *Not Whether But When: The U.S. Decision to Enlarge NATO* (Washington, D.C.: Brookings Institution Press, 1999); and George W. Grayson, *Strange Bedfellows: NATO Marches East* (Lanham, MD: University Press of America, 1999).

[7] For a sample of relevant studies, see Charles L. Glaser, "Why NATO Is Still Best: Future Security Arrangements for Europe," *International Security*, 18:1 (Summer 1993): 5–50; John J. Mearsheimer, "False Promises of International Institutions," *International Security*, 19:3 (Winter 1994): 5–49; Robert B. McCalla, "NATO's Persistence After the Cold War," *International Organization*, 50:3 (Summer 1996): 445–475; John Gerald Ruggie, "Consolidating the European Pillar: The Key to NATO's Future," *Washington Quarterly*, 20:1 (Winter 1997): 109–125; Charles Kupchan, "After Pax Americana: Benign Power, Regional Integration, and the Sources of Stable Multipolarity," *International Security*, 23:2 (Fall 1998): 40–79; *idem.*, ed., *Atlantic Security: Contending Visions* (New York: Council on Foreign Relations, 1998); Dan Reiter, "NATO Enlargement and the Spread of Democracy," *International Security*, 25:4 (Spring 2001): 41–67; and the contributions to Robert W. Rauchhaus, ed., *Explaining NATO Enlargement* (London: Frank Cass, 2001).

I

The Pros and Cons of Further Enlargement

In 1999 three East-Central European countries – the Czech Republic, Hungary, and Poland – joined NATO. Less than a decade prior to the Alliance's enlargement, these three states (the Czech Republic then was still a part of Czechoslovakia) were members of NATO's Cold War nemesis, the Warsaw Pact. The expansion of NATO was the result of a controversial decision surrounded by much public debate. Because this debate is quite relevant to the matter of the Alliance's further expansion, I will briefly revisit the reasoning of its supporters and detractors in Part I of this chapter.

NATO leaders and, more importantly, politicians in Washington, have committed themselves to further expand the Alliance. In June 2002 President George W. Bush signed a measure supporting NATO's enlargement. In October 2002 the U.S. House of Representatives passed a resolution which recommended a "big bang" expansion at the Prague NATO Summit in the following month. Although this decision is just as important as the first round of enlargement was, the debate concerning the desirability of additional expansion has been at best muted. It seems as if scholars, pundits, and public policy experts had said all they wanted to say about NATO enlargement already in the 1990s. In Part II I will examine the arguments (and the logic behind them) for and against the additional expansion of the Alliance. Moreover, I will briefly address such related issues as the future expansion of the European Union and Russian views of NATO expansion. Finally,

The Future of NATO Expansion

the objective of Part III is to answer the question of "What does NATO expect from the states that aspire for membership?"

The expansion of NATO has been a complex issue that reasonable people can disagree about. As I shall demonstrate, both proponents and detractors have made persuasive arguments and, if one fairly weighs the strengths of their reasoning, it is difficult to be unequivocally for or against enlargement. In other words, this is not a black-and-white issue; both alternative decisions – to enlarge or not to – have a number of associated costs and benefits.

PART I. BACKGROUND: NATO ENLARGEMENT, ROUND ONE

The Idea of NATO Expansion

At the July 1990 London Summit Meeting, NATO invited Hungary, Czechoslovakia, Poland, Romania, Bulgaria, and the Soviet Union to establish regular diplomatic liaisons with the Alliance. The founding of the North Atlantic Cooperation Council (NACC) in 1991 signified a further step in the evolution of NATO's relationship with the former communist states by institutionalizing the dialogue between NATO and the former Soviet Bloc. The breakup of the USSR later that year indicated that the NACC would scarcely be the most appropriate vehicle to improve cooperation between NATO and members of the former Warsaw Pact. The inauguration of NATO's Partnership for Peace (PfP) program in 1994 created a more suitable framework in which further interaction and cooperation could be pursued.[1] An equally ambitious undertaking was the establishment of the NATO-Russia Permanent Joint Council in 1997. It preserved the Alliance's latitude to act militarily and circumvent Russian interference but also promised collaboration and consultation between Brussels and Moscow.

Article 10 of the 1949 Washington Treaty, NATO's founding document, states that the Alliance remains open to new members if they

---

[1] For a more detailed discussion, see Jeffrey Simon, *Central European Civil-Military Relations and NATO Expansion* (Washington, D.C.: National Defense University, McNair Paper 39, 1995), 1–9; *NATO Handbook* (Brussels: NATO, 1995), 31–58; Nicholas Williams, "Partnership for Peace: Permanent Fixture or Declining Asset?" *Survival*, 38:1 (Spring 1996): 98–110; and *idem.*, "The Future of Partnership for Peace," *Balkan Forum* 4:2 (June 1996) 255–283.

The Pros and Cons of Further Enlargement

fulfill certain criteria. The centerpiece of NATO is still the Treaty's Article 5 which considers an armed attack against any alliance member as an attack against all of them and prescribes taking action "including the use of armed force to restore and maintain the security of the North Atlantic area." As former West German Chancellor Helmut Schmidt has pointed out, however, the territory protected by this obligation is clearly delineated in Article 6 and it includes neither the Balkans nor the Middle East.[2] With the joining of Greece and Turkey in 1952, NATO's North Atlantic geographical character changed irrevocably and the Alliance's post-1989 expansion obviously promises to shift its posture further still.

By the early 1990s a growing number of East European states came to the conclusion that the only logical solution to their countries' security dilemmas was full membership in NATO. Their governments began to lobby the Alliance and its member states through diplomatic channels and the media, and, once PfP created a more suitable framework, through NATO itself.

At the same time, the Alliance, in the midst of an identity crisis in the wake of the Cold War, had to reassess its strategic concept, its views of the types of war or hostilities it could expect to deter and fight and, more broadly, reevaluate its role in international security and politics.[3] Some observers suggested that the expansion of the Alliance, precisely owing to its post-Cold War identity crisis, gave it a new lease on life, a new raison d'être. It was also important to recognize, as U.S. Senator Richard Lugar famously noted in 1993, that "The common denominator of all the new security problems in Europe is that they all lie beyond NATO's current borders."[4] In other words, promoting stability in non-NATO Europe – an effort that became linked with the Alliance's expansion – now became one of the key objectives of NATO. Lugar's colleague, Senator Joseph Biden asserted that "approving enlargement

---

[2] See Schmidt, "The Transatlantic Alliance in the 21st Century," *NATO Review: 50th Anniversary Edition*, 22. For a more general discussion of NATO's origins see Francis H. Heller and John R. Gillingham, eds., *NATO: The Founding of the Atlantic Alliance and the Integration of Europe* (New York: St. Martin's Press, 1992).

[3] See, for instance, Joseph Lepgold, "NATO's Post-Cold War Collective Action Problem," *International Security*, 23:1 (Summer 1998): 78–106; and *The Alliance's Strategic Concept* (Brussels: NATO, 1999).

[4] Richard G. Lugar, "NATO: Out of Area or Out of Business," press release, 2 August 1993.

12   *The Future of NATO Expansion*

was essentially a referendum on the Alliance itself."[5] Others argued that expansion was merely symptomatic of, rather than central to, NATO's deeper transformation.[6]

The prospect of including former members of the Warsaw Pact in NATO generated a spirited debate both in member states and in countries desiring to join. Not unexpectedly, the enlargement process had a strong and negative impact on Russia as well. The changes in the balance of forces in Europe implied by the NATO accession of East European states could not but incite Moscow's protest.

The debate produced some odd intellectual couplings suggestive of the intricate nature of the matter. After all, there are not many issues on which Bill Clinton, Václav Havel, Jesse Helms, and Henry Kissinger find themselves on the same side opposing Richard Barnett, Paul Nitze, Phyllis Schlafly, and the editors of *The Nation*.[7] (The first group was in favor while the second against enlargement.)

Arguments Supporting Enlargement

According to Deputy Secretary of State Strobe Talbott, NATO decided to accept new members for three main reasons.[8] First, collective defense remains an imperative need of European and transatlantic security. Second, the prospect of NATO membership provides the nations of Eastern Europe and the former Soviet Union with additional incentives to strengthen their democratic institutions, respect human rights, and so on. Third, the promise of membership could also foster greater willingness among these nations to resolve disputes peacefully and contribute to peacekeeping operations. Representatives of the Clinton Administration and other supporters of enlargement proposed

---

[5] Clay Clemens, "The Strategic and Political Consequences of NATO Enlargement," in James Sperling, ed., *Two Tiers or Two Speeds? The European Security Order and the Enlargement of the European Union and NATO* (Manchester, England: University of Manchester Press, 1999), 140.

[6] Daniel N. Nelson and Thomas S. Szayna, "NATO's Metamorphosis and Its New Members," *Problems of Post-Communism*, 45:4 (July–August 1998): 33.

[7] Adam Garfinkle, "NATO Enlargement: What's the Rush?" *The National Interest*, No. 46 (Winter 1996/1997): 102; and John Lewis Gaddis, "Remember the Titanic," *New York Times*, 27 April 1998.

[8] Strobe Talbott, "Why NATO Should Grow," *Balkan Forum*, 3:4 (December 1995): 28–29.

The Pros and Cons of Further Enlargement 13

numerous other arguments favoring enlargement. Let us consider them briefly.

Cheap. According to a number of analysts, NATO enlargement was a bargain. Some suggested that the cost to the United States, perhaps $150 to 200 million a year, was well worth it and ought to be considered as an investment in democracy.[9] Others argued that even though the estimates of the Pentagon, the Congressional Budget Office (CBO), and the RAND Corporation varied widely, the price of enlargement was "moderate and affordable." The costs were modest especially when considering that they stretched out through ten to fifteen years and the United States was responsible for only a fraction of the total bill.[10] NATO military leaders believed that the expansion could be accomplished for a maximum of $2 billion over ten years. This number, however, was less than one-tenth of the Pentagon's exceedingly modest estimate, and one-fortieth of the CBO estimate.[11]

Fostering Democracy. One of the main arguments of enlargement supporters was that democracy and free markets were the best bases on which to build prosperity, security, and international peace. President Clinton noted that NATO could "do for Europe's East what it did for Europe's West: prevent a return to local rivalries, strengthen democracy against future threats" and create the conditions for prosperity.[12] Not to enlarge NATO would be to encourage the division of Europe to a self-confident and secure West and an unstable and insecure East. This argument had nothing to do with military power and the political aspirations of other countries. Rather, members of the Clinton Administration made a concerted effort to convince Congress that NATO membership for Eastern Europe was key to safeguarding and promoting democracy and free markets there. They were unable to

---

[9] See, for instance, David C. Gompert, "NATO Enlargement: Putting the Cost in Perspective," *Strategic Forum*, no. 129 (October 1997): 1–5.

[10] See Richard L. Kugler, "Costs of NATO Enlargement: Moderate and Affordable," *Strategic Forum*, no. 128 (October 1997): 1–6.

[11] Amos Perlmutter and Ted Galen Carpenter, "NATO's Expensive Trip East: The Folly of Enlargement," *Foreign Affairs*, 77:1 (January–February 1998): 2.

[12] Cited by Stephen A. Cambone, "The Strategic Implications of NATO Enlargement," in Stephen J. Blank, ed., *From Madrid to Brussels: Perspectives on NATO Enlargement* (Carlisle, PA: U.S. Army War College, Strategic Studies Institute, 1997), 9.

make a good case, however, as to "why a cold-war military alliance, rather than the European Union, [was] the best way to secure those aims."[13]

Benefits for NATO and the United States. The proponents of NATO enlargement admitted that East European armed forces added little to the Alliance's capabilities but they argued that new NATO members in the region would provide crucial forward-basing options. Such options, especially considering the volatility of the Balkans, represented an important benefit for NATO. The enlargement of NATO, the argument went, would place the Alliance and the United States firmly in the middle of Europe, between Berlin and Moscow, and thereby in position to secure lasting stability for Eastern Europe. Although gaining this strategic foothold in East-Central Europe was important, the significance of developing security arrangements with the much more sensitive Baltic states and with the far more explosive Balkans was even more so.

Enlargement supporters suggested that fearing NATO expansion was unfounded because adding qualified members would only have a positive effect on the Alliance. Enlargement would increase the effectiveness of NATO's deterrents against potential regional aggressors and provide NATO with a wider pool of participants in future operations.[14] Few of those championing enlargement, however, bothered to discuss the extent to which those countries considered for membership were "qualified."

NATO – the only international organization in Europe of which the United States was a recognized leader – would continue to be the institution through which the United States could best pursue its interests in Europe.[15] Therefore, NATO expansion would increase Washington's ability to shape East-Central and Southeastern European political developments and security.

Security for Eastern Europe. Following the fall of state socialism, East European countries found themselves in a security vacuum. After the

---

[13] "Tinkering with Europe," *New York Times*, 12 December 1996.

[14] See, for instance, Janusz Bugajski, "Key Elements of Romania's Security Strategy," in Kurt W. Treptow and Mihail E. Ionescu, eds., *Romania and Euro-Atlantic Integration* (Iasi: Center for Romanian Studies, 1999), 57.

[15] Cambone, "The Strategic Implications of NATO Enlargement," 14.

dissolution of the Warsaw Pact and the subsequent withdrawal of Soviet troops, the region's governments realized that they lacked the capacity to defend themselves. In some cases, such as Hungary, countries possessed virtually no air defense. Although they did call to life a number of regional organizations, these had minimal or no military-security dimensions. The most important of these bodies, the Visegrad Four (Czech Republic, Hungary, Poland, Slovakia), for instance, paid scant attention to security concerns.[16]

The post-Cold War period presented East European states with a host of security threats for which they were woefully unprepared owing to lacking political commitment, missing experience, and the absence of financial resources. The magnitude of these challenges was graphically illustrated by the wars in the former Yugoslavia which directly affected several states aspiring to NATO membership. But other, less conventional security challenges for Eastern Europe are also abound. These include growing organized crime that respects no international boundaries; terrorism; money laundering; illegal cross-border trafficking in humans, drugs, and arms; and unchecked international migration. In this type of security environment it was important to prevent neighbors from exploiting each other's weaknesses. Furthermore, to discourage Germany and Russia, the two regional heavyweights, from reasserting their influence was also a key consideration.

Leaders of the Alliance recognized that NATO was the only institution that could guarantee East European security. Thus, they believed, actual membership in the Alliance for these states was the way to go.

Good for Russia. The Clinton Administration and its supporters insisted that NATO enlargement was not directed against anyone. The Administration rejected the notion of expansion as an anti-Russian measure and suggested that, in fact, it was going to benefit Russia by stabilizing a historically volatile region. The Administration admitted that there was no Russian threat but did not address the obvious

---

[16] See, for instance, Zoltan Barany, "Regional Security: Visegrad Four Contemplate Separate Paths," *Transition*, 1:14 (11 August 1995): 56–60; and Valerie Bunce, "Regional Cooperation and European Integration: The Visegrad Group," in Peter Katzenstein, ed., *Mitteleuropa: Between Europe and Germany* (Providence, RI: Berghahn Books, 1998), 240–284.

question of "why not invite Russia, too?"[17] Finding a satisfactory answer to this query could have prevented a lot of potential problems.

Incidentally, other proponents of the enlargement, like Zbigniew Brzezinski, Henry Kissinger, and William Odom, contended that the outcome of Moscow's democratization experiment was far from certain and though Russia might have lost its empire it did not lose its imperial ambitions. NATO's enlargement, then, was an insurance policy against the potential future reassertion of such aspirations.[18] In other words, given its size and historical proclivities, a resurgent Russia in the future was likely to threaten Eastern Europe again. Therefore, it made eminent sense to seize the opportunity and incorporate lands vulnerable to Russia into NATO.

Yet other enlargement backers pointed out that there was no evidence of any "implicit bargain" as Russian and other politicians claimed, that the Western alliance would not expand if the Warsaw Pact dissolved. That is, NATO had no "moral obligation" to limit its own membership. Moreover, not to expand NATO would be taken by the Russians as tacit U.S. acceptance of Moscow's right to define Eastern Europe as its own security sphere.[19]

Arguments Opposing Enlargement

In a *New York Times* article George F. Kennan, the grand old man of American foreign policy, called NATO expansion into Eastern Europe "the most fateful error of American policy in the entire post-Cold War era."[20] Another prominent observer of U.S. foreign affairs, Yale University historian John Lewis Gaddis, noted in the same newspaper that though normally historians agreed on little, he "had difficulty finding any colleagues who think NATO expansion is a good idea. Indeed, I can recall no other moment when there was less support in our profession for a government policy."[21]

---

[17] Jack Mendelsohn in "The Case against NATO Expansion," *Current History*, 97:617 (March 1998): 134.

[18] See William E. Odom, "NATO's Expansion: Why the Critics Are Wrong," *The National Interest*, No. 39 (Spring 1995): 39–40.

[19] See Garfinkle, "NATO Enlargement: What's the Rush?" 102–103.

[20] George F. Kennan, "A Fateful Error," *New York Times*, 5 February 1997.

[21] Gaddis, "Remember the Titanic," *New York Times*, 27 April 1998.

The Pros and Cons of Further Enlargement

A June 1997 open letter signed by former senators Bill Bradley, Gary Hart, and Sam Nunn, as well as foreign policy experts such as Robert S. McNamara, Jack Matlock, and Paul H. Nitze, called the decision to expand NATO "a policy error of historic proportions."[22] As Michael Mandelbaum, one of the signatories and perhaps the most eloquent representative of enlargement opponents, succinctly summarized, "NATO expansion, under the present circumstances and as currently envisioned, is at best premature, at worst counterproductive, and in any case largely irrelevant to the problems confronting the countries situated between Germany and Russia."[23]

Kennan, Gaddis, Mandelbaum, and others on this side of the debate were skeptical about enlargement for several important reasons.

Expensive. The cost of enlargement was one of the few areas in which substantial disagreement centered not on the issue of expansion per se, but on the magnitude of American, NATO, and East European contribution to its considerable cost. Amos Perlmutter and Ted Galen Carpenter convincingly argued not only that if NATO expansion was taken as more than an empty political gesture, it was going to be extremely expensive, but also that the Clinton Administration was quite unaware of the real costs. Moreover, they contended that it was the United States, not our NATO allies or the East Europeans, who would have to foot the lion's share of the bill.[24]

One reason why the administration may not have had a clear idea of the price tag of expansion was that the three major analyses of the issue came up with very different conclusions. The 1996 study of the Congressional Budget Office (CBO) suggested that the cost of the enlargement process during 1996–2010 was $61 billion to $125 billion of which the U.S.'s share was between $5 billion and $19 billion. The cost calculations of the RAND report, based on optimistic evaluations of the future strategic environment, arrived at figures between $30 billion to $52 billion. Its authors argued not

---

[22] "Open Letter to President Clinton," in Robert W. Rauchhaus, ed., *Explaining NATO Enlargement* (London: Frank Cass, 2001), 203–206.

[23] Michael Mandelbaum, "Preserving the New Peace: The Case Against NATO Expansion," *Foreign Affairs*, 72:3 (May–June 1995): 9. See also *idem.*, *The Dawn of Peace in Europe* (New York: Twentieth Century Fund, 1997).

[24] Perlmutter and Carpenter, "NATO's Expensive Trip East," 2–6.

only that this price was affordable for all concerned but also that alternative arrangements to ensure East European security would be far more costly.[25] The Defense Department's own report concluded that NATO's expansion would cost no more than $27 billion to $35 billion.

All of these studies and, implicitly, the figures they generated had serious limitations. Although the CBO report's upper limit was based on plausible assumptions about future security situations, the RAND and Pentagon estimates, according to Perlmutter and Carpenter, were "based on Pollyannaish security scenarios."[26] The former essentially discounted any future security threat from Russia (which could have easily multiplied their cost estimates) whereas the latter's calculations were clearly affected by political speculation. More precisely, as off-the-record comments acknowledged, the Defense Department's main priority was "to keep costs down to reassure Congress as well as the Russians.... There was a strong political imperative to low-ball the figures."[27]

Unnecessary. Mandelbaum argued that, in contrast to what enlargement supporters were saying, there was no security vacuum in Europe.[28] Instead, a common European security system was taking shape complete with nuclear and conventional arms control agreements and a number of treaties concluded without outside pressures and after serious negotiations. Moreover, military forces across Europe were reshaped and were far more suitable for defensive than for offensive operations. Furthermore, as a result of verification acts and programs like "Open Sky" agreements, each country was cognizant of what its neighbors were doing with their forces. Others claimed that extending NATO membership to Poland, Hungary, and the Czech Republic was doubly unnecessary because these countries faced neither external nor internal threat of any sort.[29] In other words, since

---

[25] See Ronald D. Asmus, Richard L. Kugler, and F. Stephen Larrabee, "What Will NATO Enlargement Cost?" *Survival*, 38:3 (Autumn 1996): 5–26.

[26] Perlmutter and Carpenter, "NATO's Expensive Trip East," 2.

[27] Ibid., 4.

[28] Mandelbaum, "Preserving the New Peace," 11.

[29] See, for instance, Michael E. Brown, "Minimalist NATO: A Wise Alliance Knows When to Retrench," *Foreign Affairs*, 78:3 (May–June 1999): 206.

The Pros and Cons of Further Enlargement

there was no Russian threat and there was no security vacuum, NATO enlargement would represent a geopolitical overreach of a dangerous kind.[30]

NATO and Democracy. The Clinton Administration and other NATO states portrayed membership in the Alliance as a reward for states that succeeded in consolidating democracies and establishing market economies. But, opponents argued, democracy was its own reward. Besides, NATO was in the "security business" not in the "democratization business." In any event, if the Alliance was truly interested in protecting democracy then it should have extended membership to states where democracy was far from consolidated (e.g., Albania, Romania, Russia, Ukraine) and not to those where these objectives had already been reached.[31]

Opponents also noted that the primary aim of NATO was never that countries within the Alliance remain free-market democracies.[32] Greece and Turkey were hardly consolidated democracies when they joined. Furthermore, there was no solid evidence that NATO had a decisive influence on its members' progress toward democracy, witness the generals' rule in Greece and Turkey's lackluster democratic development. Brussels was interested in these countries not as models of democracy but as strategically important real estate.

Potential Entanglements. By extending membership to East European states, NATO and the United States could become party to flare-ups in the traditional animosities among the region's states. Hungary, with over three million of its co-nationals living in neighboring states, has had tense relations with Romania, Slovakia, and Serbia (Yugoslavia) since the 1920s. Neither could relations between Poland and Belarus or Romania and Bulgaria, be described as stable or

---

[30] Garfinkle, "NATO Enlargement," 106.

[31] See Dan Reiter, "Why NATO Enlargement Does Not Spread Democracy," *International Security*, 25:4 (Spring 2001): 41–67; and correspondence on "NATO and Democracy" by Harvey Waterman, Dessie Zagorcheva, and Dan Reiter in *International Security*, 26:3 (Winter 2001/02): 221–235.

[32] James Chace, "A Strategy to Unite Rather Than Divide Europe," in Carpenter and Conry, eds., *NATO Enlargement: Illusions and Reality* (Washington, D.C.: Cato Institute, 1998), 179–180.

20   *The Future of NATO Expansion*

harmonious. Future membership for the three Baltic States – all with large ethnic Russian minorities – opened yet another cluster of delicate questions.

Why Antagonize Russia? Opponents of the enlargement suggested that NATO expansion *was* about Russia, which was sure to be displeased by it. The Soviet Union had militarily occupied several of the aspiring NATO members for decades. Moscow agreed to the reunification of the two Germanies in 1990 and to withdraw its forces from East-Central Europe in the early 1990s. According to Russian politicians including former President Mikhail Gorbachev, the West implicitly agreed not to expand NATO in return for Soviet acquiescence.[33] Although NATO leaders suggested that diplomatic overtures made by the United States and NATO and the creation of the NATO-Russia Permanent Joint Council pacified Russian political elites; they were clearly wrong.[34]

Those skeptical about expansion argued that an economically and militarily emaciated Russia ridden with enormous internal problems could hardly pose a security threat to Eastern Europe. Ironically, the Baltic states, the only countries that could credibly portray themselves as potential future victims of Russian imperialism, were not seriously considered for membership in the first round of enlargement, even though they had surpassed all others in the consistency with which they regarded NATO as the only suitable safeguard of their security.[35]

The expansion of NATO was certain to encourage anti-Western political forces in Russia. This expected result squarely contradicted the Clinton Administration's objective to strengthen the liberal democratic elements in the Russian political scene. NATO enlargement, an issue that even the most pro-Western Russian politicians vocally opposed, was scarcely conducive to the promotion of Russian democracy. In essence, one could have hardly designed a program that was more likely to enable Russian nationalists. Furthermore, since Russia was

---

[33] See Anatol Lieven, "A New Iron Curtain," *The Atlantic Monthly* (January 1996), 22; and George F. Kennan's letter in *The National Interest*, no. 51 (Spring 1998): 118.

[34] See Owen Harries, "The Danger of Expansive Realism," *The National Interest*, No. 50 (Winter 1997/98): 4; and Brown, "Minimalist NATO," 206–207.

[35] Vojtech Mastny, "Reassuring NATO: Eastern Europe, Russia, and the Western Alliance," *Forsvarsstudier* (Oslo), no. 5 (1997): 71.

militarily weak, politically chaotic, and preoccupied with its internal problems (e.g., Chechnya, economic crises) the West had a great deal of time to expand NATO if and when Russia did become a threat to its neighbors. In sum, as Carpenter and Conry pointed out, there was a profound conceptual contradiction in Washington's enlargement policy and the way it related to Russia.[36]

EU, not NATO. Most East European states have always been far more interested in EU rather than NATO membership. The accession criteria for joining the EU, however, are infinitely more complex and difficult to satisfy than the conditions NATO set. Many observers have suggested that, in all likelihood, the EU's expansion would make NATO enlargement unnecessary. Although EU membership for some of the region's states was not going to be realistic in the short term (say, within a decade), there was also no compelling reason why they had to be integrated into NATO quickly given the absence of security threats to them.[37] As Mandelbaum asked, "What would be the adverse consequences of delaying NATO expansion or deciding on a better course?" His answer ("There would be none.") rang true to those who doubted the need for rapid action.[38]

Militarily Makes Little Sense. It has been widely acknowledged from the beginning of the debate that the enlargement of NATO is a political decision not a military one. After all, even the best prepared East European armed forces were light-years behind NATO armies in terms of combat readiness, equipment, training, and other factors. Alliance leaders readily admitted that the military preparedness of aspiring members would not be a key criterion of accession. Javier Solana, NATO's former Secretary-General, conceded in 1996 that the Alliance would not place "undue emphasis on military aspects of

---

[36] Ted Galen Carpenter and Barbara Conry, "Introduction," in Carpenter and Conry, eds., *NATO Enlargement: Illusions and Reality* (Washington, D.C.: Cato Institute, 1998), 5–6. See also Bruce M. Russett and Allan C. Stam, "Courting Disaster: An Expanded NATO vs. Russia and China," *Political Science Quarterly*, 113:3 (Fall 1998): 361–382.

[37] See, for instance, Amos Perlmutter, "Political Alternatives to NATO Expansion," in Carpenter and Conry, eds., *NATO Enlargement*, 238–240.

[38] Michael Mandelbaum in "The Case against NATO Expansion," *Current History*, 97:617 (March 1998): 133.

enlargement."[39] Hungarian Prime Minister Viktor Orbán openly admitted that "our contribution to security should be measured by more than the strength of our tanks and fighters." He, too, acknowledged, that NATO membership for his country was regarded as "recognition of the success our nation has achieved in the last decade."[40] Anyone familiar with the state of East European armies knew that their transformation from "security users" to "security contributors" would take many years and hundreds of millions of dollars.

Where Will It End? NATO committed itself to an open door policy, meaning that those European states that satisfy admission criteria would be eligible for membership. As Robert C. Tucker lamented, "the extent of future NATO has never been specified and the logic of the administration's policy ... point to the eventual inclusion of virtually all states situated between the old NATO and the present Western border of Russia."[41]

The question that was voiced by a number of observers was how large would NATO eventually become? If the nine Membership Action Plan (MAP, a program initiated for candidate members at the 1999 Washington Summit) states were to become members along with Austria, Finland, and Sweden – where there was considerable domestic political support for NATO accession – the Alliance could have as many as thirty member states. The opponents of expansion argued that if the open door policy was taken literally, enlargement would result in a weakened NATO in which consensus was arrived at with difficulty, obligations were diluted, and actions were enfeebled.[42] Quite simply, they argued, there were limits as to how far could the Alliance grow in the short and medium term. Moreover, the willingness of established NATO members to make a serious commitment to the security of an ever growing number of East European states was questionable at best.

[39] Javier Solana, "NATO and the New Security Architecture," *Balkan Forum* 4:2 (June 1996): 8.

[40] See Orbán's contribution to *NATO Review: 50th Anniversary Edition* (Brussels: NATO, 1999), 26.

[41] Robert W. Tucker, "Reflections of a Repentant Sinner," *The National Interest*, No. 51 (Spring 1998): 125.

[42] See, for instance, Lev Voronkov, "The Challenges of NATO Enlargement," *Balkan Forum*, 5:2 (June 1997): 5–46; and Clay Clemens, "The Strategic and Political Consequences of NATO Enlargement," 139–159.

The First Round of Enlargement: Selecting New Members

As James Goldgeier argues, it would have been hard to find individuals in the executive and legislative branches of the U.S. government in 1993 who thought enlarging NATO was a good idea.[43] And yet, in the end, it was the United States, NATO's undisputed leader, that led the Alliance throughout the process.

When considering NATO's expansion, it is useful to remember that all member states must approve this action. Therefore, when the Clinton Administration committed itself to enlargement, it had to restrict its support to countries whose inclusion would be met with support in Congress.[44] The most support was garnered by states with consolidated democracies and relatively well-functioning market economies. Of these, Poland was clearly the front-runner. The Czech Republic received somewhat less support owing to its particularly weak military, and limited enthusiasm about membership and stepped up military expenditures. Hungary proved a somewhat less popular choice mostly for two reasons. First, it did not share a border with the other two or any other NATO member, thus it would have to become an "island" in the Alliance. Second, and more importantly, large Hungarian ethnic minorities lived in virtually all of Hungary's neighbors and with several of these Budapest's relations were not devoid of tension. It was not unreasonable to surmise that Hungary, once it enjoyed NATO's protective umbrella, might be more aggressive in demanding improvements in the conditions of its co-nationals.

The State Department was against the inclusion of Romania and Slovenia because, they argued, if these two countries were included then membership for the three Baltic states would at least had to be addressed. The Administration, however, wanted to postpone a serious consideration of Estonia, Latvia, and Lithuania for as long as possible. In any event, Romania and Slovenia had several strikes against them.

---

[43] See James M. Goldgeier, *Not Whether But When: The U.S. Decision to Enlarge NATO* (Washington, D.C.: Brookings Institution Press, 1999), 3.

[44] For the account of a participant, see Gerald B. Solomon, *The NATO Enlargement Debate, 1990–1997: Blessings of Liberty* (Westport, CT: Praeger, 1998). For a more scholarly look at how the campaign for NATO enlargement was conducted in Washington, see George W. Grayson, *Strange Bedfellows: NATO Marches East* (Lanham, MD: University Press of America, 1999).

Romania, though the most ardent campaigner for membership, only elected a government seemingly committed to substantial political and economic reforms in late 1996 and was far from consolidating its democracy. Moreover, it did not have a functioning market economy. Slovenia's military power was insignificant and its status as a former republic of Yugoslavia raised – mostly unjustified – doubts in many minds. Furthermore, Ljubljana behaved in a rather withdrawn manner during the crises in the former Yugoslavia and its uncooperative stance earned it few friends in Washington. The question of why not Slovakia is an obvious one (after all, Slovak membership would have permitted Hungary to share boundaries with another NATO member) but it also has an easy answer. Until 1998 Slovakia was under the quasi-authoritarian rule of Vladimír Mečiar which effectively disqualified it.

It should be noted that within the Alliance both Slovenia and Romania had powerful backers. Though France expressed doubts about enlargement until Jacques Chirac became president in May 1995, afterward Paris was aggressively pursuing Romanian membership. French support for Bucharest was based on strong historical and cultural ties, in order not to separate Romania and Hungary (given the minority problem), to foster "Balkan stability," and because Romania could be a future supporter of France in the Alliance.[45] According to some observers, the French backing of Romania was also calculated on the assumption that Paris could not lose by supporting Bucharest: If Romania was rebuffed, France would not lose face but if it were accepted, Paris could take credit.[46]

Slovenia's backers included senior U.S. Senators, such as Joseph Biden as well as NATO member states, especially Italy. The main arguments in Slovenia's favor were its consolidated democracy and market economy, its fine record of minority policies, its aforementioned advantageous geographical situation, and the relatively small expected cost

---

[45] David S. Yost, *NATO Transformed: The Alliance's New Roles in International Security* (Washington, D.C.: United States Institute of Peace Press, 1998), 114–115. See also, Karl-Heinz Kamp, "NATO Entrapped: Debating the Next Enlargement Round," *Survival*, 40:3 (Autumn 1998): 175–177.

[46] Jonathan Eyal, "NATO's Enlargement: Anatomy of a Decision," *International Affairs*, 73:4 (October 1997): 708.

The Pros and Cons of Further Enlargement

of its integration.[47] The Baltic states also had some important support from NATO's Nordic members (Denmark and Norway). Nonetheless, Copenhagen and Oslo seemed to realize that Baltic membership at the time was a more sensitive issue than what the Alliance was prepared to tackle.

Eventually, supporters of additional prospective NATO members had to defer to the United States. Expansion clearly hinged on Washington's willingness to provide its indispensable strategic commitment and it was the United States that would incur the principal liability for honoring NATO security guarantees.[48] The disagreements over the merits of NATO's enlargement did not divide the Alliance as much as spurred debates in every member state. Ultimately, as Michael Howard has written, "The decision to expand was forced through by the United States, yet opposition to this step has been more extensive in the United States than anywhere else."[49]

PART II. NATO ENLARGEMENT, ROUND TWO

The 1997 Madrid Summit, at which the three new East-Central European members were invited, represents a milestone in the history of NATO but by no means the end of the enlargement process. In accordance with Article 10 of the North Atlantic Treaty, the Alliance remains open to further accessions.[50] In fact, NATO leaders have maintained that NATO's expansionist agenda had to be extended and that it had to come to represent yet another mission in the Alliance's repertoire. At NATO's 1999 Washington Summit aspiring states became participants of the Membership Action Plan (MAP)

[47] Goldgeier, *Not Whether But When*, 120. Slovenia was the only state, other than the three eventually invited, whose NATO membership received the explicit support of the United Kingdom. See Jiří Šedivý, "The Puzzle of NATO Enlargement," *Contemporary Security Policy*, 22:2 (August 2001): 7.

[48] Robert E. Hunter, "Maximizing NATO: A Relevant Alliance Knows How to Reach," *Foreign Affairs*, 78:3 (May–June 1999): 195.

[49] Michael Howard, "An Unhappy Successful Marriage: Security Means Knowing What to Expect," *Foreign Affairs*, 78:3 (May–June 1999): 174. See also Charles A. Kupchan, "The Origins and Future of NATO Enlargement," in Robert W. Rauchhaus, ed., *Explaining NATO Enlargement* (London: Frank Cass, 2001), 130–135.

[50] See the NATO communique, "NATO's Enlargement," Press Info, Madrid Summit, 8–9 July 1997.

The Future of NATO Expansion

program. The MAP was conceived to assure candidates that Article 10 was not a hollow promise and to assist them in preparing for membership. MAP states were told that their progress in satisfying membership criteria would be reviewed annually by NATO foreign and defense ministers and, more comprehensively, at the Alliance's Prague Summit in late 2002.[51] At that event seven of the nine MAP participants received invitations and should become full members of NATO in May 2004.

Arguments Against Further Enlargement

Lessons from the First Round. The first round of NATO's enlargement was indisputably a political decision in full recognition of the fact that the new members had profound and long-term military deficiencies. Having said this, the integration of Poland, the Czech Republic, and Hungary into NATO has been more difficult than expected. Their armed forces are poorly equipped, inadequately and/or inappropriately trained (save for a few specialized units), and insufficiently reformed. Several experts contend that the military models (force structure, doctrine, personnel policies, etc.) and ways of thinking and problem-solving inherited from Soviet/Warsaw Pact times remain firmly embedded in East-Central European defense establishments.[52]

All three states have needed continuous NATO prodding to increase their defense expenditures, notwithstanding their ardent promises to meet NATO guidelines *prior* to the invitation.[53] Modernization of equipment, reduction of manpower, and bringing training and

---

[51] See "The Reader's Guide to the NATO Summit in Washington, 23–25 April 1999" (Brussels: NATO Office of Information and Press, 1999), 83.

[52] A good summary along these lines is Marybeth Peterson Ulrich, "The New Allies: Approaching NATO Political and Military Standards," in Sabrina Crisen, ed., *NATO and Europe in the 21st Century* (Washington, D.C.: Woodrow Wilson Center, 2000), 37–48; Stuart Croft, "Enlarging NATO Again," *International Affairs* (U.K.), 78:1 (January 2002): 97–114; and Zachary Selden and John Lis, "NATO's New Members," *Problems of Post-Communism*, 49:4 (July–August 2002): 3–11.

[53] Interview with Péter Deák, Director of the Center for National Security and Defense (Budapest, 21 October 1999); and see Radio Free Europe/Radio Liberty Newsline, Part II (henceforth RFE/RL II), 5:16 (24 January 2001); and 5:49 (12 March 2001).

language skills to NATO standards are still a long way off and in many cases little progress has been made. Politicians and generals in Budapest, Prague, and Warsaw are intent on purchasing costly and unnecessary fighter jets – driven by national pride and the self-interest of generals – even though their forces often do not possess fundamental equipment. For instance, Poland was unable to get a few hundred soldiers to Central Asia because it lacks transport aircraft while the Hungarian air force had to rely on the United States to patrol its own air space during the Kosovo operations. In April 2002 Czech Defense Minister Jaroslav Tvrdik revealed that four Soviet-era fighter jets are all that remain of the Czech Republic's combat-ready air force.[54] The three new members are not expected to achieve "mature capability" before 2009, that is, not until a decade after they joined the Alliance.[55]

NATO Secretary-General Lord George Robertson and Joseph Ralston, Supreme Commander of NATO forces in Europe, have repeatedly expressed their concern and displeasure with the pace of military reforms and the lack of proper coordination and supervision in the Czech Republic and Hungary.[56] A February 2001 report lamented that the Czech army was paralyzed by financial problems to the extent that training exercises had to be postponed.[57] In March 2001 Petr Mareš, Deputy Chairman of the opposition Freedom Union party in the Czech legislature said that "We perceive the second anniversary of our entry into NATO ... as a commemoration of unfulfilled obligations and wasted chances."[58] "Hungary has won the prize for most disappointing new member of NATO, and against some competition" according to a senior European security official.[59] Hungary's defense minister, Ferenc Juhász, conceded that his country used up much of NATO's patience owing to its lackluster military reform and low defense spending.

---

[54] RFE/RL II, 6:63 (4 April 2002) citing reports from the Prague dailies *Pravo* and *Lidové noviny*.

[55] Šedivý, "The Puzzle of NATO Enlargement," 1. See also Martin Dokoupil, "Can Central Europe Afford Costly Fighter Jets?" Reuters (Prague), 24 February 2002.

[56] See, for instance, RFE/RL II, 4:208 (26 October 2000); 5:6 (10 January 2001); 5:37 (22 February 2001).

[57] See the reports by CTK (Prague), 1 February 2001; and *Mlada fronta Dneš*.

[58] Cited in RFE/RL II, 5:50 (13 March 2001).

[59] Cited by Celeste Wallander, "NATO's Price," *Foreign Affairs*, 81:6 (November–December 2002): 5.

28   The Future of NATO Expansion

Moreover, he claimed that Hungary was so far from meeting its commitments that it would have been expelled if there were a mechanism for expulsion.[60] Even if one allows for Juhász's political posturing – as a new defense minister he wanted to shift the blame on his predecessors – it is clear that Budapest has a long way to go to satisfy NATO's requirements.

Equally troubling was the lackluster support of the Czech Republic and Hungary for NATO operations in Kosovo that began two weeks after they officially joined the Alliance. While Poland provided unwavering support, the Czech Republic actually resisted NATO's objectives. Prime Minister Miloš Zeman referred to NATO (i.e., the alliance of which his country was a member) as "warmongers." Hungary, the only NATO member that bordered on Yugoslavia which, not coincidentally was home to a sizable Hungarian ethnic minority, did not conceal its reservations about the airstrikes though lent its airspace and landing strips to the campaign.[61] Before further enlargement, then, it is imperative to effectively integrate the three East-Central European states into NATO.

The decidedly mixed record of the first round of enlargement may have been on Lord Robertson's mind when he addressed a conference of the aspiring countries' defense ministers in Sofia in October 2000. He said that accession to the Alliance could not be regarded as "a political award" and added that expansion would take place when both NATO and the candidates were ready for it. Robertson noted that "NATO wants [those] countries not only to consume, but also to generate security" perhaps insinuating that the first three states have been free riders.[62] In any event, there is broad consensus among experts

---

[60] See, for instance, Róbert Kovács, "Türelmet kér a hadsereg a NATO felajánláshoz," *Népszava*, 31 July 2002; "Juhász a magyar NATO szerepvállalásról," *Magyar Nemzet*, 31 October 2002. For a contradictory view, see "Dícsérik Magyarország szerepét a NATO-tisztek," *Magyar Hírlap*, 26 November 2002.

[61] See Ryan C. Hendrickson, "NATO's Visegrad Allies: The First Test in Kosovo," *Journal of Slavic Military Studies*, 13:2 (June 2000): 25–38; Gary Dempsey, "Headaches for Neighboring Countries," in Ted Galen Carpenter, ed., *NATO's Empty Victory: A Postmortem on the Balkan War* (Washington, D.C.: Cato Institute, 2000), 59–76; and F. Stephen Larrabee, "The Kosovo Conflict and the Central European Members of NATO: Lessons and Implications," in Crisen, ed., *NATO and Europe in the 21st Century*, 32–36.

[62] Radio Free Europe/Radio Liberty Newsline, Part I (henceforth RFE/RL I), 4:200 (16 October 2000).

The Pros and Cons of Further Enlargement

that the problems of the three new members' military transformation were grossly underestimated by the Alliance.[63]

Critics of further enlargement lament that few politicians in both Eastern Europe and in the Alliance are concerned with the military issues pertaining to expansion. Rather, as Carpenter has remarked, NATO has seemingly become a "political honor society" that grants membership to all consolidated democracies regardless of their capacity to make military-security contributions to the Alliance.[64] As I shall demonstrate, in the aftermath of the September 11, 2001 terrorist attacks on the United States and America's subsequent "war on terror," NATO's standards have been further relaxed. Even countries where democracy is far from consolidated (e.g., Romania) are invited to membership as long as they eagerly support U.S. foreign policy objectives.

Unprepared Candidates. The seven countries that were invited to become NATO members in Prague are even less qualified than those in the first round of enlargement. Romania and Bulgaria have weak economies, Romania and Slovakia have yet to consolidate their democracies, and Slovenia's contribution would be little more than symbolic to NATO's capabilities. The Baltic republics, on the other hand, open an entire new cluster of issues that NATO may not want to confront.[65] In the foreseeable future none of these states can make a significant contribution to the Alliance's military strength.

Some experts have suggested that NATO's enlargement is tantamount to the expansion of the West. Still, the West and NATO, they argue, cannot simultaneously integrate states which have little in common with Western culture, democratic traditions, and economic progress. Proponents of this argument, strongly influenced by Samuel Huntington's "clash of civilizations" thesis, have particularly

[63] See, for instance, Chris Donnelly and Jeffrey Simon, "Roadmaps to NATO Accession: Preparing for Membership," East European Studies (Woodrow Wilson Center) Meeting Report no. 242 (January 2002).

[64] Carpenter's remarks at the Conference on NATO Enlargement in the Baltic States, University of Washington (Seattle, 29 November 2001).

[65] See, for instance, Yaroslav Bilinsky, *Endgame in NATO's Enlargement: The Baltic States and Ukraine* (Westport, CT: Praeger, 1999); and Roland Dannreuther, "Escaping the Enlargement Trap in NATO-Russia Relations," *Survival*, 41:4 (Winter 1999–2000): 145–164.

30   *The Future of NATO Expansion*

Albania, Bulgaria, Macedonia, and Romania as "incompatible states" in mind.[66]

Leave Expansion to the EU. The issue of the European Union and its expansion has been mentioned with reference to the second and subsequent enlargement process with much greater frequency than during the first enlargement. In fact, by the late 1990s an incremental connection developed between NATO and EU enlargement. The United States, trying to preserve as much room for decision as possible, has been anxious to avoid linkage related to the pace of the two enlargement processes. At the same time, Washington has been keen to ensure that EU enlargement takes place and that membership between the two organizations overlap to the greatest possible extent.[67]

Many analysts in aspirant countries believe that accession to NATO will strengthen their chances of joining the EU, the prize they are really after.[68] They are well aware that the NATO enlargement decision is much more subjective and is tied to fewer technical requirements than that of the EU. As former German defense minister Volker Rühe said, "You can join the Atlantic Alliance with old tanks, but joining the EU with old farm tractors causes problems.[69] Further, East European politicians reckon that being considered "important" and having passed muster with NATO would serve them well in their negotiations with the EU.

Amos Perlmutter has even suggested that, in all likelihood, EU enlargement would make NATO expansion unnecessary.[70] EU membership has certainly far more tangible benefits for these countries than

---

[66] See, for instance, Gusztáv Molnár, "Romania Has Lost Its Way ...," in Imre-József Balázs, Andor Horváth, and Lajos Kántor, eds., *Alternatives for Romania* (Cluj: KompPress, 1999), 134; and Robert D. Kaplan, *Eastward to Tartary: Travels in the Balkans, the Middle East, and the Caucasus* (New York: Random House, 2000), 53–55.

[67] Martin A. Smith, "The NATO Factor: A Spanner in the Works of EU and WEU Enlargement?" in Karen Henderson, ed., *Back to Europe: Central and Eastern Europe and the European Union* (London: UCL Press, 1999), 54–56.

[68] See, for instance, Valeri Ratchev, "Bulgaria and the Future of European Security," in Stephen J. Blank, ed., *European Security and NATO Enlargement: A View from Central Europe* (Carlisle, PA: U.S. Army War College, Strategic Studies Institute, 1998), 168.

[69] Cited in Lev Voronkov, "The Challenges of NATO Enlargement," *Balkan Forum*, 5:2 (June 1997): 21.

[70] Perlmutter, "Political Alternatives to NATO Expansion," 233–242.

belonging to NATO. Unlike NATO, the EU has been deeply involved in fostering democracy, enhancing market reforms, and supporting a plethora of projects in East European states. Furthermore, the EU possesses an intricate web of political institutions (such as European Commission, Council of Europe, European Parliament, European Court of Justice) that can contribute to conflict resolution in the region.

The East European countries have achieved widely varying levels of preparation for EU membership.[71] Not unexpectedly, the governments and populations of those countries whose chances for rapid EU integration seem slim (e.g., Romania) demonstrate far more enthusiasm toward NATO than those which appear to have a realistic shot at EU membership in the foreseeable future.

Russia. Although Russia acknowledged early on that it could not halt NATO's further expansion, Moscow also made it clear that it did not support it. In spite of the warming in U.S.–Russian relations following the terrorist attacks on New York and Washington in September 2001, Russia has remained skeptical about the need for and wisdom of a second wave of enlargement, particularly since, in all likelihood, it was going to include the three Baltic states. The implications of the fact that approximately 40% of Latvia's, 30% of Estonia's, and 7% of Lithuania's population are ethnic Russians hardly escape those who oppose Baltic membership. As Mendelsohn argued, "expanding NATO to include the Baltics would aggravate relations with the one country we need for out-of-area operations: Russia."[72] The minimalist expansion strategy – i.e., one that is limited to the first round – would bring about the best of both worlds, contended the opponents of further enlargement: It would maximize East-Central European security and would also give Russia a powerful incentive to continue to cooperate with the West.[73]

Cost. The economies as well as the armed forces of the countries that want NATO membership are, with the exception of Slovenia and

---

[71] On this point, see Helena Tang, *Winners and Losers in EU Integration: Policy Issues for Central and Eastern Europe* (Washington, D.C.: World Bank, 2000).

[72] Jack Mendelsohn in "The Case against NATO Expansion," *Current History*, 97:617 (March 1998): 134.

[73] Brown, "Minimalist NATO," 214.

32   *The Future of NATO Expansion*

Slovakia, in far worse shape than those of the first group. Moreover, the legislatures of these states are hardly likely to approve the additional taxation that increased military spending would necessitate. Therefore, it is reasonable to conclude that the costs of integrating new members would be higher than in the first round and that the bulk of these costs would have to be borne by the Alliance and, quite possibly, the United States.

Arguments Supporting Further Enlargement

A New NATO Should Have an Open Door. Those who support further enlargement believe that the Alliance's oft-repeated promises to aspiring countries must be honored. NATO leaders explicitly pledged to keep the door open for any European country "ready and willing" to shoulder the obligations of membership in the Alliance at the Madrid Summit. As Robert Hunter notes, however, notwithstanding the declarations of a continued enlargement process, there are several allies who do not want expansion in the near future. Their rationale is that NATO's goal is to be an encompassing institution without predetermined limits, *provided* that new members can meet exacting membership requirements at the time of entry and that the Alliance can maintain its strength and purpose.[74] In July 2001, U.S. President George W. Bush steered away from discussing the issue of preparedness and contended that "we should not calculate how little we can get away with, but how much we can do to advance the cause of freedom" when deciding on which countries to accept into NATO.[75]

The Countries that Really Need It Do Not Yet Have It. In a recent book Robert Kaplan argued that more than anything else, the first NATO enlargement institutionalized the divide between the Christian West and the Orthodox East in Europe. In other words it was not just Russia that was cut off from the new Europe but Orthodox countries

---

[74] Robert E. Hunter, "Maximizing NATO: A Relevant Alliance Knows How to Reach," *Foreign Affairs*, 78:3 (May–June 1999): 190.
[75] "Candidate States Hail NATO Commitment to Expansion," Reuters (Tallinn), 2 July 2001.

The Pros and Cons of Further Enlargement   33

like Bulgaria and Romania as well.[76] For Hungary or Poland, this line of reasoning suggests, NATO membership was in a sense a "seal of approval" that could be used to lure further foreign investment. For countries like Romania and Bulgaria, still at least a decade removed from EU membership, accession to NATO is an absolute necessity.

Another way to look at this issue is that isolating the Balkan states from Europe and the European integration process may, in fact, be a bigger threat to European security than separating Russia from European issues.[77] Detaching the Balkans from Europe might foster the creation of political associations hostile to democratic processes and reinforce long-standing nationalist tensions in the region.

Geostrategic Position. Incorporating Bulgaria, Romania, Slovakia, and Slovenia in the Alliance will expand its deterrent potential and enhance its rapid intervention capability in the Balkans and elsewhere in the region. Such further expansion would also improve NATO's geostrategic position by linking up Hungary with new members on its borders (Slovakia, Romania, and Slovenia) and Greece and Turkey with the rest of the Alliance through Bulgaria.

Russia. Many proponents of further enlargements believe that Russia is an inherently expansionist country and while efforts should be made to assuage its fears of a potentially hostile NATO, it should not be given any say in the Alliance's enlargement. Understandably, Moscow has been sensitive about further expansion and particularly troubled by the prospect that it might include the Baltic states. Strobe Talbott's suggestion that "Quite bluntly, Russians need to get over their neuralgia on the subject" expresses well the view of many backers of further enlargement.[78] I do not agree with this mentality. While I certainly do not believe that the Kremlin should have the right to veto enlargement decisions, a more conciliatory approach that mollifies Russia and addresses its concerns is more conducive to constructive relations between Brussels and Moscow.

---

[76] Kaplan, *Eastward to Tartary*, 46–47.
[77] Interview with Col. Valeri Ratchev, MOD (Sofia, 13 November 1999).
[78] Cited by Tucker, "Reflections of a Repentant Sinner," 125.

Russia's Position

Soviet Defense Minister Marshal Evgenii Shaposhnikov said in September 1991 that NATO did not present a threat to the USSR.[79] Shortly after his speech, however, Russia became an impassioned opponent of NATO enlargement.[80] Moscow has long argued that NATO expansion would create new divisions in Europe and, as a result, new tensions would flare up that would spoil the post-Cold War political climate and destroy mutual trust. Explaining the dangers NATO expansion posed to his country Russian Foreign Minister Andrei Kozyrev declared in 1995 that "Two things will kill the democratic experiment here – a major economic catastrophe and NATO enlargement."[81] No significant segment of Russian political or military elites has supported the expansion of the Alliance. In 1997, the liberal reformer Anatolii Chubais noted that this issue was the only one on which he agreed with communist leader Gennadii Zhuganov and nationalist maverick Vladimir Zhirinovsky.[82]

Nonetheless, when considering the evolution of Moscow's position vis-à-vis NATO it may be instructive to remember that, as Robert Legvold cautions, Russia is seeking status, not responsibility in Europe.[83] The Kremlin's strategic thinking may have remnants of imperial expansionism but it is international prestige and leverage that Moscow is most interested in. Russian military planners know the limited capacity at their disposal to project Russian power and cannot fail to realize the pitiful state of even the elite units of their armed forces.[84]

---

[79] "Shaposhnikov Comments on Defense Ministry Tasks," Radio Rossii, 18 September 1991, in *Foreign Broadcast Information Service – Soviet Union*, 20 September 1991.

[80] For analyses of Russian views of NATO enlargement, see N. N. Beliakov, and A. Iu. Moiseev, *Rasshierenie NATO na vostok: k miru ili voine?* (Moscow: Klub "Realisty," 1998); Margot Light, Stephen White, and John Löwenhardt, "A Wider Europe: The View from Moscow and Kyiv," *International Affairs*, 76:1 (January 2000): 77–88; and J. L. Black, *Russia Faces NATO Expansion: Bearing Gifts or Bearing Arms?* (Lanham, MD: Rowman & Littlefield, 2000).

[81] Cited in Michael Mihalka, "Continued Resistance to NATO Expansion," *Transition*, 1:14 (11 August 1995): 38.

[82] Alexii K. Pushkov, "Don't Isolate Us: A Russian View of NATO Enlargement," *The National Interest*, No. 47 (Spring 1997): 58–63.

[83] Robert Legvold, "The Russian Question," in Vladimir Baranovsky, ed., *Russia and Europe: The Emerging Security Agenda* (Oxford: Oxford University Press, 1997), 34.

[84] In Kosovo in 1999, for instance, Russian parachutists often ate what they could steal from nearby fields and did not have their own source of drinking water.

The Pros and Cons of Further Enlargement

The fact that Russia asked NATO for assistance in restructuring its armed forces is another sign of the improvement in U.S.–Russian relations.[85]

The idea of Russian membership in the Alliance has actually surfaced time and again. German Defense Minister Volker Rühe and his U.S. colleague, William Perry openly disagreed on this point (Perry insisting that the issue was not closed) in 1994 and subsequent events indicated that the latter was right.[86] In May 2000 Lord Robertson, in reference to President Putin's floating of the idea, said that Moscow could one day join NATO though avoided to say when that might be.[87] In the summer of 2001, President Bush and National Security Advisor Condoleezza Rice allowed that, in principle, a democratic Russia should be eligible for NATO membership. According to proponents of Russia's inclusion in NATO, it ought to be done because (a) without Russia there will not be durable peace in the new Europe; (b) integrating Russia into NATO will prevent the emergence of a grey zone in the heart of Europe; and (c) a new NATO that includes Russia would have far more influence over developments in the former Soviet space.[88] Still, many fear that Russian membership in NATO would fundamentally alter the character of the Alliance and could turn it into an ineffective Kantian or Wilsonian collective-security regime, another Organization for Security and Cooperation in Europe (OSCE) with guns.[89]

Interview with MarekČalka, Councillor of the Polish Embassy in Budapest (Budapest, 21 October 1999). See also Zoltan Barany, "Controlling the [Russian] Military: A Partial Success," *Journal of Democracy*, 10:2 (April 1999): 54–67.

[85] Judy Dempsey, "Moscow Asks NATO for Help in Restructuring," *Financial Times*, 26 October 2001.

[86] Tom Shanker, "Bonn Rebuffs US Over NATO's Role for Russia," *Chicago Tribune*, 10 September 1994.

[87] "Robertson says Russia could one day join NATO," Reuters (Moscow), 23 May 2000. For good discussions of potential Russian membership, see Charles A. Kupchan, "Rethinking Europe," *The National Interest*, No. 56 (Summer 1999): 73–80; and Henry Kissinger, "Russia: A Partner, But Not in NATO," *Washington Post*, 7 December 2001.

[88] See Charles A. Kupchan, "The Origins and Future of NATO Enlargement," in Robert W. Rauchhaus, ed., *Explaining NATO Enlargement* (London: Frank Cass, 2001), 138–139.

[89] See David S. Yost, "The New NATO and Collective Security" *Survival*, 40:2 (Summer 1998): 139; "Albright Urges Further Expansion of NATO, EU, Report Says," Reuters (Venice, Italy), 18 March 2000; Timothy Garton Ash, "Russia's Eventual Place in NATO," *New York Times*, 22 July 2001; Lawrence Freedman, "The Transformation

In early 2002 NATO has offered to form a new NATO–Russia Council that would allow a Russian ambassador to attend meetings and discuss issues of mutual concern. Russian diplomatic sources have suggested that while Moscow – whose generals continue to regard NATO with suspicion – wants to maintain ties with the Alliance, it was not interested in membership in it. A recent article in the Russian army's daily, *Krasnaya Zvezda*, maintained that "NATO [was] an American organization living on mostly American money and implementing mostly American interests." Moreover, the article contended, given Moscow's improving relations with European NATO members, Washington should worry not about including Russia in the Alliance but about being pushed away from the construction of a new European security architecture.[90]

Those who warned that relations between the United States and Russia would worsen following the expansion of the Alliance were right. After 1997 Russian–American ties had deteriorated, at least partly owing to NATO's expansion. Kremlin leaders have fiercely denounced and NATO's war in Kosovo and brashly interfered in its operations after the cease fire. As Oksana Antonenko argued, the NATO air campaign against Yugoslavia precipitated the most dangerous turn in Russian-Western relations since the heady days of the first Reagan Administration. Further, she contended that a return to cordial Russian-NATO relations would require not only political realism in Moscow but also a degree of restraint from the Alliance.[91]

The temporary worsening of U.S.–Russian relations was also manifested by the shifting emphases in Russian foreign policy. Since the late 1990s Moscow has been selling weapons to Iran, Syria, and other states

---

of NATO," *Financial Times*, 6 August 2001; Klaus-Dieter Frankenberger, "Mehr als längerfristig: Eine NATO, in der Rußland Mitglied wäre, hätte mit dem alten Bündnis wenig gemein," *Frankfurter Allgemeine Zeitung*, 11 August 2001.

[90] Yuri Pankov, "Why Russia Is Invited to NATO," *Krasnaya Zvezda*, 11 August 2001, translated in Johnson's Russia List, No. 5389 (13 August 2001); and "Russia Wants Ties with NATO, But Not Membership," Interfax (Moscow), 9 August 2001.

[91] Oksana Antonenko, "Russia, NATO, and European Security after Kosovo," *Survival*, 41:4 (Winter 1999–2000): 124, 140. See also Roland Dannreuther, "Escaping the Enlargement Trap in NATO-Russia Relations," *Survival*, 41:4 (Winter 1999–2000): 145–64; Dmitri Trenin, "Russia-NATO Relations: Time To Pick Up the Pieces," *NATO Review*, 48 (Spring/Summer 2000): 19–22; and S. Neil MacFarlane, "NATO in Russia's Relations with the West," *Security Dialogue*, 32:3 (September 2001): 281–296.

over U.S. objections.[92] A December 2000 poll revealed that the majority of Russian elites considered China a more reliable partner than the United States.[93] In July 2001 Moscow and Beijing signed the first "friendship treaty" between the two states in fifty years.[94] Ordinary Russians, too, seem to have become more suspicious of NATO enlargement: In 1999, 66 percent saw it as a threat to Russia in contrast with 51 percent two years earlier.[95] Since the September 2001 terrorist attacks on the United States, however, Russia has actively backed American actions against terrorism, including the air-strikes and other military operations against Afghanistan. Not incidentally, Washington has become less critical of Russia's own war in Chechnya and more supportive of Vladimir Putin's increasingly authoritarian regime.

In fact, as NATO Secretary-General George Robertson wrote, "everything changed" after September 11, 2001.[96] Russia is now considered a key U.S. and NATO partner in fighting against terrorism and Moscow's continuing genocidal war against its own people in Chechnya no longer seems to trouble American political elites. As NATO was gearing up for the Prague Summit, Alliance leaders had done their best to assure Russia of their good intentions. Alexander Vershbow, the U.S. Ambassador to Moscow declared that Russia was "key to [NATO's] new agenda" while high-ranking NATO officials repeatedly sketched a bright future for NATO-Russia cooperation.[97]

---

[92] See, for instance, "Russian minister counters US arguments over ties with Iran," ITAR-TASS (Vienna), 6 January 2001; "Russian security chief defends arms sales to Iran," *Komsomolskaya Pravda* (in Russian), 17 March 2001; and RFE/RL Part I, 5:99 (24 May 2001).

[93] Evan A. Feigenbaum, "The United States Is Driving Russia and China Together Again," *International Herald Tribune*, 28 December 2000.

[94] See Barry Schweid, "Bush: Russia-China Pact No Threat," AP (Washington), 16 July 2001; Patrick Cockburn, "Russia and China Revive Their Strategic Alliance," *Independent*, 17 July 2001; Constantine C. Menges, "Russia, China, and What's Really on the Table," *Washington Post*, 29 July 2001; and Valerie M. Hudson, "China-Russia: It's More Than Hot Air," *Newsday*, 30 July 2001.

[95] "Poll: 66% of Russians See NATO Enlargement as Threat," Interfax (Moscow), 30 July 1999.

[96] George Robertson, "A New Quality in the NATO-Russia Relationship," *International Affairs* (Moscow), 48:1 (2002):32.

[97] See, for instance, "Vershbow Says Russia is Key to NATO's New Agenda," United States Department of State bulletin, 18 October 2002; and "NATO Official Sees 'Bright Future' for Cooperation with Russia," ITAR-TASS (Moscow, 19 September 2002.

38   *The Future of NATO Expansion*

President Bush did his own part by habitually referring to his colleague, the former KGB colonel, as "my good friend Vladimir." Russian military elites seem less affected by the love-fest between Washington and Moscow.[98]

The Case for Postponing Enlargement

Karl-Heinz Kamp, among others, has suggested that it would be wise to wait with further enlargement till Russia consolidates its democracy and enters the path of economic prosperity. If Russia had a robust democracy and market economy it might view NATO's continuous expansion with fewer misgivings.[99] Kamp writes that this escape route has been blocked by the open-door policy conceived at the Madrid Summit. I disagree for two reasons. First, one could plausibly argue that democracy may not be consolidated in Russia in the short or medium term (say, in the next decade). Therefore, it would be a folly to make the timetable of expansion dependent on Russian democratization.

Second, the open door policy should not mean that candidate countries would be rushed to membership. It is important to learn from the mistake of the first round of enlargement when countries that were obviously unprepared to shoulder the responsibilities of membership were invited to Brussels. The Alliance ought to support the aspiring countries' progress in fully satisfying rigorous conditions of membership *at the time* of accession. It should be made clear to them that they will become members of the Alliance but only *after* they actually fulfill membership criteria.

It is useful to remember that NATO membership confers not just benefits but also obligations and costs that aspirant countries often do not anticipate. Let me relate an example from personal experience. In late 2000 I gave some lectures at the U.S. Air Force Academy. When I asked my colleagues where the Polish, Czech, and Hungarian exchange students were – after I was introduced to Romanian and

---

[98] See Olga Koleva's interviews with leading Russian generals in *Vremya Novostei*, 21 November 2002.

[99] See Karl-Heinz Kamp, "NATO Entrapped: Debating the Next Enlargement Round," *Survival*, 40:3 (Autumn 1998): 170–186.

The Pros and Cons of Further Enlargement

Slovak cadets – I was told that they could no longer afford to come. The Partnership for Peace program does fund such exchanges but once a country becomes a full-fledged NATO member, it has to pay its way.

As Michael Mandelbaum, Adam Garfinkle, and others asked before the first round of enlargement: "What's the rush?" At the November 2002 NATO summit in Prague, the same question should have also been asked. What compelling arguments are there to further expand NATO in two or three years as opposed to in ten years' time? This question is especially germane in view of (a) the fact that currently there is no security threat to the four countries this book focuses on; (b) the absence of an aggressive Russian posture toward these states; and (c) NATO's difficulties to integrate the three new members. The change in NATO's mission toward the "war on terror" does not warrant haste either, given that the two geostrategically important states from this perspective (Romania and Bulgaria) have unconditionally supported Alliance activities for years.

NATO expansion is urgent only from the perspective of the aspirants. The Alliance should not, however, base its enlargement decisions on the exigencies of East European governments. Politicians who desperately need the political benefits to be reaped from NATO membership usually lack successes in other areas of governance. The time NATO needs to properly integrate the first three new members might well be used by the newly invited countries to improve their preparation for membership in the Alliance.

PART III. NATO'S EXPECTATIONS

The fundamental reasons why East European states desire NATO membership are because the Alliance would provide them with (a) a system for conflict prevention; (b) a forum of policy coordination; and (c) collective defense. Before we move on to the analyses of the four NATO aspirants it seems useful to briefly review what the Alliance expects of them in return.[100]

---

[100] An excellent general discussion of the subject is Jeffrey Simon, "Post-Enlargement NATO: Dangers of 'Failed Suitors' and Need for a Strategy," in Blank, ed., *From Madrid to Brussels*, 29–47.

Democracy

New NATO member states should be consolidated democracies. This means not only that a democratic institutional framework has been established but also that individual liberties are observed and interactions are governed by rule of law. Preferably they will have had some changes of government between rival political forces to demonstrate that such shifts occur without political upheavals and without any alterations of the political system. An issue that has received growing attention from NATO is the proper treatment of ethnic, religious, and other minorities in candidate countries. In Eastern Europe, where ethnic minorities had been comprehensively marginalized by the state-socialist system, it is particularly important that states establish and enforce minority rights. In general, NATO has urged them to adhere to the norms and principles advocated by the OSCE.

Market Economy

States desiring membership should have functioning market economies, commitment to economic liberty and to free markets. Implicitly, they ought to have economies robust enough to permit increased defense outlays and the development of military arsenals compatible with that of NATO. Generally speaking, candidate states should be sufficiently prosperous to be able to shoulder the costs of membership in the Alliance.

Good Neighborly Relations

NATO expects new member states to have resolved major disputes with the countries on their borders. Most importantly, candidate countries should have settled with their neighbors whatever disagreements they might have had regarding territorial boundaries. Another crucial component of good neighborly relations is the proper treatment of national minorities whose mother state is bordering on the candidate country. The Alliance anticipates that "basic treaties" are concluded between the applicant and its neighbors prior to membership. Generally speaking, Brussels wants new members to improve relations with neighboring countries, particularly PfP states, as much as possible.

The Pros and Cons of Further Enlargement

Campaign and Support for NATO Membership

NATO is obviously interested in integrating states and nations that overwhelmingly support membership in the organization. The "proper" campaign for NATO is rooted in substantive achievements and progress toward satisfying criteria rather than facile verbal and written reports stressing plans rather than implementation. States that want to join the Alliance should actively participate in international peacekeeping operations and, more generally, should enhance regional stability and security.

Aspirant countries are also expected to be active in a broad spectrum of PfP projects from joint exercises and defense planning to exchange programs and specialized workshops. Although at its inauguration in 1994 Partnership for Peace (PfP) was dismissed by some as a quick fix allowing NATO to postpone the expansion issue, the PfP has become extremely valuable for its members. The PfP enables its thirty-one participants – not all of whom are candidates for membership in the Alliance – to develop military-to-military relationships with NATO member states. It allows its participants to see at first hand how NATO operates and permits them to develop useful contacts. The PfP has created a useful framework in which visits, exchanges, and, in general, communication between NATO members and PfP states could proceed. Moreover, through PfP programs NATO units and soldiers from participating countries have worked shoulder-to-shoulder in joint peacekeeping operations, disaster relief, and emergency drill activities.

Democratic Control of the Military

Proper civilian authority over the armed forces is a relatively complex matter and deserves a more detailed exposition. There are several components of successful democratic consolidation insofar as the military is concerned:[101] (a) the armed forces must be subordinated to institutionalized control balanced between the executive and legislative branches; (b) the military's chains of command and   the political

---

[101] This discussion draws on Zoltan Barany, "Democratic Consolidation and the Military: The East European Experience," *Comparative Politics*, 30:1 (October 1997): 21–44; and *idem.*, "Controlling the Military: A Partial Success," *Journal of Democracy*, 10:2 (April 1999): 54–67.

institutions' areas of responsibility over the armed forces must be codified for all potential scenarios (peacetime, emergencies, war); (c) the conditions that warrant the military's utilization in peacetime must be constitutionally regulated; (d) the executive and legislative branches must share exclusive fiscal responsibility over defense expenditures; (e) the armed forces must be depoliticized and its members must not be permitted to play any political role other than exercising their civic right to vote; (f) the military establishment itself must be democratized; and (g) civilian experts must be trained to provide objective advice to politicians on defense-related issues and to staff pertinent state institutions (including the ministry of defense).

Several additional conditions facilitate the development of democratic civil–military relations. A weighty decision facing democratizers is the manner in which political institutions exercise control over the military. Dividing civilian oversight responsibility between the president, government, and legislature strengthens the prospects of effective civilian control and reduces the likelihood of abuses of power by any one of these institutions. Appointing an authoritative civilian defense minister reduces the danger of the formation of military opposition to the democratizing state.

Proper balance must be found between civilian oversight on the one hand, and granting the armed forces a significant amount of autonomy to exercise their professional judgment within the broad policy parameters set by civilian institutions of the state (e.g., promotions, training methods, tactics) on the other.[102] The democratizing state should consolidate its authority over military affairs decisively while acting with restraint to avoid unnecessary conflict with the armed forces. To prevent civil–military strife, the state should follow the principle of incrementalism particularly in matters of personnel (i.e., when pruning the armed forces of elements suspected of potential disloyalty to the new democratic state), force restructuring, and the implementation of new military doctrine. Optimal military democratization processes are marked by negotiations and consensus building between civilian and military elites. Civilian authorities should assure the armed forces

---

[102] Larry Diamond and Marc F. Plattner. "Introduction," in Larry Diamond and Marc F. Plattner, eds., *Civil-Military Relations and Democracy* (Baltimore, MD: Johns Hopkins University Press, 1996), xxviii.

The Pros and Cons of Further Enlargement   43

that national security would not be compromised and ensure, as far as circumstances allow, the officers' continued high social status and remuneration.

Like democracy itself, civilian control is not a fact but a process that must be continually developed and perfected.[103] The best guarantee against military interference in politics is a smoothly functioning democratic government and strong political institutions supported by the public that is able to withstand the challenges of anti-democratic political forces.

Military Reform and Expenditure

Military reform is a fundamental requirement of NATO membership. Chapter five of the Alliance's own 1995 *Study on NATO Enlargement* stipulated a number of conditions pertaining to the preparation of candidate states' armed forces.[104] These include, most generally, the "sharing of roles, risks, responsibilities, benefits, and burdens of common security and collective defense." New members should also pursue the objectives of standardization to Alliance strategy and interoperability and focus on the language training of officers and NCOs in order to reduce difficulties in communication. Military reform also needs to incorporate the reduction of the armed forces' personnel, restructuring the standing forces (introducing corps in place of divisions and brigades instead of regiments) according to NATO standards, and a number of other major undertakings. Moreover, NATO member states should be able to shoulder much of the financial burden of their military reforms which requires them to spend a certain share of their Gross Domestic Product (GDP; the Alliance asked the first three entrants to devote 2 percent of their GDPs on defense) on their armed forces. The *Study on NATO Enlargement* also stipulated a number of more specific conditions posed to new members. These included mostly commonsensical requirements such as firm commitment to building consensus within the Alliance, establish permanent representation at

---

[103] See Richard H. Kohn, "How Democracies Control the Military," *Journal of Democracy*, 8:4 (October 1997): 143.
[104] See *Study on NATO Enlargement* (Brussels: NATO, 1995). The document is also available on the internet at www.nato.int/docu/basictxt/enl-9506.htm; quotations are taken from this version.

44 The Future of NATO Expansion

NATO headquarters, and to "keep the door open" for later candidate members.

CONCLUSION

This chapter examined the arguments favoring and opposing NATO expansion. I attempted to demonstrate that there were perfectly reasonable cases to be made for both sides of the issue. Although I agreed with enlargement skeptics prior to the first round, once expansion did take place, I became a supporter of NATO's open door policy. I also tried to explain the reasons why Russia's skepticism regarding further enlargement has been entirely in line with its national interests.

In the last section I outlined the broad conditions Brussels has set for states intending to join the Alliance. It is important to realize, however, that only a handful of NATO's original members would have satisfied all the criteria that are now in place for new members. As Christopher Jones has pointed out, in 1949, the year NATO came to life, the United States still had Jim Crow laws while France and Great Britain were repressing independence movements in Asia and Africa.[105] Other experts, like Jacob Kipp, contend that in some respects NATO's admission requirements are simply unrealistic. For instance, pursuing exacting military-security prerequisites such as interoperability as a make-or-break condition of membership is nonsensical given the current state of East European armed forces and their arsenals.[106] The things that are important, says Kipp, are transparency in civil–military relations and the determination of defense budgets, English language facility, familiarity with NATO procedures, and understanding how candidate countries fit into the Alliance's European security concepts. I do agree with him but, as I shall demonstrate, even on the issues he considers crucial several candidate states fall far short of NATO's criteria.

An essential argument of this study is that further NATO expansion should be preceded by the fulfillment of membership criteria by aspirant states. In the balance of this book I will assess the preparedness of four East European countries for joining the Alliance.

---

[105] Christopher Jones, "NATO Enlargement: Brussels as the Heir of Moscow," *Problems of Post-Communism*, 45:4 (July–August 1998): 45.
[106] Telephone conversation with Dr. Kipp (23 March 2001).

2

Slovakia

Catching Up to Its Neighbors

This chapter analyzes political, economic, and military-security developments in Slovakia since the fall of communism and, especially, since it became independent on January 1, 1993. In Part I I review Slovakia's democratization process, its economic performance, and the security situation it found itself in after achieving sovereignty. Part II examines Slovak foreign policy since 1993 and Bratislava's campaign for NATO membership. Part III concentrates on matters pertaining to civil–military relations. In the last section of the chapter the focus shifts to military reform and the state of the Slovak armed forces.

PART I. DOMESTIC POLITICS, ECONOMIC PERFORMANCE, SECURITY STATUS

Domestic Politics

The postcommunist era in Slovak politics may be conveniently divided into three distinctive periods. The first, December 1989–December 1992, spans from the fall of communism to the breakup of federal Czechoslovakia. The second phase, January 1993–September 1998, embraces the nearly six-year period in which Slovakia was ruled – with a brief interruption in March–October 1994 – by Vladimír Mečiar and his semi-authoritarian populist-nationalist coalition government. The third stage, September 1998 to the present, represents the tenure

45

46 *The Future of NATO Expansion*

of liberal democratic coalition governments under the premiership of Mikuláš Dzurinda.

The improbably peaceful "velvet revolution" was initiated and led by Czech dissidents in Prague. From the beginning, their Slovak colleagues were followers rather than leaders of the democratization process which made them vulnerable to being portrayed as insufficiently dedicated to pursuing specifically Slovak interests.[1] After the collapse of the communist state, Czechoslovak politics were repluralized quickly. In Slovakia an organization called the Public Against Violence (PAV) – its Czech counterpart was the Civic Forum – laid the foundations of systemic political change and economic reform. In the June 1990 Slovak elections, the PAV secured nearly one-third of the votes, far ahead of the Christian Democratic Movement and the Communist Party of Slovakia.

The emergence of politicized ethnic relations between Czechs and Slovaks was nearly simultaneous with the fall of the ancien régime. The deepening tensions were mainly rooted in the widely shared Slovak perception that Czechs mistreated them. There is little doubt that another source of apprehension was prompted by the desire for independence given that the Slovak nation had no history of sovereignty (aside from the ill-fated and short-lived fascist state during World War II). In fact, much of the domestic politicking of 1990–1992 was dominated by public speculations, proposals, and disputes about the future of Czechoslovakia.

The June 1992 elections did not generate the mass fervor for independence in either the Czech Lands or in Slovakia, though they did produce two charismatic and sharply dissimilar leaders at loggerheads with one another. Václav Klaus, the pragmatist Prime Minister of the Czech Lands and Vladimír Mečiar, his Slovak counterpart, whose populist Movement for a Democratic Slovakia (HZDS) garnered the largest share (roughly one-third) of the vote, could hardly have been more different in their political and economic agendas.

Indirectly, the 1992 elections resulted in the breakup of the federal state and the establishment of independent Slovakia. A considerable

---

[1] Sharon L. Wolchik, "Democratization and Political Participation in Slovakia," in Karen Dawisha and Bruce Parrott, eds., *The Consolidation of Democracy in East-Central Europe* (New York: Cambridge University Press, 1997), 197.

Slovakia: Catching Up to Its Neighbors

proportion of the Slovak (and Czech) public felt frustrated since they were deprived of their right to express their opinion about the splitting up of Czechoslovakia in a referendum. The way Mečiar and his political allies drove independence through the legislature also foreshadowed the style of government Slovaks were to have through much of the rest of the 1990s.[2] The Slovak Constitution, approved by the legislature in September 1992, also hinted at potential future problems by stressing national rather than civic aspects of citizenship.

Mečiar's new coalition government held power, with a short break, until September 1998. It consisted of the HZDS and its "red-brown" partners: the ultranationalist Slovak National Party (SNS) and the neo-Stalinist Workers' Party (ZRS), though nearly all cabinet members were ex-communists. In March 1994, a parliamentary no-confidence vote allowed Jozef Moravčik to form a coalition government. During the Moravčik cabinet's six-month tenure Slovakia showed signs of returning to the mainstream of the developmental trajectory of its partners in the Visegrad Group: the Czech Republic, Hungary, and Poland. Prior to the fall 1994 elections, however, the coalition partners were unable to effectively cooperate and the biggest vote-getter, once again, was the HZDS. During the 1994 electoral campaign Mečiar revved up crowds with anti-Hungarian and anti-Gypsy rhetoric and struck a chord with many by casting himself as the "father of the nation" and liberally using phrases like "being a good Slovak" in a country where less than 80% of the population was comprised of the titular nationality.[3]

After 1994, Slovak politics had come to be increasingly dominated by nationalist and authoritarian trends and independent Slovak analysts have aptly described the political system as the "democratic despotism" of Mečiar and his cronies. During Mečiar's tenure the governing elites considered laws with open contempt with the prime minister himself setting the example. A 1997 Freedom House survey provided

---

[2] See Zora Bútorová and Martin Bútora, "Introduction," in Zora Bútorová, ed., *Democracy and Discontent in Slovakia* (Bratislava: Institute for Public Affairs, 1998), 8; and idem., "Slovakia After the Split," *Journal of Democracy*, 4:2 (April 1993): 71–83. For comparative studies of Czechoslovakia's breakup, see Andrew C. Janos, *Czechoslovakia and Yugoslavia* (Berkeley: International and Area Studies, University of California, 1997); and Valerie Bunce, *Subversive Institutions* (New York: Cambridge University Press, 1999).

[3] See Jane Perlez, "Voters Back Ex-Premier in Slovakia," *New York Times*, 3 October 1994.

a concise summary for the Mečiar era placing Slovakia with Moldova and behind Russia in terms of level of democracy. The Slovak case also shows that a system of "pure parliamentarism with an overwhelming prime minister can lead to political outcomes disturbingly reminiscent of the interwar years."[4] A few examples should explain why. In December 1996 the house of František Gaulieder, a founding member of the HZDS, was bombed the day after he was unconstitutionally expelled from parliament by his own party. Prior to resigning from the HZDS, Gaulieder accused it of "striving to seize power in order to dominate society at the whim of Mečiar." Mečiar tried to twist the constitution in order to squeeze an opposition party out of parliament, proposed laws that would make "defamation of the country" an offense to be punished by a maximum five-year prison sentence, and attempted to ease the imposition of martial law. The minister of culture repeatedly purged the country's theaters, colleges, and museums, directly intervening in matters belonging to the jurisdiction of universities and independent institutions. The government's approach to ethnic minority rights had also been a cause for strong Western criticism. As one expert lamented, "Slovaks tend to equate democracy with economic prosperity."[5] In sum, by East-Central European standards, Slovakia's democratization process was extremely deficient.

Although the relationship between presidents and prime ministers was rarely placid in the region, the incessant feud between Mečiar and President Michal Kováč had a particularly disruptive impact on Slovak politics. The fundamental source of conflict was that Kováč, Slovakia's first president who was elected in February 1993, remained the last main safeguard between the prime minister and unlimited power.

---

[4] M. Steven Fish, "Postcommunist Subversion: Social Science and Democratization in East Europe and Eurasia," *Slavic Review*, 58:4 (Winter 1999): 804. For excellent summations of "Meciarism," see *idem.*, "The End of Meciarism," *East European Constitutional Review*, 8:1/2 (Winter/Spring 1999): 47–55; and Josette Baer, "Boxing and Politics in Slovakia: 'Meciarism' – Roots, Theory, Practice," *Democratization*, 8:2 (Summer 2001): 97–116.

[5] Martin Bútora, "Slovakia: A New State One Year Later," *East European Studies Newsletter* (Woodrow Wilson Center), no. 93 (May–June 1994), 3. See also Michael Carpenter, "Slovakia and the Triumph of Nationalist Populism," *Communist and Post-Communist Studies*, 30:2 (June 1997): 205–220; and Juraj Podoba, "Rejecting Green Velvet: Transition, Environment, and Nationalism in Slovakia," *Environmental Politics*, 7:1 (Spring 1998): 129–145.

Slovakia: Catching Up to Its Neighbors

The secret service, presumably with Mečiar's full knowledge, had kidnapped the president's son (one policeman familiar with the case who fed information to investigating journalists was killed when his car was blown up), and continuously harassed the president and his family. Kováč accused Mečiar's government of "violence, physical liquidation, setting off bombs, making threats, spreading fear, causing the moral decay of our public life, corrupting and criminalizing all sorts of state organs as well as political life, misusing police and prosecutors, controlling the state media and manipulating public opinion."[6]

After Kováč's tenure expired in March 1998, the National Council (the legislature) failed to elect a successor allowing Mečiar to inherit the mantle of the presidency with many of the competencies of the head of state.[7] Slovaks had to wait for a new president until May 1999 when former Košice mayor and Slovak Communist Party chief, Rudolf Schuster, received 57.2 percent of the vote to defeat Mečiar (42.8 percent) in the elections in which more than 75 percent of the electorate participated.

By this time Vladimír Mečiar was out of government owing to the defeat he suffered in the September 1998 national elections at the hands of a four-party coalition. The 85 percent voter participation was indicative of the polarization of the Slovak political scene. Although Dzurinda's coalition governments have faced several crises, they have improved the standards of governance immeasurably. The rule of law has replaced the arbitrary decision-making of Mečiar's administration. The cabinet, which includes an ethnic Hungarian deputy prime minister, Pál Csáky, has taken serious steps to improve the situation of ethnic minorities and observe minority and human rights. It has created and financed programs to help Slovakia's large and socioeconomically marginal Gypsy/Romani minority – mostly ignored under Mečiar – that have been deemed the conceptually most sound in the region. Owing to its commitment to democratic procedures and numerous substantive improvements in all areas of domestic politics, the government succeeded in transforming Slovakia's international image in a short time.

---

[6] Cited in "Nice New Friends," *The Economist*, 21 December 1996, 64. See also *Transitions*, 4:5 (October 1997): 9.

[7] Trevor Waters, "Building an Army from Scratch: Slovakia's Uphill Struggle," *Medzinárodné Otázky*, 7:4 (1998): 57. See also, "A Meciar Coup?" *The Economist*, 7 February 1998, 55.

At the same time, holding a broad-based coalition together in the face of high unemployment, a hard-to-please Hungarian coalition partner, and an unusually destructive and nationalist opposition was anything but easy. The only main uniting forces of the coalition were its anti-Mečiar (and HZDS) and pro-European integration stances. Corruption even in the highest echelons of public life remains widespread; a recent World Bank study found that it improved "only slightly" under the Dzurinda government.[8] In the first five months of 2001 alone, President Schuster fired Deputy Prime Minister Pavol Hamžik in charge of EU integration; Ronald Toth, the government's coordinator for distribution of EU funds was dismissed; and Defense Minister Pavol Kanis resigned, all because of financial improprieties.[9]

The potential of NATO membership has had some discernable impact on Slovak domestic politics. Even Mečiar allowed, in 1994, that the "price" of NATO admission was respect for individual rights for ethnic minorities as well as improved relations with Hungary. Nevertheless, after his return to power in the fall of that year, his view of NATO membership became increasingly ambivalent. It is clear that one of the major attractions of the opposition parties that won the 1998 election to the electorate was their commitment to European integration. More recently, weighing the possibility of the former premier's political comeback in 2002, President Schuster said that "everybody realizes that if we want to get into NATO and the EU, this must be granted by certain personalities" and people like Mečiar, the obstacle to Slovakia's European integration, must be ruled out.[10] Furthermore, several Slovak party leaders denied the possibility of forming an electoral coalition with the HZDS precisely because it could "jeopardize the acceptability of Slovakia to foreign structures."[11] In February 2001, the Slovak parliament approved a key constitutional bill – setting into motion the reform of the civil service and dividing powers between

---

[8] Cited in RFE/RL II, 4:120 (21 June 2000). A year later, the EU also strongly criticized the distribution of its assistance funds. See RFE/RL II, 5:121 (26 June 2001).

[9] See Tom Nicholson, "Mansion-Building Defense Minister's Luck Running Out," *Slovak Spectator*, 18–24 December 2000; and RFE/RL II, 5:86 (4 May 2001) and 5:121 (26 June 2001).

[10] RFE/RL II, 5:31 (14 February 2001).

[11] See Lucia Nicholsonová, "Opposition Seen as Potential NATO Barrier," *Slovak Spectator*, 26 March–1 April 2001. Incidentally, Mečiar also ruled out partnership with the HZDS's former allies (RFE/RL II, 5:107 [6 June 2001]).

the central and local governments – considered necessary for NATO- and EU-oriented transformations. An additional hopeful sign was that the HZDS which labeled the vote as an "ominous day for Slovakia" failed to attract a single person for its announced protest in front of the parliament building.[12]

Nonetheless, even after the post-1998 shrinking of the HZDS membership by half, it remains the largest party in the country and was likely to be a contender in the 2002 national elections.[13] According to a June 2001 poll, the HZDS was by far the most popular party and Mečiar the most "trustworthy" politician in Slovakia. True to expectations, the HZDS won the December 2001 regional elections by a landslide and continued to increase its support.[14] By January 2002 the party's popularity had further increased and according to polls, if elections were held then, the HZDS would have garnered 32.5 percent of the vote, far ahead of the *Smer* (Direction) formation which had 13 percent support, let alone the 7.2 percent of the respondents favoring Premier Dzurinda's Slovak Democratic and Christian Union.[15]

The return of "old forces" in the September 2002 elections clearly worried politicians and representatives of international organizations on both sides of the Atlantic. European Union Commissioner for Enlargement, Günter Verheugen, publicly stated that "We want to tell people in Slovakia that there is no reasonable alternative to the principled direction the country took [after 1998]" and that Bratislava's EU bid might suffer if Mečiar returned.[16] A number of NATO and U.S. officials including U.S. Ambassador to NATO Nicholas Burns, U.S. Ambassador to Slovakia Ronald Weiser, NATO Secretary General George Robertson, and Elizabeth Jones, the head of the U.S. State Department's European and Euro-Asian Affairs have repeatedly warned that Mečiar and his party "did not demonstrate a commitment to democracy and

---

[12] RFE/RL II, 5:39 (26 February 2001).

[13] See HZDS MP Olga Keltošová's interview in *Pravda* (Bratislava), 5 April 2001; and RFE/RL II, 5:67 (5 April 2001).

[14] See Deirdre Tynan, "HZDS Wins Regional Landslide on Low Turnout," *The Slovak Spectator*, 10–16 December 2001.

[15] CTK (Bratislava), 16 January 2002; RFE/RL II, 6:10 (16 January 2002).

[16] See "Snap and Snarl," *The Economist*, 9 June 2001; CTK (Bratislava), 19 June 2001; RFE/RL II, 5:118 (21 June 2001), and 5:122 (27 June 2001).

52 *The Future of NATO Expansion*

the rule of law" and Slovakia's NATO accession chances might well suffer if he and his party managed to stage a political comeback.[17]

The voters obviously did not want to hazard Slovakia's European integration, especially not after Mečiar's campaign antics (which included, a week before the elections, punching a reporter that was caught on videotape).[18] Although the HZDS managed to gain the most votes (19.5%) at the September 2002 elections, the four Western-oriented center-right parties led by Prime Minister Dzurinda's Slovak Democratic and Christian Union (15.9%) gained a narrow two-seat majority in the 150-mandate parliament. Dzurinda's new cabinet once again includes Deputy Prime Minister Csáky as well as three more ministers from the ranks of the Hungarian Coalition Party.

Economic Performance

Notwithstanding its political problems, the marketization of the Slovak economy has been relatively successful, especially so compared to the two Balkan states in this study. According to the United Nations' Human Development Index – based on life expectancy, education, and real income – Slovakia places higher than Hungary and Poland and just behind Slovenia and the Czech Republic.[19] To be sure, Slovakia's developmental level was one of the highest in the region at communism's end even if a great deal of the country's industrial capacity was tied up in defense-related enterprises. Still, nearly a decade after the split, it is clear that Slovakia has fared worse economically than the Czech Republic. A 1996 *New York Times* article suggested that the Czechs'

---

[17] See, for instance, RFE/RL II, 5:217 (15 November 2001); 6:3 (7 January 2002); 6:28 (12 February 2002); 6:39 (28 February 2002); and 6:52 (19 March 2002); as well as "Robertson Says Elections Decisive for NATO Hopes," *Slovak Spectator*, 5–11 November 2001; "Robertson Again: 'Eyes Wide Open," *Slovak Spectator*, 10–16 December 2001; and Deirdre Tynan, "Mečiar: A Date with NATO," *Slovak Spectator*, 17–23 December 2001.

[18] Tom Nicholson, "Losing It," *The Slovak Spectator*, 8:36 (September 23–29, 2002).

[19] See *National Human Development Report – Slovakia 1998* (Bratislava: United Nations Development Program, 1998); and *Human Development Report 2001* (New York: Oxford University Press for the UNDP, 2001), 141. See also Anton Marcinčin and Miroslav Beblavý, eds. *Economic Policy in Slovakia, 1990–1999* (Bratislava: Centre for Social and Media Analysis and Institute for Economic and Social Reforms, 2000).

Slovakia: Catching Up to Its Neighbors

greatest economic asset was that they no longer had to "carry as a liability" Slovakia.[20]

Slovak privatization proceeded relatively slowly and was mired in corruption.[21] Double-digit unemployment, relatively high inflation, and modest levels of foreign investments during the Mečiar years were nonetheless complemented with high (nearly 6 percent per year in 1995–1998) growth rates. The Dzurinda government implemented several austerity measures that have paid dividends though made the cabinet unpopular. Unemployment rates have decreased and foreign investment has increased substantially, especially with the large-scale investment of U.S. Steel in Slovakia's biggest steel mill in Košice in October 2000.

There is far more popular and political elite support in the country for joining the EU than for NATO membership. Since 1998 Slovakia has made impressive progress in its candidacy for European Union accession. In January 2000 Deputy Premier Hamžik contended (entirely reasonably) that the EU should not place his country on the same level as Bulgaria or Romania because their economies were not in the same league as Slovakia's.[22] In August he urged the EU to admit Slovakia with the first group of aspirants (Slovenia, Estonia, and the other Visegrad states). An October 2000 report of the European Parliament supported his view, recommending that EU countries abolish visas for Slovak citizens and praising the actions of the Dzurinda government.[23] By October 2002 Bratislava had largely caught up with its Visegrad partners in terms of their membership preparations, having reached agreement with the EU on twenty-nine (of the total of thirty-one) chapters of the *acquis communautaire*.[24] In that month the

---

[20] Peter Passell, "Czechs Are Doing Well, with Luck and without Slovakia," *New York Times*, 23 May 1996.

[21] See, for instance, Jane Perlez, "Slovakia Suffers in Leaving Czechs," *New York Times*, 2 February 1994; and Sharon Fisher, "Meciar Retains Control of the Political Scene," *Transition*, 2:16 (9 August 1996): 32–36.

[22] RFE/RL II, 4:18 (26 January 2000). See also Heather Grabbe and Kristy Hughes, "Central and East European Views on EU Enlargement: Political Debates and Public Opinion," in Karen Henderson, ed. *Back to Europe: Central and Eastern Europe and the European Union* (London: UCL Press, 1999), 185–202.

[23] RFE/RL II, 4:163 (22 August 2000); and CTK (Czech news agency, Prague), 4 October 2000.

[24] See Ed Holt, "Slovaks Leap Forward in EU Entry Race," *Slovak Spectator*, 28 May–3 June 2001, and RFE/RL II, 6:204 (29 October 2002).

54   *The Future of NATO Expansion*

EU announced that Slovakia would be among the ten countries to be included in its 2004 enlargement.

Security Situation

After the breakup of Czechoslovakia the new Slovak Republic's geopolitical center of gravity shifted eastward. The Czech Republic was now cut off from the "Carpathian arc of instability" and gained, in Slovakia, a buffer between itself and the former Soviet Union.[25] Politicians in Bratislava like to insist that Slovakia does not have any traditional enemies. Nonetheless, given Slovakia's history of conflict with Hungary in the twentieth century, the anti-Hungarian theme of Slovak nationalism, and its frequently tense relations with Budapest owing primarily to its treatment of the Hungarian minority, Hungary is clearly the traditional adversary of Slovakia. A 1991 survey found that the majority of Czechoslovak citizens (67 percent) thought that whatever danger was posed to their country came from the former Soviet Union, while 25 percent perceived a united Germany or the United States as a threat to Czechoslovak security.[26]

In a speech delivered to military officers a few days after achieving independence, Prime Minister Mečiar noted that "we have no enemies" adding that the country had no allies either.[27] Things changed rather quickly, however. Relations with Russia became so central to Slovak security and foreign policy that, in October 1995, Slovak Deputy Prime Minister Sergej Kozlík proposed a customs union between Bratislava and Moscow.[28] The suggestion did not lead anywhere and one of the first substantive policy shifts of the Dzurinda cabinet

---

[25] See Ivo Samson, "Transformation and Structural Change: Slovakia's Postcommunist Security and Military Adjustment to NATO Integration," in Piotr Dutkiewicz and Robert J. Jackson, eds., *NATO Looks East* (Westport, CT: Praeger, 1998), 123–138.

[26] Cited in Jan Obrman, "The Czechoslovak Armed Forces: The Reform Continues," *RFE/RL Research Report*, 1:6 (7 February 1992): 50–51.

[27] "Meciar Unwilling to Reduce Arms Production," *Národná Obroda*, 5 January 1993 translated in *Foreign Broadcast Information Service-Eastern Europe* (henceforth *FBIS*), 14 January 1993, 23. See also Ivo Samson, *Die Sicherheits- und Aussenpolitik der Slowakei in der ersten Jahren der Selbstständigkeit* (Baden-Baden: Nomos Verlagsgesellschaft, 2000), which provides solid coverage of the Mečiar years.

[28] See Miroslav Wlachowský, "Foreign Policy," in Martin Bútora and Péter Hunčik, *Global Report on Slovakia: Comprehensive Analyses from 1995 and Trends for 1996* (Bratislava: Sándor Márai Foundation, 1997), 43.

Slovakia: Catching Up to Its Neighbors

was an unambiguous reorientation of security policy toward the West.

According to government officials in Bratislava, Slovakia's current security challenges are "soft" ones, meaning drug trafficking, organized crime, and illegal migration rather than a conventional military threat from any specific state.[29] An interministerial commission devoted much attention to the elaboration of Slovakia's new national security strategy which closely follows the methodological conception of NATO.[30] The Slovak National Council overwhelmingly approved the document in March 2001.

Slovakia's military doctrine has also undergone several changes in the 1990s reflecting both the shifts in the constellation of political forces and the unbalanced judgment of some politicians in Bratislava. In 1991, for instance, Mečiar openly exploited the population's irrational fears of millions of refugees arriving from the Soviet Union, and called for a redeployment of troops to Eastern Slovakia.[31] After independence the first Slovak Defense Minister, Imrich Andrejčák, quickly turned his attention to the elaboration of a national military doctrine.[32] The new doctrine – entirely defensive and committed to political trust and military transparency – was approved by the Mečiar government in March 1994.

A few months later the Moravčik cabinet initiated changes in the document placing more emphasis on closer relations with European and transatlantic security structures and unambiguously identifying the goal of NATO membership.[33] The current Slovak military doctrine is in line with NATO desiderata and is based on the position and needs of the Slovak Army while also taking long-term projections of the political-military and military-strategic environment into account. Jeffrey Simon's supposition, that if the 2002 round of NATO enlargement excluded Slovakia, Bratislava might well have declared

---

[29] Interview with Miroslav Wlachowský, Head of the Department of Analyses and Policy Planning at the Ministry of Foreign Affairs (Bratislava, 7 September 1999).

[30] Interview with Lt. Col. Dušan Kulik, Department of Integration and International Relations, MoD (Bratislava, 9 September 1999).

[31] "Interview with Meciar," Prague Television 1, 26 January 1991; translated in *FBIS-EEU*, 28 January 1991, 22.

[32] See "Základná služba iba rok," *Národná obroda*, 20 April 1993.

[33] Trevor Waters, "Building an Army from Scratch: Slovakia's Uphill Struggle," *Medzinárodné Otázky*, 7:4 (1998): 51–52.

56 *The Future of NATO Expansion*

its neutrality is reasonable, especially when considering the lackluster popular support for and some of the opposition parties' (especially the communists') resistance to membership in the Alliance.[34]

PART II. FOREIGN POLICY AND THE CAMPAIGN FOR NATO MEMBERSHIP

Slovak Foreign Policy from Independence to 2001

Slovak foreign policy and its institutional framework – even more than the military realm – had to be built from scratch after the breakup of Czechoslovakia. Just as domestic politics, Slovak foreign policy can also be split into "Mečiar" (1993–1998) and "after Mečiar" (1998–) periods.

Even though during 1993–1998 Slovakia had five different foreign ministers, these personnel changes reflected shifts in domestic politics rather than major foreign policy alterations. In fact, all of them declared the continuity in foreign policy and stressed its principal aim of European integration.[35] At the same time, Bratislava's proclamations were often contradicted by its actions at home and abroad. According to some MOD officials, Mečiar's foreign policy was predicated on the assumption that "if the West doesn't want us, the East will." The underlying argument supporting warm relations with Moscow was that "Russia is an important country, it is not a direct neighbor, and we are totally dependent on it for our energy supply."[36]

Slovak-Russian relations under Mečiar were close. The first country outside the Commonwealth of Independent States that Moscow granted a loan to was Slovakia. Russian Prime Minister Viktor Chernomyrdin repeatedly praised Mečiar and his policies while politicians in Moscow declared that "Slovakia today is the one country of Central Europe in which no prejudices are held against Russia."[37] Relations between Bratislava and Moscow also extended to cooperation in military and security affairs. The two defense ministers negotiated several arms

---

[34] Jeffrey Simon, "Central and East European Security: New National Concepts and Defense Doctrines," *Strategic Forum*, no. 151 (December 1998): 5.

[35] Wlachowský, "Foreign Policy," Bútora and Hunčik, *Global Report on Slovakia*, 33.

[36] Interview with Col. Marian Božik (Bratislava, 9 September 1999).

[37] Wlachowský, "Foreign Policy," 43.

Slovakia: Catching Up to Its Neighbors 57

agreements, most having to do with the transfer of Russian weapons to Slovakia in lieu of payments on Russia's debt. According to some Slovak experts the most important attribute of the Bratislava–Moscow nexus under Mečiar was its asymmetrical character: Slovakia chiefly interested in economic benefits whereas Russia primarily being concerned with the political significance of friendly bilateral relations with an East-Central European state.[38]

On a superficial level the Mečiar government's relations with the West were cordial. Still, Slovakia's domestic policies and close camaraderie with Russia simply precluded the type of substantive progress in European integration the other Visegrad states had achieved. Although there were no sharp conflicts in Slovakia's relations with the West, international organizations as well as representatives of West European and North American governments repeatedly criticized Bratislava's minority policies and the shortcomings of its democratization process.

The very same policies also diminished the prospects of meaningful cooperation with the other members of the Visegrad group, even though Slovakia had few notable disagreements with Prague and Warsaw.[39] The Mečiar government's poor treatment of the country's large ethnic Hungarian community, however, prompted a major deterioration of Slovak-Hungarian relations. The high point of Bratislava's relations with Budapest was the signing of the so-called basic treaty ("Treaty on Good Neighborliness and Friendly Cooperation") in March 1995. The treaty, which Hungary signed because political elites correctly perceived it as a prerequisite of NATO membership, was ratified only with difficulties in both legislatures and its subsequent implementation left a great deal to be desired. The low point came in August 1997 when Mečiar suggested a government-supported voluntary exchange of ethnic minorities between the two states at a meeting with Hungarian premier Gyula Horn.[40] The offer was not only preposterous given the profound disparities in the number, treatment, and

---

[38] See Alexander Duleba, *Slepý pragmatizmus slovenskej východnej politiky* (Bratislava: Štúdie k medzinárodným otázkam, 1996).

[39] See, for instance, Zoltan Barany, "Regional Security: Visegrad Four Contemplate Separate Paths," *Transition*, 1:14 (11 August 1995): 56–60.

[40] See, for instance, Daniel Borský, "Mečiar Call for Ethnic Minorities to Be Swapped Between Slovakia, Hungary," *Slovak Spectator*, 25 September-8 October 1997; and Wlachovský, et al., "The Foreign Policy of the Slovak Republic," 85–86.

58   *The Future of NATO Expansion*

level of social integration of Hungarians in Slovakia versus Slovaks in Hungary, but also evoked the memory of World War II-era forced deportations. President Kováč signed a basic treaty with his Ukrainian counterpart, Leonid Kravchuk, in 1993 but Ukraine remains not only Slovakia's largest but also its least known neighbor.

As a Slovak foreign ministry official told me, after the "years of hibernation" under Mečiar, his ministry had no alternative but to try to catch up to Slovakia's Visegrad Four partners.[41] Eduard Kukan, the Dzurinda cabinet's Foreign Minister, wasted no time to declare that Slovak foreign policy goals in the wake of the Mečiar era were to improve relations with its neighbors and to join the EU and NATO as soon as possible. At his swearing-in ceremony in June 1999, President Schuster declared that in view of Slovakia's NATO and EU orientation it would be "unrealistic" to expect Bratislava to be neutral.[42]

Slovakia's relations with NATO member states improved rapidly. High-ranking state visits took place with virtually every NATO country from Denmark to Turkey, and the leaders of NATO states had repeatedly assured Bratislava of their support of Slovak membership in the Alliance.[43] In August 2000 Slovakia became a member of the Organization for Economic Cooperation and Development (OECD), a milestone hailed by Prime Minister Dzurinda as "confirmation that Slovakia is becoming part of the world of freedom and wealth."[44] Representatives of the U.S. government and Congress have also expressed their approval of Slovakia's changed policies on innumerable occasions since 1999.[45]

The new Slovak government made numerous efforts to change its minority policies (particularly vis-à-vis the Hungarians). Strains in the

---

[41] Interview with Wlachowský (Bratislava, 7 September 1999). See also, Marián Leško, "Príbeh sebadiskvalifikácie favorita," in Martin Bútora and František Šebej, eds., *Slovensko v Šedej Zóne? Rozširovanie NATO, zlyhania a perspektívy Slovenska* (Bratislava: Institute for Public Affairs, 1998), 15–80.

[42] CTK (Bratislava), 15 June 1999; and RFE/RL II, 3:117 (16 June 1999).

[43] See, for instance reports of meetings with leaders of the UK: RFE/RL II, 4:47 (7 March 2000); France: 4:76 (17 April 2000); Denmark: 4:95 (17 May 2000); Belgium: 4:163 (22 August 2000); Germany: 5:14 (22 January 2001); and Vladimír Bilčík, et al., "Slovakia's Foreign and Defense Policy," 248–257.

[44] CTK (Bratislava), 1 August 2000; and RFE/RL II, 4:147 (2 August 2000).

[45] See, for instance, RFE/RL II, 3:8 (13 January 1999); 3:80 (26 April 1999); 4:223 (16 November 2000).

relations between Bratislava and Budapest have eased markedly although several remain. These include Hungary's concern with the adverse affects of redistricting in Hungarian-majority areas of Slovakia, continuing problems with the Gabčikovo-Nagymaros dam on the Danube, and Slovak opposition to Hungary's "status law" that would grant privileges to ethnic Hungarians living in neighboring states.[46] Hungary, along with Austria and Germany, have also called for the revisiting of Czechoslovakia's so-called Beneš decrees of 1945, that allowed for the postwar deportation, resettlement, and confiscation of the property of hundreds of thousands German speakers and Hungarians. Another bone of contention has been the 2001 Slovak Local Public Administration Law referred to by Hungarian Prime Minister Viktor Orbán as "the worst possible" for ethnic Hungarians. As a result of the law, which failed to set up a region with an ethnic Hungarian majority in southern Slovakia, the Hungarian Coalition Party (SMK) voted unanimously to leave the ruling coalition in August 2001.[47] At the urging of EU officials and the president, the SMK – whose defection would have jeopardized Dzurinda's coalition government – decided to stay in the government. The tensions between the two countries prompted Prime Minister Dzurinda to boycott the March 2002 Visegrad Four summit to be held in Budapest. Nonetheless, Budapest has supported Slovak NATO membership partly because – as Hungarian Foreign Minister János Martonyi has said – it is in the interest of Hungarians living in Slovakia.[48] The new (after May 2002) center-left government of Péter Medgyessy is interested in improving Hungary's relations with Bratislava and has repeatedly indicated that an amendment of the status law was in the offing. Slovak relations with Prague and Warsaw have been essentially free of any tension.

[46] Interview with Col. Jozef Kapcala, Military Attache at the Slovak Embassy in Budapest (Budapest, 22 October 1999). See also Zsuzsa Csergő and James M. Goldgeier, "Hungary's 'Status Law': A Post-Territorial Approach to Nation-Building?" presented at the Annual Meeting of the American Association for the Advancement of Slavic Studies (Pittsburgh, PA, November 21–24, 2002).

[47] RFE/RL II, 5:150 (9 August 2001), 5:152 (13 August 2001); and "Csáky Pál szerint korai a kilépés," *Magyar Nemzet*, 15 August 2001.

[48] See Sándor Neszményi, "Martonyi látogatása Pozsonyban," *Magyar Nemzet*, 15 February 2001; and "Szilárd a Visegrádi együttműködés," *Magyar Nemzet*, 4 June 2001.

60 The Future of NATO Expansion

Bratislava's relations with other neighboring countries have also improved although the Austrian government remains concerned about the Slovak nuclear plant near Mochovce and has been lukewarm in its support of Slovakia's EU accession. Ukraine, on the other hand, was none too pleased about the visa requirements Slovakia established for Ukrainian citizens in the summer of 2000, in order to bring its visa policy in line with that of the Czech Republic. Kyiv quickly reciprocated though, given the nature of cross-border travel, Ukrainian citizens are affected far more adversely.

Slovakia also made an effort to raise the level of cooperation with other NATO candidate states. Bratislava initiated several meetings for states aspiring to join NATO in order to create a forum at which their plans could be discussed and their progress compared. Bratislava continuously coordinated its position on EU and NATO enlargement with Bucharest, Sofia, and Ljubljana, and intensified economic cooperation with them. Slovakia's relations with Romania have been especially cordial, in part because the two countries share the problem of a relatively large and contumacious Hungarian ethnic minority.[49] An enduring foreign policy problem Slovakia has had to face since the Dzurinda government took office has been the imposition, retraction, and reimposition of visa requirements on Slovak citizens by several West European states, owing to the influx of Slovak Roma. This issue elicited frequent international criticism of Bratislava's treatment of its Gypsy minority. The Dzurinda government has responded with new policies and programs designed to better the Roma's conditions.

In the spring of 1999 Slovak and Russian officials agreed that weapons and armaments would no longer be accepted in exchange for Russia's debt (energy sources would be substituted). More importantly, the new Slovak government decided to refuse the Russian S-300 anti-missile system as part of the debt settlement, even though it was already agreed upon by its predecessor.[50] In short, after 1998 Bratislava's flirting with Moscow ended. Its intention now was to conduct cordial

---

[49] See, for instance, OMRI Daily Digest, Part II, no. 97 (19 May 1997); and RFE/RL II, 4:68 (5 April 2000).

[50] See, for instance, Daniel Domanovský, "Migaš Trip to Russia Raises MP's Eyebrows," *Slovak Spectator*, 11–17 October 1999.

Slovakia: Catching Up to Its Neighbors

relations with Russia but to make no concession to its ultimate goal of Euro-Atlantic integration.

Slovakia's Unsteady Campaign for NATO Membership

In sharp contrast to its Visegrad Four partners, Bratislava was not invited to join the Alliance at the July 1997 NATO summit and the Luxembourg EU summit, held five months later, relegated Slovakia to the slower track toward membership. Although Prime Minister Mečiar declared that opposition parties and the "anti-Slovak" media were primarily responsible for NATO's snub, the real culprit was none other than his own coalition government. Although the short-lived Moravčik administration attempted to strengthen Slovakia's credentials for membership in the Alliance, until 1998 Bratislava's campaign to join NATO was uneven at best.

Slovakia joined the Partnership for Peace program in February 1994 without any major political debates. Nonetheless, the public could not but doubt the sincerity of official declarations in favor of NATO integration in view of very friendly relations with Moscow and due to the fact that two of the three parties in Mečiar's coalition government did not support this objective.[51] An October 1997 poll revealed that a large majority of the voters supporting all three coalition parties (HZDS, ZRS, SNS) overwhelmingly opposed NATO membership.[52] In April 1998 Defense Minister Ján Šitek, a member of the extreme right Slovak National Party, went so far as to sign a petition calling for Slovakia's neutrality, even though joining NATO was an official government policy.[53] SNS leaders have continued to voice their conviction that membership in NATO was both unnecessary and enormously expensive, threatening the fiscal health of the country.

---

[51] For a more detailed account, see Ivo Samson, "Transformation and Structural Change: Slovakia's Postcommunist Security and Military Adjustment to NATO Integration," in Piotr Dutkiewicz and Robert J. Jackson, eds., *NATO Looks East* (Westport, CT: Praeger, 1998), 131–134.

[52] See Zora Bútorová and Olga Gyárfášová, and Vladimír Krivý, "Parties, Institutions, and Politicians," in Zora Bútorová, ed., *Democracy and Discontent in Slovakia: A Public Opinion Profile of a Country in Transition* (Bratislava: Institute for Public Affairs, 1998), 85; and Vojtech Mastny, "Reassuring NATO: Eastern Europe, Russia, and the Western Alliance," *Forsvarsstudier* (Oslo), no. 5 (1997): 75–76.

[53] RFE/RL II, 2:73 (16 April 1998); and Reuters (Bratislava), 15 April 1998.

Perhaps the most unseemly moment in the Mečiar government's incongruous "quest" for membership in the Alliance was the May 1997 national referendum on NATO (and on direct presidential elections). The referendum was mainly demanded by the coalition parties in the legislature, especially the SNS. Experts contended that its timing (a month before the Madrid Summit) and the complicated wording of the questions signified an "obvious attempt at shifting the responsibility to citizens for the looming failure of the government's integration efforts."[54] In any event, the HZDS's two junior coalition partners openly opposed NATO membership despite the fact that their members held key positions in government: Šitek was Defense Minister and Jozef Kalman (ZRS) was deputy premier in charge of European integration. Mečiar's own party donated its pre-referendum television slots to opponents of the issue.[55] There were a number of irregularities with the ballots and the binding nature of the referendum itself was questioned by the Constitutional Court. In the end less than 10 percent of registered voters turned out and thus the results were invalid.

According to the Dzurinda cabinet, NATO membership will safeguard Slovak security, allow Slovakia to participate in joint exercises, provide financial assistance to restructure its military, and strengthen cooperation in the area of defense production.[56] On 30 October 1998, one of the first actions of the new government was to send an open letter to NATO Secretary-General Javier Solana, pledging to "introduce significant political and economic changes" and to set up a government "firmly devoted to democratic principles with full respect for the rule of law."[57] Representatives of the Slovak government have time and again expressed the crucial importance of NATO membership on their agenda. On a few occasions some politicians, like former Defense Minister Pavol Kanis, even suggested that NATO expansion to East-Central

---

[54] Zora Bútorová, "Public Reactions to Domestic Political Issues," in Zora Bútorová, ed., *Democracy and Discontent in Slovakia: A Public Opinion Profile of a Country in Transition* (Bratislava: Institute for Public Affairs, 1998), 120.

[55] Wlachovský, et al., "The Foreign Policy of the Slovak Republic," in Bútora and Skladony, *Slovakia 1996–1997*, 99. See also Martin Simecka, "Slovakia's Lonely Independence," *Transitions*, 4:3 (August 1997): 16–17.

[56] *White Paper on Defense of the Slovak Republic* (Bratislava: Ministry of Defense, 1998), 16.

[57] AP (Bratislava), 30 October 1998.

Slovakia: Catching Up to Its Neighbors 63

Europe that leaves Slovakia out "will create problems" in the relations between countries that joined and those that did not, playing to NATO fears of regional instability.[58] (Romanian politicians also repeatedly resorted to this tactic.)

On 6 October 1999, the Bratislava government approved the first annual National Program for NATO accession, based on the Membership Action Plan (MAP). On the same day Foreign Minister Kukan announced that President Clinton "promised" Dzurinda that Slovak accession could take place by 2001.[59] In October 2000 a conference entitled "Slovakia Belongs in NATO" was convened in Bratislava. Then-Deputy Prime Minister Hamžik said that "We realize that NATO members are not discussing enlargement much nowadays, and our task is to get that discussion going."[60] In early 2001 Dzurinda pleaded with top-ranking army officers to "identify themselves" with the "national priority" of Slovakia's admittance to NATO and promised to launch a "personal foreign political offensive" during his visit to the U.S. in February 2001.[61] The prime minister also formally agreed with President Schuster and Jozef Migaš, the parliamentary chairman, to put their differences aside and coordinate their approaches as Slovakia attempts to gain NATO and EU membership.[62]

The Dzurinda government has also taken a number of tangible steps to convince NATO of its commitment. As early as in February 1999 Bratislava gave the U.S. Air Force unescorted access to the Malacky airport near the capital and to the aerial training grounds nearby; since then this cooperation has expanded to include a growing number of Slovak airfields and USAF aircraft.[63] The cabinet also agreed to destroy its short-range SS-23 missiles – something its predecessor refused to do – albeit with U.S. funds. The last one was ceremoniously demolished in October 2000. In the wake of the September 2001 terrorist attack on the United States, Bratislava permitted U.S. military transport planes to overfly Slovak territory.

---

[58] See CTK (Bratislava), 21 January 1999.
[59] CTK (Bratislava), 7 October 1999.
[60] RFE/RL II, 4:209 (27 October 2000).
[61] RFE/RL II, 5:21 (31 January 2001); and 5:22 (1 February 2001).
[62] CTK (Bratislava), 20 June 2001.
[63] See, for instance, Keith Miller, "US Air Force Returns to Kuchyňa," *Slovak Spectator*, 31 July–6 August 2000.

64 The Future of NATO Expansion

In April 1999 Slovakia agreed to allow NATO to use the country's transport infrastructure system and air space in conjunction with its operations in the Balkans. This was a particularly beneficial measure from NATO's point of view since the two neutral states of the region, Switzerland and Austria, could not allow overflights without constitutional contravention. In May 2000, NATO Secretary-General Robertson thanked Slovakia for its assistance to the Alliance during the 1999 war in Yugoslavia. The Dzurinda government deployed a military engineering unit to Afghanistan in August 2002 to participate, under U.S. command, in Operation Enduring Freedom. From the early 1990s Slovakia participated in a number of regional organizations in addition to the Visegrad Group, such as the Carpathian-Euroregion.[64] These activities have intensified since 1998, in part undoubtedly to satisfy the NATO condition of cooperative relations with neighboring states. Slovakia has also been increasingly active in Partnership for Peace and has gained a great deal from its participation from proliferating individual contacts to professional exchange programs.

The Slovak public's support for NATO membership has been unenthusiastic perhaps because, as Štefan Sarvaš, a prominent Czech expert on the Slovak military has noted, the question of national sovereignty has been closely linked with neutrality.[65] In 1996 only 35%, in 1997 52%, and in 1998 58% of Slovaks supported NATO membership.[66] The government's decision to cooperate with NATO in 1999 not only divided the coalition but also went against popular views. Slovaks opposed NATO's airstrikes by a margin of 64%–32%,

---

[64] See, for instance, Vasil Hudák, "Transfrontier Cooperation in Central Europe," in Hudák, ed., *Building a New Europe* (Prague: Institute for East-West Studies, 1996), 1–10.

[65] Štefan Sarvaš, "The NATO Enlargement Debate in the Media and Civil-Military Relations in the Czech Republic and Slovakia," *European Security*, 9:1 (Spring 2000): 122. See also Ivo Samson, *Integracia Slovenska do bezpečnostného systemu Zapadu* (Bratislava: Slovak Foreign Policy Association, 1997).

[66] See Ivo Samson, "Transformation and Structural Change: Slovakia's Postcommunist Security and Military Adjustment to NATO Integration," in Piotr Dutkiewicz and Robert J. Jackson, eds., *NATO Looks East* (Westport, CT: Praeger, 1998), 134; and Zora Bútorová and Martin Bútora. "Slovakia and the World," in Zora Bútorová, ed., *Democracy and Discontent in Slovakia* (Bratislava: Institute for Public Affairs, 1998), 179.

Slovakia: Catching Up to Its Neighbors

and during the war their support for joining the Alliance dropped to 30%.[67]

A 29 June 2001 poll conducted by the UVVM Institute showed that 41% of the respondents supported, 46% opposed, and 13% were undecided about NATO membership.[68] Another survey carried out by the MVK polling agency two weeks later found, however, that 52.5% of Slovaks favored and 37.5% disapproved of joining the Alliance.[69]

This substantial disparity is likely due to errors in survey methods but the point is – regardless of which of the two polls is more reliable – that popular support for NATO remained lukewarm as confirmed by a February 2002 poll in which 53% were in favor and 35% against.[70] The endorsement of NATO accession by professional officers, on the other hand, has been quite high; according to Defense Minister Jozef Stank, it stood at 65% in March 2001.[71] In April 2001 Kukan admitted that raising the level of public support for membership "from the current 50% to 60% in 2002 was an important task" for the government which has been conducting a publicity campaign.[72] The government seems not to have reached its objective. Although a March 2002 poll found 57% support for NATO membership another survey conducted in October 2002 registered only 52.1% of those asked in favor.[73] In any case, Dzurinda, Kukan, Stank, and other members of the cabinet repeatedly declared that they fully expected an invitation to join the Alliance at the 2002 Prague NATO summit.[74]

---

[67] Inštitút pre Verejné Otázky (Institute for Public Affairs) poll on April 16–18, reported in TASR (Bratislava), 21 April 1999 (www.tasr.sk); and Jeffrey Simon, "NATO's Membership Action Plan (MAP) and Prospects for the Next Round of Enlargement," Woodrow Wilson Center (Washington, D.C.), Occasional Paper No. 58 (November 2000), 13.

[68] RFE/RL II, 5:125 (2 July 2001).

[69] RFE/RL II, 5:140 (26 July 2001).

[70] RFE/RL II, 6:27 (11 February 2002).

[71] RFE/RL II, 5:56 (21 March 2001).

[72] RFE/RL II, 5:78 (23 April 2001); and Martina Pisárová, "NATO Entry To Be Focus of Intense Media Campaign," Slovak Spectator, 4–11 February 2002.

[73] "NATO Entry Support Tops 57 percent," The Slovak Spectator, 8:11 (March 25–31, 2002); and RFE/RL II, 6: 197 (18 October 2002).

[74] See, for instance, RFE/RL II, 4:63 (29 March 2000); 4:119 (20 June 2000); 5:25 (6 February 2001); 5:89 (10 May 2001); 5:113 (14 June 2001); and Tom Nicholson, "Defense Ministry Starts 'Spring Cleaning' To Impress NATO," Slovak Spectator, 19–25 February 2001.

66 *The Future of NATO Expansion*

Opposition among political elites to joining NATO has hardly subsided since the Dzurinda government took office in 1998. In February 2001, for instance, in his meeting with NATO Secretary General Robertson, Róbert Fico, leader of the Smer Party, lambasted Premier Dzurinda for traumatizing Slovak society in preparation for NATO membership.[75] Nonetheless, Robertson said that the enlargement decision was unlikely to be influenced by the outcome of the 2002 Slovak elections – in which the current coalition parties could easily lose – since all major parties were committed to NATO membership.[76] Robertson may have been mistaken. The HZDS voiced its support for joining NATO and even lobbied members of the U.S. Congress emphasizing that the party guarantees to continue Slovakia's NATO accession process should it win the 2002 elections. Still, the HZDS's commitment to the cause has been widely questioned while the SNS remained unambiguously opposed.[77] Moreover, a July 2001 article in the Bratislava daily *Pravda* charged that parliamentary parties lacked the courage to admit that NATO costs were likely to prove much higher than they estimated and, as a result, defense expenditures would have to rise to 3 percent of the GDP (as opposed to 1.7% in 2001).[78]

A few words should also be said about military diplomacy, particularly because even during the Mečiar era military-to-military relations between Slovakia and its Visegrad partners (and particularly Hungary) were far better than interstate relations. Since 1998, the relations between the region's armed forces have further improved. In cabinet level meetings defense ministers of the Visegrad Group have continuously assured Bratislava of their support for Slovak NATO membership. Military cooperation between the Czech Republic and Slovakia has been especially strong given common traditions, compatible equipment, and the absence of language barrier. The Slovak army has

---

[75] Robin Sheeran, "News from Slovakia," *Central Europe Review*, 3:5 (5 February 2001).

[76] RFE/RL II, 5:100 (25 May 2001).

[77] See Daniel Domanovský and Tom Nicholson, "HZDS Apologizes, Embraces West," *Slovak Spectator*, 27 March–2 April 2000; Nicholsonová, "Opposition Seen as Potential NATO Barrier," *Slovak Spectator*, 26 March–1 April 2001; Štefan Sarvaš, "One Past, Two Futures?: The NATO Enlargement Debate in the Czech Republic and Slovakia," *Harmonie Paper 11*, 36–40; and RFE/RL II, 5:108 (7 June 2001), 5:133 (17 July 2001); and CTK (Bratislava), 6 May 2002.

[78] Cited by CTK (Bratislava), 1 July 2001.

conducted numerous joint exercises with Czech units. The Bratislava government also approved the formation of a joint peacekeeping battalion with Czech forces which began operating in Kosovo in March 2002.[79] Moreover, just days before the November 2002 Prague NATO Summit Slovakia signed an agreement with Hungary, Romania, and Ukraine to set up the "Tisa" international battalion to tackle natural disasters. Bratislava also backs the Czech proposal for joint air defense, a project that will also be advanced to Budapest and Warsaw.

The Slovak armed forces have been participating in a growing number of peacekeeping operations in Bosnia, Kosovo, and Moldova in Eastern Europe and, farther afield in the Golan Heights, and Angola. In fact, though Slovak involvement in peacekeeping has been relatively modest, it has been considerably more intensive than that of the Czech Republic.[80] Bratislava has also concluded a number of defense cooperation agreements with NATO members and other states. Especially important among these are the intergovernmental agreement on protecting secret military information with the U.S. (1995) and the accord with the U.K. regarding cooperation between the two armed forces and the sharing of know-how in strategic planning (1998).

PART III. CIVIL–MILITARY RELATIONS

Depoliticizing the Armed Forces

Following the demonstrations in November 1989 several strong signals – including a speech by Defense Minister Milan Vaclavik and the attempted information freeze in some bases – suggested that the military was taking the Czechoslovak Communist Party's side. Moreover, there is also evidence that a segment of the armed forces and political elites was contemplating the use of force during the brief upheaval that led to the fall of the communist regime in Czechoslovakia. Still,

---

[79] RFE/RL II, 5:75 (18 April 2001), and 5:98 (23 May 2001), and 5:155 (16 August 2001); and CTK (Bratislava), 15 August 2001.

[80] Ivo Samson, "Transformation and Structural Change," 128. See also Bilčík, et al., "Slovakia's Foreign and Defense Policy," 257–258. See also, Martina Pisárová, "Slovak Military Missions Aiding Country's NATO Ambition," *Slovak Spectator*, 27 August–2 September 2001.

68   *The Future of NATO Expansion*

the military did not play an active role in the transition of political power.[81]

The history of the Czechoslovak armed forces does little to dispel the stereotype of the "good soldier Švejk" created by the novelist Karel Čapek. It had no tradition of defending its country; in fact, it remained passive as Czechoslovakia was run over by Nazis (1938), communists (1948), and the Soviet-dominated Warsaw Pact (1968). In the communist era the military profession was unpopular, the educational level of officers was low, and the public had little respect for the armed forces particularly since the country was occupied by Soviet troops (1968–1991). Consequently, the army had faced constant challenges in recruitment, morale, and combat readiness.

Following the transfer of power to the democratically elected government, the first task was to depoliticize and democratize the Czechoslovak military. Already in December 1989 party organizations were banned from the armed forces and, as early as March 1990 the new defense minister, Miroslav Vacek, ordered soldiers and officers to resign membership in political parties. They could still run for public office but once elected they had to leave the armed forces. The Czechoslovak defense law of 1990 reduced compulsory military service from twenty-four to eighteen months, provided the option of alternative service, prohibited the drafting of women in peacetime, and guaranteed "full freedom of religion" to soldiers. The law also imposed strict limitations on the use of army units as a labor force and singled out only one scenario in which the armed forces could be used in internal security actions: in a direct armed attack on the constitutional system of the country. The decision to use the military rested with the Commander-in-Chief (CIC), the President of the Republic.[82]

In addition, a massive purge of the military was carried out in order to depoliticize the officer corps of whom as many as 90 percent were

---

[81] For a comparative analysis, see Zoltan Barany, "Civil-Military Relations in Comparative Perspective: East-Central and Southeastern Europe," *Political Studies*, 41:3 (December 1993): 594–610.

[82] See Zoltan Barany, *Soldiers and Politics in Eastern Europe, 1945–90* (New York: St. Martin's, 1993), 161; Dale R. Herspring, "The Process of Change and Democratization in Eastern Europe: The Case of the Military," in John R. Lampe and Daniel N. Nelson, eds., *East European Security Reconsidered* (Washington, D.C.: Woodrow Wilson Center Press, 1993), 58–59; and Carol Skalnik Leff, *The Czech and Slovak Republics* (Boulder, CO: Westview Press, 1997), 233–235.

Slovakia: Catching Up to Its Neighbors

Communist Party members. As a result of the "political screening" of all military officers, by September 1990 9,460 (15% of the corps) left the services. Of these, more than 52% did so voluntarily before the lustration process; 24% refused to sign the loyalty oath to the democratic state; 18.5% retired; and the rest were dismissed for incompetence.[83] It bears mentioning that many young officers refused signing the oath not for political reasons but because this way they could leave the military with impunity and be freed from their contractual obligations.

As the June 2001 discovery by the Czech Ministry of Interior that at least 114 screening certificates were forged in 1991–1992 shows, lustration was only relatively successful in Czechoslovakia. Czech security officials rushed to inform their Slovak counterparts that fifteen employees in the Bratislava MOD (Ministry of Defense) were agents of the former communist counterintelligence unit.[84] The screening of military officers did not continue in Slovakia after 1993 and this allowed certain figures from the pre-1989 army to remain in the service which prevented younger officers, untainted by their political past, to be promoted.[85] NATO's Office for Security has expressed its dissatisfaction about the fact that there are approximately 5,000 Slovak officials with potential access to classified information who have been exempted from security screening.[86] The renewed efforts of the Military Intelligence Service to weed out unreliable individuals yielded a "big fish" in September 2002 when Deputy Chief of Staff Jan Cmilansky failed to pass the vetting process and was asked to leave the armed forces.[87]

Slovak soldiers are permitted to be members of political parties but they may not participate in party functions during working hours or in uniform.

---

[83] Jan Obrman, "The Czechoslovak Armed Forces: The Reform Continues," *RFE/RL Research Report*, 1:6 (7 February 1992): 46–47.

[84] See Martina Pisárová, "Defense Officials Defuse Fears of VKR Agents in Ranks," *Slovak Spectator*, 18–24 June 2001; and idem., "What Is the Lustration Law?" in the same issue.

[85] See Silvia Mihalikova, "Political Culture and Civil–Military Relations in Slovakia," *Harmonie Paper 11* (Groningen, Holland: Centre of European Security Studies, University of Groningen, April 2000), 49. In June 2001 Vladimir Palko, chairman of the Slovak legislature's Defense and Security Committee said that lustration laws had not applied in Slovakia "practically since 1993." Cited in CTK (Bratislava), 6 June 2001.

[86] RFE/RL II, 6:20 (31 January 2002).

[87] TASR and CTK (both Bratislava), 7 September 2002.

Institutional Arrangements of Civilian Oversight

The current Slovak system of civilian control over the armed forces generally satisfies democratic requirements, although some pertinent laws could be clearer. During the Mečiar era – and particularly prior to the 1998 national elections when the governing coalition's defeat appeared increasingly likely – the ambiguity of some legislation coupled with the frequent disregard of the Constitution by the cabinet and its political allies led to a number of incidents unacceptable in a democratic state.

According to the Slovak Constitution the National Council (legislature) is the supreme authority of the state and it is empowered to amend the basic law and to ratify all laws regarding defense matters. The National Council solicits and deliberates reports submitted by the State Defense Council, ensures transparency, exercises its control through the budget process, and oversees the Minister of Defense who is answerable to parliament. The National Council also makes resolutions on declaring war and provides political and legal legitimacy to the armed forces. The parliament has two special committees directly pertaining to the armed forces: the Committee on Defense and Security and the Committee on Finance, Budget, and Currency through which civilian control is realized. There is an additional body, the Special Committee for the Control of the Activities of Military Intelligence.[88]

The President of the Slovak Republic is the Commander-in-Chief of the armed forces but does not get involved in day-to-day operations. In the peacetime chain of command (Chief of the General Staff [CGS] – Defense Minister [DM] – Prime Minister [PM] – parliament) the president is "out of the loop." In wartime, however, the President chairs the State Defense Council (*Rada obrany štátu*) and the CGS is directly responsible to him. The president personifies civilian control over the military, but he does not have the power to make any serious decisions on his own.[89] As in other "pure parliamentary systems," presidential powers in Slovakia are mostly ceremonial (i.e., similar to

---

[88] See Mihalikova, "Political Culture and Civil–Military Relations in Slovakia," 40; and interview with Miroslav Wlachowský (Bratislava, 7 September 1999).

[89] See William A. Walski, "Comparative Analysis of the Systems of Civilian Control over the Armed Forces in Slovakia and the USA," M.A. Thesis, Department of Politics, Comenius University (Bratislava, 2000), 37.

Slovakia: Catching Up to Its Neighbors

that in Slovenia or Hungary). During the Mečiar era the prime minister's dogged efforts to undermine and usurp presidential authority actually decreased presidential entitlements vis-à-vis the military. For instance, a 1995 constitutional amendment transferred the previously presidential power to promote generals to the government although the Constitutional Court later reversed this action.[90]

The government is responsible for carrying out parliamentary decisions and it recommends "draft issues" for the consideration of the legislature. The State Defense Council, whose members are ministers and other high-ranking officials engaged in military-security related fields, is a special governmental body that has primary responsibility for organizing the country's defense. It also makes decisions about the direction of Slovakia's military doctrine, approves major defense-related investments, and proposes measures to the government for the safeguarding of national interest.[91] In addition, there are interministerial committees that draft plans and recommend measures to the government regarding military-security affairs. The interministerial committee on NATO enlargement, for instance, consists of representatives from the ministries of defense, foreign affairs, finance, interior, education, environment, and the state resource administration. Among other things it drafts the Annual National Plan which includes reports on political, economic, defense, security, and legal aspects and is required by the MAP.[92]

The most important governmental body for defense is, of course, the Ministry of Defense which has been led by a civilian from the beginning of Slovak independence. The MOD is a conservative ministry, where few people work who were not politically active before 1989. Approximately half of the ministry's employees are civilians and half are military personnel. Nonetheless, just as in other East European states, retired military officers are often rehired and reclassified as civilians by the MOD, owing to the dearth of people with expertise and for personal reasons.[93] According to a 2001 interview with Martin Bruncko, a Slovak defense expert, many MOD employees who were educated

---

[90] Mihalikova, "Political Culture and Civil–Military Relations in Slovakia," 45.
[91] See, for instance, Ed Holt, "Ageing MiGs To Be Jettisoned," *Slovak Spectator*, 19–25 February 2001.
[92] See Simon, "NATO's Membership Action Plan (MAP) and Defense Planning: A Preliminary Assessment," 13.
[93] Interview with Wlachowský (Bratislava, 7 September 1999).

72 *The Future of NATO Expansion*

under the communist regime in Moscow, still think along Cold War policy lines, do not speak Western languages, and NATO is "naturally suspicious about these people's Soviet ideological thinking."[94]

Imrich Andrejčák (HZDS), a former general in the Czechoslovak army, was the first Slovak (1993–1994), and the last Czechoslovak defense minister. Andrejčák's was a formidable task: to build a new Slovak army from the remnants of the Czechoslovak military on Slovak territory. His successor was a civilian, Pavol Kanis of the reformed Communist Party of the Democratic Left (SDL), who served in Moravčik's short-lived cabinet (1994) and again, in Dzurinda's government until forced to resign (1998–2001). Kanis was not only a famously corrupt politician but he also filled the MOD with incompetent former communist officials and bureaucrats.[95]

During Mečiar's "long run" (1994–1998) the DM was Ján Šitek. When Mečiar's coalition government was taking shape after the 1994 elections, the SNS demanded for itself the defense portfolio so it could oversee and benefit from the privatization of the arms industry, most of which was located in the traditional SNS stronghold of the Váh river valley. Šitek became a weak Defense Minister, however, and the MOD was in effect run by Jozef Gajdoš, a HZDS-appointed State Defense Secretary.[96] In 1995 Šitek announced his plans to create a militia, subordinated to the Chief of the General Staff, which would be staffed by army veterans and "employed for the protection of objects and in the case of mobilization."[97] The legislature did not fund his request and the proposal fell by the wayside.

For years a sharp conflict persisted between the MOD and the general staff (GS) stemming in part from the breakup of Czechoslovakia. The Slovak army's command that officially became the GS after 1994, was established before the MOD was. Until 2000, when it moved to

---

[94] Martina Pisárová, "Stank Bolsters NATO Entry Plans," *Slovak Spectator*, 8–14 January 2001.

[95] Interview with Wlachowský (Bratislava, 7 September 1999). See also Matúš Korba, "Civil–Military Relations in Slovakia from the Perspective of NATO Integration," *Slovak Foreign Policy Affairs*, 2:2 (Fall 2001): 50–63 and Szayna, "Slovak Civil–Military Relations," 8.

[96] Antonietti, "Civil–Military Relations in Slovakia," 70.

[97] Jeffrey Simon, *Central European Civil–Military Relations and NATO Expansion*, McNair Paper 39, Institute for National Strategic Studies (Washington, D.C.: National Defense University, 1995), 148.

Bratislava and became a part of the MOD, the GS was based in Trenčín at the former headquarters in Czechoslovakia's Eastern Military District. The MOD had to be built up from scratch and it became, according to its critics, the bailiwick of inept political appointees and politicized generals. Officers at the GS perceived themselves as "real soldiers" versus the "politicians in uniform" at the MOD. People at the MOD, however, felt that the GS had no use for them whatsoever.[98] Even recent analyses contend that the MOD leadership has been extremely deficient in staffing the ministry with competent people.

An important source of tension between the MOD and the GS was that until recently there was no clear separation of functions between the two and their activities were often duplicated. According to the Law on the Army, the Chief of the General Staff (CGS) is appointed by the president based on the recommendation of the DM. The long-serving CGS, Pavol Tuchyňa (1994–2000), enjoyed extensive political support to replace DM Pavol Kanis (following his resignation due to financial misdeeds) in January 2001. Nonetheless, owing to the NATO norm that the minister is a civilian, the job went to a diplomat, Jozef Stank of the reformed communist SDL, the party to which the post belonged as a result of a coalition agreement. After the 2002 elections Stank resigned to run President Schuster's office. His Successor, Ivan Šimko, is a politician from the Slovak Democratic and Christian Union.

Finally, a few words should be said about the deliberation of defense expenditures because one of the most effective ways of civilian control is legislative oversight of the military's budget. Slovak parliamentary oversight is extremely limited over the country's defense budgeting process. One reason is that most legislators are ignorant about and seem to have little interest in defense matters. Partly as a result, the MOD has been able to pretty much prepare its budget request as it did under the communist system. That is, first the MOD and the GS draft their requirements which may or may not be subsequently modified by the government. Finally, the cabinet presents this budget to the legislature as a fait accompli.[99] There are few financial details provided and it is often unclear what the precise breakup of expenditures might be because the MOD provides the legislature only with aggregate numbers.

---

[98] Mihalikova, "Political Culture . . . ," 42.
[99] See Mihalikova, "Political Culture . . .", 51–52.

74   *The Future of NATO Expansion*

According to a 1996 statement by an official of the MOD's Economic Policy Section, "budgetary oversight does not yet exist" and "it is not yet possible to determine how much money is allocated per soldier, platoon, or company."[100]

The Dzurinda government promised more transparency in the budgetary process but shortcomings remain. Stanislaw Zatorsky of the MOD's Department of Financial Planning claims that the MOD's budget now includes approximately 800 items and all expenditures over 10,000 crowns and durable goods with a "life expectancy" of more than one year are in a separate register which is specially approved.[101] The budget is public, only some spheres of military research are classified. The MOD typically gets all the money approved by the legislature from the Ministry of Finance but in special cases (such as in 1998, when Slovakia suffered a debilitating flood) actual disbursements may be reduced.

Shortcomings of Civil–Military Relations

As the discussion above strongly suggests, all has not been well in Slovak civil–military relations although most of the problems occurred prior to the Dzurinda government's tenure. The legislature's role in defense matters was weak under Mečiar and members of his administration repeatedly attempted to crack and politicize the armed forces prior to the 1998 national elections.[102]. Parliamentary officers time and again ignored the Constitution and pertinent laws. For instance, in August 1998 parliamentary chairman Ivan Gašparovič dismissed the CGS, Jozef Tuchyňa, and appointed Marian Mikluš as his successor breaking the law which clearly states that the CGS is appointed by the head of state based on the DM's recommendation. When taken to task, Gašparovič said that "there is no point in discussing legal questions now."[103] He also appointed eight new brigadier generals and promoted five officers to major general without consulting with the DM

---

[100] Interview with Colonel Jozef Zadzora in *Obrana*, 16 March 1996; cited by Mihalikova, "Political Culture ...," 52.
[101] Interview with Zatorsky (Bratislava, 9 September 1999).
[102] Telephone conversation with Jeffrey Simon (19 July 1999).
[103] See Jeffrey Simon, "Transforming the Armed Forces of Central and Eastern Europe," *Strategic Forum*, no. 172 (June 2000): 5; and RFE/RL II, 2:161 (21 August 1998).

Slovakia: Catching Up to Its Neighbors

or the CGS, as prescribed by law. State Secretary Gajdoš repeatedly criticized his minister, Jan Šitek, who, Gajdoš said, should be replaced. More importantly, he also publicly castigated President Kováč commenting that "I do not find anything that would support his authority as commander-in-chief of the Slovak Armed Forces."[104]

Although the Slovak army is depoliticized, the actions of leading politicians have occasionally raised questions about how seriously they take the military's political impartiality or democratic civilian oversight. For example, Gajdoš publicly noted that the salaries of the professional soldiers might increase, but only after the 1998 elections and on the condition that the professional corps "will not fall short of expectations."[105]

The effectiveness of the legislature and its committees as civilian watchdogs over the armed forces are limited by their lacking expertise over defense issues. There are few civilian defense experts and this robs political institutions of objective advice on military matters. As a result, members of parliament do not have defense specialists on their staffs and they are rarely well informed about military-security issues.[106] The absent civilian awareness of defense-related matters diminishes the chance for substantive discourse between armed forces and society. In order to remedy this problem, foundations (e.g., the Slovak offices of the Friedrich Ebert and Konrad Adenauer foundations) and universities (in Bratislava, Banská Bystrica, and Prešov) have created the opportunity for civilians to learn about civil–military relations and defense issues. Civilians have also been able to take courses at the Military Academy at Liptovski Mikuláš.

The Slovak MOD has been no stranger to scandals and serious allegations of corruption at the very highest levels. Charges were most often associated with Jozef Gajdoš who, according to a number of military organizations like the Association of Slovak Soldiers, was guilty

---

[104] Interview with Gajdoš in *Slovenská Republika*, 29 December 1995, cited by Antonietti, "Civil–Military Relations in Slovakia," 71.

[105] *Národná obroda*, 6 February 1998, cited by Sarvaš, "One Past, Two Futures?," 54.

[106] See, for instance, Françoiş de Coulon, "Problems and Prospects in the Reform of the Defence Establishment in Slovakia: The Case of the Military Academy of Liptovsky Mikuláš in Central Slovakia," NATO Fellowship Programme (Bratislava, Summer 1996), 8–11; and Patrick Antonietti, "Civil–Military Relations in Slovakia," M.A. Thesis, Department of Politics, Comenius University (Bratislava, 1997), 65–66.

of corruption in a 1998 deal involving the repayment of Russian debts to Slovakia with the delivery of military equipment. The Mečiar cabinet's spokesman rejected DM Šitek's demand that Gajdoš resign on the ground that he was a political appointee.[107] A year later the MOD had to deny recurring allegations of bugging companies to be privatized in cahoots with National Property Fund officials.

The 2000 "A Study of Defense Reforms in the Slovak Republic" compiled by U.S. experts under the leadership of the U.S. Army's Major-General Joseph Garrett and with cooperation from the Slovak MOD, identified several major problems in civil–military relations. First, there is a troubling coexistence of military and quasimilitary elements in the defense sector. Second, the control of armed forces may be difficult in certain circumstances because they are under the jurisdiction of three ministries (MOD, Ministry of Interior, and the Ministry of Transport, Post, and Telecommunications). Third, in its personnel policies, the army still operates according to principles inherited from the communist regime. Not only are there too many former communists in the MOD's ranks but many of the key people are former generals ill-prepared to communicate at the highest levels with officials in Brussels. Finally, the report criticizes the government for the lack of a unified or national standard for planning the use of funds despite the relatively high annual GDP growth of the past and politicians' expectations that this trend is going to continue.[108]

PART IV. MILITARY REFORM AND THE STATE OF THE ARMED FORCES

Military Reform

In building a new Czech army political and military elites could use the federal structures based in Prague whereas their Slovak counterparts had to start with a clean slate. For instance, there was no military academy for training ground forces in Slovakia (it was located

---

[107] RFE/RL II, 2:171 (4 September 1998). Matúš Korba ably describes the tensions between Šitek and Gajdoš in his "Civil–Military Relations in Slovakia," 6.

[108] Tom Nicholson, "Defense Ministry Starts 'Spring Cleaning' to Impress NATO;" and "Garrett Report's Findings on Slovakia," both in *Slovak Spectator*, 19–25 February 2001.

Slovakia: Catching Up to Its Neighbors 77

in Bohemia) whereas the only air force academy in Czechoslovakia was based in the Slovak city of Košice. After the breakup of the federal state, Czech and Slovak officials agreed to split military assets on a two to one ratio, a process that was completed smoothly. Unfortunately for the Slovaks, however, most of the military infrastructure – not only repair and storage facilities but also housing for officers and soldiers – was based in the Czech lands. The 229 Slovak Air Force aircraft deployed in Slovakia, for instance, had to be lined up on airfields because there were no hangars in the country to house them.[109]

Although a number of steps were taken in the areas of force restructuring (e.g., establishing corps in place of divisions, brigades in place of regiments) and the redeployment of units, military reform was at best halfhearted in Slovakia between 1993 and 1999. The best that can be said is that the country laid the institutional groundwork for implementing NATO's Membership Action Plan. A comprehensive military reform concept – prepared by fourteen working groups in different ministries (four in the MOD) – was approved by the government in October 1999 and it produced some results by 2002. An integral part of this plan is that by 2002 the army's personnel should be levelling off at 30,000 (which would signify an approximately 45 percent reduction from the 1992 high of 54,000). Another important part of the reform is (especially English) language training for officers and NCOs. In 1999 the MOD issued an order called the "Strategy for Foreign Language Education at the Ministry of Defense" to ensure that by 2002 a minimum of 20 percent of professional soldiers reach some level of linguistic ability. As I noted above, the MOD and the GS were fused in early 2000 bringing the structural side of armed forces leadership in line with NATO requirements.

The centerpiece of current military reform is the "Concept for Reform of the Ministry of Defense Until 2002" which, according to Slovak experts, "deals with neither a concrete program or strategy for military

---

[109] Francine S. Kiefer, "Breakup of Army Is Technically Smooth, Socially Rough," *Christian Science Monitor*, 24 December 1992. See also, Milan Štembera, "ČSFR-Streitkräfte und Rüstung," *Österreichische Militärische Zeitschrift*, 30:5 (September–October 1992): 390–396; and Erich Schulz, ed., "Neuaufbau und Umstrukturierung der tschechoslowakischen Streitkräfte vor der Teilung," *Osteuropa* 43:1 (January 1993): A22–A40.

78   *The Future of NATO Expansion*

reform nor the entire system of defense" but merely the MOD.[110] The goal of these reforms is to create an army that would be able to guarantee to defense of the country on its own prior to membership in NATO. Closer scrutiny of the proposals reveals, however, that many unforeseen problems which can endanger the entire reform concept are concealed or taken as givens. The reform is based on successful application of the MAP and "will demand enormous effort" from Slovakia. The financial shortfall between reform requirements and designated funds is, again, according to Slovak experts, "alarming" and it is difficult to see how the fancy reform proposals and defense concept studies will amount to more than just words.[111]

Politicians and military leaders have innumerable times publicly contended that the Slovak armed forces were already prepared for NATO membership. Then-DM Kanis noted in February 2000 that unlike the members of NATO who joined in 1999, Slovakia would carry out its "radical military reforms" before joining the organization.[112] But four months later, when responding to criticisms of the armed forces, Kanis said that since 1998 when he took office, no one had taken seriously his warnings about the state of the army.[113] In reference to U.S. criticisms of the Slovak military's combat readiness Foreign Minister Eduard Kukan told a NATO Parliamentary Assembly subcommittee in June 2000 that "we must not forget that the aim of the Alliance is above all the protection and implementation of certain [democratic] values."[114] These and many other such declarations confirm doubts about Slovak commitments to substantive military reform prior to joining NATO.

Since early 2001, when Jozef Stank took over the defense ministry, several positive developments have taken place in the area of military

---

[110] Vladimír Bilčík, Martin Bruncko, Alexander Duleba, Pavol Lukáč, and Ivo Samson, "Slovakia's Foreign and Defense Policy," in G. Mesežnikov, M. Kollar, and T. Nicholson, eds., *Slovakia 2001: A Global Report on the State of Society* (Bratislava: Institute for Public Affairs, 2001), 256. See also Margriet Drent, et al., "Organising National Defences for NATO Membership: The Unexamined Dimension of Aspirants' Readiness for Entry," *Harmonie Paper 15* (Centre of European Security Studies, University of Groningen, October 2001), 81.

[111] Ibid.

[112] RFE/RL II, 4:33 (16 February 2000).

[113] Kanis in an interview with CTK (Bratislava), 2 June 2000; cited in RFE/RL II, 4:109 (6 June 2000).

[114] Cited by RFE/RL II, 4:119 (20 June 2000).

Slovakia: Catching Up to Its Neighbors

reform. During 2001 the MOD underwent a major reorganization as a result of which it employed 850 individuals in early October, 418 less than in the beginning of the year.[115] In the same year, Slovakia adopted a National Security Strategy and a draft military strategy, and took other important steps (which included the removal of antipersonnel mines and SS-23s from its arsenal). The MOD also committed itself to the abolition of the draft by 2006. Still, Slovak experts repeatedly charged that actual defense reforms did not proceed according to the government's ambitious plans.[116]

When I voiced my skepticism about Slovakia's military preparedness for joining the Alliance during my interviews with MOD and government officials, several of them told me that Slovakia would be ready by 2003.[117] By all impartial accounts (Slovak and foreign) it appears that they actually have a much longer way to go before they could satisfy NATO's criteria. According to the Garrett report, basic documents such as the Security Law and the National Military Strategy do not even correspond to defense requirements. After numerous reductions the army is still too large. At the same time, the level of professionalization and combat readiness are woefully low, especially in the many units that are staffed at less than 70 percent of their calculated wartime levels. Training is similarly inadequate owing to financial and professional causes. The Slovak army has not organized a single combined arms exercise nor has there been any joint training for ground and air forces.[118] In January 2001 Prime Minister Dzurinda found it necessary to call on the top brass to "identify itself" with the "national priority" of Slovak NATO membership warning that the effort they put forth would decide their future career.[119] In March 2001 his cabinet approved an updated "National Program for Preparations for Joining

---

[115] See, for instance, Waters, "Building an Army from Scratch," *Medzinárodné Otázky*, 7:4 (1998): 51; and the Defense Minister Stank's news conference, CTK (Bratislava), 5 October 2001 and RFE/RL II, 5:191 (9 October 2001).

[116] See, for instance, Korba, "Civil–Military Relations in Slovakia," 9–10.

[117] Meeting at the MOD with Stanislaw Zatorsky, Department of Financial Planning, Army Col. Marian Božik, Department of Defense Planning, Air Force Lt. Col. Dušan Kulík, Department of Integration and International Relations (Bratislava, 9 September 1999).

[118] This paragraph draws heavily on "Garrett Report's Findings on Slovakia," *Slovak Spectator*, 19–25 February 2001.

[119] RFE/RL II, 5:21 (31 January 2001).

80   *The Future of NATO Expansion*

NATO" the implementation of which for 2001 is estimated to cost 2.3 billion crowns (US$ 48.2 million).

Officers and Soldiers

The Slovak officer corps is depoliticized and officers seem averse to publicly voice political preferences but, of course, they do have them. According to Sarvaš there are three trends within the officer corps.[120] First, there is a pro-Western contingent which is comprised of those who studied in the West and share their democratic orientation. Second, there is a nationalistic element linked to the Slovak National Party (SNS) which advocates national principles of military organization. Finally, there is a populist faction linked with the HZDS. Although there is no official military trade union in Slovakia (they are forbidden by law), there are as many as 16 professional and social organizations in the military. Some of these – like the Association of Slovak Soldiers (ASS), the Slovak Liberation Army, and the Military Forum – originate from the time of the communist regime's fall, when they quickly became active in calling for an independent Slovakia and a separate Slovak army. Some have identifiable political leanings: for instance the first political orientation mentioned above is represented by the Association of Slovak Military Professionals and the Military Association of Slovak "Renewal" while the second by the most influential among these organizations, the ASS. During the Mečiar era the officer corps was considered to be far more Western oriented than the government of which they were quietly critical.[121]

Of the 8,686 Slovak officers based in the Czech lands in 1992, only 747 showed any interest in returning to Slovakia whereas most of the Czech officers deployed in Slovakia did return to their home region.[122] One of the biggest problems that affect military reform in Slovakia is the lack of money for adequate housing for officers and their families. The dearth of available housing compelled many Slovak officers – mostly

---

[120] This discussion draws on Sarvaš, "One Past, Two Futures?," 58.

[121] Ben Lombardi, "An Overview of Civil–Military Relations in Central and Eastern Europe," *Journal of Slavic Military Studies*, 12:1 (March 1999): 23.

[122] "Career Soldiers Prefer To Remain in Czech Army," *Pravda* (Bratislava), 5 March 1993; translated in *FBIS-EEU*, 9 March 1993.

Slovakia: Catching Up to Its Neighbors

those whose skills enabled them to find work outside of the military – to leave the service.

Although prospective military officers now can study at civilian institutions, professional training is based at the two military colleges: the Military Academy at Liptovski Mikuláš and the Military Aviation College at Košice. They confer two degrees which are also recognized by civilian institutions: a three-year bachelor's degree and five-year master's degree. Currently there are approximately 1,300 students at these institutions (including civilians). Although the opportunity to study in one of the many Western military academies is open to Slovak officers, such training does not necessarily denote a major benefit for the armed forces. First, the officers who participate in these programs are often the least qualified ones because commanders have a stake in keeping their more indispensable officers around. Second, many of the hundreds of Slovak officers who study abroad join the private sector upon their return. A recent decree obligates the returnees to serve a certain amount of time proportionate to their training period abroad in the military, but some officers have joined private companies anyway since their new employers are willing to pay the penalty assessed by the MOD.[123] Third, some officers expect or demand immediate career advancement upon their return thereby causing tension and antagonisms. Finally, an even more common phenomenon is when nothing happens to those who return due to lacking personal connections, professional jealousy, etc.

Training problems which originate in the absence of resources constitute one of the major problems for the Slovak armed forces. Owing to the lack of money to conduct regular training and for equipment maintenance officers and soldiers often do not have the opportunity to preserve their skill levels let alone raise them. For instance, Slovak air force pilots – those that actually fly since many have been made redundant by budget cuts – are in the air for 45 hours per year in contrast with the 160 to 180 hours customary for NATO states.[124] Moreover, the equipment in the Slovak arsenal – mostly Soviet-made airplanes

---

[123] Interviews with Wlachowský (Bratislava, 7 September 1999); and Col. Jozef Kapcala, Slovakia's military attache to Hungary (Budapest, 22 October 1999).

[124] See *The Military Balance, 2000–01* (London: International Institute for Strategic Studies, 2000), 102; and Bilčík, et al., "Slovakia's Foreign and Defense Policy," 255.

like MiG-21s and MiG-29s – are far more expensive to operate than Western aircraft. Still, there have been areas of substantial improvement. At the air force academy in Košice, for example, the quality of education is said to be very high and it is available entirely in English. Some experts have argued, however, that even though more and more Slovak officers acquire some foreign language facility, the situation is actually getting worse because the demand for such skills is increasing much faster than the supply of new language speakers.[125]

The prestige of the military profession in Slovakia is extremely low and the officer corps' morale is best described as lethargic. In a poll gauging the occupational preferences of conscripts, "army officer" ranked forty-third out of fifty professions.[126] Officers are poorly paid compared to the remuneration for similar qualifications in the private sector. The most important problem remains the absence of adequate housing which forces many officers to rely on their wives or families in obtaining houses. Single officers ordinarily live in shoddy dormitories or with extended families. Many commute from long distances. Recently salaries have become somewhat more competitive with the introduction of bonuses and incentives for special assignments.[127] Not surprisingly, the Slovak military also struggles with recruitment and replacement problems. In 1999 the MOD introduced some incentives for officers to stay; for instance, the payment of ten-to-thirteen-month salary tax free after twenty years of continuous service.[128]

Slovak officers nevertheless enjoy a great deal of public support. In public opinion surveys the military is rated consistently as the most trustworthy institution in the land. The media has been broadly supportive of the armed forces but few journalists are critical or have the expertise to provide real insight into military affairs. In a country with such a large proportion of ethnic minorities it is important to ask

---

[125] See François de Coulon, "Problems and Prospects in the Reform of the Defence Establishment in Slovakia: The Case of the Military Academy of Liptovsky Mikuláš in Central Slovakia," North Atlantic Fellowship Programme (Bratislava, Summer 1996), 5–7.

[126] Cited in Szayna, "The Military in a Postcommunist Czechoslovakia," Rand Note (N-3412-USDP, 1992), 60.

[127] See Mihalikova, "Political Culture . . . ," 55; Antonietti, "Civil–Military Relations," 71–73; and interview with officers (Bratislava, September 1999).

[128] Interview with Col. Kapcala (Budapest, 22 October 1999).

Slovakia: Catching Up to Its Neighbors

the question of how well are they integrated in the armed forces. By all accounts there are few problems with members of the Hungarian minority – although proportionately many fewer are interested in the military as a career choice than Slovaks. According to some experts there have been some difficulties communicating with Magyar conscripts who speak only Hungarian.[129] Much more problematic has been the training of Gypsy conscripts who are often illiterate and have a higher-than-average incidence of physical and mental health problems.[130] There is a growing number of female officers and NCOs in the armed forces most of whom are employed in administration.

The period of compulsory military service has been reduced repeatedly since 1989. It was shortened from twenty-four to eighteen months in 1991, then to twelve months in 1992. In November 2000 lawmakers overwhelmingly voted for a bill to cut mandatory service to nine months, a period so brief that it effectively limits the type of duties conscripts can be trained to perform. Finally, in January 2002 Defense Minister Stank announced that the conscription period would be shortened to six months in 2003 prior to the abolition of the draft in 2006.[131] The compulsory service is vastly unpopular among young men. With the fall of the communist regime and the introduction of unarmed service, they could freely express their opposition to it. By the end of 1991, a total of 38,000 men had refused to serve in the army but there were not enough alternative service positions for them. Moreover, a 1991 call-up of reservists became a disaster when more than 40 percent simply refused to participate as if to confirm survey results that suggested that 70 percent of reservists "have no interest in the defense of the state."[132]

There have been efforts to humanize military service with the reintroduction of chaplain's offices still, thousands refuse to fulfill their conscript obligations. A common complaint among men who enter the Slovak army is that they are wasting their time, that the bases are extremely disorganized, and that living conditions are poor. Moreover,

---

[129] Waters, "Building an Army from Scratch," 53.
[130] Interview with Col. Kapcala (Budapest, 22 October 1999).
[131] See Martina Pisárová, "Army Reform 2006: Conscripts No Longer Wanted," *Slovak Spectator*, 5–11 November 2001; and "Stank Briefs Army Officials," *Slovak Spectator*, 8:1 14–20 January 2002.
[132] Obrman, "The Czechoslovak Armed Forces," 47–48.

84   *The Future of NATO Expansion*

their military service is extremely boring mainly because there is no money to properly train soldiers so they end up literally marking time. As a result, some people are willing to bribe physicians (to the tune of 50,000 or 60,000 crowns) to receive "medically unfit" classifications.[133]

The State of the Forces

Slovakia's armed forces (38,600 [13,600 conscripts and 25,000 officers and NCOs] active personnel in 2000) are large for the size of country, its population (5.4 million), and in proportion to the country's borders. Although, as I noted above, the Slovak military, especially the ground forces, have already been reduced by nearly 16,000 since 1993, one of the major goals of the ongoing military reform is to cut the forces to 30,000 by 2004 and to 24,500 by 2006. The most important objective, as I was told on numerous occasions by Slovak officers, is "to have an army that is interoperable with NATO and can defend Slovakia." At present though, the quality of the forces leave much to be desired. The unusually frank Garrett report noted that the army's combat readiness was "virtually nil" and it had been equipped to "only about 70% of its needs in 2000."[134]

Like nearly all post-Warsaw Pact countries, Slovakia has also decreased its military spending. This trend started with the end of the communist regime. The Czechoslovak defense budget was slashed from 33 billion crowns in 1989 to 30.5 billion crowns in 1990, to 26.5 billion crowns in 1991 (without adjusting for inflation).[135] The budgetary problems of the last years of Czechoslovakia foreshadowed similar difficulties for independent Slovakia. The defense budget was cut from 2.2% of the GDP in 1995 to 1.69% in 1999. In 1998 it was 14.6 billion crowns (US$ 416 million) but sharply decreased in 1999, the first full year of the Dzurinda government, to 13.8 billion crowns (US$ 311 million) and increased only moderately in real terms to 15.8 billion (US$ 348 million) in 2000.

---

[133] See Ivan Remiaš, "Conscripts Resent Army Service," *Slovak Spectator*, 30 August–5 September 1999.

[134] RFE/RL II, 4:107 (2 June 2000).

[135] Thomas S. Szayna and James B. Steinberg, *Civil–Military Relations and National Security Thinking in Czechoslovakia* (Santa Monica, CA: RAND, 1992), 13.

Slovakia: Catching Up to Its Neighbors 85

According to recent forecasts defense expenditure in the 2003 budget will represent 2 percent of the GDP.[136]

Owing to the chronic shortage of resources, in 1997 the army could not call up 6,000 draftees (one-fourth of the annual conscription). And, in the second half of 1999 the Slovak armed forces had to be practically shut down and only vital programs – such as PfP participation which takes up roughly 5 percent of the defense budget – were permitted to continue.[137] In June 2000 DM Kanis said that the army needed 21 billion crowns for its modernization while the budget provided only 15 million crowns (i.e., less than 1 percent of the required amount!) for that purpose.[138] According to the MOD, the country's military outlays amounted to 1.74 percent of its GDP in 2001 which they were hoping to raise to 1.89 in 2002.[139] In short, as General Garrett noted, it is clear that Slovakia did not have sufficient financial resources to implement the Membership Action Plan.[140]

Because most of Slovakia's meager defense outlays are spent on personnel-related costs, since 1993 the military's arsenal has changed little. In February 2001 the MOD said that it would need $353 million to meet all (equipment-related) requirements for NATO membership but only $52 million was earmarked for that purpose in 2001. Considering such disparities it may be reasonable to assume that Slovakia will need a decade or more to modernize its aging fleet of MiG-29 combat aircraft and Mi-24 and Mi-17 attack and transport helicopters.[141] It is questionable, though, whether such aircraft is truly useful for Slovakia

---

[136] RFE/RL II, 6:218 (20 November 2002).

[137] See Simon, "Transforming the Armed Forces of Central and Eastern Europe," *Strategic Forum*, no. 172 (June 2000): 6. On these issues, more generally, see Gabriel Palacka, *NATO a cena za bezpečnost: Porovnavacia studia o nakladoch prijatia a neprijatia Slovenska do NATO* (Bratislava: IVO, 1997); and interviews with MOD State Secretary Jozef Pivarci in *Národná obroda*, 16 June 1999 and *Pravda*, 7 September 1999.

[138] Kanis in an interview with CTK (Bratislava), 2 June 2000; cited in RFE/RL II, 4:109 (6 June 2000).

[139] RFE/RL II, 5:36 (21 February 2001).

[140] Reported by TASR (Slovak telegraph agency) (Bratislava), 14 April 2000.

[141] Ibid.; and Holt, "Ageing MiG's To Be Jettisoned," *Slovak Spectator*, 19–25 February 2001. As of early November Slovakia possesses two fewer MiG-29s owing to the midair collision that took the life of one of the country's most experienced pilots (the other pilot managed to eject to safety). See "Jet Crash Takes One Life," *Slovak Spectator*, 11–17 November 2002.

86   *The Future of NATO Expansion*

at all. What the country does need, however, is the modernization of its radar and other air defense equipment.

Since 1993 Slovakia has managed to reduce its arsenal in accord with the Conventional Forces Europe Treaty, eliminating over half of its main battle tanks (currently 478), armored vehicles (683), aircraft (94), and nearly two-thirds of its artillery pieces (383).[142] Until 1998 Slovakia did receive some new equipment – MiG-29s, cargo planes, parts – as payment on Russia's debt. Other additions to Slovakia's arsenal have been limited to upgrades in a handful of artillery pieces and a few helicopters. In May 2001 Bratislava conducted negotiations on a barter deal in which it would receive thirty-six Czech-made L-159 subsonic aircraft from Prague in return for Slovak-made "Zuzana" howitzers.[143]

During the Cold War Slovakia was home to a relatively large defense industry. Actually, in the 1980s Czechoslovakia (in fact, largely Slovakia) ranked seventh among the world's arms exporters.[144] By 1991, however, arms exports had fallen to one-eighth of their former levels to traditional clients, several of whom would not pass muster with the West. For instance, a tank deal with Syria, designed to rescue Slovakia's tank producing enterprises that ran out of orders triggered U.S. presidential protests.[145] Incidentally, the production of tanks – mostly modified and updated versions of the Soviet-made T-72s – had been for years the bread-and-butter of Slovak defense industry. The drastic drop in production went hand in hand with major losses of revenue and increasing unemployment in some industrial areas. The privatization of the defense sector has been slow and, according to one expert, the old bureaucratic, centrally-directed system continues with a state-owned holding company coordinating the industry as a whole.[146]

---

[142] See *Armáda Slovenskej Republiky 1999* (Bratislava: MOD, 2000), 33.

[143] CTK (Prague), 17 May 2001.

[144] Samson, "Transformation and Structural Change," 129–130; see also Yudit Kiss, "Sink or Swim? Central European Defense Industry Enterprises in the Aftermath of the Cold War," *Europe-Asia Studies*, 47:5 (1995): 787–812; and idem., "Trapped in Transition: Defence Industry Restructuring in Central Europe," *European Security*, 4:1 (Spring 1995): 56–84.

[145] Leff, *The Czech and Slovak Republics*, 229.

[146] Thomas S. Szayna, "Central European Defense Industries and NATO Enlargement," Rand Report (MR-717.0-RC, 1996), 25; and interview with Col. Kapcala (Budapest, 22 October 1999).

Slovakia: Catching Up to Its Neighbors 87

It may be on the verge of a modest recovery, however. In October 1997 Turkish Defense Minister Ismet Sezgin, and in May 2000 Pham Van Tra, his Vietnamese colleague, expressed interest in cooperating with the Slovak armaments industry.[147]

CONCLUSION

Slovakia was turned down by NATO in 1997 primarily because of its poor record of democratic consolidation. NATO Secretary-General Javier Solana openly criticized the Mečiar government in 1998 warning that "the decision on NATO membership will be made in Slovakia and if there are any problems, these problems are not in Brussels … but in Bratislava."[148] Since the 1998 elections the new government has drastically improved the country's political climate. Although the Dzurinda cabinet has been unable to significantly weed out corruption, its domestic and foreign policies have strongly supported its key objective of Euro-Atlantic integration. The 2002 elections confirmed that Slovakia was firmly committed to consolidate its democracy.

The Dzurinda government's campaign for NATO membership has been committed and intensive. Some opposition political forces have actually felt that the cabinet has uncritically served NATO's interests while defying public opinion prior to and since the Kosovo crisis when it surrendered control over its railways, air space, and military bases to the Alliance. Moreover, the Slovak population has had no more than half-hearted support for their country's membership in NATO. Just how tenuous this support was was clearly shown during NATO's 1999 Kosovo operation.

Although civil–military relations are by and large democratized this is not an area without problems either. Legal ambiguities have encouraged some public officials to subvert the intention of laws and high-ranking politicians have actually repeatedly broken the law and violated the principle of the military's political neutrality. Thousands of Slovak public officials are potential security risks from NATO's perspective since they have not gone through a security clearance process. At present Slovakia does not have an adequate pool of civilian military

---

[147] RFE/RL II, 1:146 (24 October 1997); and 4:97 (19 May 2000).
[148] Reuters (Bratislava), 6 March 1998.

experts who could provide objective information about defense and security issues to lawmakers. Consequently, the latter are ill-informed, a fact that has had serious ramifications to the budgetary process.

As a number of domestic and foreign critics have convincingly demonstrated, the effectiveness of Slovakia's military reforms has left a great deal to be desired. The armed forces have yet to overcome major shortcomings in downsizing, combat readiness, training, morale, the budgeting process, equipment, English (and generally foreign) language facility, and several other areas. A 2001 NATO report has found fault with Slovakia's basic security documents, many of which were outdated or irrelevant and problems remain with the planning and distribution of resources. In a candid moment in April 2001, Defense Minister Jozef Stank himself admitted that "the current state of the armed forces does not correspond" with NATO requirements.[149] Six months later, Stank conceded that reform of the Slovak Army along NATO guidelines *will take until 2015* rather than 2010 as previously thought.[150]

In short, it seems safe to assume that the Slovak armed forces will not satisfy NATO's accession criteria in the foreseeable future and certainly not by 2004 when it is scheduled to become a full member of the Alliance.

[149] RFE/RL II, 5:78 (23 April 2001).
[150] "Army Reshape To Last Until 2015," *Slovak Spectator*, 7:37 1–7 October 2001, my emphasis.

3

Slovenia

A Regional Leader

This chapter, like the next two, will follow the thematic framework familiar from Chapter 2. Thus, in Part I I review Slovenia's democratization process, its economic performance, and the security situation it found itself in after gaining independence on 25 June 1991. Part II examines Slovene foreign policy since 1991 and Ljubljana's campaign for NATO membership. Part III concentrates on matters pertaining to civil–military relations. In the last portion of the chapter the focus shifts to military reform and the state of Slovenia's armed forces.

At the outset I should like to point out a common misconception according to which contemporary Slovenia is a part of the Balkans. Slovenia "became" a Balkan state after World War I owing only to its incorporation into what was to become Yugoslavia. Once it obtained independence in 1991, Slovenia should once again be categorized as an East-Central European (or Central European) state. Apart from its unambiguous geographical position, it was ruled for nearly eight hundred years by the Austrian Habsburgs prior to 1918 and, in terms of its economic and cultural orientation, Slovenia may well be the most "Western" of East European states. At the beginning of the new millennium Slovenia is indisputably the most prosperous state with the cleanest government in postcommunist Europe, in many respects far ahead of its closest rivals, the Czech Republic, Hungary, and Poland.[1]

---

[1] See the table in "Ex-communist Europe: Is Democracy Working?" *The Economist*, 23 June 2001, 47.

89

90 *The Future of NATO Expansion*

PART I. DOMESTIC POLITICS, ECONOMIC PERFORMANCE,
SECURITY STATUS

Domestic Politics

On 25 June 1991, the Slovene legislature passed a Declaration of Independence which effectively signified Slovenia's separation from the federal state of Yugoslavia. This act was the logical culmination of a five-year long liberalization process. It began in 1986, when reform-minded and younger cadres led by Milan Kučan became the dominant force in the League of Communists of Slovenia. Thus, Slovenia may have been the first East European country – albeit not yet an independent one – that set out on a path toward democratization.[2]

In the first post-World War II multiparty elections held in April 1990, Slovenes elected the former communist leader, Kučan, who represented the new Social Democratic Party, as their president. He has been serving in that capacity ever since, having been repeatedly reelected by large margins. He is likely to be succeeded, after the December 2002 run-off presidential elections, by long-time prime minister Janez Drnovšek. Kučan is one of the few erstwhile communists in the region who seems to have made a complete personal transition and become a genuine social democrat. Even his detractors allow that he has a clear vision of his country's future that few East European politicians share.[3]

Slovene independence is rooted in a December 1990 plebiscite in which 88 percent of the participants had voted in favor of sovereignty. Although the EU, the United States, and the federal Yugoslav government all stressed their opposition to Slovene independence, politicians in Ljubljana forged ahead.[4] From 27 June to 4 July 1991, units of

---

[2] Sabrina Petra Ramet, "Democratization in Slovenia – the Second Stage," in Karen Dawisha and Bruce Parrott, eds., *Politics, Power, and the Struggle for Democracy in South-East Europe* (New York: Cambridge University Press, 1997), 191. On Kučan, see "Canny Survivor," *The Economist*, 22 November 1997, 60, 62.

[3] Interview with Damjan Perlovšek, Slovenia's Ambassador to the Czech Republic (Prague, 25 August 1999).

[4] See Milan Andrejevich, "Slovenia: Politics and the Economy in the Year One," *RFE/RL Research Report*, 1:36 (11 September 1992): 16; and Bojko Bučar, "The International Recognition of Slovenia," in Danica Fink-Hafner and John R. Robbins, eds., *Making a New Nation: The Formation of Slovenia* (Brookfield, VT: Dartmouth, 1997), 31–45.

Slovenia: A Regional Leader 91

the federal Yugoslav Army and the Slovene territorial defense forces engaged in clashes that resulted in fifty-four casualties, over three hundred wounded, and considerable property damage. In early July international mediators met with federal and Slovene emissaries who agreed to a cease fire and to the gradual withdrawal of Yugoslav troops from Slovenia. Belgrade's willingness to leave undoubtedly had much to do with its concern with Croatia's substantial Serbian minority, given that Croatia also declared its independence on June 25, 1991. In late October the last Yugoslav soldier left Slovene territory and President Kučan could jubilantly announce: "Citizens of Slovenia, the Republic of Slovenia is free."[5]

Since 1992 Slovenia has been a pure parliamentary system, dominated by the ninety-member National Assembly. Similarly to Slovakia but in contrast with Romania, presidential powers in Slovenia are limited. Sabrina Ramet, an American expert on Slovenia contended in 1997 that "Slovenia's gravitation toward a stable party system has been nothing but robust"[6] but, two years later, she wrote of the "continued instability of political parties, as parties continue to split and recombine with other parties."[7] I agree with her 1997 opinion: the Slovene party system has been relatively stable, especially in comparison to other East European states like Romania, and the changes that have occurred may be considered the normal "growing pains" of a new polity. Since independence the main political parties have been the Liberal Democratic Party of Slovenia (LDS), the United List of Social Democrats of Slovenia (ZLSD), the Party of Pensioners of Slovenia (DeSUS), the Christian Democratic Party (SKD), the Slovene People's Party (SLS), Social Democratic Party of Slovenia (SDS), and the Slovene National Party (SNS).

Slovenia's first freely elected prime minister was a Christian Democrat, Lojze Peterle, who held the office for two years (April 1990 to April 1992). Peterle's SKD was a member of DEMOS, a six-party coalition of center and center-right parties. Peterle's government succeeded in guiding the country from a constituent republic in a federal state to

---

[5] *Večerno delo* (Ljubljana), 27 October 1991.
[6] Ramet, "Democratization in Slovenia," 205.
[7] Ramet, *Balkan Babel: The Disintegration of Yugoslavia from the Death of Tito to the War for Kosovo* (Boulder, CO: Westview Press, 1999, 3rd ed.), 181.

a sovereign democracy. It could not achieve consensus on a number of major issues ranging from foreign policy to privatization and was unable to avert a governmental crisis in early 1992. In May 1992 the Slovene National Assembly elected the leader of the leftist Liberal Democrats, Janez Drnovšek as prime minister. Since then, apart from a six-month interruption, Drnovšek has headed Slovenia's coalition governments prompting two British specialists to entitle a chapter in their book on the country "Hiatus: Drnovšek and Kučan for ever?"[8] Nonetheless, the governing coalitions at times were born after difficult negotiations following long delays which in 1998 and 2000 resulted in problems for Slovenia's ability to deal with both its NATO and EU accession processes.[9]

The "hiatus" James Gow and Cathie Carmichael refer to occurred during April–October 2000. On 8 April Drnovšek lost a vote of confidence which turned into the biggest political crisis in post-independence Slovenia. Andrej Bajuk, the candidate of the center-right opposition succeeded in securing parliamentary approval for his proposed government only on his third attempt. The new cabinet was the first since independence that was not led by former members of the communist-era nomenclature. Nonetheless, it did not last long. In the October 2000 elections Drnovšek and his Liberal Democrats once again garnered the largest number of votes.[10] A new coalition, controlling fifty-eight of the ninety seats in parliament, took shape in the following month. It includes the Liberal Democrats, the conservative People's Party, the former communists known as the United List of Social Democrats, and the Pensioners' Party.

The Liberal Democrats' chief political rival has been the right-wing and thus misnamed Social Democrats (SDS) led by the most controversial Slovene politician, Janez Janša. It is no exaggeration that much of what has been objectionable in Slovene politics from the perspective of

---

[8] James Gow and Cathie Carmichael, *Slovenia and the Slovenes: A Small State and the New Europe* (Bloomington: Indiana University Press, 2000). See also "Janez Drnovsek, Slovenia's Dogged Guardian," *The Economist*, 22 April 2000.

[9] See Gow and Carmichael, *Slovenia and the Slovenes*, 170, 173; "Bridging Europe," *The Economist*, 11 January 1997, 49; and Radio Free Europe/Radio Liberty, Newsline, Part II (henceforth: RFE/RL II), 4:100 (24 May 2000).

[10] See Brian J. Požun, "Slovenia's Return to the Left," *Central Europe Review*, 2:36 (23 October 2000).

Slovenia: A Regional Leader 93

democratic consolidation has been, in some way, connected to Janša himself. A journalist who wrote critical articles about the Yugoslav armed forces, Janša was arrested with three of his colleagues in 1988. The botched trial at the end of which they were sentenced to eighteen-month prison terms galvanized Slovenia's opposition and became a mile-post in the Slovene path to independence. In the first multiparty government in 1990 Janša became a defense minister, a portfolio he retained until 1994. In his early life, Janša was a leading figure of the communist youth organization but by the late 1980s he adjusted his sails to the changing political winds and began his ideological jour-ney "from radical Marxist left to the extreme anti-communist and nationalist-xenophobic right."[11] His stance on national defense has evolved from pacifism to neutrality to ardent support of Slovene NATO membership.

Slovene politics has certainly lacked the antidemocratic features and frequent political dramas of Mečiar's Slovakia. Nonetheless, some con-troversies in public affairs have occurred. Especially in the early 1990s, the Roman Catholic Church – to which over 90 percent of the country's religious belong – attempted to get abortion criminalized and make Catholic instruction at schools mandatory by intensively campaign-ing for the Christian Democrats and urging voters to cast their ballots to those representing "Christian" as opposed to "communist" values. As Anton Bebler, his former professor at the University of Ljubljana's program on defense studies and an aspirant to his job has written, Janša, a veteran of four parties who founded the SDS, used it as a pool for political appointees in the Slovene Ministry of Defense (MOD).[12] While he was defense minister and since his dismissal from the MOD in 1994 (decided by a National Assembly vote), Janša has repeatedly sought to embarrass President Kučan, shamelessly castigating him for his communist past even as he overlooked his own.

During the mid-1990s, the prime minister and cabinet members ac-quired more power in practice than constitutional provisions would

---

[11] Anton Bebler, "Civil–Military Relations in Slovenia," in Constantine P. Danopoulos and Daniel Zirker, eds., *Civil–Military Relations in the Soviet and Yugoslav Successor States* (Boulder, CO: Westview Press, 1996), 207. See also, James Gow, "Slovenia: Stabilization or Stagnation," *RFE/RL Research Report*, 3:1 (7 Jan 1994): 135–136.

[12] Bebler, "Civil–Military Relations in Slovenia," 208; Ramet, *Balkan Babel*, 181; and Ramet, "Democratization in Slovenia," 212–213.

have suggested and ministers – particularly in the case of Janša – could get away with using their ministries as their personal fiefdoms.[13] Although according to Transparency International's 2002 report Slovenia was the least corrupt East European country it is not immune to the problem.[14] In November 2000, for instance, Boris Šustar, a well-known official and economics professor who oversaw the privatization of state-owned companies was arrested on charges of blackmailing and bribe-taking.[15] Still, this was the first corruption charge against a high-ranking government official in independent Slovenia.

Slovenia has been easily the most stable polity and the most democratic state among the four countries this book focuses on.[16] Even so, according to the Ljubljana government, one of the reasons for its quest for NATO membership is "to strengthen and enhance democratic standards."[17] Ethnic minorities make up roughly 10 percent of the country's population and they benefit from one of the most liberal minority policies in the region although xenophobia is not entirely absent from Slovene society.[18] The EU's 2000 report on Slovenia's progress toward accession recognizes that Ljubljana essentially meets all political criteria and identifies only a few areas for improvement. The most important of these is the relative slowness of the legislative process – there is a large backlog of pending court cases – which itself points to the need for comprehensive judicial reform. The process to overhaul Slovenia's electoral system, for instance, has lasted for nearly five years. The affair has included a referendum, a controversial Constitutional Court decision, and endless debates between parliamentary parties. In the end, the resulting legislation is unlikely to change Slovene politics.[19]

---

[13] Gow and Carmichael, *Slovenia and the Slovenes*, 142.

[14] RFE/RL II, 4:178 (14 September 2000).

[15] RFE/RL II, 4:218 (9 November 2000); and 5:51 (14 March 2001).

[16] This discussion draws on Brian J. Požun, "EC 2000 Progress Report on Slovenia," *Central Europe Review*, 2:39 (13 November 2000).

[17] "National Strategy for Integration of the Republic of Slovenia into NATO," *Facts about Slovenia* (Ljubljana: Government Public Relations and Media Office, 1998).

[18] See, for instance, Miran Komac, ed., *Protection of Ethnic Communities in the Republic of Slovenia* (Ljubljana: Institute for Ethnic Studies, 1999); and Sabrina P. Ramet, "The Slovenian Success Story," *Current History*, 97:617 (March 1998): 116.

[19] Andrej Auersperger Matič, "Electoral Reform as a Constitutional Dilemma," *East European Constitutional Review*, 9:3 (Summer 2000): 77–81.

Economic Performance

Slovenia was one of the most prosperous regions in communist Europe. It only had about 8 percent of Yugoslavia's population but its export share was nearly 30 percent.[20] In the 1990s, Slovenia's economic performance was the envy of East-Central Europe. It is the only postcommunist economy to have attained A-grade ratings from risk-assessment agencies like Standard & Poor's as early as 1996. Its per capita income has already surpassed that of Greece and Portugal, two EU member states. Since 1992, it has had single-digit inflation, positive economic growth (one of the highest percentage of sustained growth in the region), and budget deficits of less than 1 percent.[21]

This is not to say that the Slovene economy has not faced adversities. As a result of the collapse of Yugoslavia, Slovenia lost 70 percent of its traditional markets and faced short-term economic problems as it encountered problems in shifting trade to new markets. By 2000, however, over 70 percent of Slovenia's trade was with the European Union though Slovene businesses remained hopeful to regain the Yugoslav market.[22] Slovenia has also compiled a lackluster record of attracting foreign direct investment (FDI), obtaining only one-third of that of Estonia. In 1996 Prime Minister Drnovšek blamed low FDI on certain political parties that, fearing loss of sovereignty, contended that the country should "protect itself" from outside investment.[23] Although unemployment rates through most of the 1990s were relatively high, in the summer of 2001, after a sustained decline, it dropped to 6.7 percent.[24]

More importantly, owing to the difficulties of reaching political compromises about the appropriate method of denationalizing state property, privatization did not start in earnest until 1994. By 1996,

---

[20] Duncan Shiels, "Slovenia Shines in Shadow of War," *Central European Times On-Line*, 2:32 (14 February 1995).

[21] See Michael Wyzan, "A Reluctant Star in the Economic Sphere," *Transition*, 2:25 (13 December 1996): 41–43, 64; and Michael Huelshoff, "CEE Financial Reform, European Monetary Union, and Eastern Enlargement," in James Sperling, ed., *Two Tiers or Two Speeds? The European Security Order and the Enlargement of the European Union and NATO* (Manchester, England: University of Manchester Press, 1999), 71–72.

[22] RFE/RL II, 5:11 (17 January 2001).

[23] Quoted by Wyzan, "A Reluctant Star," 41.

[24] "Labour Market: Record Fall in Unemployment," *Slovenia Weekly*, 16–22 July 2001.

96 The Future of NATO Expansion

however, only 555 out of about 1,500 enterprises slated for privatization had their programs approved by the privatization agency. The slow progress in this area was also demonstrated by the fact that in late 2000 Prime Minister Bajuk still identified privatization as his government's key priority. As he said, "The need for privatization is an urgent problem because too many firms are directly or indirectly owned by the state," an unacceptable situation by international standards.[25]

Notwithstanding some remaining problems, Slovenia is likely to face fewer problems once it obtains EU membership than any other East European state. Nicole Fontaine, the president of the European Parliament said in April 2000 that she fully expected Slovenia to be among the first group of new members and "be among the countries that will participate in the 2004 election to the European Parliament."[26] The head of the Slovene Office for European Affairs, Janez Potočnik, announced in November 2000 that Ljubljana was going to be ready to join the EU as early as 2002. According to recent EU reports, Slovenia is expected to work on privatization, public administration reform, setting up regional development offices, and improving border regulations. In early 2001 Foreign Minister Dimitrij Rupel said that Slovenia's chances of joining the EU would be boosted if it were admitted to NATO.[27] In fact, Slovenia could hardly be better positioned for EU accession with or without membership in the Alliance. It surprised no one that Slovenia received an invitation from the EU in October 2002.

Security Situation

In the aftermath of Yugoslavia's breakup it would be hard to come up with even a marginally realistic scenario in which Slovenia would be invaded. It is bordered by two NATO members, Italy and Hungary, neutral Austria (an EU member), and Croatia. Slovenia's relations are cordial with all of its neighbors but it has sparred with Austria, Croatia, and Italy concerning a number of unresolved issues. These, however, in no way constitute any form or level of threat to Slovene security.

---

[25] RFE/RL II, 4:193 (5 October 2000).
[26] Reuters (Ljubljana), 18 April 2000.
[27] RFE/RL II, 5:28 (9 February 2001).

After independence, Slovenia's only direct experience with the wars in Yugoslavia was a few incidents of Croatian military aircraft (ostensibly accidentally) violating Slovene airspace and Serbian surface-to-surface missile strikes on Croatia within five miles of the Slovene border.

Slovene political elites recognize the need to maintain armed forces for two reasons. First, to possess a force capable of reacting to or deterring cross-border incursion; and second, to be able to utilize the armed forces as a part of a broader security policy for the country while also demonstrating that Slovenia was a responsible member of the international community.[28]

Owing to the lacking statehood tradition and a Slovene military doctrine as well as to the frequent changes of personnel at the top of the ministries of defense and foreign affairs, Slovene elites needed a great deal of time to define key national interests in the security and foreign policy field. As the country's current Defense Minister, Anton Grizold, wrote in a 1995 article, Slovenes recognize that there are no military threats to their country and whatever security challenges do exist are of a social and economic character, for example, economic crisis, drugs, crime, and natural disasters.[29] In fact, the Slovene case of a complete lack of a security threat has raised the question in many an analyst's mind whether – considering its small size and population – the Alliance really needed new members whose only substantial contribution could be to provide overland connection between other members (in Slovenia's case, between Italy and Hungary).[30]

In concert with its favorable security situation, Slovenia's military doctrine does not identify any foes and the Slovene Army has an entirely defensive configuration. In the field of national security the legislature has approved three major documents: the "Resolution on General Principles of National Security" (1993), the "Military Defense Doctrine" (1995), and the "Military Defense Strategy" (1998). According to Jeffrey Simon, Slovenia's defense doctrine exists only in name; to complete it has been a difficult task owing to disagreements regarding who should prepare and approve the document and because

---

[28] Gow and Carmichael, *Slovenia and the Slovenes*, 187.
[29] Anton Grizold, "The National Security of Slovenia: The View of Public Opinion," *Balkan Forum*, 3:3 (September 1995): 184.
[30] See, for instance, Vojtech Mastny, "Reassuring NATO: Eastern Europe, Russia, and the Western Alliance," *Forsvarsstudier* (Oslo), no. 5 (1997): 74.

98 *The Future of NATO Expansion*

parliamentary parties do not have a clear concept of defense policy.[31] Following a great deal of legislative work, in a July 2002 interview Defense Minister Grizold contended that Slovene strategic and doctrinal documents were entirely comparable with those of developed countries.[32]

PART II. FOREIGN POLICY AND THE CAMPAIGN FOR NATO MEMBERSHIP

Slovene Foreign Policy from Independence to 2001

From the moment of its independence, Slovenia has conducted an unambiguously pro-Western foreign policy having abandoned the former Yugoslavia's active non-alignment approach. This uncompromised Western orientation has continued under all Slovene governments. The top priority of Slovene foreign policy has been full-fledged membership in the EU followed by joining NATO.

After obtaining sovereignty, foreign policy makers in Ljubljana had two immediate tasks. First, to gain influential supporters willing to recognize Slovenia as an independent state. Second, to convince the international community to view Slovenia not as a part of the Balkans but as a viable, stable, and democratic Central European state without ethnic minority problems. Slovenia accomplished the first objective (the EC officially recognized it in January 1992) by appealing to historically sympathetic sponsors: Austria and especially Germany. Among "Western European states Serbophile France was the last" to recognize Slovene independence in April 1992, two weeks after the United States.[33]

Ljubljana attempted to achieve the second goal by distancing itself from the on-going crisis in the former Yugoslavia. In fact, as Vojtech Mastny points out, "Slovenia's desire to dissociate itself from the other heirs of the former Yugoslavia by dwelling on its Central European heritage was an important initial motive in its bid for NATO

---

[31] Jeffrey Simon, "Central and East European Security: New National Concepts and Defense Doctrines," *Strategic Forum*, no. 151 (December 1998): 4.

[32] "Compatible with Other Armed Forces," *Slovenia Weekly*, 23 July 2002.

[33] Ramet, *Balkan Babel*, 178.

Slovenia: A Regional Leader

membership."[34] This policy had mixed outcomes. On the positive side, Slovenia succeeded in being compared in international forums not to the rest of Yugoslavia but to other East-Central European states. At the same time, this policy has, in some respects backfired. Slovenia received some international criticism for its "constructive disengagement" policy in the first half of the 1990s, that is, for not supporting NATO operations in Bosnia and for being reluctant to take part in Western efforts to promote stability and development in the former Yugoslavia. Slovene experts say, however, that Ljubljana's options were limited and its key objective was to avoid being dragged into the war on any level.[35]

By the late 1990s Ljubljana realized that rather than isolating itself from the difficulties in the Balkans, Slovenia could actually benefit from its Yugoslav heritage by acting as a bridge between Central Europe and the Balkans. As Czech President Václav Havel said in 2000, "Slovenia, which is closest to [the crisis region] not only geographically but also owing to its insight and understanding, can play an important role in this field."[36] Foreign policy officials in Ljubljana insist that they fully recognize that Slovenia's long-term security depends on promoting stability and prosperity in southeastern Europe which is why it has not only welcomed but has become an active participant in the EU's 1999 Stability Pact for Southeastern Europe.[37]

From its independence Slovenia has conducted a responsible, mature, and constructive foreign policy. In May 1993 Slovenia obtained full membership in the Council of Europe. It has been one of the four candidates (along with the Czech Republic, Hungary, and Poland) that have earned at least passing marks in fulfilling the overlapping EU and NATO criteria for membership.[38] Slovenia has had excellent relations

---

[34] Mastny, "Reassuring NATO: Eastern Europe, Russia, and the Western Alliance," *Forsvarsstudier* (Oslo), no. 5 (1997): 73.

[35] Interview with Marjan Malešič (Ljubljana, 2 December 1999) and Andrej Slapničar (Ljubljana, 3 December 1999).

[36] RFE/RL II, 4:84 (28 April 2000).

[37] See Boris Frlec, "Slovenia's Perspective on Promoting Stability in South-eastern Europe," *NATO Review*, no. 4 (Winter 1999): 16; interview with Andrej Slapničar of the Department for Political Multilateral Relations/NATO Section, Ministry of Foreign Affairs (Ljubljana, 3 December 1999); and "Stable SE Europe a Common Task," *Slovenia Weekly*, 20 March 2001.

[38] Anton Bebler, "NATO's Enlargement and Slovenia," (Ljubljana, 1999), 12.

with the new East-Central European members of NATO as well as with the other NATO aspirants discussed in this book. Ljubljana has been a vocal supporter of their candidacies and has actively cooperated with them in their quests for EU and NATO membership. Given Slovenia's geographical distance and miniscule trade with Russia, relations with Moscow have played an inconsequential role in Slovene foreign policy.

Slovenia's relations with other Western states have also been exemplary. On innumerable visits Ljubljana has received the support of virtually all NATO member states. NATO membership has been the most important issue in Slovene-U.S. relations. Representatives of the U.S. government from former secretaries of defense William Perry and William Cohen to Senators Joseph Biden and George Voinovich have time and again expressed their approval of Slovenia's development. During his 1995 tour of Eastern Europe, Secretary Perry said that "of all these countries, I believe that Slovenia has made perhaps the greatest progress in the transition to democracy, the transition to a market economy, and the smooth turnover of the military to civilian control."[39] It is the only East European state that, in 2001, met the standards to join the U.S.'s visa waiver program.[40] On the eve of his first European trip as president, George W. Bush hailed Slovenia as "an example of what can happen if freedom-loving people insist upon institutions that free people [support]."[41]

Ljubljana's relations with Budapest have been free of strains. Slovenia actually supports Hungary's status law – that extends benefits to Hungarian minorities in neighboring states – which has been controversial in both Slovakia and Romania.[42] Then again, Slovenia's treatment of its Hungarian minority has long been exemplary. Slovene relations with other neighbors – Austria, Croatia, and Italy – have been frustrated by some troublesome issues. This has naturally been of some concern in Ljubljana given that Italy and Austria are EU members and could conceivably thwart Slovene membership therein, as they

---

[39] Cited by Stan Markotich, "A Balancing Act Between NATO and the EU," *Transition*, 1:23 (15 December 1995): 55.

[40] "Only CEE Country in Visa Waiver Programme," *Slovenia Weekly*, 5–11 February 2001.

[41] RFE/RL II, 5:111 (12 June 2001).

[42] "Szlovénia támogatja a státustörvényt," *Magyar Nemzet*, 15 January 2002.

Slovenia: A Regional Leader   101

have repeatedly threatened to do so.[43] Relations with Italy were impeded primarily by the issue of Italian property in Slovenia, confiscated by communist Yugoslavia in the 1940s. Relations worsened in 1994, after Silvio Berlusconi's conservative cabinet took office. The Italian government blocked Slovenia from becoming an associate EU member which was a necessary step prior to attaining full membership. Partly in order to pacify Italy, Slovenia changed its constitution in 1997 to allow foreigners to buy real estate in the country.[44] After Romano Prodi's government took office in May 1996, relations between the two countries became more cordial and, since then, Italy has become perhaps the most active proponent of Slovenia's EU and NATO membership. Moreover, in 2000 the Italian legislature passed the "Law on the Global Protection of the Slovenian Minority" which has satisfied Ljubljana.

Tensions between Slovenia and Austria emerged only after the electoral success of Jörg Haider's nationalist Freedom Party in October 1999. On the one hand, Slovenia's concerns centered on the conditions of the Slovene minority in an Austria ruled by the Freedom Party. On the other hand, Vienna expressed its doubts about the safety of Slovenia's Krsko nuclear power plant, its anxiety about the tens of thousands of Slovenes who were expected to "overrun" Austria were Slovenia to become an EU member, and its displeasure with Ljubljana's reluctance to address the issue of the post-World War II expulsion of German-speakers from Slovenia and the confiscation of their property. Despite these disagreements, however, Slovene-Austrian relations have been cordial and continuously improving. In February 2002 Austrian Chancellor Wolfgang Schüssel declared that any open questions between the two states would not be an obstacle to Slovenia's joining the EU.[45]

Slovenia's relations with Croatia have been by far the most contentious. Although Ljubljana and Zagreb have been quarreling about

---

[43] Open Media Research Institute Daily Digest, Part II (henceforth: OMRI DD II), no. 49 (9 March 1995).

[44] Interview with Mitja Močnik of Slovenia's embassy in Hungary (Budapest, 22 October 1999). See also, Júlia Sárközy, "Nincs barátsag olaszok, horvátok, és szlovénok között," *Magyar Hírlap*, 8 December 2001.

[45] *Die Presse* (Vienna), 21 February 2002 cited in RFE/RL II, 6:34 (21 February 2002).

several matters, three major issues dominated the agenda. First, the nuclear power plant Krsko, opened in 1982 and planned to shut down around 2020, was owned jointly by Slovenia (51%) and Croatia (49%) in the Yugoslav era. The dispute between the two countries centered on financial issues and the proportion of Slovene/Croat representation in management. Second, a subsidiary of the Slovene-owned bank, Ljubljana Banka-Zagreb, lost its license after the dissolution of Yugoslavia when no foreign banks were allowed to operate in Croatia. The crux of the matter is the approximately DM400 million assets that the bank has yet to recover. A number of trade disputes and the issue of hazardous materials transport have also surfaced as problems troubling enough for Ljubljana to contemplate requesting World Trade Organization mediation. Finally, there was a contentious border issue between the two states. The Bay of Piran, Slovenia's access to the Adriatic, was overseen by Ljubljana in Yugoslav times but since then Croatia has demanded control of the bay. In July 2001 the two sides reached compromises on the Krsko nuclear power plant issues and expected to settle the bank affair shortly. They have also resolved some other outstanding issues ranging from foreign-owned properties to local residents' access to border regions. Nonetheless, the Bay of Piran issue has thus far eluded resolution. In August 2002 Drnovšek described relations with Zagreb at "their lowest level since our countries became independent" and suggested that the two sides might seek international arbitration.[46]

Slovenia's Campaign for NATO Membership

According to former Foreign Minister Boris Frlec, Slovenia needs NATO membership because in an unstable southeastern Europe the country's long-term security can only be safeguarded and consolidated within NATO's collective defense system.[47] Given that Slovenia is the militarily weakest country in the region that could not resist claims of larger states on its territory, NATO membership is in Slovenia's national

---

[46] See "Property Accord with Croatia," *Slovenia Weekly*, 6:35 (12 October 1999); interview with Andrej Slapničar (Ljubljana, 3 December 1999); and RFE/RL 6:53 (20 March 2002) and 6:163 (29 August 2002).

[47] Boris Frlec, "Slovenia's Perspective on Promoting Stability in South-eastern Europe," *NATO Review*, no. 4 (Winter 1999): 18.

Slovenia: A Regional Leader

interest. The "National Strategy for Integration of the Republic of Slovenia into NATO," adopted by the government in 1998, views NATO as the "only efficient organization for collective security in the existing European security architecture." According to this document, the fundamental reasons for Slovenia to pursue NATO membership are to (1) strengthen the security of the country and add to its long-term development; (2) to gain advantages in foreign policy, economic, scientific research, and technological and organizational issues; and (3) to be included in the political and security framework of the most developed countries which promote economic and social cooperation, strengthens Slovenia's credibility, upgrades its international status, and consolidates the international identity of Slovenia as a democratic and peaceful country.[48] As one Slovene official succinctly put it, NATO membership is important because we "do not want to be pushed back to the Balkans."[49]

Ljubljana's NATO campaign began in earnest in December 1993 when the legislature adopted a "Resolution on the General Principles of National Security" which was, in essence, the first formal document to identify accession to NATO as a Slovene objective. In March 1994 Slovenia joined the Partnership for Peace program. Slovene politicians have on many occasions pointed out that their country was the only serious NATO aspirant that never belonged to the Warsaw Pact and that it was situated in the geographical proximity of Balkan crises and therefore could provide a crucial foothold for NATO operations. Slovene political and military leaders have made hundreds of official visits to NATO countries and hosted their counterparts in Ljubljana and elsewhere.

From the beginning of its campaign, NATO leaders and Western politicians recognized Slovenia's prominent position in postcommunist democratization and market reform. In fact, in 1995 Slovene Defense Minister Jelko Kačin said that he was told by Secretary Perry that the United States wanted Slovenia to be a member of NATO "as soon as possible."[50] There were other indications, especially from

---

[48] Malesic, "Slovenian Security Policy and NATO," 16.
[49] Cited in Bogomil Ferfila and Paul Phillips, *Slovenia: On the Edge of the European Union* (Lanham, MD: University Press of America, 2000), 82.
[50] *Foreign Report (Economist)*, no. 2345 (30 March 1995): 7.

Washington, that Slovenia would be invited to join NATO in the first round (Slovenia, for instance, was included in the Pentagon's cost estimates).[51]

As noted earlier, one of the reasons why Slovenia was not included in the first round of enlargement in 1997, as U.S. Secretary of State Madeleine Albright acknowledged, was its reluctance to get involved in any way in the war in Bosnia.[52] The anticipated French opposition to an invitation to Slovenia but not to Romania – notwithstanding the enormous disparity between the two states in terms of democratization, marketization, and other areas – was likely to have been an even more important deterrent. In fact, in off-the-record conversations several Pentagon and State Department officials admitted that "Slovenia was sacrificed for Romania."[53] Furthermore, as Gow and Carmichael pointed out, instead of underscoring the ways in which Slovenia could have been a strategic asset and contributor to NATO, Ljubljana's campaign kept stressing Slovene stability, democracy, prosperity, and civilian control over the armed forces which were less persuasive reasons to be granted membership.[54] In any event, both of these countries were singled out in Madrid as the states with the best chances of inclusion in the following round enlargement.

Although Slovenes were disappointed by NATO's decision, the political elites continued to lobby Western states prior to the 1999 Washington Summit. Slovenia established a mission to NATO Headquarters in Brussels as well as to SHAPE (Supreme Headquarters Allied Powers Europe) in Mons as part of its sustained membership campaign, and beefed up the NATO sections in its MOD and Ministry of Foreign Affairs (MFA). In addition, an interdepartmental commission consisting of twelve governmental sectors was established to coordinate the NATO-related activities of the executive branch. In 1998 Slovenia approved the National Strategy for Integration in NATO

---

[51] See Gow and Carmichael, *Slovenia and the Slovenes*, 198; and James M. Goldgeier, *Not Whether But When: The U.S. Decision to Enlarge NATO* (Washington, D.C.: Brookings Institution Press, 1999), 119.

[52] Interview with Marjan Malešič (Ljubljana, 2 December 1999).

[53] Off-the-record interviews (Washington, D.C., September 1996 and March 2000). See also Jiří Šedivý, "The Puzzle of NATO Enlargement," *Contemporary Security Policy*, 22:2 (August 2001): 7.

[54] Gow and Carmichael, *Slovenia and the Slovenes*, 195–196.

Slovenia: A Regional Leader

and a year later became actively involved in the Membership Action Plan by adopting the first Annual National Plan for its enforcement. An October 1998 North Atlantic Assembly report singled out Slovenia as the only state included in all five potential future enlargement scenarios.[55] According to the 2000 Defense Assessment Study on Slovenia, prepared by a group of experts from the Pentagon, since 1997 the country has made excellent progress in meeting NATO entrance criteria.[56]

Since 1997 Slovenia has been far more willing to get involved in mediating and peace-keeping activities in the Balkans. During the 1999 Kosovo war the government not only supported NATO policy but opened Slovene airspace to the Alliance. In 2001 Ljubljana signed a free-trade agreement with Bosnia, opened the largest Slovene embassy in Belgrade, and offered to mediate in the dispute between Serbia and Montenegro, demonstrating its commitment to good relations with the states of the former Yugoslavia. Slovenia has been active in a range of international endeavors to promote security, including SFOR and the Multinational Specialized Unit in Bosnia, KFOR and the UN Interim Administration Mission in Kosovo, and the West European Union-led Multinational Advisory Police Element in Albania.[57] It has participated even more energetically in PfP projects and has become active in regional military cooperation.

In 2000 and 2001 Slovenia organized several major military exercises (with the participation of at least 1,000 troops) which, according to leading politicians, have been important in persuading NATO that Ljubljana took defense reforms seriously.[58] In recent years, Slovene forces have taken part in over fifty joint events in various fields with their Italian colleagues annually. Perhaps the most important of these is the joint peacekeeping brigade called the Multinational Land Force,

---

[55] Bebler, "NATO's Enlargement and Slovenia," 16.

[56] "NATO Accession Activities Gather Momentum," *Slovenia Weekly*, 10 October 2000.

[57] Frlec, "Slovenia's Perspective on Promoting Stability in South-Eastern Europe," *NATO Review*, no. 4 (Winter 1999): 18. Actually, during the Kosovo crisis MFA officials found a law inherited from the legal system of federal Yugoslavia that no overflight of armed man was allowed but this law was quickly modified. Interview with Andrej Slapničar (Ljubljana, December 1999).

[58] "Resolute Response 2001," *Slovenia Weekly*, 23 October 2001; and "Realistic Program to Meet Standards," *Slovenia Weekly*, 2 October 2001.

established by Slovenia, Italy, and Hungary.[59] Slovenia has also been an active member of the Southeastern Europe Defense Ministerial (a group that includes nine states from the region along with the United States and has ambitions to set up a 3,000-strong joint peacekeeping force) and CENCOOP, a similar organization among Central European states. Slovenia has also taken part in dozens of NATO workshops and exercises fostering its preparation for membership.[60] Slovene soldiers have participated in peacekeeping operations in Cyprus, the Middle East and elsewhere. The results of Slovenia's dynamic military diplomacy include bilateral military cooperation agreements with twenty-four states and participation in numerous joint exercises with partners ranging from Ukraine to the United States.

The desire to join NATO and thus to some extent compromise sovereignty has not been shared by an overwhelming majority of the Slovene population. Polls had shown that, in 1991 38 percent of the population favored demilitarization.[61] In addition, many Slovenes preferred neutrality and were concerned that NATO membership might mean that Slovene territory could be used to deploy nuclear weapons and Slovene soldiers might fight and die abroad. The general crisis in the former Yugoslavia and the war on Slovenia's borders, however, shifted public opinion toward NATO. Still, according to a summer 2002 poll, only 38.8% of Slovenes are supportive of the country's NATO membership which is lower than comparable figures for virtually all East European states. Not surprisingly, NATO has repeatedly expressed concern about low levels of Slovene public support in the Alliance.[62] The Slovene government has conducted a low intensity public campaign to convince people of the necessity and benefits of NATO membership. This enterprise has included the dissemination of information about national security and

---

[59] "NATO Accession Activities Gather Momentum," *Slovenia Weekly*, 10 October 2000.
[60] See, for instance, "Information Workshop for Latvia and Slovenia Held in Brussels," *NATO Update*, 14 March 2001.
[61] On this issue see Gow and Carmichael, *Slovenia and the Slovenes*, 192–194.
[62] See, for instance, Bebler, "NATO's Enlargement," 13; Malešič, "Slovenian Security Policy," 45–48; Grizold, "The National Security of Slovenia;," interviews with Mitja Močnik (Budapest, 22 October 1999) and Marjan Malešič (Ljubljana, 2 December 1999); and RFE/RL II, 6:11 (17 January 2002); 6:71 (16 April 2002); and 6:102 (3 June 2002).

NATO, translation of NATO documents, a free telephone service to provide answers to questions about NATO, putting on conferences, conducting public debates, and providing relevant materials to the media. The campaign has been coordinated through the MFA's NATO department and through NGOs like the Atlantic Council of Slovenia.

Though the media has been somewhat more critical of NATO membership – highlighting the costs, the nuclear issue, and ecological concerns – political elites have steadily voiced their support. Among the major political parties three (LDS, SDS, SKD) have consistently and strongly backed joining NATO for several years. By 1996 the two other parties, the Slovene People's Party (SLS) and the United List of Social Democrats (ZLSD), that earlier harbored reservations about the benefits of NATO membership, also fell in line. At a January 2002 National Assembly debate, however, the representatives of the extraparliamentary New Party voiced their opposition to NATO membership – claiming that Slovenia did not need NATO – and that of the ZLSD contended that joining at all cost was a poor policy. Moreover, the leader of the Slovenian National Party, Zmago Jelinčič insisted that entering NATO must be supported by a public referendum, a proposal that has also been made by President Kučan.[63] After Slovenia was invited to NATO membership at the Prague Summit, Prime Minister Drnovšek announced that a referendum on the issue would be held in the first half of 2003.

In April 1997 the National Assembly adopted a joint declaration by parliamentary parties stating that the Republic of Slovenia met all the requirements for joining NATO and was capable and willing to cover its share of expenses linked to full membership in the Alliance.[64] Most Slovene politicians were extremely optimistic about their country's chances of receiving an invitation from NATO in 2002. They were not disappointed.

---

[63] RFE/RL II, 6:11 (17 January 2002); "Membership in NATO: Pros and Cons," *Slovenia Weekly*, 22 January 2002.

[64] See, for instance, "Slovenia/U.S. Assistance in Meeting NATO Standards," *Slovenia Weekly*, 3 October 2000; "Ready for Membership," *Slovenia Weekly*, 29 January– 4 February 2001; "NATO Accession: Fulfilling Membership Criteria," *Slovenia Weekly*, 5 June 2001; and "Membership in NATO: Pros and Cons," *Slovenia Weekly*, 22 January 2002.

108   The Future of NATO Expansion

PART III. CIVIL–MILITARY RELATIONS

Depoliticizing the Armed Forces

Unlike in Slovakia and Bulgaria, the armed forces in Slovenia played an important role in the fall of the ancien régime. The Yugoslav federal state was held together by Josip Broz Tito, the League of Yugoslav Communists and the federal army (JNA). Ethnic Serbs dominated the JNA's professional personnel as they comprised two-fifths of the population but over three-fifths of the officer corps. Slovenes – along with ethnic Albanians, Muslims, and Hungarians – were the most disproportionately underrepresented nationality among JNA officers.[65] Yugoslavia was the only communist state, however, where there were territorially based militias under the control of the local (republic) authorities.[66] This institutional detail became extremely important and auspicious for Slovenia. Beginning in the mid-1980s a group of young journalists – among whom the most charismatic was Janez Janša – had been increasingly and openly contemptuous of the JNA (because it was expensive, over-politicized, and antidemocratic). To some extent their views mirrored those of the relatively liberal Slovene communist leadership which allowed their critical articles to be published in the magazine *Mladina*. The fact that in 1990 a non-Slovene general was appointed to head the Slovene Territorial Defense (TD) even though that position was always held by a general of Slovene origin contributed to sharpening tensions.[67] In the "Ten-Day War" that followed the Slovene declaration of independence, the high-spirited TD bolstered by good intelligence triumphed over and humiliated the small and dispassionate JNA contingent sent by Belgrade to reestablish order.[68] The hostilities

---

[65] See Robin Alison Remington, "The Yugoslav Army: Trauma and Transition," in Constantine P. Danopoulos and Daniel Zirker, eds., *Civil–Military Relations in the Soviet and Yugoslav Successor States* (Boulder: Westview Press, 1996), 167; and Anton Grizold, "The Defence of Slovenia," in Danica Fink-Hafner and John R. Robbins, eds., *Making a New Nation: The Formation of Slovenia* (Brookfield, VT: Dartmouth, 1997), 46–55.

[66] Valerie Bunce, *Subversive Institutions: The Design and the Destruction of Socialism and the State* (New York: Cambridge University Press, 1999), 118.

[67] Bebler, "Civil–Military Relations in Slovenia," in Danopoulos and Zirker, eds., *Civil–Military Relations in the Soviet and Yugoslav Successor States*, 196.

[68] Three excellent books on this subject are James Gow, *Legitimacy and the Military: the Yugoslav Crisis* (New York: St. Martin's, 1992); Janez Janša, *Premiki. Nastajanje*

Slovenia: A Regional Leader

were confined to the two regular armed forces and were not accompanied by intercommunal violence. As Anton Bebler noted, the success of the TD was widely and wrongly interpreted as a victory of amateurs over professionals.[69]

After the JNA left, Slovenia's armed forces underwent substantial changes. Today the Slovene army is the only regular military force in Slovenia combining elements of a standing army and of dispersed territorial units.[70] The TD was authenticated by the 1991 Constitution as an institution of the Slovene nation, serving its national interests. The first task was to break up the party-army symbiosis that is the most fundamental characteristic of civil–military relations in communist states. The political weight the military was allowed to have in the republics of the former Yugoslavia was greatly reduced in Slovenia. The entire defense sector became far more transparent and more accessible to parliamentary and media scrutiny. The internal security role of the armed forces was discontinued.

The access of the communist party to the military was terminated, political directorates and the hierarchy of political officers were abolished. Active members of the armed forces were prohibited to join political parties. Political indoctrination as a component of military education and training was discontinued. These measures resulted in a substantial shift away from a politicized military toward a professionalized one. In order to make a clean break with the past and to enhance the TD's national character, no former JNA general received commissions in the new Slovene national force. More generally, major personnel changes were instituted particularly in the upper echelons of the ranks and, wherever possible – particularly in the MOD – civilians were hired to replace officers.

---

in *Obramba Slovenske Države, 1988–1992* (Ljubljana: Založba Mladinska Knjiga, 1992); and Janez J. Švajncer, *Obranili Domovino: Teritorialna Obramba Republike Slovenije v Vojni za Svobodno in Samostojno Slovenijo, 1991* (Ljubljana: Viharnik, 1993).

[69] See two of Anton Bebler's articles, "The Armed Conflicts on the Balkans, 1990–1993," *Balkan Forum*, 1:4 (September 1993): 14; and "Civil–Military Relations in Slovenia: Temporary Reduction to Irrelevance?" (Ljubljana, 1997), 42.

[70] Anton Grizold, "Civil–Military Relations in Slovenia," in Bebler, ed., *Civil–Military Relations in Post-Communist States* (Westport, CT: Praeger, 1997), 106.

Institutional Arrangements of Civilian Oversight

The most important Slovene institutions relevant to defense are the president, the cabinet, and the defense minister (DM). The Slovene president is the head of state and the titular commander-in-chief but he has no specific powers relating to the armed forces. Slovenia's is a bicameral legislature composed of the National Council (upper house) with forty members and the National Assembly (lower house) with ninety directly elected deputies. The National Council can veto the lower house's draft bills but its veto is not final as the ultimate decision rests with the latter. The legislature defines the basic directives for defense organization and implementation. Several committees in the legislature are specialized for defense-security affairs. These include the Defense Committee; the Committee for Budget, Finance, and Monetary Policy; the Committee for Budget and Public Finance Control; the National Security Resolution Committee; as well as additional committees for supervising intelligence organizations, internal policy, and judicial matters. A practice that has received some criticism is that some MPs sit on more than one defense-related legislative committee.

The government organizes preparations for defense and leads its implementation. It controls the defense budget (and coordinates the activities of the MOD and the Ministry of Finance) and, since military personnel are considered public servants, also oversees the armed forces' personnel or cadre policy. In Slovenia all executive responsibility related to defense is invested in the MOD which prepares changes for the defense law, elaborates strategic documents (to be debated by parliament), and devises and implements development and modernization programs. Since 1991 the MOD has been thoroughly civilianized and its managerial style has come to stress inter-departmental participation. The majority of positions in the MOD are now filled by civilians. Some critics of the ministry have noted that the civilianization process may have gone too far given that specialized military expertise is at times lacking.[71] The military officers employed at the MOD are from the territorial defense units, former JNA officers, or defense experts with military training.

---

[71] Interview with Arnejčič (Ljubljana, 3 December 1999).

Slovenia: A Regional Leader

As a result of differences between the president and the government, the Slovene National Security Council was only established in 1998. It is a consultative and advisory body comprised of "strategic" ministers (e.g., defense, interior, foreign affairs). This body has lacked both dynamism and transparency. Drago Demšar, who was DM for a brief period (1999–2000), set up a Strategy Council within the MOD to facilitate regular discussions of policy issues. Twelve experts constitute the Council that meets monthly to prepare and debate policy.[72] The General Staff (GS) is integrated into and housed in the same building complex as the MOD. The Chief of the General Staff (CGS) answers to the minister of defense who, in turn, is accountable to the prime minister. The GS is responsible for military readiness, and executes tasks concerning the organization, training, and performance of the armed forces.

The civilian DM is responsible to execute defense policy, manage defense matters, and propose to the government the CGS. As I noted above, Slovenia has not been particularly fortunate with its defense ministers. Janša, who was heading the MOD in 1990–1994 and briefly again, in 2000, was the cause of more political problems in the 1990s than any other Slovene politician. The tenure of his successor and former colleague, Jelko Kačin (1994–1997) was also marked by controversies as Kačin found it difficult to control MOD personnel loyal to Janša. Tit Turnšek, a complete newcomer to defense issues, who followed Kačin, was forced to resign in early 1998 when Croat officials arrested two operatives of the MOD's Security and Intelligence Service and impounded the $1 million worth of surveillance equipment they were using. Turnšek's successor, Alojz Krapež resigned in October 1998, after less than eight months in office, in the wake of a corruption scandal.[73] After the brief tenures of two more DM, Lojze Marinček (1998–1999) and Drago Demšar, Janša briefly returned to the MOD in Andrej Bajuk's short-lived cabinet and implemented extensive changes in personnel described by the Ljubljana daily, *Dnevnik*, as political purges.[74] The latest Drnovšek government seems to have made a more inspired choice by appointing Anton Grizold, a

---

[72] Interview with Arnejčič.
[73] RFE/RL II, 2:39 (26 February 1998); and 2:204 (21 October 1998).
[74] See *Dnevnik*, 25 September 2000; and RFE/RL II, 4:185 (25 September 2000).

respected professor of the defense studies program at the University of Ljubljana.

In contrast to other postcommunist states, Slovenia has not had the problem of an insufficient number of civilians with the requisite knowledge and skill to advise politicians on defense matters. Rather, the civilianization of the MOD and the army may have gone a little too far, and some politicians in their zeal to fill the MOD with civilian workers may have overlooked their qualifications. Military officers employed in the MOD are encouraged to wear civilian clothes and not to display their military credentials.[75] As the case of Janša and others had shown, there are actually quite a few individuals with expertise on military affairs. To a large extent this is the legacy of the Yugoslav government's policy to establish defense studies departments in all republic capitals (except for Montenegro) starting as early as the mid-1970s. The Department of Defense Studies at the University of Ljubljana accepts fifty freshmen a year (more than three times as many apply ordinarily).[76] Consequently, in Slovenia there appears to be a sufficient number of qualified civilian defense specialists.

The Slovene defense budget is established and implemented much like that of other consolidated democracies. The process itself is open to media scrutiny. The DM, together with his top civilian and military colleagues (especially the CGS), prepares a budget proposal including the MOD's needs and, after consultation with the Ministry of Finance, sends it to the government. The latter might modify the budget according to priorities and then presents the aggregate budget to the legislature. After close scrutiny and consultation with the government, which may result in further modification, the legislature adopts the budget. Parliament also controls the implementation of the budget for which the defense minister is accountable.[77]

---

[75] Joseph Derdzinski, "Ten Years After Independence: Consolidation of Democratic Control of the Slovene Armed Forces," paper presented at the "War in the Balkans" Conference, Florida Atlantic University (Boca Raton, 23 February 2002), 9.

[76] Interview with Professor Marjan Malešič of the Department (Ljubljana, 2 December 1999).

[77] See Bogomil Ferfila and Paul Phillips, *Slovenia: On the Edge of the European Union* (Lanham, MD: University Press of America, 2000), 31–61 and especially 34; and Arnejčič "Some Aspects of the Accountability," 79.

Shortcomings of Civil–Military Relations

Although fundamentally civil–military relations are democratized and civilian oversight is secure, there have been more problems in this sphere than one would expect given Slovenia's outstanding record in most areas. Especially until the mid-1990s far too many troublesome incidents occurred.

As defense minister, Janez Janša tolerated public verbal attacks on the Commander-in-Chief (Kučan) by serving military officers, used state-subsidized military organizations to promote himself, exploited the mass media to bolster his popularity, and oversaw virtual witch hunts of his critics. Bypassing the GS, he subordinated a special commando unit (the Republic of Slovenia Brigade, its Slovene acronym is MORiS) to himself alone. The outfit was comprised of several hundred elite troops trained as a rapid mobilization force. Janša viewed it as his own band and on occasion interfered in the judicial process to obtain dismissals of criminal charges against MORiS members.[78] Janša also "utilized the legal void created by the new Constitution (which was not accompanied in time by new corresponding legislature) – as he effectively made himself the commander-in-chief," pressuring the President into signing an order dismissing the Chief of the Territorial Defense (TD) Staff, deprived the President of relevant official information on the army, issued important orders without proper authorization, and so on.[79]

Some individuals with lacking professional and personal ethics were able to cause strains in interinstitutional relations because there were no clearly set procedures to coordinate the defense-related responsibilities of the government, the prime minister, the president, and the MOD. Many problems in civil–military relations took place because a great deal of necessary legislation was not prepared on time. Janša and others were able to exploit the fact that, due to quarrels among political leaders and parliamentary parties, the (imperfect and incomplete) Law on National Defense was only passed in 1994. There are also, as DM Anton Grizold wrote, varying degrees of institutionalization within the existing security arrangements and a lingering ambivalence in the

---

[78] Ramet, "Democratization in Slovenia – the Second Stage," 212–213.
[79] Bebler, "Civil–Military Relations in Slovenia," in Danopoulos and Zirker, eds., 208.

distribution of authority in national security matters.[80] According to Slovene analysts, other related problems include the unclear division of authority between the defense minister, his deputy, and the CGS and the far too rapid decision-making process in the MOD due to short deadlines. Moreover, as the director of the MOD's Center for Strategic Studies told me, in many ways cadre policy is still based on old legislation and the Law on National Defense did not sufficiently clarify the differences between the status of professional soldiers and public officials.[81]

In a sense, the turbulence around Slovene defense ministers has reflected the insufficiently developed democratic political culture, the deficient art of pluralist consensus, and the low levels of political tolerance among top politicians.[82] The aforementioned transgressions can be and have been countered by additional legislation. It should be remembered that most of these incidents took place in the first half of the 1990s and that they were connected to a single person, Janša, who managed to jeopardize civilian rule and personified the threat of populist authoritarianism to the country.[83] At the same time, notwithstanding the abundance of civilian defense expertise at the MOD, most members of parliament are ignorant of military issues which, in practice, impedes the close parliamentary scrutiny of defense matters.[84] It ought to be underscored that in spite of these problems, Slovene civil–military relations have been thoroughly democratized.

---

[80] Grizold, "Civil–Military Relations in Slovenia," in Bebler, ed., *Civil–Military Relations in Post-Communist States*, 107–108.

[81] Interview with Beno Arnejčič, Acting Director, Center for Strategic Studies, MOD (Ljubljana, 3 December 1999); see also Beno Arnejčič, "Some Aspects of the Accountability of the Slovenian Minister of Defense and Head of the General Staff of the Slovenian Defense Forces," paper presented at the "Democratic Civil–Military Relations Conference" (Ottawa, 26 March 1999).

[82] Bebler, "Civil–Military Relations in Slovenia," 15.

[83] For a good portrait of Janša and his supporters, see Rudolf M. Rizman, "Radical Right Politics in Slovenia," in Sabrina P. Ramet, *The Radical Right in Central and Eastern Europe since 1989* (University Park: Pennsylvania State University Press, 1999), 147–171.

[84] Neil Grayston also makes this point in his "Democratic Control of the Armed Forces of Slovenia: A Progress Report," in Graeme P. Herd, ed., *Civil–Military Relations in Post Cold War Europe* (Camberley, UK: Conflict Studies Research Centre, 2001), 7.

Slovenia: A Regional Leader

PART IV. MILITARY REFORM AND THE STATE OF THE ARMED FORCES

Military Reform

The breakup of the former Yugoslavia, unlike the former Czechoslovakia's "velvet divorce," was not followed by a fair and proportionate distribution of military assets. Consequently, Slovenia was even more disadvantaged than Slovakia when it started to build up its armed forces in 1991. After the withdrawal of the JNA the only military force in the country was the Territorial Defense which was later renamed "Slovene Army" (*Slovenska Vojska*), one of the youngest armed forces in Europe. Slovene defense experts like to point out that the Slovene Army was not "reformed" after 1991; it was started from scratch.

Since 1991, the defense-security sector has been civilianized to a larger extent than that of any other East European state. According to a Slovene expert, MOD officials made a mistake when they did not make a more spirited effort to recruit ethnic-Slovene officers and NCOs serving in the other republics of Yugoslavia because thereby they limited the pool of qualified individuals. As a result, in the early 1990s some low-ranking officers and NCOs had to be rapidly promoted even though some of them were unqualified. Nevertheless, the Slovene military has become far more professional while at the same time its social importance and the political role it could play in the former Yugoslavia plummeted.[85]

After Slovenia signed the Membership Action Plan (which allows aspirant states organized, transparent, and all-round preparation for membership) in 1999, the government formed an interministerial working group for the enforcement of Annual National Plans (ANP). This group organizes and manages all the activities associated with NATO in Slovenia. More specifically, in designing and adopting the ANP, it comprehensively analyzes the Individual Partnership Programs and Slovene participation in the Planning and Review

---

[85] Bebler, "Civil–Military Relations in Slovenia: Temporary Reduction to Irrelevance?" 8, 14; and *East European Constitutional Review*, 4:2 (Spring 1995): 32.

Process (PARP).[86] DM Grizold admitted in a July 2001 interview, that Slovenia's first two ANPs (1999–2000, 2000–2001) set unrealistic goals. In the third (2001–2002) ANP the emphasis was on identifying attainable objectives and, judging by the praise it received in Brussels, the government succeeded.[87]

The long-term goal of the Slovene MOD is to develop a three-tier army that relies less on traditional territorial defense forces. The lowest component of this is the "support defense forces" consisting of the reserves (made up of discharged draftees and professionals). In the middle are the "main defense forces," the biggest part of the Slovene Army, consisting of professional and reserve units. The first level of defense, the modern, well-equipped rapid reaction force will be the key instrument of Slovene security policy.[88]

Slovenia's military reform concept places the emphasis on the first and second tiers, and especially on developing lighter, leaner, and more mobile forces with multiple capabilities, in many ways similar to those of Austria and Switzerland.[89] Slovene defense experts contend that in the short-term (i.e., by 2003) the new force and unit structure will be established along with the rapid reaction forces. Moreover, in concert with the overall reform plan, the main brigades will be upgraded and the territorial forces will be reorganized. In the longer-term (i.e., between 2003–2010) the final structure and size of all three tiers of forces will be implemented.[90] The MOD also intends to outfit a seven hundred-man Peace Support Battalion but Jeffrey Simon is probably right in suggesting that this might exceed Slovene capabilities and would unnecessarily divert scarce resources from the main defense

---

[86] "The Annual National Programme for the Implementation of the Membership Action Plan – Executive Summary" (Ljubljana: Government Public Relations and Media Office, 1999), 2.

[87] "Contributing to NATO's Policy: Interview with Defense Minister Anton Grizold," *Slovenia Weekly*, 3 July 2001; and "Membership Action Plan Praised in Brussels," *Slovenia Weekly*, 30 October 2001.

[88] Gow and Carmichael, *Slovenia and the Slovenes*, 189–190; and interview with Malešič (Ljubljana, December 1999).

[89] For more detail, see Bebler, "Civil–Military Relations in Slovenia," in Danopoulos and Zirker, eds., *Civil–Military Relations*, 201–203.

[90] This discussion draws Marjan Malesic, "Slovenian Security Policy and NATO," *Harmonie Paper 13* (Centre of European Security Studies, University of Groningen, The Netherlands, June 2000): 69–71.

forces.[91] According to a February 2002 press conference by army leaders, Slovenia planned to field an armed force with "no more than 26,000 members" (or 1.3% of the population) by 2004, establish and arm intervention forces, bolster command-and-control systems, and make units more independent in terms of logistics.[92] Conscription is planned to be ended by 2004. Several of these reforms, as DM Grizold has recently admitted, are still in the planning stages but, as he frequently notes, the objective is to persistently, if slowly, reshape the Slovene Army into a proud force that can strike fear into potential enemies.[93]

The MOD's Defense Research Center has focused its efforts on another priority, the improvement of defense planning. One of NATO's particular criticisms pointed at the incompatibility of Slovene defense documents with those of the Alliance. In the late 1990s the Center submitted to the government the drafts of nine new documents (ranging from "National Security Strategy" to "Civilian Protection Strategy") that conform to NATO standards. In 2000, the comprehensive "1993 Resolution on the National Security Strategy" was updated, and other similarly important documents on defense and military strategy were being drafted.

Ljubljana satisfied the political and economic requirements of NATO membership even before 1997. There are numerous remaining military areas where Slovenia needs to improve its preparations. They include the development of a national security and defense system by adopting the principles of NATO's strategic concept, integration into the Alliance's collective defense planning, cooperation in its military structure, interoperability, and standardization.[94] The army's structure needs further changes and its size additional reduction (a problem that could possibly lead to civil-military discord), the system of defense planning should be improved along with the logistical

---

[91] Jeffrey Simon, "Transforming the Armed Forces of Central and Eastern Europe," *Strategic Forum*, no. 172 (June 2000): 7.

[92] RFE/RL II, 6:24 (6 February 2002).

[93] "Carrying Out the Written Word" (an interview with Grizold), *Slovenia Weekly*, 8 January 2002; and "Compatible with Other Armed Forces," *Slovenia Weekly*, 23 July 2002.

[94] "Putting the NATO Membership Action Plan into Effect," *Slovenia Weekly*, 6:35 (12 October 1999): 7.

independence of some military units.[95] The Slovene military also lacks an effective personnel management system which has led to some politicized appointments and the MOD continues to have too many military directorates which leave the General Staff with too few competencies and contributes to poor communication between the ministry and the military headquarters.[96] In a November 2001 visit to Slovenia, NATO Secretary-General Lord George Robertson claimed that Ljubljana was not ready for NATO and it needed to do a great deal more in the area of military reform and to concentrate on "producing armed forces which are usable and deployable."[97]

Officers and Soldiers

The attributes of the Slovene Army's personnel have changed substantially in the last decade. The status of professional soldiers is now the same as that of civil servants with the exception that the former do not have the right to strike. The small size of the armed forces, the lack of a notable military tradition, the low profile of the army leadership, in addition to the underdeveloped corporate identity of Slovene military officers all contribute to the high degree of civilian domination of the military.[98]

In Yugoslav times Slovene officers received their specialized education in military academies, most of them in Belgrade. There are no such institutions in contemporary Slovenia, however. Prospective officers need to have a university degree (all major concentrations are accepted) and then continue their studies at the MOD's Military School Center (MSC) in Ljubljana by enrolling in one of its one-year programs. Since 1993 a growing number of Slovene officers have attended military colleges in Western (particularly NATO-member) states. By 2000, 320 Slovene officers and MOD employees were educated in the United

---

[95] "NATO Accession: Fulfilling Membership Criteria," *Slovenia Weekly*, 5 June 2001.

[96] See Grayston, "Democratic Control of the Armed Forces of Slovenia," 9, and Margriet Drent, et al. "Organising National Defences for NATO Membership: The Unexamined Dimension of Aspirants' Readiness for Entry," *Harmonie Paper 15* (Centre of European Security Studies, University of Groningen, October 2001), 57.

[97] AP (Brdo Pri Kranju, Slovenia), 12 November 2001; and RFE/RL II, 5:215 (13 November 2001).

[98] Bebler, "Civil–Military Relations in Slovenia: Temporary Reduction to Irrelevance?" 1.

Slovenia: A Regional Leader 119

States alone. The MSC actively cooperates with military schools in the United States, Germany, Austria, the Czech Republic, and Hungary. It has had especially successful exchange programs with the Theresian Academy in Wiener Neustadt (Austria) and with the Military School at Vyškov (Czech Republic).[99] As virtually all other East European states, Slovenia has also faced the problem of retaining officers returning from academies abroad who often receive lucrative offers from the private sector.

The military profession in Slovenia does not have a great deal of prestige. The Slovene armed forces do not possess an illustrious history given that the nation lived under foreign occupation for the last nine centuries. On a ten-point scale the prestige of the military profession scored 5.3 in a recent survey; respondents generally did not firmly oppose their children taking up the military as a profession but only 3.8 percent said that they would be happy about it.[100] At the same time, the morale and motivation of the officer corps are considerably higher than in Yugoslav times given that the army has become the hallmark of Slovenia's newly acquired sovereignty.[101] The remuneration of professional officers and NCOs is similar to that of other civil servants. Especially when considering the relatively high unemployment in the country until recently, the military occupation is better rewarded than in many other postcommunist states. Nonetheless, there is no long-term security in the profession owing to the MOD's view that individuals should not spend their entire productive life in the service. Upon being commissioned, officers sign a ten-year contract with the MOD which can be extended twice for five years each.[102] In the 1990s the Slovene Army became more socially representative and it has become open to women who now comprise 13 percent of the professional personnel.[103]

The public view of the Slovene Army is very favorable. In opinion polls it consistently ranks as one of the most trusted institutions. Most Slovenes are extremely positive on concepts like "Slovenia" and

---

[99] "The Republic of Slovenia: Ministry of Defense Military School Center" at www.mo-rs.si/mors/eng/usposeng.htm

[100] Grizold, "The National Security of Slovenia," 200.

[101] Bebler, "Civil–Military Relations in Slovenia: Temporary Reduction to Irrelevance?" 5.

[102] Interview with Marjan Malešič.

[103] See "Force Composition" www.mo-rs.si/mors/eng/sestavasileng.htm

120   *The Future of NATO Expansion*

"nationhood" and this patriotism – at least in an abstract sense – is also reflected on the army.[104] Nonetheless, many respondents to public opinion surveys would prefer if the state could provide security through greater reliance on nonmilitary means (diplomacy, politics) and by joining NATO.[105]

The majority of Slovene youngsters, just like their counterparts elsewhere, display limited enthusiasm about the mandatory military service even though it has been considerably democratized and generally eased since independence. The official service period is seven months but in practice it is a month shorter given the tradition according to which President Kučan signs a decree to discharge conscripts after six months. Conscientious objection to bearing arms has been decriminalized thus conscription-age young men may opt for alternative service. According to a recent survey, 66 percent of the youngsters surveyed chose armed service while 34 percent would rather serve without arms. Especially since 1994, the high ratio of the latter has become a serious problem and an additional reason for the increasingly serious discussions about the desirability of an all-professional military.[106] Those participating in alternative service also serve only seven months but they do not get reprieve of the last month. Conscripts spend three months with basic training and the rest with specialized training in combat units. The service itself is low key and draftees can go on leave for virtually every weekend. Following their active service they are transferred into the territorial reserve.

The State of the Forces

The current Slovene Army approximately equals 50 percent of the JNA's previous strength in Slovenia. Since 1991 the MOD has given up a great deal of its real estate and many of the former federal barracks

---

[104] See Beno Arnejčič, "National Value Orientation of Slovenian Citizens and Their Trust in the Armed Forces," in Erich Reiter, ed., *Österreichisches Jarhbuch Internationale Sicherheitspolitik* (Vienna, 1997), 338–342. See also, *Public Opinion, Mass Media, and the Military* (Ljubljana: Ministry of Defense, 1999).

[105] Grizold, "The National Security of Slovenia," 191–192.

[106] Interviews with Močnik (Budapest, October 1999); Malešič (Ljubljana, December 1999); and "NATO Accession Activities Gather Momentum," *Slovenia Weekly,* 10 October 2000.

Slovenia: A Regional Leader

and bases were converted to civilian use. Furthermore, the army's size and heavy armaments have been drastically reduced. The Slovene Army is comprised of approximately 4,200 officers, NCOs, and professional soldiers, 5,000 to 6,000 conscripts, and about 56,000 reserves. The objective is to reduce the active military to about 9,000 and the reserve component to no more than 33,000.[107] As a number of observers have noted, the combat readiness of the Slovene military as a whole is inadequate.[108]

Slovenia with a 1999 per capita GDP of $11,100 is by far the most prosperous among MAP member states (the figure for the runner-up, Slovakia, is $8,487). Freed from its obligations to federal Yugoslavia, Slovenia was able to reduce its defense expenditures from $900 million in 1990 to about $165 million in 1993.[109] Since 1998, Slovene defense budgets have increased from $241 million to $373 million in 2001. In 1998, 1.53% of the GDP was spent on defense and, according to the DM Grizold, the figure will stay between 1.5% and 1.6% in upcoming years.[110] In 1994 the Slovene government unveiled its armament acquisition strategy, the Basic Development Program, initially planned for ten years. It is often referred to as the "defense tolar" (the tolar being the national currency) similarly to other special programs like the "highway tolar" and "school tolar," which are not part of the regular budget. In 1994 the government earmarked DM1 billion for weapons procurement development. According to experts the procurement of new equipment has been managed erratically and imprudently.[111] A Long-Term Basic Development Program for Equipping the Slovene Army (by 2015) has also been drawn up by the MOD and the Ministry of Finance. Slovene officials take pains to point out that Slovenia will have no problem meeting the financial responsibilities NATO membership entails.

---

[107] Malesic, "Slovenian Security Policy and NATO," 70; "Contributing to NATO's Policy;" *The Military Balance, 2000–2001* (London: IISS, 2000), 102–103; and Szayna, *NATO Enlargement, 2000–2015,* 108.

[108] Drent, et al., "Organising National Defences for NATO Membership," 58.

[109] Bebler, "Civil–Military Relations in Slovenia," in Danopoulos and Zirker, eds., *Civil–Military Relations,* 200.

[110] Interviews with Močnik (Budapest, 22 October 1999); Malešič (Ljubljana, 3 December 1999); "Fulfilling Membership Criteria," "The Annual National Programme," and "Realistic Programme."

[111] Grayston, "Democratic Control of the Armed Forces of Slovenia," 10.

As I noted above, Slovenia received less than its fair share of the federal Yugoslav army's assets. Moreover, from September 1991 until spring 1996 there was a United Nations arms embargo on the entire territory of the former Yugoslavia. As a result, the Slovene arsenal is short on heavy weapons (especially artillery and armor) and has no combat jet aircraft or substantial naval weapons. The bulk of the arsenal is comprised of one hundred main battle tanks (updated T-55s and M-84s), some Pilatus training planes, a dozen Bell helicopters, and a recent purchase: Israeli-made Howitzers. The Slovene navy's first ever ship – purchased in 1993 but, due to the embargo, delivered only in 1996 – is a 25-meter military patrol boat, equipped with two 20-millimeter canons, also of Israeli manufacture.[112] In sum, Slovenia's arsenal corresponds to the modest size of its armed forces.

Perhaps the most important problem of the Slovene defense industry has been that all the military-related products in the former Yugoslavia relied on parts and suppliers from different republics, so few of these products can now be produced in one republic. Nonetheless, the small-scale Slovene defense industry manages to turn out an impressive array of sophisticated products.[113] One of the best firms is "Fotona" that has produced world-class high-tech military optics, particularly for foreign consumers. In 1996, the government established a special commission to ensure that the defense industry's products do not get into the wrong hands.

CONCLUSION

A decade after it achieved independence, Slovenia is a prosperous and stable state with a consolidated democracy. Human rights and basic freedoms are consistently observed and enforced. Its economy in many ways is the envy of the region. Slovene foreign policy has been unwavering in its Western orientation from the moment of independence. Political elites in Ljubljana realized that their reluctance to get involved in Balkan affairs – however rationalized – was a mistake and, taking international criticism to heart, after 1997 Slovene policy toward the region became constructive and beneficial. Slovenia's geographic

[112] OMRI DD II, no. 148 (1 August 1996).
[113] See *Slovenian Defence Products, 1999–2000* (Ljubljana: MOD, 1999).

Slovenia: A Regional Leader   123

position between two NATO member states and abundant experience with the Balkans are advantages to be exploited. Ljubljana's campaign for joining the Alliance has been steady although it has not enjoyed the support of the overwhelming majority of the population.

Slovenia conforms with the overlapping EU/NATO expectations. It complies with NATO-specific criteria concerning civilian control of the military though some areas of civil–military relations could be improved and more clearly legislated. Ljubljana should also accelerate certain aspects of its military reform and it seems willing and financially capable to do so. In recent consultations with NATO Slovenia received positive evaluations of its progress toward fulfilling the Alliance's military criteria of membership.[114] In fact, the aforementioned 2000 Defense Assessment Study on Slovenia found that at least 90 percent of its key recommendations had already been achieved.[115] At a February 2001 conference on security Foreign Minister Rupel stressed that at the next NATO summit Slovenia would be waiting prepared, as it was waiting prepared in 1997 in Madrid.[116]

Although Slovenia has been clearly qualified with respect to non-military criteria of membership, it is important to realize that, as an October 2001 Dutch study has pointed out, "[a]t the moment, Slovenia does not have a single unit prepared for international operations, although the manning and equipping of the 10th Motorised Battalion for this role has been underway since 1998."[117] As NATO Secretary-General Robertson and others have often pointed out, Slovenia's greatest contribution to NATO as a military alliance remains its geographical location. At present it adds little if anything to the military force of the Alliance. Apparently this notion troubled NATO leaders little prior to extending Ljubljana an invitation to the Alliance in November 2002.

---

[114] See, for instance, "Accession Activities Praised," *Slovenia Weekly*, 29 January–4 February 2001.

[115] "NATO Accession Activities Gather Momentum," *Slovenia Weekly*, 10 October 2000.

[116] "Ready for Membership," *Slovenia Weekly*, 29 January–4 February 2001.

[117] Drent, et al., "Organising National Defences for NATO Membership," 57.

4

Romania

Twelve Years of Disappointments

The objective of this chapter is to examine the political, economic, and military-security developments in Romania since the fall of Nicolae Ceauşescu's hard core communist regime. In Part I I review Romania's democratization process, its economic performance, and security situation. Part II examines Romanian foreign policy since 1989 and Bucharest's campaign for NATO membership. Part III concentrates on matters pertaining to civil–military relations. In the last portion of the chapter the focus shifts to military reform and the conditions in the Romanian armed forces.

The second largest state in Eastern Europe, Romania has encountered immense difficulties in meeting its considerable potential. Its example shows the significance of the long-standing legacies of communism. There was minimal opposition to Ceauşescu's sultanistic regime evidenced by the fact that Romania was the only authoritarian state in Europe or South America where not a single full-blown samizdat (or underground) publication appeared.[1] Extensive police terror made the development of any organized opposition to the regime all but impossible. Thirteen years after the Romanian Revolution, the country is ruled by former communists whose metamorphosis to genuine democrats is far more doubtful than that of their colleagues elsewhere in the region.

---

[1] Juan J. Linz and Alfred Stepan, *Problems of Democratic Transition and Consolidation: Southern Europe, South America, and Post-Communist Europe* (Baltimore: Johns Hopkins University Press, 1996), 352–353.

PART I. DOMESTIC POLITICS, ECONOMIC PERFORMANCE, SECURITY STATUS

Domestic Politics

The defining moment of the fall of the communist regime in Romania was the execution of the former dictator and his wife on 25 December 1989, as the culmination of a swift and farcical trial closed to the public. It foreshadowed the difficulties Romania was to face with democratic transition and consolidation. It was the only former Warsaw Pact state where the postcommunist order was born in violence and Romania has also been the country where the most troubling continuities with the ancien régime remain. If one uses regularly recurring elections and a pluralist political system as the key hallmarks of democracy then Romania has become one. Yet the Romanian case also demonstrates the problems with such a minimalist definition. In fact, Romanian politics since 1989 has been characterized by populist, authoritarian, and illiberal features, and the absence of a decisive break with the centralized, bureaucratic, and statist traditions inherited from the past.[2] The lack of real bargaining, compromise, and power sharing has been a nagging reminder that the transition to polyarchy has been severely hampered.[3]

Romania's has been one of the least stable party systems in Eastern Europe. According to a 2000 EU report its legislature is "dogged by bureaucracy and lacks an organized and efficient consultation process" (in 1999 only 59 of the 453 draft laws submitted to parliament were adopted).[4] Unlike Slovakia and Slovenia, Romania's is a presidential-parliamentary polity with broad presidential powers. Since 1989

---

[2] See Vladimir Tismaneanu and Dorin Tudoran, "The Bucharest Syndrome," *Journal of Democracy*, 4:1 (January 1993): 41–52; and Vladimir Tismaneanu, "Romanian Exceptionalism? Democracy, Ethnocracy, and Uncertain Pluralism in Post-Ceausescu-Romania," in Karen Dawisha and Bruce Parrott, eds., *Politics, Power, and the Struggle for Democracy in South-East Europe* (New York: Cambridge University Press, 1997), 403–451.

[3] Helga Welsh, "Political Transition Processes in Central and Eastern Europe," *Comparative Politics*, 26:4 (July 1994): 385. For a prescient article about the superficiality of Romania's early transition see Vladimir Tismaneanu, "New Masks, Old Faces," *The New Republic*, 5 February 1990, 17–21.

[4] Catherine Lovatt, "EC 2000 Progress Report on Romania," *Central Europe Review*, 2:39 (13 November 2000).

Romania has had two presidents. Under the former communist-turned-populist Ion Iliescu (1990–1996, 2000 to present) political elites squandered nearly seven years' worth of opportunities to consolidate a liberal democracy and plundered national resources instead of implementing substantive economic reform. Emil Constantinescu's presidency (1996–2000) was as disappointing as Iliescu's but for different reasons. Perhaps more than anything, four years of relatively liberal rule showed that the forces of progress in Romania were fragmented, inefficient, incompetent, and in some respects scarcely superior to their political foes.

After the popular revolution in December 1989, Iliescu and other former communists quickly managed to seize control over the National Salvation Front (NSF). In the 1990 presidential and parliamentary elections the NSF garnered two-thirds of the vote and therefore, was able to impose its agenda on the country. As Vladimir Tismaneanu noted, "Iliescu's strategy was to cater precisely to the fears, neuroses, and phobias among Romania's industrial workers, peasants in the less developed regions, and the retired population."[5] In 1992 he was reelected by a large margin (his opponent in the run-off was Constantinescu). Iliescu's renamed Democratic National Salvation Front (DNSF), dominated by former communists, also came out on top but lost a great deal of support and was forced to form a minority government. It had to rely on three other parliamentary factions: the rabidly anti-Hungarian Party of Romanian National Unity led by Cluj mayor Gheorghe Funar, the neocommunist and anti-Western Socialist Labor Party headed by Ceauşescu henchman Ilie Verdet, and the anti-Semitic and populist–nationalist Greater Romania Party led by Corneliu Vadim Tudor.[6] The 1992 elections were surrounded by questions of electoral intimidation and manipulation; as many as 30 to 40 percent of the ballots at some voting stations were said to have been annulled.[7]

---

[5] Tismaneanu, "Romanian Exceptionalism?" 426.

[6] See Michael Shafir, "Ruling Party Formalizes Relations with Extremists," *Transition*, 1:5 (14 Apr 1995): 42–46, 64; and Walter M. Bacon, Jr., "Romanian Civil–Military Relations after 1989," (unpublished ms., 1996), 12. For a more comprehensive analysis, see Shafir's "The Mind of Romania's Radical Right," in Sabrina P. Ramet, ed., *The Radical Right in Central and Eastern Europe since 1989* (University Park: Pennsylvania State University Press, 1999), 213–332.

[7] "Recount Is Called in Romanian Vote," *New York Times*, 1 October 1992.

Romania: Twelve Years of Disappointments

The minority government of ex-communists, against the expectations of many – there were five no-confidence votes against it in twenty months – managed to serve out its tenure. Largely thanks to the tough policies of central bank governor Mugur Isarescu, Nicolae Vacaroiu's government was able to bring inflation down to about 30 percent and increase economic growth in 1995. It was, nonetheless, unable to substantially improve Romania's economy. Social relations also suffered during Iliescu's reign. Nationalism was one of the more prominent ideological influences on his cabinets which at times exploited the anti-minority sentiments of some political parties and certain segments of society. Iliescu's coalition governments needed the support of nationalist parties for their survival and he shied away from antagonizing them by championing the cause of ethnic minorities (especially Hungarians and Gypsies). Unlike virtually all other East European presidents, Iliescu did not condemn anti-Gypsy violence in the early 1990s.

Finally, the tables turned in 1996. In the June local elections opposition parties scored a number of impressive victories. Even the former tennis star, Ilie Nastase – supported by the Party of Social Democracy in Romania (PDSR, formerly DNSF) – was unexpectedly routed in his quest for the mayoralty of Bucharest. The November 1996 national and presidential elections resulted in the triumph of the Democratic Convention of Romania (CDR) – comprised by fifteen disparate groups including greens, liberals, and Christian Democrats – and its presidential candidate, Constantinescu. These developments were widely anticipated to signal the advent of a positive shift toward more democratic politics.[8] In a short time, the president and Victor Ciorbea's new coalition government made some painful but necessary economic decisions and embarked on an enlightened minority policy (the Hungarian Democratic Federation of Romania [UDMR] became a member of the coalition and had cabinet-level positions in it). The favorable reception of the new Romanian political and economic orientation was also reflected by the country's improved international prestige. Still, as Tom Gallagher noted, by late

---

[8] See Michael Shafir, "Romania's Road to Normalcy," *Journal of Democracy*, 8:2 (January 1997): 144–159; and Tom Gallagher, "Ceausescu's Legacy," *The National Interest*, no. 56 (Summer 1999): 107–111.

1997 it looked as though the well-meaning liberals had no idea how to pull the country out of the black hole into which it had fallen.[9]

Ciorbea and his government were unable to control the coalition plagued by incessant squabbles, and encountered trouble consolidating the early achievements of their reform program. During his short tenure inflation had increased dramatically and corruption – involving even top level politicians – failed to subside. Following his resignation in March 1998, Radu Vasile, another Christian Democrat, formed a new government. He, too, was forced to quit in late 1999 to be replaced by Isarescu. By 2000, the poor state of the largely unreformed economy had further detrimental effects on Romanian society. For instance, Romania's per capita GNP was $1,562 in 1995 and $1,515 in 1999.[10] Social reforms – including education, healthcare, and social security – have been largely neglected and popular discontent was clearly on the rise. Moreover, under Constantinescu the practice of ruling by ordinances – authorized by the Constitution as an extraordinary legislative measure – became commonplace even though Iliescu's cabinets were fiercely criticized by the opposition every time an ordinance was issued. In fact, during the six years of Iliescu's presidency twenty-eight ordinances were issued in contrast to more than 450 under Constantinescu's four-year rule, signifying a shift toward a more fully presidential system.[11]

The June 2000 local elections provided the first clear sign that the electorate drew its conclusions from the CDR's lackluster performance. The PDSR came in well ahead of other parties while the CDR received a mere 7.3 percent for mayoral elections and 6.5 percent for local councillors. In the following month Constantinescu withdrew from the presidential race publicly lamenting that "a Mafia-type system with links to official institutions" was dominating and destroying Romania's economic and political structures and "people buy and sell principles, ideologies, seats in the parliament and cabinet, making use to that

---

[9] Gallagher, "Ceausescu's Legacy," 110.

[10] Marian Chiriac, "Deadlocked Romania," *Current History*, 100:644 (March 2001): 126.

[11] Correspondence with a Romanian political analyst (10 June 2000). See also M. Steven Fish, "Postcommunist Subversion: Social Science and Democratization in East Europe and Eurasia," *Slavic Review*, 58:4 (Winter 1999): 804–806.

Romania: Twelve Years of Disappointments

end of lies, blackmail, vulgarity, and manipulation."[12] According to observers, however, Constantinescu himself was hardly less corrupt than those he criticized.[13]

"Let no one entertain illusions," cautioned Michael Shafir, an eminent analyst of Romanian politics in 1999, "that the PDSR, once it will gain power again will mean a decrease of chances for European integration."[14] The Romanian electorate, even more impoverished and dispirited in 2000 than it was four years before, did not heed his warning. The PDSR – in Shafir's words, "the unreformed 'successor' party to the Communists" – received 37% of the votes for the Senate and 36.6% for the Chamber of Deputies, followed by the extremist Greater Romania Party (PRM, 21% and 19.4% respectively). The Democratic Party (7.5%/7%), the National Liberal Party (7.4%/6.8%) and the UDMR (6.9%/6.8%) were the only other formations passing the 5% electoral hurdle necessary for parliamentary representation. In the 10 December presidential run-off elections Iliescu defeated the PRM leader, former Ceauşescu court poet and perhaps the most viciously xenophobic East European politician, Corneliu Vadim Tudor, by a margin of two-to-one (i.e., one-third of the voters preferred Tudor).[15] This electoral choice was depicted by a leading Romanian newspaper as a choice between AIDS and cancer while the

---

[12] Radio Free Europe/Radio Liberty Newsline, Part II (henceforth, RFE/RL II), 4:136 (18 July 2000).

[13] Interview with Andrea Bartosin, foreign editor of the Romanian daily *Adevărul* (Austin, TX, 29 August 2000). For instance, Constantinescu proposed that former heads of state should get a lavish house in the center of Bucharest, the same salary as the sitting president, a chauffeur-driven car, and two bodyguards for life. In 1994–1995 the PDSR suggested the same for Iliescu who turned it down. Interview with Larry Watts (Bucharest, 2 November 1999).

[14] Michael Shafir in Imre-József Balázs, Andor Horváth, and Lajos Kántor, eds., *Alternatives for Romania* (Cluj: Komp-Press, 1999), 33. See also interviews with Marius Tabacu (Cluj, 25 October 1999); and Andor Horváth (Cluj, 26 October 1999).

[15] For an insightful analysis of the election, see Michael Shafir, "Counting and Accounting after the Romanian Election," End Note, RFE/RL II, 4:231 (30 November 2000). In August 2001 Romanian journalists published a book entitled "The Anthology of Shame" – it includes Tudor's poems in praise of the Ceauşescus and "venomous stories" about other writers – in order to show Romanians his "real face." See *Evenimentul zilei*, 15 August 2001; RFE/RL II, 5:155 (16 August 2001) and; "A Nastase Shock for NATO?" *Economist*, 6 April 2002, 46.

influential German daily *Die Welt* called it "another giant step in the wrong direction."[16]

Since it took office in December 2000, Prime Minister Adrian Nastase's government has been connected to a number of scandals which, along with some questionable policies, have given ammunition to its critics in Romania and abroad. As a recent European Parliament report noted, a rising number of specialized independent intelligence and security services were created in each ministry while the executive branch has repeatedly and brashly interfered in the judiciary.[17] Lucian Mihai, a judge on the Constitutional Court who resigned in June 2001, said that his experience gained on the bench of the country's highest court showed that Romania was "still a partially totalitarian country" and that the executive and legislative branches handled the judiciary "as if it were merely a decorative artifact."[18] Domestic and foreign critics have castigated Nastase for surrounding himself with individuals with ties to the *Securitate*, Romania's infamous communist-era secret police. In late March 2002, NATO called upon the Romanian government to bar former communist secret police staff from holding sensitive positions. The following month Ioan Talpes, a former security service chief and current presidential adviser speculated that Romania, indeed, "might have to part" with Securitate operatives employed by the state.[19] In November 2002, a week after Romania received its invitation to NATO, Iliescu declared that the issue of former *Securitate* agents still active in state organizations had to be resolved.[20] Though the president publicly refuted the persistent rumors of deepening conflict between himself and the prime minister, they have failed to subside.[21]

---

[16] Cited in "Gulp," *Economist*, 16 December 2000, 57; and by Jiří Šedivý, "The Puzzle of NATO Enlargement," *Contemporary Security Policy*, 22:2 (August 2001): 15, respectively. For an excellent article on the elections, see Alina Mungiu-Pippidi, "The Return of Populism: The 2000 Romanian Elections," *Government and Opposition*, 36:2 (Spring 2001): 230–352.

[17] "Draft Report on Romania's Membership Application to the European Union and the State of Negotiations" (European Parliament, 23 May 2001), 11, 14. See also the strong criticisms of Amnesty International in its annual report, RFE/RL II, 6:99 (29 May 2002).

[18] RFE/RL II, 5:107 (6 June 2001).

[19] AP report cited by RFE/RL II, 6:54 (21 March 2002) and 6:65 (8 April 2002).

[20] RFE/RL II, 6:222 (26 November 2002).

[21] RFE/RL II, 5:63 (29 March 2001); and conversations with Bucharest political analysts (April–May 2001).

Romania: Twelve Years of Disappointments

A few days after entering office, the Nastase government dismissed the head of the national news agency, Rompres, and placed it under the supervision of the Orwellian Ministry of Public Information. As a result of international outcry (even from the Balkan Stability Pact of which Romania is a member), control over Rompres was returned to the legislature in February 2002.[22] According to a recent independent content analysis of five television stations, the government and the ruling party have been allotted ten times more coverage than opposition parties.[23]

In June 2001 the cabinet finally decided to suspend the international adoption of Romanian children. This step was in response to criticisms by the European Parliament that Romanian "government officials [were] involved in lucrative moneymaking from trading with adopted children," charges by the Council of Europe that legislation turned Romania into "a heaven for pedophiles and child traffickers," and the United States' placing Romania in the category of states that "make no significant effort" to combat international trafficking in human beings.[24]

In June 2001, with an eye to joining the Socialist International which refused to admit it in the past, the PDSR merged with the Social Democratic Party of Romania (PSDR) and became the Social Democratic Party (PSD). The PSD minority government envisions constitutional changes which would include reducing the cabinet's prerogative of ruling by governmental orders (a license that was badly abused under Constantinescu) and to limit parliamentary immunity to cover only expressions of political opinion.

The new Romanian legislature includes individuals like Senate Deputy Chairman Gheorghe Buzatu of the PRM, a Holocaust minimizer and member of the Marshall Antonescu (Romania's wartime leader) League.[25] Iliescu and the government could have been more sensitive to foreign concerns about rehabilitating Antonescu. In Bucharest and across the country, there are new statues of the Marshall, who was at least partially responsible for the deaths of tens of thousands

---

[22] See RFE/RL II, 5:9 (15 January 2001) and 6:24 (6 February 2002).
[23] RFE/RL II, 5:214 (9 November 2001).
[24] See RFE/RL II, 5:119 (22 June 2001), and 5:132 (16 July 2001), and the report in *The Guardian*, 31 October 2001.
[25] RFE/RL II, 4:244 (19 December 2000).

132 *The Future of NATO Expansion*

of Jews and Gypsies.[26] Even though there are only about 12,000 to 14,000 Jews (most over the age of sixty-five) in Romania's population of twenty-two million, Tudor and other prominent politicians have publicly and often blamed the country's ills on them.[27] As Senator Adrian Paunescu, a member of Prime Minister Nastase's party recently said, the Holocaust "is reality but not a part of Romanian history."[28]

In October 2001 lawmakers approved a governmental ordinance prohibiting discrimination but eliminated from the law the prohibition of discrimination against national minorities.[29] At the same time, some recent developments are more hopeful. In March 2002 a governmental decree banned the public display of statues and naming of streets in honor of Antonescu. The first Antonescu statue was dismantled in the town of Piatra-Neamt "on orders from Bucharest" though the fact that it was to undergo restoration and placed in a museum is hardly reassuring.[30] In August 2002 the municipal council of Botosani revoked its earlier refusal to change the name of a street named after Antonescu. And, in September 2002 a presidential advisor demanded that the xenophobic television channel Oglinda TV be taken off the air.[31]

Under the new government the state's treatment of the Hungarian minority has somewhat improved, even after Budapest passed a "status law" which gives certain social and economic privileges to ethnic Hungarians in neighboring states while in Hungary. Although various EU bodies found the law to satisfy EU norms and Slovenia, a country that is also home to a Hungarian minority actually supported it, Romanian reactions were quite different. Iliescu said he "hoped" the

---

[26] See Mediafax (Bucharest), 19 January 2001; RFE/RL II, 5:14 (22 January 2001), 5:21 (31 January 2001), and 5:26 (7 February 2001). According to recent surveys 75 percent of Romanians believe that Antonescu, who was executed in 1946, was not a war criminal. *Ziua*, (Bucharest), 25 June 2001, reported in RFE/RL II, 5:121 (26 June 2001). For an early assessment of Antonescu's postcommunist "historical restoration," see Michael Shafir, "Marschall Ion Antonescu: Politik der Rehabilitierung," *Europäische Rundschau*, 22:2 (1994): 55–70.

[27] Interview with Shafir (Prague, 23 August 1999); *The American Jewish Yearbook* (New York: American Jewish Committee, 1999), 384; and "Gulp," *The Economist*, 16 December 2000, 57.

[28] RFE/RL II, 5:211 (6 November 2001).

[29] RFE/RL II, 5:192, 10 October 2000.

[30] Mediafax (Bucharest), 29 March 2002.

[31] Mediafax (Bucharest), 12 September 2002.

Romania: Twelve Years of Disappointments 133

basic treaty with Budapest would not have to be "suspended," Nastase noted that Romania was "no colony from which Hungary can recruit workforce," and Tudor suggested the immediate outlawing of the UDMR and "preparing the army for a crisis situation."[29] Cooler heads prevailed, however, and a compromise was reached between Nastase and his Hungarian colleague, Viktor Orbán, in December 2001. According to this agreement, all Romanian citizens, regardless of their ethnic background, would be allowed to apply for work permits in Hungary. The new government in Budapest is expected to amend the law. As a result of a political compromise, the UDMR has supported the PSD's initiatives in parliament and has held some government positions.

Although after years of criticism from the EU, the Council of Europe, and human rights groups, in June 2001 the Romanian cabinet approved a draft law to decriminalize homosexual relations, some reports have suggested that the Ministry of Justice intended to again designate them as a criminal offense.[32] In fact, the Chamber of Deputies' Judicial Commission changed the government's amendment to the Penal Code a few days later, restoring the punishment to same-sex relations "if they occur in public." As UDMR Deputy Ervin Székely, the only member of the commission who opposed the decision said, the other members believed that they could thus "fool the Council of Europe" which insisted on the legislation.[33] Finally, in September 2001 the Romanian Senate voted 83 to 32 in favor of decriminalizing homosexual relations, a move that was called a "fatal error," a "brutal [European] interference in Romanian legislation" by Greater Romania Party Senator Aron Belascu.[34]

Economic Performance

Romania's economy is arguably the least reformed in Eastern Europe. As the Hungarian liberal political analyst, László Lengyel, noted in 1999, "The way I see it, Romania is now at the stage that Hungary was

---

[32] RFE/RL II, 5:110, 11 June 2001. See also "Council of Europe Report Slaps Romania on Rights," Reuters (Bucharest), 19 May 1994.

[33] RFE/RL II, 5:118 (21 June 2001).

[34] RFE/RL II, 5:170 (7 September 2001).

134 *The Future of NATO Expansion*

in the mid-sixties. Romania cannot escape its own Kádár regime."[35] His Romanian colleague, the liberal intellectual Adrian Marino, contends that in contemporary Romania the right to property is not ensured and regulations concerning foreign investment remain uncertain; consequently the country has attracted one of the smallest amounts of foreign direct investment in postcommunist Europe. Moreover, the absence of genuine law and order, the murky legislations, and the all-pervasive corruption have effectively thwarted business activities.[36]

In 1993 Iliescu said on national television that his government made significant strides toward a market economy but one of his own ministers rebutted him, saying economic reform had not even started.[37] Actually, after 1990 the country's leaders allied themselves with the segments of the working class least interested in radical reform and made an effort "to discredit the very notion of privatization or foreign investments by brandishing the horrors of capitalism and sounding the alarm that the country was about to be sold out to foreigners."[38] In other words, privatization and economic restructuring were viewed in political terms.

From the early 1990s Romania has been dependent on loans from the International Monetary Fund. The IMF has demanded spending cuts in all fields, controls on the budget deficit, limits to foreign borrowing, and the immediate closure of indebted state companies. The governments after 1996 remained hesitant given protests involving tens of thousands of potentially unemployed workers demanding that their inefficient factories remain open. The Ciorbea cabinet did have some successes, including slashing the budget deficit from 10% of the GDP in 1996 to 4.5% in 1997, but this was accompanied by 120% inflation and a 6.5% shrinkage of the economy in the same year and no growth at all in 1998.[39] According to a 2001 Organization for Economic Cooperation and Development (OECD) study, the traditionally

---

[35] László Lengyel, "Economic Traumatology," in Imre-József Balázs, Andor Horváth, and Lajos Kántor, eds., *Alternatives for Romania* (Cluj: Komp-Press, 1999), 74.

[36] Marino in Balázs, et al., *Alternatives for Romania*, 25.

[37] Jane Perlez, "Bleak Romanian Economy Growing Even Bleaker," *New York Times*, 24 November 1993.

[38] Nestor Ratesh, "Romania: Slamming on the Brakes," *Current History*, 92:577 (November 1993): 391.

[39] "Emerging-Market Indicators," *The Economist*, 28 February 1998, 112.

Romania: Twelve Years of Disappointments

strong Romanian agriculture lacked an overall reform framework until 1997 and the country had become a net importer of food. Private farmers do not have access to national markets because links between state farms and food processing companies are still very strong.[40]

In March 2000 Prime Minister Mugur Isarescu admitted that Romania did not have a functional market economy – given that it had neither the requisite institutions nor the flow of information – but rather a "substitute with many malfunctions."[41] The 2000 EU Progress Report agreed, stating that "Romania cannot be regarded as a functioning market economy and is not able to cope with competitive pressure and market forces within the Union in the medium term. It has not substantially improved its future economic prospects."[42]

Living standards in 2000 were "edging toward those of India or Africa: 40% of the population lived on less than $35 a month.... In a population of 23 million, there are 6 million retirees and only 4.3 million registered workers supporting them. Between 25 and 40% of the economy goes untaxed. The young flee west."[43] In July 2001 a new study by the Institute for Research on Life Quality reported that 44% of the population were destitute and that the rate of poverty increased by 60% in the previous two years."[44] According to Prime Minister Nastase, only Albania, Russia, and Moldova had a higher proportion of impoverished people than Romania.[45] In August 2001 a government-commissioned poll found that 56% of the respondents (aged 15 to 29) would leave the country if given the opportunity and 68% were extremely dissatisfied with the political environment.[46] The fact that, according to the British weekly *The Economist*, barely a fifth of Romanians pay income tax, makes matters all the more difficult.[47]

---

[40] Ron Synowitz, "OECD Praises Bulgarian Farm Reforms, Concerned about Romania," RFE/RL II End Note, 5:11 (17 January 2001).

[41] RFE/RL II, 4:61 (27 March 2000).

[42] See "Draft Report on Romania's Membership Application to the European Union and the State of Negotiations," 12; and Lovatt, "EC 2000 Progress Report on Romania."

[43] Donald G. McNeil, Jr., "Long-Suffering Romanians To Vote for a Leader Today," *New York Times*, 26 November 2000.

[44] Mediafax (Bucharest), 13 July 2001; and correspondence with Cătălin Zamfir of the Institute (August 2001).

[45] RFE/RL II, 5:99 (24 May 2001).

[46] Mediafax (Bucharest), 2 August 2001; and RFE/RL II, 5:146 (3 August 2001).

[47] "Easy To Preach, Harder To Do," *The Economist*, 31 August 2002.

As of March 2001, none of the many agreements with the IMF signed by successive Romanian governments was implemented. In fact, the Fund repeatedly suspended delivery of monies due to nonfulfillment of agreements. Romania is the last among all EU candidates having closed only eight chapters of the *acquis communautaire* by August 2001. Günter Verheugen, the European Commissioner for Enlargement, told Nastase in Brussels that "We want to see clear results. Promises, written papers, are not sufficient."[48] In his address to the Romanian legislature a few months later, Verheugen said that the EU "is not expecting from Romania miracles from one day to the next" but "wants to see clear-cut, unequivocal proof" that "substantial reforms" will be implemented in the "short term."[49] Given that Iliescu is first and foremost a populist who at a March 2000 PDSR conference declared that he supported the state ownership of major enterprises, it is difficult to envision the political will for a comprehensive reform of the economy in the foreseeable future.[50] In spite of ominous signs, in 2001 the Romanian economy registered modest growth and some economic reforms started to be implemented. The European Commission's October 2002 report did not include Romania among the ten countries it recommended for EU admission in 2004 assigning for it the provisional target date of 2007 instead.

Security Situation

Romania is a Balkan state whose leaders have often been uncomfortable with this geographical identity and have portrayed their country as a Balkan or East-Central European state depending on the occasion.[51] As Marino writes, "Geopolitically speaking, Romania is in the 'grey zone' on a borderland at the interference of East and West politically, and in the risk zone economically."[52] Romania is bordered by

---

[48] Reuters (Brussels), 25 January 2001 cited in RFE/RL II, 5:18 (26 January 2001).
[49] RFE/RL II, 5:81 (26 April 2001).
[50] Interview with Andrea Bartosin (Austin, TX, 29 August 2000).
[51] Compare two excellent articles, Tom Gallagher's "To Be Or Not To Be Balkan: Romania's Quest for Self-Definition," *Daedalus*, 126:3 (Summer 1997): 63–83; and Tony Judt's, "Romania: Bottom of the Heap," *The New York Review of Books*, 1 November 2001, 44; with the contributions to Kurt W. Treptow and Mihail E. Ionescu, eds., *Romania and Euro-Atlantic Integration* (Iasi: Center for Romanian Studies, 1999).
[52] Marino in Balázs, et al., *Alternatives for Romania*, 26.

one NATO member, Hungary, and Ukraine, Moldova, Bulgaria, and Yugoslavia (Serbia). In public opinion polls most Romanians identify Russia and Hungary as the two sources of external threat to their country but, according to Ion-Mircea Plangu, a former State Secretary for Defense Policy, this perception has more to do with historical animosities than with realistic fears.[53]

"The main danger threatening Romania is not coming from outside, but from inside subversion" said Ioan Mircea Pascu, a former state secretary at the Ministry of Defense (MOD) and current defense minister (DM) in a 1994 news conference.[54] Although he failed to elaborate, he may well have referred to the potential of ethnic Hungarian insurrection supported by Budapest, the favorite boogeyman of both former communists and nationalists in Romania. The Romanian-Hungarian relationship, while far from a current security threat, is undoubtedly one of the most tense in the region. In 1991, for instance, former DM Victor Stanculescu could convince the legislature to increase the MOD's budget in part to counter the military threat from Hungary.[55]

When I asked Pascu in late 1999 about the security challenges his country faced, he mentioned only cross-border smuggling of strategic materials, illegal trade of conventional weapons, drug trafficking, and illegal immigration.[56] Presumably he did not mean that Romanian security was threatened by Jiu Valley miners who staged demonstrations, went on rampages, and clashed with the police and unsympathetic civilians on five occasions in nine years (the last time in January 1999) in Bucharest, resulting in dozens of deaths. In July 1990 the miners actually heeded the request of Pascu's boss, President Iliescu, to "restore order" against anticommunist protesters who criticized the government for hijacking the revolution.[57]

---

[53] Interview with Plangu, MOD (Bucharest, 5 November 1999).
[54] "Greatest Danger Awaiting Romania Comes from Inside, Defence Official Says," Rompres (Bucharest), 15 April 1994.
[55] Dale R. Herspring, "The Process of Change and Democratization in Eastern Europe: The Case of the Military," in John R. Lampe and Daniel N. Nelson, eds., *East European Security Reconsidered* (Washington, D.C.: Woodrow Wilson Center Press, 1993), 66.
[56] Interview with Pascu (PDSR), Chairman of the Chamber of Deputies' Committee on Defense, Public Order, and National Security Committee (Bucharest, 3 November 1999).
[57] On this point, see Chiriac, "Deadlocked Romania," 126–127.

138   *The Future of NATO Expansion*

Romania's porous frontier with Moldova has been a concern because it made a lot easier the introduction of Russian and Chinese mafias, illegal immigrants, and drugs to Romanian territory.[58] According to Romanian officials, in July 1998 "at least eight terrorist groups, including the 'Muslim Brothers,' Hezbollah, 'Western Front,' and the Kurdistan Workers' Party were active on Romania's territory."[59] Constantin Dudu Ionescu, a former Minister of Interior, noted that the risk factors for Romania were major economic and financial imbalances and crimes, tax evasion, and organized crime which might threaten the functioning of fundamental state institutions.[60]

The trade embargo against Yugoslavia and the disruption of shipping on the Danube in the wake of NATO's 1999 bombing of bridges in the country very adversely affected the Romanian economy. Romanian politicians have often complained that Bucharest received no compensation for its sacrifices. When asked about oil smuggling to Yugoslavia during 1994–1995, Prime Minister Vacaroiu said that only private individuals did so, but in November 2000 President Constantinescu admitted that 30,000 tons of fuel was illegally shipped to Yugoslavia in breach of the international embargo with the connivance of the border police and the Ministry of Transportation.[61]

Researchers at the Institute for Political Studies of Defense and Military History began to work on Romania's national security concept by 1990, in order to identify fundamental national interests and formulate the most suitable strategy. In 1994 the Supreme Council of National Defense (SCND) approved the concept, a modified version of which became the National Security Strategy in 1999.[62] The five major issue areas considered for the strategy were (1) defense of fundamental

---

[58] Adina Stefan, "Romania's Engagement in Subregional Co-operation and the National Strategy for NATO Accession," *Harmonie Paper 10* (Groningen, Holland: Centre of European Security Studies, University of Groningen, December 1999), 13.

[59] General Stan Stangaciu, commander of the gendarmes, reported in *Azi*, 13 July 1998, cited in Stefan, "Romania's Engagement," 13.

[60] Constantin Dudu Ionescu, "Romania's Defense Policy and Regional Cooperation for National Security," in Treptow and Ionescu, eds., *Romania and Euro-Atlantic Integration*, 75–76.

[61] RFE/RL II, 4:141 (25 July 2001); and "Long-Suffering Romanians," *New York Times*, 26 November 2001.

[62] Interview with Teodor Repciuc and Cristian Mureşanu of the Institute (Bucharest, 4 November 1999). See also "Romania's Strategy of National Security" (Bucharest: Government of Romania, June 1999), 10 pp.

Romania: Twelve Years of Disappointments

rights of civic and minority rights; (2) consolidation of democratic changes; (3) defense prerogatives of the state, such as independence, territorial integrity, national unity; (4) incentives of international relations (i.e., future membership in international organizations); and (5) active participation to foster regional/international security. Once Romania joined the Partnership for Peace program, its integrated strategy of national security and national military doctrine were harmonized with PfP mechanisms.[63] In 1998 the General Staff revamped the defense doctrine which now identifies the risks and threats to Romania and the armed forces' objectives in crises, peace, and war and reiterates the country's commitment to Euro-Atlantic integration.

PART II. FOREIGN POLICY AND THE CAMPAIGN FOR NATO MEMBERSHIP

Romanian Foreign Policy

Romania had a hesitant start in reshaping its foreign and security policies after the Revolution of 1989. During 1990–1993, Bucharest even adopted pro-Eastern postures that contrasted sharply with Ceauşescu's traditional policies. Romania was the last East European state to call for the dissolution of the Warsaw Pact, and to establish diplomatic ties with NATO.[64] Nonetheless, after 1993, its foreign policy has been more consistently Western-oriented than Slovakia's. In February 1993 Bucharest signed an association agreement with the European Community (the EU's former name). In October 1993, after several delays caused by serious doubts about Romania's democratization and human rights records, it was admitted to the Council of Europe as a full member. After Constantinescu took over the presidency, Bucharest's foreign policy orientation became even more unambiguously oriented toward the EU and NATO as the government attempted to make up for the country's poor international reputation. During the 2000 electoral

---

[63] "Defense Minister on Reform in the Armed Forces, Partnership for Peace," Rompres (Bucharest), 9 February 1994.

[64] Dan Ionescu, "Hammering on NATO's Door," *Transition*, 2:16 (9 August 1996): 39. For an early assessment of post-Ceauşescu foreign policy, see Ronald H. Linden, "After the Revolution: A Foreign Policy of Bounded Change," in Daniel N. Nelson, ed., *Romania after Tyranny* (Boulder, CO: Westview Press, 1992), 203–238.

140   *The Future of NATO Expansion*

campaign Iliescu insisted that there would be no changes in foreign policy were he elected president. In 2001 Romania took over the rotating presidency of the Organization for Security and Cooperation in Europe (OSCE) which Foreign Minister Mircea Geoana called "the most important international task Romania had in decades."[65]

During the first presidency of Iliescu, himself a graduate of a Soviet university, Romania had close relations with the USSR/Russia. In April 1991 Bucharest concluded a basic treaty with the former Soviet Union. Romania also has the distinction of signing a military cooperation agreement with the USSR in the last month (December 1991) of its existence. In March 1993 Defense Minister Pavel Grachev became the first Soviet/Russian military leader to set foot on Romanian soil in over two decades on the occasion of the signing of a military cooperation agreement.[66] Under Constantinescu, Bucharest's relations with Moscow were reevaluated. Not surprisingly, Romanian-Russian relations are expected to improve once again during Iliescu's second presidency. Early in his new administration Iliescu declared that there should be "normal relations" between the two countries adding that there could be no European stability without the "active role" of Russia.[67] He noted that he expected to sign the pending basic treaty with Russia before the end of his mandate in 2004 and it would be "far less problematic" than that signed with Ukraine in 1997.[68]

Romania's relations with two of its neighbors, Ukraine and Moldova, both republics of the former Soviet Union, have been mixed. Although in 1997 Bucharest concluded a "Good Neighborliness Treaty" with Kyiv which recognized their common border as permanent, the two governments since then have locked horns over the ownership of the Serpents Island in the Black Sea and future Ukrainian oil drilling in its vicinity. The issue remains unresolved and Prime Minister Nastase has suggested that Bucharest might request the U.N. International Court of Justice to rule on the dispute.[69] There have not been

---

[65] Mediafax (Bucharest) interview with Geoana, 2 January 2001.

[66] Stéphane Lefebvre, "Changes in the Romanian Armed Forces," *Jane's Intelligence Review*, 7:1 (January 1995): 10.

[67] Mediafax (Bucharest), 27 February 2001.

[68] RFE/RL II, 5:120 (25 June 2001) and 5:228 (4 December 2001).

[69] See "Akadályozzák Romániát?" *Magyar Nemzet*, 1 August 2001; and RFE/RL II, 5:198 (18 October 2001); and 6:190 (8 October 2002).

Romania: Twelve Years of Disappointments

major conflicts between Romania and Moldova but a number of controversies pertaining to Moldovan ethnic and national identity remain. Bucharest, for good reasons, views Moldovans "as part of the Romanian ethnic group" which Moldovan politicians occasionally interpret as Romanian interference.[70] Nonetheless, after considerable difficulty the two states signed a basic treaty in 2000, expressed their commitment to the improvement of bilateral ties which was renewed by Iliescu after taking office.[71] Bucharest's relations with rump Yugoslavia shifted drastically in January 1997, when Constantinescu sent a personal emissary to meet opposition leaders in Serbia, thus abandoning his predecessor's stance of identifying with the hard-line Slobodan Milošević.[72]

All in all, Romania has maintained good relations with its fellow NATO aspirants discussed in this book. It has the best contacts with Slovakia with which Bucharest shares the challenges of a relatively large, well-organized, and troublesome Hungarian minority. Iliescu and Mečiar met on numerous occasions to exchange ideas about effective minority policies.[73] Romania's relations with Sofia have been less cordial owing to a number of troublesome issues, including environmental problems and the unresolved matter of a Danube bridge between Calafat and Vidin. Romania has also been irked by the repeated declarations from Sofia that Bulgaria did not want international organizations to consider it in the same category as its neighbor to the north, given that both in terms of democratic consolidation and economic transition Bulgaria was far ahead. In late October 2002 Nastase suggested that the Romanian and Bulgarian governments should work together to lobby for the two countries, EU admission but was, once again, rebuffed by his Bulgarian counterpart.[74] Vasile Pascas,

---

[70] On this issue, see Janusz Bugajski, "Key Elements of Romania's Security Strategy," in Treptow and Ionescu, eds., *Romania and Euro-Atlantic Integration*, 53.

[71] See Stefan, "Romania's Engagement," 26–29; Michael Shafir, "Romania, Moldova Conclude Problematic Basic Treaty," End Note, RFE/RL II, 4:85 (2 May 2000); and 5:71 (11 April 2001).

[72] Gallagher, "To Be Or Not To Be Balkan," 75.

[73] See, for instance, Open Media Research Institute Daily Digest, Part II (henceforth: OMRI DD II), no. 57 (21 March 1995); and no. 97 (19 May 1995).

[74] See, for instance, RFE/RL II, 4:215 (6 November 2000); and 6:205 (30 October 2002). Robert Kaplan writes about the minimal interest in each other and the mutual disdain between Romania and Bulgaria. See his *Eastward to Tartary: Travels in the Balkans, the Middle East, and the Caucasus* (New York: Random House, 2000), 60–61.

Romania's chief negotiator with the EU, contended that Sofia's "dissociation from Romania in the accession process" demonstrated that Bulgaria "lies at the gates of the Orient" and that he wished them "the success they wish for us."[75] Romanian-Slovene relations have been cordial although Ljubljana did not always respond to Bucharest's initiatives with the enthusiasm expected.[76]

Romania's relations with the three new East European NATO members have been mixed. All of them have backed its NATO bid although Czech President Havel contended in June 2001 that Romania and Bulgaria were the least likely to join in 2002.[77] In essence, after 1997 Bucharest upgraded its contacts with the three East-Central European states. Although since 1989 Romanian-Hungarian ties have somewhat improved, they remain strained primarily owing to Bucharest's treatment of the approximately 1.6-million strong Hungarian minority. In September 1996 the two states finally signed a basic treaty after numerous postponements. As U.S. Ambassador to NATO Robert Hunter noted, the Treaty was signed not "because they like each other" but because both governments realized that their chances of NATO membership would be increased with the agreement.[78] Relations perceptibly improved during 1996–1998, that is, after the Democratic Convention took power in Bucharest and before the Young Democrat-dominated government, keenly interested in the conditions of Hungarian minorities abroad, won the elections in Budapest. They have become far less cordial since the "second coming" of Iliescu as the aforementioned controversy around the Hungarian "Status Law" shows.[79] Moreover, UDMR leaders have charged that the long-overdue 2000 Public Administration Law which ordained the installation of bilingual street signs and a number of other concessions to Hungarians

---

[75] "Romania Has No Inferiority Complex with Bulgaria," *Nine O'Clock* (Bucharest), 6 October 2002.

[76] See, for instance, the Romanian suggestion of a "quadripartite cooperation between Italy, France, Slovenia, and Romania," RFE/RL II, 3:133 (12 July 1999).

[77] RFE/RL II, 5:115 (15 June 2001).

[78] Hunter quoted in *The Wall Street Journal*, 2 January 1997. For an insightful article on the relations between Bucharest and Budapest, see Ronald H. Linden, "Putting on Their Sunday Best: Romania, Hungary, and the Puzzle of Peace," *International Studies Quarterly*, 44:1 (March 2000): 121–146.

[79] See, for instance, Mediafax (Bucharest), 19 June 2001 and 13 July 2001; "Martonyi: Megalapozatlan fenntartások," *Népszabadság*, 23 June 2001; and "Státustörvény: maradt a vita Bukaresttel," *Népszabadság*, 14 July 2001.

Romania: Twelve Years of Disappointments 143

in areas where they comprise at least 20 percent of the population is simply ignored by authorities.[80] With the new center-left Hungarian government relations between the two states should improve yet again.

After 1993 relations with EU and NATO states became a priority of Romanian foreign policy. Bucharest took pains to court all European NATO members and received their verbal support for membership on numerous occasions prior to and after 1997. (It might be pointed out that such gestures are not terribly courageous given that any one country can veto a new member and it is the leader of the Alliance, the United States, that is expected to do so. In other words, European states that assure aspirants of their support have nothing to lose by doing so.) President Jacques Chirac of France, a traditional patron of Romania, declared that he wanted "privileged relations" with Romania, "the only Latin country in Eastern Europe."[81] In 2001 Chirac said that Romania has the "right" to join NATO at the Alliance's 2002 Prague Summit, and that Romania was "naturally" among the first countries that should join.[82]

Bucharest's relations with the United States were rather contentious in the early 1990s given American reservations about Romanian democratization and minority policies. In September 1992 the U.S. House of Representatives overwhelmingly (283 to 88) defeated the Administration-backed bill to restore Most Favored Nation (MFN) trade status to Bucharest.[83] Romania was finally granted MFN status a year later and permanent MFN status in 1996. Romanian-American ties improved during Constantinescu's presidency. Even though the United States (along with Britain, Denmark, and Iceland) was strongly opposed to Romanian NATO membership in 1997, it did offer a "Strategic Partnership" to Bucharest in order to enhance cooperation with and democratization in Romania.[84] Following the 2000 Romanian elections Washington repeatedly expressed its concern over

---

[80] Iulia Trandafir, "UDMR Discontented with Public Local Administration Law Enforcement," *Nine O'Clock* (Bucharest), 16 August 2001.

[81] *Adevărul* (Bucharest), 22 January 1996, cited by OMRI DD II, no. 16 (23 January 1996).

[82] Interview with Chirac in *Adevărul*, 14 June 2001.

[83] "Recount Is Called in Romanian Vote," *New York Times*, 1 October 1992.

[84] See Sean Kay, "What Is a Strategic Partnership? *Problems of Post-Communism*, 47:3 (May–June 2000): 15–24.

144   *The Future of NATO Expansion*

the emergence of extremists and its displeasure about the appointment of former *Securitate* officers to high positions; nonetheless, as NATO's recent criticism indicates, they remain in the government.[85] Nevertheless, Bucharest's immediate and strong expressions of support for Washington in the aftermath of 9/11 placed U.S.-Romanian relations on a new footing.

Bucharest eagerly offered its troops to participate in the U.S.-led military operations in Afghanistan, against Iraq, along with Romanian airspace and military bases. Washington's goodwill toward Bucharest was further cemented when the latter became the first state in August 2002 to sign an agreement with the United States on exempting U.S. peacekeepers from prosecution under the International Criminal Court.[86] The Nastase government went to great length to defend its decision about the controversial treaty which, incidentally, is opposed by the EU and much of the international community.[87] After Bucharest secured an invitation to NATO in November 2002, Romania volunteered to host U.S. missile bases on its territory and Iliescu decorated George Bush with Romania's highest state order. In his speech to a cheering crowd in Bucharest's Revolution Square, the U.S. President asserted that Romania "brings moral clarity to our NATO alliance."[88] Thus, in the course of little over a year Romania, whose NATO accession chances seemed exceedingly doubtful, has become, in Bush's word, the "spearhead of the Alliance."[89] The question that remains, as Walter Bacon has put it, "where is the spear headed?"[90]

Romania's Campaign for NATO Membership

It is fair to say that no state has conducted a more vehement campaign for NATO membership than Romania. Because Bucharest could not

---

[85] See, for instance, RFE/RL II, 4:232 (1 December 2000); and Mediafax (Bucharest), 4 April 2001.

[86] RFE/RL II, 6:144 (2 August 2002).

[87] See, for instance, RFE/RL II, 6:155 (19 August 2002); 6:158 (22 August 2002); and 6:167 (5 September 2002).

[88] RFE/RL II, 6:221 (25 November 2002).

[89] See Robert G. Kaiser, "Romania Seeks NATO Membership as Remedy for Post-Communist Ills," *Washington Post*, 21 October 2002.

[90] Bacon's presentation at the Annual Meeting of the American Association for the Advancement for Slavic Studies (Pittsburgh, PA, 23 November 2002).

Romania: Twelve Years of Disappointments

portray itself as a leader in democratization or economic reforms, it has put the emphasis in its campaign on Romania's "strategic location" in the Balkans. Although politicians in Bucharest like to go on about how much NATO needs Romania, former Chief of the General Staff (CGS) Constantin Degeratu believes it is the other way around: "Romania is the only country in Europe between the two great regions of instability and uncertainty, the former Yugoslavia and the former Soviet Union. For the sake of ourselves and Europe, we require stability. No other country in Europe needs NATO as much as we do."[91] With the admission of Hungary to NATO there is "a risk that Romania's northeast frontier will become a new partition line, dividing a stable Europe from a peripheral group of countries deemed to fall short of Western political and economic standards."[92]

After the first Iliescu administration decided to seek NATO membership, its campaign largely involved a consistent attempt to eliminate the distinction between the Visegrad states and Romania. Iliescu, Constantinescu, and officials of their administrations repeatedly tried to blackmail NATO by suggesting that an expansion of the Alliance that included Hungary but not NATO could lead to sharpening tensions between the two states and growing instability in the region.[93] Then-Defense Minister Gheorghe Tinca actually declared that "an armaments race" would break out between Hungary and Romania if the former were accepted before the latter into the Alliance.[94] The November 1996 elections that brought democratic forces to the fore certainly boosted Romania's stock in Brussels and Constantinescu, in a last-ditch effort that included visits to each of the sixteen NATO capitals, tried to turn this advantage into an invitation. A 1997 Ministry of Foreign Affairs (MFA) document estimated the cost of Romania's

---

[91] Kaplan, *Eastward to Tartary*, 52.

[92] Gallagher, "Ceausescu's Legacy," 108.

[93] See, for instance, "Iliescu a NATO bővítésről," *Magyar Nemzet*, 1 July 1996; Defense Minister Victor Babiuc in Reuters (Bucharest), 17 January 1997; Foreign Minister Severin cited in OMRI DD II, no. 12 (17 January 1997); and former Romanian King Mihai, Reuters (London), 25 March 1997. For a more general analysis of Romania's NATO campaign, see Alfred H. Moses, "Romania's NATO Bid," *SAIS Review*, 18:1 (Winter–Spring 1998): 137–143.

[94] *Vocea României*, no. 715 (8 April 1996), cited in Adrian Stan, "The Euro-Atlantic Structures and Romania," *Euro-Atlantic Studies* (Centre for Euro-Atlantic Studies, University of Bucharest, 1998), 123.

146 *The Future of NATO Expansion*

NATO integration at $3.8 billion "affordable," especially as the "economic reform progresses."[95]

During his 1997 visit to Bucharest (just days after the Madrid Summit), a conciliatory President Clinton – perhaps overwhelmed by the frenetic reception in spite of his opposition to Romanian membership – remarked that "I can see no stronger candidate" when referring to Romania's chances for NATO membership. Basing his comments on this lapse of presidential realism, Romanian Foreign Minister Adrian Severin said that "Romania could be labeled a leading candidate and a motor of further NATO enlargement."[96] Oleg Serebrian, a Moldovan foreign policy analyst had a different view. He noted that

The Romanian NATO campaign was a big mistake. It is silly to undervalue your own nation's strategic interest and prefer those of the USA.... The most shocking part of this absurd drama was Clinton's visit to Bucharest. I was wondering which of the countries aware of the concept of "minimal pride" would have greeted the president of a country opposing Romania joining NATO with such silly admiration?[97]

More sensible messages emanated from Brussels. In 1998 NATO Deputy Secretary-General Klaus-Peter Kleiber told Prime Minister Vasile that whether Romania was in the next round depended on the progress of reform.[98] Kleiber might have politely referred to the fact that notwithstanding the flurry of diplomatic activity, very little was done under Constantinescu's watch to substantially reform the Romanian military.

According to several observers, the Constantinescu administration's groveling NATO campaign was downright counterproductive. During the Kosovo crisis, for instance, Bucharest voluntarily satisfied NATO's every request without asking for anything in return (not even

---

[95] *White Book on Romania and NATO* (Bucharest: Ministry of Foreign Affairs, 1997), 38.

[96] See Severin, "Romania Endeavors to Join NATO," in Anton A. Bebler, ed., *The Challenge of NATO Enlargement* (Westport, CT: Praeger, 1999), 161.

[97] Oleg Serebrian, "Romanians between East and West," in Balázs, et al., *Alternatives for Romania*, 168. For a Romanian view, see Constantin Ene, "Romania Sets Its Sights on NATO Membership," *NATO Review*, no. 6 (November–December 1997): 8–11.

[98] Joseph Harrington and Scott Karns, "Romania's Ouestpolitik: Bucharest, Europe, and the Euro-Atlantic Alliance, 1990–1998," in Treptow and Ionescu, eds., *Romania and Euro-Atlantic Integration*, 45.

Romania: Twelve Years of Disappointments

compensation for the considerable losses of Danube shipping). Ioan Mircea Pascu – the current DM – told me that given Bucharest's sycophantic behavior, NATO leaders could reasonably ask, "why should we extend membership to Romania when it gives us what we want for nothing anyway?"[99] He was not entirely correct, however, since Romania did get NATO security guarantees in exchange for its support and additional benefits of its stance included a promise of British backing for Bucharest's accession to the EU. James Rosapepe, a former U.S. ambassador to Bucharest, suggested that the Romanian experience demonstrates that "excessive anxiety about getting into NATO quickly can be counterproductive."[100]

Since the new administration took office in late 2000, Bucharest's view of NATO membership has become more realistic. Both Iliescu and Prime Minister Nastase have repeatedly said that though they fully supported NATO accession, it would not be a "tragedy" or reasons for "exasperation and despair" if it did not happen in 2002.[101] This more realistic attitude did not mean a lack of commitment, however. In March 2001 Iliescu announced the launching of a new propaganda and diplomatic campaign – the measures of which include the coordination of the activities of all ministries and intensive international lobbying – to boost the country's NATO accession chances and asked for the support of parliamentary parties, the media, and nongovernmental organizations.[102] This strategy provided for not only fulfilling membership admission conditions but also for promotion activities in NATO member states. Since then, Bucharest has conducted a self-described "diplomatic offensive" in Brussels, Washington, and

---

[99] Interview with Pascu (Bucharest, 3 November 1999). When the Danube was closed, 126 Romanian and 18 foreign barges destined for Romania carrying 60,000 metric tons of merchandise were suddenly stranded. See Gary Dempsey, "Headaches for Neighboring Countries," in Ted Galen Carpenter, ed., *NATO's Empty Victory: A Postmortem on the Balkan War* (Washington, D.C.: Cato Institute, 2000), 69–71. On this issue, see also Stephen J. Flanagan, "NATO and Kosovo: Lessons Learned and Prospects for Stability in Southeastern Europe," in Sabina Crisen, ed., *NATO and Europe in the 21st Century* (Washington, D.C.: Woodrow Wilson Center, 2000), 52–53.

[100] James C. Rosapepe, "Romania and NATO; 'Knocking on an Open Door'," *Central European Issues: Romanian Foreign Affairs Review*, 5:1 (1999): 50.

[101] See, for instance, RFE/RL II, 5:64 (2 April 2001), 5:86 (4 May 2001), and 5:115 (15 June 2001).

[102] Mediafax (Bucharest), 26 February 2001.

148   *The Future of NATO Expansion*

points in-between.[103] Following the 2001 terrorist attack on the United States, Romania declared that it would emulate the Bulgarian example and grant NATO use of a military base on its territory and would offer the Alliance full access to Romanian airspace, land, and waterways.[104]

As is clear from the above, Romania did its best to curry favor with NATO after 1997. NATO Secretary-General Robertson and U.S. Secretary of State Albright thanked Bucharest for its cooperation during the 1999 war in Yugoslavia. The United States has repeatedly extended grants to Romania to help its armed forces make progress in reaching compatibility with NATO.[105] Romania was the first signatory to the PfP and has been one of the most active participants in the program. Among the many processes that are supposed to ease the modernization of its armed forces, Romania has participated in the PfP Council and "Operational Partnership" concept – NATO's basic tools for the twenty-first century – which offer new possibilities of strengthening military cooperation, as well as more politically involved relationships with NATO and its member states.[106] Romania has participated in a number of regional organizations including the Southeastern Cooperation Initiative; the Charter on Good-Neighborly Relations, Stability, Security, and Cooperation in Southeastern Europe; the Black See Littoral Cooperation; the Carpathian Euroregion; the Multinational Peace Force Southeastern Europe, and a number of other multilateral cooperative arrangements.[107] Since the early 1990s Romanian troops

---

[103] See, for instance, "NATO Supreme Allied Commander To Make Official Trip to Bucharest," *Mediafax* (Bucharest), 18 January 2002; RFE/RL II, 6:13 (22 January 2002), 6:14 (23 January 2002), 6:24 (6 February 2002).

[104] RFE/RL II, 5:179 (20 September 2001); and 5:222 (26 November 2001).

[105] The last one of these grants, $17 million, was transferred in late June 2001. See Reuters (Bucharest), 27 June 2001.

[106] "Romania's Pro-NATO Option," *Panoramic Militar*, nr. 3 (1999): 3. See also, Gheorghe Tinca, "Reflections on Armed Forces Day," *Romania Today*, no. 9 (October 1996): 1, 4; *Romanian Armed Forces: In the Service of Peace* (Bucharest: Ministry of Defense, 1997); and Constantin Degeratu, "Romania: Five Years in Partnership for Peace," *Central European Issues: Romanian Foreign Affairs Review*, 5:1 (1999): 36–46.

[107] See, for instance, Vasil Hudák, "Transfrontier Cooperation in Central Europe," in Hudák, ed., *Building a New Europe: Transfrontier Cooperation in Central Europe* (Prague: Institute for EastWest Studies, 1996), 1–10; and Stefan, "Romania's Engagement in Subgregional Cooperation," 18–25.

Romania: Twelve Years of Disappointments

have also done more than their fair share in international peacekeeping assignments.

According to the MFA, the Romanian public's support for NATO membership has been consistently in the range of 90–95%, though MOD officials contended that it plummeted to 60–65% following the war in Yugoslavia.[108] Vojtech Mastny cautions though that the 95% support scores for membership are not necessarily reliable "in a country notorious for the skill of its ruling cliques in manipulating a politically inexperienced citizenry."[109] A public opinion survey conducted by the INSOMAR polling institute showed that 88 percent of the respondents supported Romania's NATO membership in October 2002.[110] During the mid-1990s the MFA established some programs and supported some NGOs (such as the Euro-Atlantic Center and the Manfred Wörner Association in Bucharest) to increase public awareness in NATO. In the MOD, a Public Relations Directorate was created with a nation-wide staff of 300 to 350 employees both to increase the military's prestige and to educate the public about NATO.[111] All Romanian parliamentary parties support joining NATO although in the case of the Greater Romania Party, as its leader, Vadim Tudor said, only because Hungary was a member and this was "the only way to keep an eye on it."[112]

In August 2001 Democratic Party leader Traian Başescu revealed that NATO reports indicated that Romania was facing problems of political stability, corruption, and with military reforms, as well as with the integration of the Hungarian and Jewish minorities. Prime Minister Nastase admonished Başescu for "washing the dirty linen in public" and said that the opposition should heed his call for "an armistice on NATO accession." His call has been rejected by both the Democratic Party and the National Liberal Party.[113]

---

[108] See *White Book on Romania and NATO* (Bucharest: MFA, 1997), 13; and interview with Col. Anghel Filip (Ret.), NATO/WEU Integration Directorate/MOD (Bucharest, 1 November 1999).

[109] Mastny, "Reassuring NATO," 74.

[110] Romanian Radio, 9 October 2002, cited in RFE/RL II, 6:192 (10 October 2002).

[111] Interview with Col. Valentin Stancu, Chief of Public Relations Directorate/MOD (Bucharest, 3 November 1999).

[112] Cited by RFE/RL II, 5:44 (5 March 2001).

[113] This paragraph is based on the report in RFE/RL II, 5:161 (24 August 2001).

150   *The Future of NATO Expansion*

Romania's military diplomacy has been more successful than the MFA and the government in developing constructive relations with its neighbors. Romania has made commitments to or has already established joint (mostly peacekeeping) units with several of its neighbors, including Bulgaria, Hungary, Moldova, and Ukraine. Romanian officer-diplomats have concluded defense cooperation agreements with numerous NATO countries, among them France, Greece, Spain, Turkey, the United Kingdom. A fitting illustration of the point that military diplomacy is distinct from inter-state diplomacy and one may not always be reflective of the other is the traditionally cordial ties between the Romanian and Hungarian armed forces. Even in the early and mid-1990s when relations between the two states were strained, the two armies maintained good relations.[114] The two defense ministries have kept close contacts on ministerial, general staff, and lower levels and have signed several important agreements. In May 1991 the two countries were the first to sign an "Open Skies" agreement allowing for four annual unarmed surveillance flights over each other's territory and they set up a joint 1,000-strong peacekeeping unit which became operational in January 2000.[115]

As I noted above, especially after 9/11 2001 Bucharest did more than any other candidate to focus its efforts on obtaining an invitation to NATO. More than mere expressions of its solidarity with the United States, a Romanian battalion joined the fighting against Taliban forces in Afghanistan. Recognizing the significance of this decision, DM Pascu said after Bucharest received the invitation at the Prague Summit that "Romania's way to Prague led through Kandahar."[116] MOD officials estimated the cost of participation at approximately $25 million (which meant a scrious sacrifice for a country where millions earned less than $80 per month).[117] In the days leading upto the Prague Summit former Romanian King Michael I even toured European

---

[114] This impression was confirmed at several rounds of interviews I conducted with numerous high ranking Romanian and Hungarian military officers and diplomats in Budapest and Bucharest in 1993, 1995, 1996, and 1999.

[115] Alfred A. Reisch, "Central and Eastern Europe's Quest for NATO Membership, *RFE/RL Research Report*, 2:28 (9 July 1993): 39; and Mediafax (Arad), 12 April 2000.

[116] DPA (Bucharest), 21 November 2002.

[117] RFE/RL II, 6:90 (15 May 2002).

countries ruled by monarchs to drum up support for Romania's NATO accession.

It is a safe bet that no government was more jubilant after receiving an invitation to the Alliance than Romania's. Nearly two months before the decision became official, the ruling PSD announced its intention to declare November 19 "NATO Day," a national celebration organized by central and local authorities complete with public events, military parades, and cultural and athletic competitions.[118] During the Prague Summit President Iliescu declared that Romania received a chance to reverse "the great historical backwardness that Romania inherited."[119] He did not say that this gap had only widened throughout his eight-year reign.

PART III. CIVIL–MILITARY RELATIONS

Depoliticizing the Armed Forces

In no East European state were civil–military relations more antagonistic in the late-communist era than in Romania. Nicolae Ceauşescu, an increasingly distrustful dictator, periodically rotated the top officials of key ministries and in the military establishment to prevent them from consolidating their power bases. Communist party control over the armed forces was more extensive and intensive than elsewhere and the Romanian military had an institutional rival, the security police (*Securitate*), which received priority treatment from the Bucharest leadership. Moreover, the army was increasingly used as a captive labor force for Ceauşescu's pharaonic construction projects.[120] In all of Eastern Europe, the fall of the *ancien régime* was most sudden in Romania where the armed forces actually decided the fate of the Revolution. Between 17–21 December 1989 the army obeyed the military elite's orders to fire on demonstrators in the Transylvanian city

---

[118] "PSD Wants to Establish 'NATO Day'," *Nine O'Clock*, 1 October 2002.
[119] RFE/RL II, 6:220 (22 November 2002).
[120] See, for instance, Zoltan Barany, "Romania and the Warsaw Pact," paper read at the U.S. Air Force Intelligence Conference on Soviet Affairs (Arlington, VA, 19–22 October 1988); and William Crowther, "'Ceausescuism' and Civil–Military Relations in Romania," *Armed Forces and Society*, 15:2 (Winter 1989): 207–225.

of Timişoara and elsewhere. After 21 December, following a few days of vacillation among its leadership, the armed forces sided with the population – "The Army is with us!" (*Armata e cu noi!*) was among the most memorable exultations of the demonstrators[121] – and fought successfully against pro-Ceauşescu forces until the end of the year. Over 1,000 people were killed during the revolution, more than 20 percent of whom were soldiers.[122]

The role of military elites during the revolution remains a disputed issue in Romania. Those siding with the former communists (generally, Iliescu's supporters) contend that the Romanian Army deserves the gratitude of the nation for its role after 21 December, not harassment. Until 1996 leading generals implicated in the shooting of civilians (Victor Stanculescu, Mihai Chitac, and Stefan Guse) were not prosecuted. During Constantinescu's presidency, however, bringing those responsible to justice became a domestic policy priority. In 1999, after years of legal wrangling, the courts convicted the two generals still alive (Guse had died in the meantime) and sentenced them to fifteen-year prison terms. Constantinescu repeatedly declared that the army had no "collective guilt" and its honor and prestige were unaffected. Still, Iliescu and his allies decried the verdict as "politically motivated" and even Senate Chairman and former Prime Minister Petre Roman suggested that it was "discrediting the army as a whole."[123] DM Victor Babiuc and CGS Degeratu defended the generals and insisted that the sentences were not only "bizarre, unfounded, and illegal" but also undermined the principle of "fulfillment of orders" by the military.[124] In February 2000 the Romanian Supreme Court upheld the sentences. The impression that this in large part has been a process dominated by political consideration was confirmed a year later, when one of the first actions of the returning Iliescu administration's prosecutor-general

---

[121] Walter M. Bacon, Jr., "Romanian Civil–Military Relations after 1989," unpublished manuscript, 1996, 1.

[122] For a detailed description of the revolution and the armed forces' role therein, see Nestor Ratesh, *Romania: The Entangled Revolution* (Westport: Praeger, 1991); and Larry L. Watts, "The Romanian Army in the December Revolution and Beyond," in Daniel N. Nelson, ed., *Romania After Tyranny* (Boulder, CO: Westview, 1992), 105–108.

[123] RFE/RL II, 3:141 (22 July 1999).

[124] RFE/RL II, 3:139 (20 July 1999).

Romania: Twelve Years of Disappointments   153

was to suspend the sentences and, later, to order a retrial for January
2002.[125]

Writing in 1993, Dale Herspring wrote that Romania's was the
least changed armed forces in the region marked by the absence of
any serious effort to democratize.[126] Although DM Colonel General
Victor Stanculescu announced four months after the Revolution that
the army's depoliticization was complete, the situation corroborated
Herspring's opinion.[127] To be sure, on paper and on the institutional
level the Romanian Army seemed to support Stanculescu's claims. The
Higher Political Council (the Romanian equivalent of the Main Political Administration) and military party organizations were abolished,
political officers were dismissed, retired, or retrained, and the military
was forbidden to develop links to any political party. Actual practice,
however, was quite another matter.

Significant problems arose during the military's depoliticization
which was resented and resisted by generals, colonels, and the corps of
former political officers. The revision of curricula in military colleges
was sluggish. Following a promising start, the intra-military interest
representational organizations were repressed. The most important of
these was CADA (Action Committee for the Democratization of the
Army), formed by disenchanted officers in February 1990 and disbanded by Iliescu in the following year.[128] Although CADA had several achievements to its credit, including the dismissal of DM General

---

[125] The decision was widely criticized by Romanian opposition parties and the media. The daily *Ziua* commented that "the heroes of Timişoara are turning in
their graves" while *Evenimentul zilei* sarcastically asked in a headline: "Revolution? When? Where?" See RFE/RL II, 5:149 (8 August 2001), and 5:150 (9 August
2001).

[126] Dale R. Herspring, "The Process of Change and Democratization in Eastern Europe:
The Case of the Military," in John R. Lampe and Daniel N. Nelson, eds., *East
European Security Reconsidered* (Washington, D.C.: Woodrow Wilson Center Press,
1993), 65.

[127] Rompres (Bucharest), 27 April 1990. In a September 1991 interview Defense Minister Lieutenant General Nicolae Spiroiu denied accusations that the armed forces still
harbored communist structures. See "Any Attack on the Army Is an Attack Against
the Country," *Curierul National* (Bucharest), 19 September 1991, translated in *Foreign Broadcast Information Service-Eastern Europe* (hereafter *FBIS-EEU*), 24 September 1991, 22. In May 1992 Spiroiu was forced to deny persistent rumors about the
repoliticization of the armed forces. See *Azi* (Bucharest), 7 May 1992.

[128] See Watts, "The Romanian Army," 99–105; and *Baricada* (Bucharest), January 26,
1993, 26.

154   *The Future of NATO Expansion*

Nicolae Militaru in 1990, it could not reach one of its major goals, a full-scale inquiry over the military's role during the revolution. Junior officers constituted the most vocal support for depoliticization and internal democratization and demanded an investigation of their commanders in some cases raising fears of insubordination and institutional paralysis.[129] The major obstacle to the efforts of both CADA and the large pool of younger officers were the uncooperative military and political elites. Quite simply, President Iliescu considered them an "illegitimate and provocative challenge."[130]

Since the early 1990s a great deal of progress has been made in the army's substantive depoliticization. Professional military personnel may not be members of political parties though they do enjoy the right to vote. The politicization of the military is not free of problems, however. A couple of recent examples[131]: In November 1999 the presidency circulated letters under official letterhead among professional personnel encouraging them to take an anti-PDSR stance on various issues. In December 1999 the spokesperson for the MOD issued an official press communique condemning the PDSR for allegedly showing contempt for the military. And, in April 2000, the Chief of the General Staff, Mircea Chelaru, publicly advocated the institutionalized involvement of the military in politics through the establishment of ten senatorial seats for military officers and the abolition of the constitutionally-mandated Supreme Council of National Defense.

Institutional Arrangements of Civilian Oversight

The most important components of the legislative framework governing national defense and the armed forces were established by 1994. In July 1994 the Law on National Defense was promulgated. Article 117 of the Law says that the armed forces may be asked to defend the constitutional order. As I noted above, during the Constantinescu presidency an unusually high number of ordinances was issued owing to the slowness of the legislative process (according to the government's supporters) and because ordinances do not receive,

---

[129] Watts, "The Romanian Army," 103.
[130] Ibid., p. 105.
[131] I draw on Larry Watts' "The Crisis in Romanian Civil-Military Relations," *Problems of Post-Communism*, 48:4 (July–August 2001): 16–17.

Romania: Twelve Years of Disappointments

at least in the short run, parliamentary scrutiny (according to its opponents).[132]

The Commander-in-Chief of the Romanian Army and the guarantor of the country's territorial integrity is the president who chairs the Supreme Council of National Defense. The SCND's members include leaders of the pertinent ministries and governmental agencies but it has no legal-constitutional authority.[133] Presidential powers also include the mobilization of the armed forces providing prior parliamentary approval (in exceptional cases she/he can do so and is allowed five days to consult with the legislature), and to make promotions to the ranks of marshall, general, and admiral. The president can also submit a list of those to be decorated with the highest distinctions, a list in which Constantinescu included himself in 2000.[134] The Prime Minister is the vice chairman of the SCND and is the Head of Civil Protection (protection of the population in case of war or other disaster). The other eight members of the SCND are the ministers of defense, interior, foreign affairs, commerce, industry, heads of domestic and foreign intelligence services, and the CGS.

The legislature maintains four committees charged with defense issues: one Defense, Public Order, and National Security Committee in each of the two chambers, and joint committees for NATO and internal affairs. The former supervise the MOD, the Ministry of Interior, the secret service, intelligence services, the government's Special Office for Military Affairs, and the penitentiary system. All of these committees can initiate legislation, organize hearings, set up ad hoc committees and subcommittees. They are actively involved in the budget debate and consider the nominations of ministers and state secretaries.[135] The

---

[132] Interviews with George-Vlad Niculescu, Assistant to the Secretary of State for Defense Planning and Monica-Mirela Malcoci, Deputy Head Directorate for Integrated Defense Planning (Bucharest, 4 November 1999), and Pascu (Bucharest, 3 November 1999). See also, "Ordinances and Orders by the Romanian Government," *Romania's Official Gazette*, no. 302 (18 August 1988).

[133] "New Law on Supreme Defense Council," *Monitorul Oficial* (Bucharest), December 13, 1990, 2–3, translated in *FBIS-EEU*, 15 February 1991, 44.

[134] "Ce vor comanda cei 100 de generali daca fortele trebuie reduse?" *Cotidianul*, 23 October 2000. See also the response to this article in *Romania Libera*, 24 October 2000.

[135] Interviews with Pascu (Bucharest, 3 November 1999) and Senator Nicolae Alexandru (Bucharest, 4 November 1999), chairmen of the Defense, Public Order, and National Security Committee of the Chamber of Deputies and the Senate, respectively.

156   *The Future of NATO Expansion*

defense budget is first drafted by the Directorate for Integrated Defense Planning, submitted to the Secretary of State for Defense Planning who turns it over to the Minister of Defense. The DM may modify the budget in consultation with the finance minister, and then present it to the government. The final arbiter of the defense budget is the legislature. According to the Defense Law of January 1991, the Ministry of Defense is the central executive organ for defense. The minister is accountable to the government for all of the Ministry's activities and, as a member of the government, he is also accountable to parliament.[136]

During his first term as president, Iliescu made a concerted effort to vest in himself increasing authority concerning defense issues and to obstruct parliamentary committees wishing to establish control over the military and the police.[137] He tried to ensure that, as in the communist period, one of the army's top priorities would remain the protection of the regime from its internal opponents. In fact, in December 1990 when the SCND was created, its explicit objectives included to initiate "cooperation between the Defense and Interior Ministries" for the "maintenance and restoration of legal order."[138]

A further troubling aspect of the SCND was that, as critics charged, it was a faithful continuation of the Political Executive Committee of the Romanian Communist Party's Central Committee and directly contradicted the separation of powers principle. As the chair of the Council, the president calls to order and controls government members who belong to it.[139] Iliescu also attempted to establish his own power base in the highest echelons of the armed forces by interfering with matters of personnel (i.e., the promotion and retirement of generals).[140] Many Romanian politicians steered clear of the military

---

[136] "Law on Ministry of National Defense," *Viitorul* (Bucharest), 19 January 1991, 3; in *FBIS-EEU*, 1 February 1991, 122.

[137] One case in point was the repeated refusal of the head of police to appear before the parliamentary Committee on Internal Affairs. Interview with Ina Bardan, Helsinki Watch/Grupul Pentru Dialog Social (Bucharest, 13 May 1993).

[138] *Monitorul Oficial al Romanei*, No. 39, 13 December 1990, cited in Watts, "The Romanian Army," 111.

[139] See Victor Ianu, "The Supreme Council for the Country's Defense," *Dreptatea* (Bucharest), 24 October 1991, 1; in *FBIS-EEU*, 4 November 1993, 23.

[140] In May 1992, for instance, Iliescu assigned eleven generals to the reserves and promoted six colonels to generals. See "Iliescu Promotes Loyal Military Officers," *Romania Libera* (Bucharest), 27 May 1992, 1; in *FBIS-EEU*, 1 June 1992, 33.

Romania: Twelve Years of Disappointments

due to their fear of opposing Iliescu and others who already wrested control over it. This notion was indicated by the fact that no political party was prepared to support anyone but an active military officer as DM in order to avoid political debates and due to views that a civilian DM would be incompetent and arrogant.[141] As a result, between 1989 and 1994 Romania had three generals as defense ministers: Nicolae Militaru, Victor Stanculescu, and Nicolae Spiroiu.

Still, in March 1994, Spiroiu – whose political liberalism and desire to maintain interethnic peace made him an anathema to the extreme nationalists[142] – was replaced by a civilian, Gheorghe Tinca who had filled a number of high-level positions in the Ceaușescu era and enjoyed Iliescu's full support. The switch was explained by the need to satisfy "accepted international standards" though opposition politicians charged that it was the result of differences of opinion between the president and Spiroiu and called for an investigation of Tinca's alleged ties to the *Securitate*.[143] For most of the Constantinescu period the DM was Victor Babiuc and, after his resignation in March 2000, Sorin Frunzaverde. Neither of them had any military experience or expertise. Their successor in the new Iliescu administration is Pascu. A political analyst under Ceaușescu, Pascu was foreign policy counsellor to Iliescu, then Secretary of State in Charge of Defense Policy at the MOD prior to 1996. He was widely seen as a gray eminence behind many NATO-related policies and one of the authors of the idea that "the world's great powers and not Romania's slow progress toward democracy should be blamed" for the latter's exclusion from the Alliance in order to exonerate the pre-1996 administration.[144] Pascu was chairman of the Defense Committee of the Chamber of Deputies during Constantinescu's presidency, and became DM in the Nastase government in 2000.

Since the mid-1990s the Romanian military-security sphere has undergone substantial civilianization. In the main military institutions, including the MOD, there has been a growing number of civilians who are now in charge of making defense policy. In recent years, more than

---

[141] Interview with Larry L. Watts (Bucharest, 31 May 1993).
[142] Tom Gallagher, *Romania After Ceausescu* (Edinburgh: Edinburgh University Press, 1995), 226.
[143] Reuters (Bucharest), 17 March 1994.
[144] Ionescu, "Hammering on NATO's Door," 39–40.

158   *The Future of NATO Expansion*

half of the graduates of the prestigious Higher Military Academy have been civilians in concert with governmental efforts to prepare a growing pool of civilian defense experts.[145] The MOD was restructured in 1993 (separate general staffs for the various services were established) and reorganized in 1997.[146] At that time, in order to strengthen the civilian role in controlling defense policy, the Head of Defense Policy and International Relations Department with the rank of State Secretary was created and the CGS's responsibilities were limited to purely military tasks. The CGS is subordinated to the DM. Until 1997 CGSs (Vasile Ionel and Dumitru Cioflina) were highly experienced commanders unlike their successors under the Constantinescu presidency, Constantin Degeratu and Mircea Chelaru, who had minimal command experience which, in turn, resulted in a major decline in the prestige and respect for the CGS in the officer corps.[147] In 2001 the Defense Planning Council (DPC), a formerly ineffectual structure was streamlined, reformed, and vested with real authority to coordinate military planning in the MOD. The DPC now oversees the formulation of a single defense plan which is based on information provided by the GS.[148]

Shortcomings of Civil-Military Relations

Since 1989 the Romanian military has been utilized on several occasions in domestic scenarios albeit never violently. Political elites have sought "to include defense of the social order and the political leadership against domestic challengers" as one of the army's legitimate

---

[145] Interview with Col. Filip (Bucharest, 1 November 1999), and Pascu (Bucharest, 3 November 1999). See also Watts, "Democratic Civil Control of the Military in Romania: An Assessment as of October 2001," in Graeme P. Herd, ed., *Civil–Military Relations in Post Cold War Europe* (Camberley, UK: Conflict Studies Research Centre, 2001), 35.

[146] *Two Years of Governance* (Bucharest: The Government of Romania, 1994), 28; Victor Babiuc, "Reform and the Romanian Armed Forces: Modernization and Interoperability," in Treptow and Ionescu, 122; and interviews with Gheorghe-Vlad Niculescu, Monica-Mirela Malcoci (Bucharest, 4 November 1999) and Col. Alexandru Grumaz (Bucharest, 8 November 1999).

[147] See Watts, "The Crisis in Romanian Civil–Military Relations," *Problems of Post-Communism*, 48:4 (July–August 2001): 20–21.

[148] Watts, "Democratic Civil Control of the Military," 28.

Romania: Twelve Years of Disappointments

tasks.[149] With the decreasing power of the security apparatus after 1989, Romanian political elites realized that the coercive authority of the state had declined. To counter this situation, the president repeatedly relied on the military by assigning it the function of defending not the constitutional order but his regime. In March of 1990, for instance, military units were deployed alongside the police in the Transylvanian city of Targu Mureş when violence broke out between ethnic Romanians and Hungarians. Army troops controlled Victory Square in front of government headquarters in central Bucharest during the two days of riots in September 1991 that brought down Petre Roman's government.[150] In order to prevent the demonstration of the notorious Jiu Valley miners in January 1999, the authorities closed down train traffic from the area several days prior to the scheduled event. DM Babiuc said that the armed forces would use all weapons at their disposal and the army was mobilized. Although hostilities were avoided, the incident pointed to another deficiency of Romanian civil–military relations, namely the absence of clear legislation pertaining to the domestic role of the armed forces, particularly in emergency situations.[151]

Party politics plays an enormous role in Romanian civil–military relations. Governmental shifts tend to signify sea changes in Romania meaning that the entire staff of ministries is fired and even desk keys are hidden just to obstruct the work of successors.[152] In 1996, for instance, the in-coming Constantinescu administration wanted to wrest control of the MOD from the General Staff, firing CGS Dumitru Cioflina and naming General Degeratu to the post. In this way, the president hoped to give his new DM, Victor Babiuc, more authority. But Degeratu, who had been a lieutenant colonel only five years

---

[149] Watts, "The Romanian Army," 108.

[150] See *The Guardian*, September 27, 1991, and the articles from the Romanian press translated in *FBIS-EEU*, 22 September 1991, 33; 30 September 1991, 24; and 9 October 1991, 27.

[151] Interviews with Larry Watts (Bucharest, 2 November 1999), Ioan Mircea Pascu (Bucharest, 3 November 1999), and Senator Nicolae Alexandru (Bucharest, 4 November 1999). See also AP (Bucharest), 26 January 1999; and Watts, "Democratic Civil Control of the Military in Romania: An Assessment as of October 2001," in Graeme P. Herd, ed., *Civil–Military Relations in Post Cold War Europe* (Camberley, UK: Conflict Studies Research Centre, 2001), 24–25.

[152] Interview with Tabacu (Cluj, 25 October 1999).

earlier, was widely regarded as unprepared for the post while Babiuc's role in day-to-day military matters was limited because of his substantial political responsibilities within the Democratic Party (a key component of the new ruling coalition).[153] In the 1990s political partisanship became a principal criterion of top postings in the MOD and the GS.

Politics affects the military in other ways, too. Just prior to the November 1998 local elections, operatives of the Democratic Convention brought to Bucharest fresh recruits a few days before the elections to vote even though according to the electoral law only those who resided in the locality for at least three months prior to the elections may cast their ballots. A disproportionate number of these conscripts (over 80 percent) voted for the Convention. The Romanian legislature's control over the armed forces is clearly limited. Even though deputies have the right of interpellation, the DM may and occasionally does refuse to answer their questions.[154] In particular, parliamentary oversight through the control of the defense budget still needs to improve. As the Romanian analyst Adina Stefan suggests, Romanian legislators who vote for military budgets must learn to ask questions on defense-related issues.[155] In the past members of the parliamentary defense committees – especially if they sat on the wrong side of the aisle – at times did not see important pertinent legislation prior to submission. The transparency of military activities and the relevant work of political institutions is in need of further improvement. It appears that since 2001 the legislature has managed to play a larger role in overseeing defense issues. Parliamentary committees concerned with military reforms, for instance, have met more frequently and these meetings have also been more substantive.[156]

On a number of occasions defense officials were forced to deny persistent but unsubstantiated allegations about impending military

---

[153] See Nelson, "Civil Armies, Civil Societies, and NATO's Enlargement," *Armed Forces & Society*, 25:1 (Fall 1998): 152–153.

[154] For instance, when Valentin Gabrielescu, Secretary General of the National Peasant Party and Vice Chair of the Senate Defense Committee, asked Spiroiu about the MOD's intentions concerning equipment modernization in June 1993, he was told that "what we are doing is our business; it is a secret insofar as Parliament is concerned." Interview with Gabrielescu (Bucharest, 2 June 1993).

[155] Stefan, "Romania's Engagement," 50.

[156] Watts, "Democratic Civil Control of the Military," 34.

Romania: Twelve Years of Disappointments

coups or increasing military activism in politics.[157] A 1994 article, entitled "The Army is Intoxicated with Politics," quoted the controversial mayor of Cluj, Gheorghe Funar, who declared that "the army is ready to take power in case of political disorder."[158] In November 2000, twenty-eight active generals and retired soldiers – including former CGS Chelaru – established a National Association of Romanian Soldiers (ANMR) in order to "prevent corruption, antisocial and antinational acts, and decrease crime." The two major extremist parties, the Party of Romanian National Unity and the Greater Romania Party welcomed the creation of ANMR, though both the MOD and the Ministry of Interior expressed its disapproval, and the Romanian media sounded alarm bells warning of a military coup. To allay their fears, the MOD banned all active military personnel from joining ANMR and promptly dismissed the officers who were its founding members – including three colonels and a general – for infringing on the Statute on Military Personnel.[159]

There are also signs that democratic values have yet to be firmly embedded in the Romanian officer corps. Several high ranking military officers – including, again, former CGS and active general Mircea Chelaru – attended the ceremony marking the fifty-fifth anniversary of Marshall Antonescu's execution in June 2001. The MOD announced that it would "not tolerate" violations of the "principle of the army's political noninvolvement" and that General Chelaru would face disciplinary action. Chelaru requested to be transferred to the reserves in order to avoid being reprimanded and Corneliu Vadim Tudor threatened to make public compromising documents on DM Pascu if the request was rejected.[160] Even more troubling, however, is the fact that

---

[157] See, for instance, *Curierul National* (Bucharest), 19 September 1991 in *FBIS-EEU*, 24 September 1991, 22; *Dreptatea* (Bucharest), 2 September 1992 in *FBIS-EEU*, 9 September 1992, 24; *Dimineata* (Bucharest), 24–25 October 1992 in *FBIS-EEU*, 4 November 1992, 23; and Dan Ionescu, "The President, the Journalists, and the KGB," *Transition*, 1:16 (8 September 1995): 36, 39.

[158] "Armata e intoxicată cu politică," *Tineretul liber* (Bucharest), 22 April 1994.

[159] See RFE/RL II, 4:213 (2 November 2000), 4:215 (6 November 2000); and "Szervezkedö román tábornokok," *Magyar Nemzet*, 3 November 2000.

[160] See RFE/RL II, 5:104 (1 June 2001), 5:105 (4 June 2001), and 5:106 (5 June 2001). In March 2002 Chelaru made a political comeback as he was elected chairman of the National Council of the extraparliamentary Party of Romanian National Unity. See RFE/RL II, 6:51 (18 March 2002).

162 *The Future of NATO Expansion*

the serving CGS, General Mihai Popescu, sent the organizers of the Antonescu commemoration a letter expressing his "regrets" that he could not attend due to family obligations.[161]

PART IV. MILITARY REFORM AND THE STATE OF THE ARMED FORCES

Military Reform

As U.S. Secretary of State Colin Powell noted in an August 2001 letter sent to his Romanian colleague, in spite of some progress the Romanian armed forces have a long way to go before they would satisfy NATO's criteria.[162] Still, especially since the mid-1990s efforts at military reform have intensified and they were impeded more by the absence of financial resources than that of determination. Romania's national defense planning and military strategy (approved in 2000) are developed by the MOD based on political and strategic decisions and the options are determined by the parliament, the president, and the government.[163]

The army's reform is the result of years of study and deliberation – three different draft programs had been prepared – and have been revised and updated with the help of American and other NATO personnel. The program the MOD is pursuing is divided into two phases, primarily owing to the anticipated budgetary situation. Thus, in the first phase, 2000 to 2003, the goal is to restructure all echelons of the armed forces by creating corps, brigades, and battalions (and gradually eliminating armies and regiments). The specific goal by 2003 is to have three active duty army corps (plus one reserve corps) and totally abolish the army-division-regiment structure. Since 1989, the manpower of the armed forces has been reduced from 250,000 to 120,000; the final objective is to cut the army to 75,000 military personnel and 15,000 civilians in 2007–2010. According to the reform, civilians will take over many of the jobs currently done by uniformed personnel.

---

[161] "Generalul Mircea Chelaru va fi convocat în fața Consilului de Judecată al MApN pentru încălcrea principiului neimplicării politice a armatei," Mediafax (Bucharest), 3 June 2001.

[162] See RFE/RL II, 5:156 (17 August 2001).

[163] Ion Mircea Plangu, "Defense Planning for 2010," in Treptow and Ionescu, 133–134.

Approximately 40,000 positions for officers and NCOs will be eliminated (they will be transferred to the reserves).[164] Moreover, special requalification programs will be established for them to ease their transition into civilian life. Per-troop expenditures need to be raised from $4,600 in 2000 to $10,000 by 2003, a goal that may be overly optimistic.

The MOD has also introduced the concept of "active reserve" in order to help terminated officers make the transition to civilian life. In practice, the program pays officers in the reserves in their first year out of active service 70 percent of their former salary and encourages them to get civilian employment. In every subsequent year their allotment is cut by 20 percent. Given the planned reduction cycle of the armed forces, the active reserve program is to be eliminated by 2005.[165]

In the second phase of the reform, 2003 to 2008, the most important objective is to build up the arsenal of the armed forces. Lack of money forced weapons procurement into a second phase in which the plan calls for increasing compatibility with NATO and for the creation of rapid and immediate reaction forces. Since 1999 Romania has pursued individual Membership Action Plans which are custom tailored to the degree of performance level already achieved by individual states and provide further assistance in evaluating and structuring reform endeavors.[166] There are Annual National Plans and year-by-year evaluations to help the implementation of these reforms.

Perhaps the most important long-term goal of Romanian military reform is to promote interoperability and compatibility with NATO forces.[167] More specifically, the tasks are to complete military legislation according to NATO integration requirements, fulfill the objectives Romania assumed within the Planning and Review Process (PARP), pursue compatibility in procurement, training of personnel,

---

[164] Interviews with Col. Filip (Bucharest, 1–5 November 1999). See also, Babiuc, "Reform of the Romanian Armed Forces," 124.

[165] Interview with General Balan, Chief of the Human Resources Management Directorate at the MOD (Bucharest, 4 November 1999).

[166] "The Washington Summit and the Continuation of NATO Enlargement: Romania's Expectations and Suggestions" (Bucharest: Government of Romania, March 1999), 1–4.

[167] The discussion in this paragraph draws on Stepan, "Romania's Engagement," 36–37; "The Rapid Reaction Force," *Panoramic Militar*, no. 3 (1999): 15–18; and interview with Gheorghe-Vlad Niculescu (Bucharest, 4 November 1999).

and modernize and integrate its information system with NATO's. In the past, however, Bucharest had at times tried to take on too much and consequently failed to achieve its goals.

For instance, in the PARP Romania accepted forty-four interoperability objectives for the 1997–1999 cycle. The MOD prepared a study to promote satisfying program objectives but things did not go according to plans because of difficulties in defining how much interoperability was needed and in what field, and priorities were not established properly. Quite simply, Bucharest was too anxious to show that its armed forces were prepared to join NATO as soon as possible and, as Stefan noted, the wrong assessment of available financial resources led to waste in terms of time and efficiency.[168] Nonetheless, Bucharest could not resist the temptation of attempting to impress NATO by taking on, with much fanfare and self-promotion, a large number of objectives in the Annual National Plans, only a small proportion of which could possibly be fulfilled. (During 1999–2000 Romania took on eighty-eight objectives and fulfilled two of them.) The fact is that under Constantinescu very little real military reform took place.

Since the Nastase government took office in late 2000, the reform has been pursued with a keener awareness of fiscal constraints. Some programs have been slowed down, others reorganized and reconsidered, but the key focus on working toward interoperability has remained. In a May 2001 meeting with NATO officials Nastase said that 4,000 officers would be discharged by the end of 2001 of whom 306 were generals; in fact the particularly bloated corps of generals was slated to be reduced by 68 percent. (In 1999 Romanian armed forces had 5,000 colonel positions; Germany, with any army twice the size of Romania, had only 1,100.[169]) In 2001 the MOD finally took the painful but necessary steps of reducing the officer corps by making 44 generals, 888 colonels, 1,400 lieutenant-colonels, and 1,200 majors redundant (at the same time, 15 colonels were promoted to general in December 2001).[170] And, in the 2000–2001 PARP cycle Romania

[168] Ibid., 37.
[169] Interview with Division General Balan (Bucharest, 4 November 1999).
[170] Presentation by Larry Watts at the Annual Meeting of the American Association for the Advancement of Slavic Studies (Crystal City, VA, 18 November 2001); and RFE/RL II, 5:215 (13 November 2001).

Romania: Twelve Years of Disappointments 165

prudently adopted a mere thirteen interoperability objectives but fulfilled all of them.

There is little doubt that since 2001 military reform has been accelerated by the Nastase government that, unlike its predecessors, has focused on actual reform and not just on self-serving propaganda. The achievements include the introduction of a new human resources management system, the implementation of program-driven rather than means-based budgeting, joint defense planning, and the establishment of a new acquisitions and management framework that satisfies NATO criteria.[171] As far as the future of Romanian military reform is concerned, it is, of course, highly dependent on Romania's economy. In any event, it is questionable how much even a most determined government can do with the scant resources available.

Officers and Soldiers

One of the biggest problems is that the armed forces continue to have too many officers. In 1999 there was one NCO to every officer, a ratio that needs to be changed to 3:1.[172] The most important problem currently is not the pace of the army's downsizing but the disproportionately large number of officers: there are still 8,000 more than required. An enormous glut has developed especially in the "lieutenant colonel and higher" category which now makes up 60 percent of the officer corps.[173] The vast majority of Romanian officers (according to some polls, more than 90 percent) are ardent supporters of NATO membership. This is hardly surprising, given Romania's socioeconomic conditions. For military officers NATO membership represents the promise of good careers, decent salaries, trips abroad, and access to international professional networks.[174] The officer corps has traditionally been supporters of Iliescu and the PDSR/PSD, especially

---

[171] Watts, "Democratic Civil Control of the Military," 14.

[172] Interview with Division General Neculai Balan, Chief of the MOD's Human Resources Management Directorate (Bucharest, 4 November 1999).

[173] *Ibid.*

[174] See Ionescu, "Hammering on NATO's Door," 37; Kaplan, *Eastward to Tartary,* 55; and interview with Col. Stancu, Chief of the MOD's Public Relations Directorate (Bucharest, 3 November 1999).

owing to their opposition to the Constantinescu government's handling of the Kosovo crisis.[175]

Romania's military educational system was reorganized after 1989 to reflect the switch to the "defense expert-manager" concept of the armed forces professional. There is a network of military high schools that encourage its graduates to adopt the army as a career choice. Four- and five-year service academies (air force in Braşov, navy in Constanţa, and ground forces in Sibiu) train officers for various military specialties and a separate Military Medical Academy educates future military physicians, dentists, and pharmacists. The purpose of the postgraduate Military Academy (Bucharest) is to train staff and command officers in its two-year programs. It is slated to be turned into a National Defense University in 2003.[176] In military schools and academies the curricula have been revamped and training methods have been updated in order to produce "NATO-compatible" officers and NCOs.

This institutional framework is complemented by additional training opportunities, such as the Romanian-British Regional Training Center in Bucharest which offers NATO-compatible staff courses. Nearly a thousand Romanian officers have received some military education or training in NATO countries during the last decade.[177] As elsewhere, it is often the most expendable (i.e., not the most prepared) officers who are sent to be educated abroad. Upon their return, they often demand promotions and better positions which may not be available.

Military training in Romania seriously suffers from the lack of resources, however. As CGS Mihai Popescu admitted in April 2001, the army was poorly trained. In 2000, for instance, pilots could only carry out 13 percent planned training and nearly 70 percent of aviators were "nonoperational" due to insufficient flying time. Popescu noted that the

---

[175] Interview with Andrea Bartosin, foreign editor of *Adevărul* (Austin, TX, 29 August 2000).

[176] "Romania Will Be Militarily Divided Into the North and the South, "*Nine O'Clock*, 28 November 2002.

[177] Babiuc, "Reform of the Romanian Armed Forces," 125. See also "Review of Parliamentary Oversight of the Romanian Ministry of National Defence and the Democratic Control of Its Armed Forces" (London: UK Ministry of Defence, February 1997), 33.

navy was in a "precarious" shape and that the army's combat training had declined owing to poor equipment. The CGS also lamented that half of the navy's ships did not leave port in 2000 because that service received only 15 percent of the fuel it needed.[178]

Still, ordinarily there are many more applicants to military academies than they can accommodate which is a reflection of the relative absence of attractive job opportunities elsewhere in the economy. Salaries in the armed forces are considerably higher than the national average. In 1999, for instance, a first-year school teacher earned about one-third of the salary of a first-year lieutenant. Nonetheless, military personnel, too, have faced a housing shortage and officers have been known to complement their salaries by taking "under-the-table" jobs. Although a 1993 law made that practice illegal it is tolerated.[179] Aside from the aforementioned intramilitary organizations (CADA and ANMR) that were subsequently banned, there have been no independent interest-representational groups for armed forces personnel. Civilians employed in the armed forces are allowed by law to join trade unions, however, although some military commanders remain suspicious of such organizations believing that they undermine their command.[180]

The military profession has been prestigious in Romania in part because even during the communist era the armed forces were not perceived as highly dependent on the Soviet Union, and because of their traditional anti-Russian stance, nationalist deviation, and perfunctory membership in the Warsaw Pact.[181] In sum, officers were able to maintain their national credentials. The military is considered a national institution; Ken Jowitt suggested that it "provides whatever glue exists in holding" Romania together.[182] Opinion polls consistently show that there is no institution that Romanians respect more than the armed forces (generally about 90 percent of respondents regard it highly,

---

[178] AFP (Bucharest, 2 April 2001) report cited in RFE/RL II, 5:65 (3 April 2001).

[179] Interviews with military officers (Braşov, June 1996; and Sibiu, October 1999).

[180] "Review of Parliamentary Oversight," 41.

[181] See Alexander Alexiev, "Party-Military Relations in Eastern Europe: The Case of Romania," in Roman Kolkowicz and Andrzej Korbonski, eds., *Soldiers, Peasants, and Bureaucrats: Civil–Military Relations in Communist and Modernizing Societies* (London: Allen & Unwin, 1982), 199–231.

[182] Ken Jowitt, "The Leninist Legacy," in Ivo Banac, ed., *Eastern Europe in Revolution* (Ithaca, NY: Cornell University Press, 1992), 221.

significantly more than the runner-up Orthodox Church).[183] Although until 1989 there were female officers and NCOs in the army – which signified another Romanian exception in the Warsaw Pact – women have not been admitted since then. In October 2001 DM Pascu suggested that the military would make it possible for women to develop a career "suitable to their valor and competence."[184]

The esprit de corps, however, has been adversely affected by the bad equipment, institutional poverty, and continued politicization of the armed forces. The widespread demoralization both among senior officers and the rank and file, the deepening intra-military cleavages (between older and younger officers, between the services, and between supporters of various political parties) have led to a "marked degradation of military effectiveness."[185] Both Iliescu and Constantinescu promoted to general dozens of incompetent officers who were their political supporters, thereby adding to the lopsidedness of the rank-pyramid (in 1999 lower rank officers [second lieutenant to major] comprised 40 percent of the officer corps) and discouraging those eligible for and deserving of promotion.[186] In 2001 the MOD established military selection boards and revised the *Military Career Guide* in order to make the promotion process more objective and transparent.

Romania maintains a universal conscription system in which draftees are obligated to serve for twelve months (to be reduced to eight months in 2003). The conscript cohort is more than sufficient to meet requirements. The MOD has made some attempts to ease the service, introducing religious assistance (a group of military chaplains have been trained) as well as a "draftees' ombudsman system" to improve commanders' approach to welfare and management issues. Although there is little doubt that as communications improve, international travel increases, and Western ideas become more fully understood there will be increasing reluctance to accept conscripted military service,

---

[183] See, for instance, "88 la sută din români continuă să aibă înredere în armată," *Evenimentil zilei*, 16 March 1994; Lavinia Stan, *Romania in Transition* (Brookfield, VT: Dartmouth, 1997), 65; and Shafir, "The Mind of Romania's Radical Right," 229.

[184] RFE/RL II, 5:193 (11 October 2001).

[185] On this point, see Watts, "The Crisis in Romanian Civil–Military Relations," 17, 25.

[186] See "Iliescu Promotes Loyal Officers," *Romania Libera*, 27 May 1992 translated in *FBIS-EEU*, 1 June 1992, 33; interview with General Balan (Bucharest, 4 November 1999); "Ce vor comanda cei 100 de generali daca fortele trebuie reduse?" *Cotidianul*, 23 October 2000.

Romania: Twelve Years of Disappointments

at the present time it is not quite as unpopular as in Slovakia or Slovenia.[187]

The State of the Forces

As mentioned above, the most important tangible achievement of military reform has been the reduction of the Romanian army's manpower. According to *The Military Balance*, the active military force of Romania was 207,000 (including 36,700 "centrally controlled units" and 108,600 conscripts) in 2000; 106,000 served in the army, 20,800 in the navy, and 43,500 in the air force.[188] In March 2002 Foreign Minister Geoana announced that the military was successfully downsized to 120,000 (in contrast to 320,000 in 1990).[189] Although there are far too many officers, the number of contract soldiers is low as the MOD has not been able to make service attractive to those potentially interested. The downsizing process has been difficult for the many thousands of officers who were led to believe until the early 1990s that they had a job for life.

Even the most reputable Western research institutions differ widely in their estimates of Romania's defense budget. According to the Stockholm International Peace Research Institute, in 1998 Romania spent $642 million and in 1999 $541 million on defense whereas the corresponding numbers provided by the International Institute for Strategic Studies are $900 million and $607 million, respectively.[190] DM Pascu, basing his estimates on Romania's projected economy growth – a chancy proposition in the past – has said that military spending will be $880 million for 2003, $1.02 billion for 2004, $1.12 billion for 2005, and $1.19 billion for 2006.[191] Romania's state budget for 2003 earmarks 2.3 percent of the GNP for defense purposes

---

[187] "Review of Parliamentary Oversight," 32.

[188] *The Military Balance, 2000–2001* (London: IISS, 2000), 100–101.

[189] Eugen Tomiuc, "Foreign Minister Says Romania Determined To Secure Invitation To Join NATO," RFE/RL II, End Note, 6:42 (5 March 2002).

[190] See http://milexdata.sipri.org/result_milex.php?send for the estimates of SIPRI; and *The Military Balance, 2000–2001*, 100.

[191] Ioan Mircea Pascu, "Defence Plannning in Emerging Democracies: The Case of Romania," in Andrew Cottey, Timothy Edmunds, and Anthony Forster, eds., *Democratic Control of the Military in Postcommunist Europe: Guarding the Guards* (Houndmills, UK: Palgrave, 2002), 138.

although CGS Popescu has said that the MOD needed at least 2.5 percent to fulfill its plans.[192] Although it may be difficult to establish precise figures, it is clear that real-term Romanian defense expenditures have declined since 1989 and that it still earmarks a respectable proportion of its GDP (1.8%–2.4% depending on the year) to military outlays.

The problem, of course, is that due to economic problems actual defense expenditures are relatively low especially when considering that, according to domestic estimates, the direct costs of Romania's NATO integration would be in the $3–$4 billion range.[193] In 1999 parliament allocated less than 2% of the GDP for the military, exposing the high political costs of defense budgets, instead of the 3% suggested by a state-funded assessment study. As Stefan observes, NATO's failure to point to a certain date for the next round of enlargement, the legislators' poor knowledge of defense-related matters, high inflation and drastic drops in the GDP, and IMF-imposed constraints on public spending have all contributed to the diminution of military budgets.[194] According to Larry Watts, an American expert who has been for many years an advisor to the Romanian military-security establishment, until 2001 the MOD had virtually no control over the defense budget given that the budget itself was not passed by the legislature until March, April, or even June of the year for which it was earmarked. For the first time since 1989, the 2002 budget was enacted in November 2001 allowing for appropriate planning.[195]

It is not surprising, then, that Romania's arsenal is outdated, inadequate, and poorly maintained. It has also decreased since 1989 owing to the stipulations of the Conventional Forces Europe Treaty, the restrictions of which Romania has meticulously satisfied. By late 1994 the MOD scrapped 945 tanks, 148 heavy artillery pieces, 484 armored cars and 47 fighter planes.[196] Five years later, a total of 5,175 artillery pieces were retired which meant, according to MOD analysts, that

---

[192] Mediafax (Bucharest), 28 May 2002 and 17 October 2002.
[193] See *White Book on Romania and NATO* (Bucharest: Ministry of Foreign Affairs, 1997), 38; and Adina Stefan, "Romania's Engagement," 43.
[194] Stefan, "Romania's Engagement," 45.
[195] See Watts, "Democratic Civil Control of the Military," 16, 28.
[196] *Two Years of Governance* (Bucharest: The Government of Romania, November 1994), 30.

Bulgaria's artillery became superior to that of its northern neighbor.[197] Because of the chronic lack of funds existing equipment is poorly maintained and frequently stands idle. In 1998, for instance, 40 percent of the navy's ships could not execute combat missions and the air force's MiG-21s were grounded. According to General Eugen Badalan, Chief of the MOD's Protection and National Security Division, the combat equipment is "far under the minimum necessary level of performance."[198]

On the positive side, Romania's existing military arsenal and on-going equipment acquisition programs are characterized by an unambiguous Western orientation. Romania recently acquired four Hercules transport planes from the United States and most of its 110 MiG-21 fighters have already been upgraded with a package developed by an Israeli firm which will result in machines on par with MiG-29s. On order are four AN/TPS-117 radar-locator systems from Lockheed-Martin which satisfy top NATO standards. There are also plans to update Romania TR-85 M main battle tanks (increasing fire power and mobility and improving communication system) and the IAR 320-SOCAT helicopters. During his July 1998 visit to Washington, President Constantinescu committed Romania to the purchase of U.S.-made Bell helicopters notwithstanding the dire economic situation at home and his finance minister's threat of resignation should the deal materialize.[199] Another problem has been that the major acquisition programs started in 1993–1994 in some cases do not correspond to subsequent plans but payments still must be made on outstanding contracts. It must be noted, however, that in the acquisitions area, too, improvements took place since 2001. A new acquisition management system has been put in place and an *Equipment Procurement Strategy for*

---

[197] Interview with Teodor Repciuc and Cristian Mureşanu, Institute for Political Studies of Defense and Military History (Bucharest, 4 November 1999).

[198] *Azi*, 16 September 1998; cited by Stefan, "Romania's Engagement," 38; and Florin Avrigeanu, "Navy Day Celebrated with Pomp in Constanta Harbor," *Nine O'Clock*, 16 August 2001.

[199] On this issue see, for instance, RFE/RL DR II, 2:147 (3 August 1998); and Zoltan Barany, "Hungary: Appraising a New NATO Member," *Clausewitz-Studien*, 1 (1999): 1–31; interviews with Ion-Mircea Plangu, State Secretary for Defense Policy, MOD (Bucharest, 5 November 1999) and Col. Grumaz, Chief of Procurement Resources Management Directorate, MOD (Bucharest, 8 November 1999).

172   *The Future of NATO Expansion*

2001–2008, and up to 2020 has been submitted to the Defense Planning Council.[200]

Starting with the 1960s Romania has developed a relatively dynamic defense industry which considerably contracted after 1989. In 1996 the new government expressed its intention to privatize parts of the industry – characterized by huge facilities, large workforces, and shortage of capital – in order to make it competitive. Although some progress has been achieved in this regard – particularly with the Braşov-based IAR-Ghimbav aircraft company – much more needs to be done. The process has been impeded by nearly omnipresent corruption scandals.[201] The outdated and inefficient state-owned plants have encountered troubles paying and continuously employing their workers. Consequently, demonstrations by defense industry workers are not uncommon; in March 2000, for instance, 10,000 of them protested outside governmental buildings in Bucharest.[202] According to the Ministry of Industry, approximately 10,000 military industry workers lost their jobs by February 2002 because the government could no longer cover 90–95% of the industry's losses as it did during 1996–2000.[203]

CONCLUSION

The vast majority of Romanian citizens rightly consider the postcommunist period an utter disappointment. The country does not satisfy any of NATO's five basic membership criteria. According to some analysts Romania has actually regressed since the 1997 Madrid summit and remains one of the most backward countries in Europe.[204] Although it is a country with enormous human and natural resources and tremendous potential, in large part owing to its incompetent elites, Romania has been the least successful former Warsaw Pact state in terms of democratic consolidation and market-oriented reforms. Romanian civil–military relations are, according to perhaps the most

[200] Watts, "Democratic Civil Control of the Military," 30–31.
[201] See, for instance, Daniel N. Nelson, "Civil Armies, Civil Societies, and NATO's Enlargement," *Armed Forces & Society*, 25:1 (Fall 1998): 148–149.
[202] Rompres (Bucharest), 1 March 2000. See also interview with Col. Grumaz (Bucharest, 8 November 1999).
[203] RFE/RL II, 6:10 (16 January 2002).
[204] Šedivý, "The Puzzle of NATO Enlargement," 15; and Tony Judt, "Romania: Bottom of the Heap," *The New York Review of Books*, 1 November 2001, 41–45.

Romania: Twelve Years of Disappointments

astute observer of the subject, in "crisis."[205] Although there are no urgent security challenges in Romania's immediate neighborhood and Bucharest has played an active role in regional stability programs, the fact that disagreements with neighbors lead the second most powerful Romanian party's leader to call for the army's mobilization might give pause to the complacent. The armed forces are impoverished and demoralized; they are unlikely to be able to make a contribution to NATO in the foreseeable future.

Romania's obsequious campaign to join NATO has been stressing the country's supposedly invaluable geographic position given that in its unreformed state it has little else to offer. Nonetheless, NATO leaders have been telling Bucharest, at least prior to 9/11/01, that the "geostrategic factor" should be, at best, of secondary importance. As former U.S. Ambassador Rosapepe has noted, the first priority for the country should be "profound, tangible, and real" economic reform.[206] Gheorghe Maior, the MOD's State Secretary for Euro-Atlantic Integration conceded recently that "Romania has wasted a lot of time in implementing NATO accession plans and is lagging 12 to 14 months behind."[207]

In May 2001 Foreign Minister Mircea Geoana admitted that while after the 1997 Madrid Summit Romania was considered a "frontrunner" for NATO membership, four years later it was in "a shadowy area" together with Bulgaria (his colleague in Sofia, would have, no doubt, protested). Geoana went on to say that the decision of further NATO enlargement would be primarily political but economic performance criteria would also be taken into consideration, perhaps seeking to exculpate his government in advance.[208] His cabinet colleagues painted a darker scenario to explain the reason why Romania might not succeed in securing an invitation from NATO in 2002 and, not surprisingly, they had nothing to do with the governing elites. In July 2001 both Minister of Public Information Vasile Dancu and DM Pascu publicly charged that "foreign espionage agencies" and a "former general close to the Constantinescu regime" intended to block

---

[205] Watts, "The Crisis in Romanian Civil–Military Relations."
[206] See OMRI DD II, no. 66 (2 April 1996); and Rosapepe, "Romania and NATO," 53.
[207] Mediafax (Bucharest), 20 March 2001.
[208] RFE/RL II, 5:92 (15 May 2001) citing Romanian radio.

174 *The Future of NATO Expansion*

Bucharest's NATO membership by spreading rumors and lies.[209] A few months later Pascu again indulged in conspiracy theories announcing that a great number of illegal immigrants were attempting to cross the Romanian frontier "to discredit Romania" and to "harm Romania's efforts at integration in Euro-Atlantic structures."[210]

But, as I noted above, 9/11 changed everything. Romania has been a major beneficiary of the new world created by the terrorist attacks on the United States. As far as the Bush White House has been concerned, Romania's frequently expressed "solidarity" and the ill-equipped (according to DM Pascu) battalion that Bucharest sent to Afghanistan has propelled Romania to the top of the accession candidates. And the Bucharest government has been eager to play the role it was given by Washington. As a perceptive *Washington Post* article noted in October 2002, few U.S. officials associate "NATO ally" with Romania, a corrupt, poverty-stricken, and incompletely reformed postcommunist state.[211] Still, Mircea Geoana, the foreign minister of the newly invited NATO candidate declared that Romania intended to become a vehicle for the "transmission of Euro-Atlantic values" to other countries in the region and "the locomotive" of NATO expansion.[212]

---

[209] See "Akadályozzák Romániát?" *Magyar Nemzet,* 1 August 2001 citing a July 2001 issue of the Bucharest daily *Curentul.*

[210] Mediafax (Bucharest), 10 October 2001; and RFE/RL II, 5:193 (11 October 2001).

[211] Kaiser, "Romania Seeks NATO Membership as Remedy for Post-Communist Ills."

[212] RFE/RL II, 6:155 (19 August 2002) and 6:191 (9 October 2002).

5

Bulgaria

Progress After Seven Wasted Years

Bulgaria has been one of the least studied countries of postcommunist Eastern Europe in part owing to its comparative political stability. This chapter analyzes its political, economic, and military–security developments since the 1989 replacement of Todor Zhivkov, the longest-serving communist leader in Eastern Europe. In keeping with the structure of the foregoing country chapters, in Part I I review Bulgaria's democratization process, its economic performance, and security situation. Part II examines Bulgarian foreign policy since 1989 and the country's campaign for NATO membership. Part III concentrates on matters pertaining to civil–military relations. In the concluding portion of the chapter the discussion focuses on military reform and the state of the Bulgarian armed forces.

PART I. DOMESTIC POLITICS, ECONOMIC PERFORMANCE, SECURITY STATUS

Domestic Politics

The subtitle of a study on Bulgaria, "7 Lost Years," suggests an accurate assessment of the country's political and economic development in the 1990–1997 period, marked by the consistent failure of Bulgarian governments to embark on radical economic reforms and foreign policy reorientation.[1] During these years four different governments not only wasted their chances to improve the conditions of their fellow citizens but, in fact, exacerbated their problems. I think of them as "four false tries," abortive attempts toward substantive reform.

Unlike in the other states discussed in this book, the communist regime fell in Bulgaria as a result of a palace coup of sorts in November 1989. Long-serving ministers Petûr Mladenov (foreign affairs) and Dobri Dzhurov (defense) – having secured the blessing of Mikhail Gorbachev – persuaded Todor Zhivkov to "voluntarily" tender his resignation. He did, and the new leadership declared its support for pluralism and the rule of law.

Similarly to Romania, there was no noteworthy organized opposition to the communist regime in Bulgaria. Not surprisingly, therefore, the first free elections in 1990 prolonged the former communists' hold on power. They defeated the Union of Democratic Forces (UDF), founded by ten parties and formations in December 1989. The new Prime Minister, Andrei Lukanov, and his government promised a gradual transition to a market economy, a slow process in which no one would suffer. The BSP did not succeed in transforming itself into a modern socialist party. It was unprepared to introduce radical market reforms and reluctant to expand political pluralism. Its failure to proceed with desperately needed reform and restructuring precipitated the further deterioration of the Bulgarian economy manifested in part by plummeting living standards. Perhaps Lukanov's single biggest mistake was to freeze payments on Bulgaria's foreign debt in 1990, a decision that raised international concerns about his government's credibility and was perceived by domestic public opinion as a major delegitimating act. This was the first false try.

The second false try commenced in late 1991 when the UDF won a narrow, four-seat plurality in the legislature and invited the Movement for Rights and Freedoms (MRF), a party primarily comprised of and supported by ethnic Turks, to form a coalition. Although the new government pledged to usher in an era of substantive reform, its program was short on conceptual clarity and its team was both

---

[1] Jeffrey Simon, "Bulgaria and NATO: 7 Lost Years," *Strategic Forum*, no. 142 (May 1998): 1–7. For a brief analysis of Bulgaria's postcommunist politics, see Zoltan Barany, "Bulgaria's Royal Elections," *Journal of Democracy*, 13:2 (April 2002): 141–155.

Bulgaria: Progress After Seven Wasted Years

inexperienced and incompetent. By 1991 corruption became endemic as the former communist ruling circles managed to convert their political clout into economic power and became a de facto corporate-oligarchic clique, not unlike its Russian counterpart. In the meantime the UDF developed an increasingly hierarchical and top-heavy structure. Its leading organ, the doctrinaire Coordinating Council (its tell-tale nickname was "Central Committee"[2]) punished deviation from the party line with suspension or excommunication. The UDF's on-going feud with its former leader, President Zhelyu Zhelev, further limited the chances of sustained governance.[3] Moreover, people did not seem to care as much as the UDF about taking revenge on the communists; they wanted jobs and better living standards and that the government could not deliver. In the fall of 1992 the BSP together with the MRF, which had become disenchanted with its senior coalition partner, managed to defeat the vote of confidence the government called for.

The third false try toward meaningful reform was the government of Lyuben Berov which, for an additional two years (until September 1994), managed to do little positive. The new government represented a flexible majority, including politicians from all three major parties. It started out to follow the policies of the UDF's moderate wing but it soon became vulnerable to intimidation by the BSP, large-scale blackmail, and bribes. The government failed to deliver its promise to privatize because of vested interests opposed to it and its supporters could not agree on what type of privatization they wanted. In the meantime, behind the scenes, the process of syphoning off the state's remaining assets continued unabated.[4]

---

[2] Deyan Kiuranov, "Salient Points of Political Behavior in Bulgaria," delivered at the Conference on East European Transitions (Bucharest, August 1994), 4.

[3] See, for instance, Andrew Nagorski, "Bulgaria's New Leaders Turn on Each Other," *Newsweek*, 12 July 1993; and Georgi Karasimeonov, "Differentiation Postponed: Party Pluralism in Bulgaria," in Gordon Wightman, ed., *Party Formation in East-Central Europe* (Aldershot, UK: Edward Elgar, 1995), 154–178.

[4] See Krassen Stanchev, "Can Economic Reforms Overcome Ethnic Tensions? The Role of Institutions in Bulgaria's Economic Reform," delivered at the Conference on Political and Economic Change in the Balkan States (Sofia, August 1994), 15–19; "Inside Crooked Bulgaria," *Foreign Report* (Jane's Information Group), no. 2364 (17 August 1995): 5–6; and Rumyana Kolarova, "Bulgaria: Could We Regain What We Already Lost?" *Social Research*, 63:2 (Summer 1996): 543–559.

As far as its societal impact is concerned, the fourth false try, the tenure of Zhan Videnov's socialist government, was clearly the most devastating. The BSP won the 1994 elections by garnering nearly twice as many votes as the UDF.[5] The BSP's program was based on orthodox leftist policies. For instance, at a time when East-Central European states were already advanced in privatizing and denationalizing loss-making enterprises, the Videnov government promised to support industries and pull them out of bankruptcies. At the same time, there was no consensus within the BSP with respect to how to deal with the quickly deteriorating economic situation and powerful interests within the party started to fight one another. In 1996 the government placed three commercial banks under the guardianship of the National Bank, thereby restricting their functioning and effectively administering a lethal blow to them. Tens of thousands were trying to withdraw their savings. A full-blown economic crisis broke out complete with three-digit inflation and governmental collapse.

The 1996 elections for the presidency – much less than executive but a good deal more than merely ceremonial – were won by Petûr Stoyanov, the UDF's candidate. The 1997 national elections, in which the UDF won 137 of the National Assembly's 240 seats, were seen by many observers as a last chance to save the country for consistent economic reform.[6] Ivan Kostov's government, the first to serve out its four-year mandate, did just that. In an astonishingly short period of time inflation dropped due to the establishment of a currency board which pegged the Bulgarian leva to the Deutschmark. By February 2000 the government privatized 70% of state assets and restored 95% of communist-nationalized land even though unemployment remained high (18.14% in that month). Respectable – although far short of miraculous – rates of economic growth returned as well.[7]

---

[5] For electoral results and analysis, see "Final Election Results; DAR Out of Parliament," Khorizon Radio Network (Sofia), 21 December 1994, translated in *Foreign Broadcast Information Service-Eastern Europe* (henceforth *FBIS-EEU*), 21 December 1994: 2.

[6] Interview with Ognyan Minchev, Executive Director of the Institute for Regional and International Studies (Sofia, 19 November 1999).

[7] Radio Free Europe/Radio Liberty, Part II (henceforth *RFE/RL II*), 4:61 (27 March 2000). For a positive appraisal of the UDF government, see M. Steven Fish and Robin S. Brooks, "Bulgarian Democracy's Organizational Weapon," *East European Constitutional Review*, 9:3 (Summer 2000): 63–71.

The crucial shortcoming of the UDF government was its inability to check the extensive and growing corruption that permeated even the highest echelons of public life, notwithstanding the repeated promises of Kostov and Stoyanov to clean up politics.[8] Owing to missing or ambiguous legislation and to the haphazard enforcement of existing laws, there were many opportunities for unscrupulous politicians. Politicians who demanded sacrifices from the people while taking bribes provides the basic explanation for the erosion of political support for the cabinet. An April 2000 Gallup poll revealed that 52% of Bulgarians did not trust the government, more than double the 25% figure of May 1997.[9] According to another poll, every fourth person admitted to taking a bribe during the previous year and more than 80% of those surveyed accepted bribe-taking as a normal practice.[10] Interior Ministry investigators revealed that in each of the criminal organizations uncovered there were police officers from the lowest to the highest offices of the national services.[11]

As late as April 2001 it appeared that the June elections were going to be decided between the BSP and the UDF. Nonetheless, in April, the former king of Bulgaria, Simeon II – exiled by the communists at the age of nine in 1946 and first returned to his homeland in 1996 – launched the Simeon II National Movement (NDSV) in order to participate in the electoral contest. Simeon proposed to bring about radical changes in "Bulgaria's economic and political outlook" and to substantially improve living standards in eight hundred days. Polls immediately suggested that voters were receptive to the NDSV's message; it won the elections by a landslide.[12] The NDSV garnered over 42% of the vote gaining 120 parliamentary seats as opposed to the UDF's 18.8% (51 seats) and the left-wing coalition's (to which the BSP belonged) 17.15% (48 seats). The NDSV entered into a coalition

---

[8] See, for instance, RFE/RL II, 4:41 (28 February 2000) and 4:61 (27 March 2000); and interview with Boyko Todorov of the Sofia Center for the Study of Democracy (Austin, TX, 27 February 2001).

[9] RFE/RL II, 4:80 (21 April 2000).

[10] Margarita Assenova, "The Schengen List Impacts on Bulgaria's Elections," RFE/RL II End Note, 4:227 (22 November 2000).

[11] "There Are Police Officers in Each Gang," *Standart* (Sofia), 7 December 2001.

[12] See "The Winner: All Eyes on Simeon II," BTA (Bulgarian Telegraph Agency) (Sofia), 18 June 2001; and "People Punished the Use of Power," *Standart*, 19 June 2001.

agreement with the MRF which gained 21 seats, having received 7.45% of the vote.[13] The ex-king became the prime minister under the name Simeon Saxecoburggotski. His new government is dominated by politically inexperienced young ministers with Western education or work experience and includes also two ethnic Turks and two BSP members.[14] By March 2002 the popularity of the NDSV declined owing to charges of incompetence, internal squabbling, and corruption.

Until a few days prior to the November 2001 presidential elections, most political analysts took it for granted that Petûr Stoyanov would easily secure another five-year term. Although he ran as an independent, he secured the support not only of the UDF but also of the NDSV which, for the sake of continuity in foreign policy and of national unity, decided not to run its own candidate. In a field of six candidates Stoyanov's only serious opponent was the BSP's leader, Georgi Parvanov. The voters apparently faulted Stoyanov for his insufficient involvement in the struggle against corruption and for his all-too-close affiliation with the UDF and Kostov's government. Parvanov, who won convincingly in the second round of the elections, is committed to continue the policy of Euro-Atlantic integration and promises to pay more attention to social problems and less to party politics than his predecessor.

The potentiality of NATO membership has been frequently tied to the irreversibility of democratic transition and consolidation by Bulgarian political elites.[15] In fact, one of the main reasons why the UDF came to power in 1997 was that its campaign platform was guided by the desire for membership in both the EU and NATO, and its domestic policies were formulated with an eye to this objective. According to a 1997 survey, 59.5% of the respondents believed that membership in NATO would promote domestic political stability, 67.9% that it would guarantee territorial integrity of country, and 71.6% that it would make political reforms irreversible.[16]

---

[13] See "Former King Won the Election in Bulgaria," *Standart*, 19 June 2001.

[14] "The Wrong Job?" *The Economist*, 21 July 2001, 45; RFE/RL II, 5:137 (23 July 2001); and AP (Sofia), 24 July 2001.

[15] See, for instance, Open Media Research Institute Daily Digest, Part II (henceforth OMRI DD), no. 87 (3 May 1996).

[16] Cited in Tsvetan Tsvetkov, "Bulgarian Security Policy: Alternatives and Choice," *Harmonie Paper 9* (Centre of European Security Studies, University of Groningen,

Bulgaria: Progress After Seven Wasted Years

It is important to note that even prior to 1997 democracy was not threatened in Bulgaria. Although its governments had been unstable, Bulgaria's party system has been perhaps the most steady in the region with the same three parties determining political outcomes from 1989 to 2000. Bulgaria did not experience the authoritarian tendencies often displayed by Slovak and Romanian politicians. In political contingencies the authorities have not interfered with demonstrations and the constitution has been generally respected by all political players.[17] The appalling treatment the country's main ethnic minority, the Turks, were subjected to under the communist period had stopped. In fact, Sofia's policies toward the Turkish minority have been described as a model for other states to emulate, though its treatment of its sizable Romani (Gypsy) minority has been far less progressive or imaginative.[18] Bulgaria's fundamental problem has been its disastrous economic performance rooted in the reluctance of its leaders to ally themselves with unpopular but necessary economic policies. As John Mueller noted, Bulgaria was a good example of a country that became a successful democracy even though very little meaningful economic reform took place for several years after the regime change.[19]

Economic Performance

Political life in Bulgaria has revolved more around economics than in the other states this book has examined. One reason for this is that

---

August 1999), 21. See also interviews with Navy Captain Ognyan Kirilov, Bulgarian Military, Naval, and Air Force Attache (Warsaw, 13 August 1999); and with Dimitûr Abadjiev, MP (Sofia, 17 November 1999).

[17] See Jacques Coenen-Huther, ed., *Bulgaria at the Crossroads* (Commack, NY: Nova, 1996); Iliana Zloch-Christy, *Bulgaria in a Time of Change: Economic and Political Dimensions* (Brookfield, VT: Avebury, 1996); and Valerie Bunce, "The Political Economy of Postsocialism," *Slavic Review*, 58:4 (Winter 1999): 772.

[18] See "BSP Deputy Chairman on Minority Issues," *Trud* (Sofia), 7 December 1994, translated in *FBIS-EEU*, 13 December 1994, 1–2; Vera Mutafchieva, "The Turk, the Jew, and the Gypsy," in Antonina Zhelyazkova, ed. *Relations of Compatibility and Incompatibility between Christians and Muslims in Bulgaria* (Sofia: International Centre for Minority Studies and Intercultural Relations, 1995), 5–63; Krassimir Kanev, "Dynamics of Inter-Ethnic Tensions in Bulgaria and the Balkans," *Balkan Forum*, 4:2 (June 1996): 213–252; Matilda Nahabedian, "EC 2000 Progress Report on Bulgaria," *Central Europe Review*, 2:39 (13 November 2000).

[19] John Mueller, *Capitalism, Democracy, and Ralph's Pretty Good Grocery* (Princeton, NJ: Princeton University Press, 1999), 233–234.

Bulgarian politics did not spawn prominent politicians with authoritarian and/or scandalous streaks like Vladimír Mečiar, Janez Janša, Ion Iliescu, or Corneliu Vadim Tudor. The other reason is that Bulgaria did experience a gradually unfolding economic disaster, the magnitude of which was unique in the region.

Until 1997, quite simply, very little economic transition took place in the country. In 1994, for instance, more than 90 percent of the Bulgarian economy was still in the hands of the state (in contrast, by this time more than half of the Polish economy was privatized).[20] By the mid-1990s the economy had become dominated by criminal activities of all sorts, some of which were connected to the government. For instance, one widespread protection racket obligated its victims to buy coverage from certain insurance companies; those who did not usually had their property damaged or destroyed. Another scam was the moonshine industry – responsible for as much as 60 percent of the alcohol for sale on the street – that had become so big that it bought used liquor bottles for $1.50 each.[21] By late 1996 the economy was beginning to fall apart. State sector production was down, the national currency depreciated against the dollar by almost 70% in six months, inflation started to spin out of control (200% in ten months), foreign exchange reserves were depleted, the grain harvest was the worst ever, and major banks went bust.[22] Moreover, under IMF pressure Prime Minister Videnov agreed to close down dozens of loss-making enterprises raising the specter of major unemployment and worker unrest.

A caretaker government led by current Sofia mayor Ivan Sofiansky in the spring of 1997 took some important steps toward economic stabilization. Ivan Kostov's cabinet managed to reverse the seven-year trend of diminishing economic performance. The most successful element of its economic program was the aforementioned currency board, urged

---

[20] See Raymond Bonner, "Bulgaria Slow To Cut Loose Its State-Owned Enterprises," *New York Times*, 20 February 1994; and "Die Schocktherapie wurde in Bulgarien zum Flop," *Die Presse* (Vienna), 30 May 1994.

[21] See "Drückende soziale Lage in Bulgarien," *Neue Zürcher Zeitung*, 21 June 1994; and "Inside Crooked Bulgaria," 6.

[22] "A Rocky Bulgarian Path Ahead," *Foreign Report* (Jane's), no. 2412 (15 August 1996): 6–7; and "Can Bulgaria Get Worse," ibid., no. 2423 (7 November 1996): 7–8.

Bulgaria: Progress After Seven Wasted Years 183

by the IMF, which reduced inflation from 1,000% (in the worst twelve-month period) to 6% by the end of 1999 and even further since then. In time exports have also increased while the trade deficit declined; the first positive trade balance was registered in December 2000. Foreign investment has also grown substantially ($800 million in 2000 alone) although it looks less impressive by comparison to Hungary which, with nearly the same population as Bulgaria, received $17 billion during 1992–2000 in contrast to Bulgaria's $2.5 billion.[23] In spite of major progress, Bulgaria remains a very poor country. According to official statistics, in 2000 40% of Bulgarians lived below the poverty line, the average monthly salary was $110, unemployment was stuck above 18%, and 60% of single mothers suffered from malnutrition because they were giving most of their food purchases to their children.[24] A December 2000 survey revealed that 54% of the respondents would advise their children to emigrate.[25]

The further liberalization and privatization of the economy are the top priorities of the Saxecoburggotski government. A number of major industrial enterprises remain under state ownership – such as the GORBUSO mining complex, the Varna shipyard, the tobacco company "Bulgartabac," and Bulgarian Telecommunications Company – that the cabinet intends to sell. Perhaps the most demanding and intricate task of the new administration, however, is to weed out the all-pervasive corruption which has been Bulgaria's chief socioeconomic and political problem.

Since 1997 Bulgaria has received positive reports from the European Union, the organization it most wants to join. In early 2001 the EU lifted visa requirements for Bulgarians which was evaluated as a foreign policy coup in Sofia. Predictably, EU officials have commended the government for its prudent economic policies that managed to keep inflation down despite relatively strong economic growth (an average of around 4% during 1998–2002), for the effective farm reform that

---

[23] RFE/RL II, 4:168 (31 August 2000), and 4:201 (17 October 2000). One of the declared priorities of the new government is attracting more investment. See "Bulgaria's New Premier Vows To Boost Investment," *Standart* (Sofia), 26 July 2001.

[24] RFE/RL II, 4:75 (14 April 2000); and Assenova, "The Schengen List Impact on Bulgaria's Elections."

[25] ALPHA Research cited by Margarita Assenova, "Bulgaria: The Rush To Build Coalitions," RFE/RL II End Note, 5:25 (6 February 2001).

has been implemented since 1997, and for the overall economic stability.[26] As of October 2001 Bulgaria closed 12 completed chapters in EU negotiations out of the 31 *acquis communautaire* (in contrast to Romania's 8). According to the EU's 2000 progress report Bulgaria "continues to fulfill" the political criteria of membership though corruption remains a "very serious issue."[27] The challenge of EU accession for Bulgaria remains "vast," as Kostov said. According to optimistic EU negotiators it would be unreasonable to expect Bulgarian membership prior to 2007.[28] That year is precisely the provisional target date suggested to Sofia (and Romania) by the European Commission in October 2002.

Security Situation

Bulgaria's southeastern Balkan location is a comparatively advantageous geostrategic position from NATO's perspective. It is bordered by the Black Sea to the east, Turkey and Greece to the south, Macedonia and Yugoslavia (Serbia) to the west, and Romania to the north. Bulgaria has no territorial claims on any of its neighbors and it does not recognize others' claims. Its main strategic goal is to develop attachments to the international security system. Like all countries in this study, Bulgaria, too, has faced fundamental changes in the character and essence of the dangers and threats to its national security in the postcommunist era.

Bulgaria will not become a geopolitical center and it does not intend to expand its influence given that such an action might lead to international conflicts. According to politicians in Sofia, what they can offer to the international community is not a rich country but an uncommonly stable one in a traditionally explosive region.[29] Foreign policy

---

[26] See interview with Georgi Prohaski, Center for Economic Development (Sofia, 13 November 1999); and Ron Synowitz, "OECD Praises Bulgarian Farm Reforms, Concerned About Romania," RFE/RL II End Note, 5:11 (17 January 2001).

[27] Nahabedian, "EC 2000 Progress Report on Bulgaria."

[28] See Reuters (Sofia), 20 April 2000; and Phelim McAleer, "Bulgaria Welcomes EU Report, But Not Its Details," *Financial Times*, 13 November 2001.

[29] See Valeri Ratchev, "Bulgaria and the Future of European Security," in Stephen J. Blank, ed., *European Security and NATO Enlargement: A View from Central Europe* (Carlisle, PA: U.S. Army War College, Strategic Studies Institute, 1998), 177–178.

professionals in Sofia are well aware that in the Balkans – the only region in Europe which was equally volatile at the beginning of both the twentieth and the twenty-first century – successful diplomatic outcomes demand that everything be done multilaterally. In concert with this realization and in order to safeguard its own security and to contribute to that of the entire region, Bulgaria has consciously shifted its emphasis from bilateral to multilateral regional cooperation in the Black Sea and inner Balkan zones.

The Bulgarian General Staff (GS) developed a new security concept as early as 1992 which reflected the shift away from the previously strong emphasis on potential threat from the south.[30] The National Security Strategy of Bulgaria was approved by the legislature in July 1999. Its most important feature is the prescription that all changes in defense and military policy should serve the foremost security objective of the country: membership in NATO.[31] Bulgaria's new military doctrine, passed by the National Assembly in 1999, prescribes the development of the Bulgarian Armed Forces (BAF) according to the principle of reasonable sufficiency and conforming to the structural framework of NATO forces (replacing divisions and regiments with corps and brigades). It is a purely defensive doctrine serving the objectives of border protection and prompt availability for peace-keeping operations and disaster relief.[32]

Bulgaria has no serious disputes with any of its neighbors that could generate a military threat. The external military threats to Bulgaria are primarily related to the serious and growing imbalance between the armed forces of the Balkan states and the possibility that the conflicts in the former Yugoslavia would spill over and grow into an all-Balkan conflict. As the prominent Bulgarian security expert Valeri Ratchev writes, "To be prepared in this case means to be prepared for a whole spectrum of conflicts" and the solution can only be found "in the

---

[30] Kjell Engelbrekt, "Bulgaria's Evolving Defense Policy," *RFE/RL Research Report*, 3:32 (19 August 1994): 48–49.

[31] See Petûr Tagarev, "Kontseptsiata za natsionalna sigurnost i informatsionnoto protivoborstvo," *Informatsiya i sigurnost: Mezhdunaroden zhurnal*, 1:2 (Fall–Winter 1998): 32–42; and Todor Koburov, "National Security Policy: Conceptional Bases, Problems and Prospects," *Security Policy*, 1 (1999): 15–20.

[32] See Bell, "Bulgaria's Search for Security," 308; and *Public Charter for the Reform in the Bulgarian Army, the Military Doctrine, and the Accession of Bulgaria into NATO* (Sofia: K & M Publishing House, 1999), 15–23.

186   *The Future of NATO Expansion*

context of growing cooperation with NATO, the EU, and the UN as well."[33]

Though from the outside it seemed unlikely that Sofia could be pulled into the Yugoslav wars, when asked in a 1993 poll what concerned them most about the future, the highest proportion of Bulgarians (41 percent) said "war."[34] Bulgaria, like Romania, *has* been a victim of the region's conflicts and its close proximity to the hostilities might have scared off potential investors. According to President Stoyanov, the 1992–1995 Bosnia war cost Bulgaria "at least $5–6 billion" and the war in Kosovo also "caused damages in the billions."[35] The 2001 crisis in Macedonia between the titular nationality and ethnic Albanians has presented Sofia with yet another security challenge. Bulgaria repeatedly declared that it would not add to the tension in any way. Chief of the General Staff (CGS) Miho Mihov confirmed that Bulgaria did not intend to deploy additional troops on its Western border and that there were no threats to the country's airspace.[36] Nonetheless, the government prepared contingency plans to be ready for a potential influx of refugees from Macedonia.

Bulgarian experts and the Ministry of Defense's (MOD) 2001 White Paper identify a host of nontraditional security risks. These include international terrorism, organized crime and the extremely slow justice system, ethno-religious conflicts, xenophobia and aggressive nationalism, economic distress, and environmental and ecological threats.[37] As far as the latter is concerned the most pressing issue is the nuclear power plant near Kozloduy which some EU and Central European states consider one of the most dangerous in Europe.[38]

---

[33] Valeri Ratchev, "Combining Political and Military Considerations in Assessing Military Conflicts," *Journal of Slavic Military Studies*, 9:1 (March 1996): 49, 54.

[34] Luan Troxel, "Bulgaria: Stable Ground in the Balkans?" *Current History*, 92:577 (November 1993): 389.

[35] See the interviews with Andrew Pierre of the U.S. Institute of Peace in "Bulgaria's Road to Reform," CNN Question & Answer Program, 21:30 CET, 22 November 1999; and with Stoyanov in the *Süddeutsche Zeitung*, 18 April 2000. Incidentally, Bulgaria received direct damage as well, caused by a missile that went astray and partially destroyed a house in a Sofia suburb.

[36] Reuters (Sofia), 22 March 2001.

[37] See Tsvetkov, "Bulgarian Security Policy," 29–32; and *White Paper on the Defence and Armed Forces of the Republic of Bulgaria* (Sofia: MOD, 2001), 13–14.

[38] See Boian Koulov, "Political Change and Environmental Policy," in John D. Bell, ed., *Bulgaria in Transition: Politics, Economics, Society, and Culture After Communism*

Bulgaria: Progress After Seven Wasted Years

PART II. FOREIGN POLICY AND THE CAMPAIGN FOR NATO MEMBERSHIP

Bulgarian Foreign Policy

Sofia was the Soviet Union's most reliable ally during the Cold War and often received more favorable treatment from Moscow than other members of the Warsaw Pact. Similarly to Slovakia and Romania, the alignment of Bulgarian foreign policy has been strongly dependent on the political forces in power. In general, BSP governments considered maintaining good relations with Russia a priority. UDF governments, on the other hand, pursued an unequivocally pro-Western foreign policy the key objective of which had been membership in NATO and the EU. Especially after 1997, Bulgarian foreign policy was completely reoriented toward the West. Saxecoburggotski's cabinet has followed this direction.

The first BSP government did not easily recognize the passing of an era. As late as November 1990 Foreign Minister Lyuben Gotsev and other officials argued that the Warsaw Pact was still useful and predicted that it would survive in the "coming two or three years."[39] Despite such early faux pas, foreign policy, by and large, became one of the more successful areas of Bulgarian politics. European organizations swiftly recognized Bulgaria's success in building democracy. Sofia gained membership in the Council of Europe in 1992, reached an association agreement with the EU in 1993, secured an invitation to participate in the EU's military branch, the Western European Union in 1994, and joined the Partnership for Peace program in the same year.

Bulgaria has signed cooperation agreements with all of its neighbors but Yugoslavia; a similar pact with Belgrade will surely be soon negotiated with the post-Milošević leadership. Bulgarian-Romanian relations have been at times wrought with tension – for example, centering on pollution, cross-border traffic, smuggling – but both states have worked

---

(Boulder, CO: Westview Press, 1998), 153. In 2001 Sofia agreed to decommission the oldest reactors at the plant by 2003.

[39] See "General Discusses Alliances, Role of the Army," *Anteni* (Sofia), 18 April 1990, translated in *FBIS-EEU*, 25 April 1990; "Bulgaria's Foreign Minister Says Warsaw Pact Still Useful," Reuters (Sofia), 14 November 1990; and Alfred Reisch, "Central and Eastern Europe's Quest for NATO Membership, *RFE/RL Research Report*, 2:28 (9 July 1993): 38.

on their differences. In March 2000, after years of dispute, they signed an agreement to build a second bridge across the Danube which will be paid for by Bulgaria. The two governments have increasingly cooperated on NATO-related subjects because, as Romanian Defense Minister Pascu recently said, they could achieve more if they worked together.[40]

Still, since the early 1990s Bulgarian politicians – pointing to Sofia's superior record in democratization and, after 1997, in economic restructuring – have pushed hard to dispel any notion that Bulgaria should be put in the same category with Romania in international talks. In August 2001, for instance, the UDF criticized the Saxecoburggotski government for agreeing to coordinate "in tandem" with Romanian efforts to join Euro-Atlantic structures because such a formula "contravenes Bulgarian interests."[41] Josef Gruver of the Konrad Adenauer Foundation agreed, saying that Bulgaria should part with its role of Romania's "Siamese twin" in its drive to join Europe, considering that it had done far better than Romania and should not be held back by assessments of Romania's progress.[42]

Sofia's relations with Macedonia have been more complex. Bulgarian governments fought in three wars during the twentieth century (1913, 1918, 1944) to unite Macedonia with the Bulgarian kingdom; all ended in disasters. Most Bulgarians believe that Macedonians *are* Bulgarians and speak essentially the same language as they do. Although Sofia was the first state to recognize the independent Republic of Macedonia, Bulgaria never acknowledged the existence of either a Macedonian nation or a Macedonian language.[43] Despite some latent tensions, Bulgarian policies toward Skopje have been cordial and constructive, particularly under Ivan Kostov's premiership. Sofia

---

[40] RFE/RL II, 5:19 (29 January 2001).

[41] BTA (Sofia), reported in RFE/RL II, 5:154 (15 August 2001). See also "Progress in Sofia," *Wall Street Journal* (European edition), 13 January 1992; interview with Lubomir Ivanov Deputy Director of the NATO, WEU, and Security Issues Directorate, Ministry of Foreign Affairs (Sofia, 19 November 1999); and Reuters (Sofia), 10 November 2000.

[42] Interview with Gruver in BTA, cited by RFE/RL II, 4:212 (1 November 2000).

[43] For analyses of Bulgarian-Macedonian relations, see Hugh Poulton, *Who Are the Macedonians?* (London: Hurst & Co., 1995), 148–162; and Ulrich Büchsenschütz, "Macedonia's 'Big Brother' – With Tied Hands," RFE/RL II End Note, 5:120 (25 June 2001).

extended military aid worth $3.5 million to Macedonia in 1999, President Stoyanov visited Skopje in 2000 (closing his speech with "Long Live Independent Macedonia!"), and Bulgaria has been supportive of Macedonia during the 2001 crisis.[44] Stoyanov and others have repeatedly declared that the destabilization of Macedonia was completely unacceptable and Sofia once again approved arms exports to Skopje in 2001.[45]

Once the new government took office in 2001, the policy toward the Macedonian crisis considerably shifted. The new foreign minister, Solomon Pasi, announced that Sofia's position would be "calmer and more moderate" and that "Bulgaria cannot act as a mediator in a conflict in which it has not been invited to mediate."[46] Macedonian politicians assured the new government that they expected its full contribution to the conflict's settlement and also asked Sofia for military aid.[47]

The conflictual Bulgarian-Turkish relations of the Cold War have fully recovered since 1989. President Suleyman Demirel and other leading Turkish politicians have repeatedly praised Bulgaria's positive treatment of its Turkish minority and assured Sofia of their support of Bulgarian NATO membership. Greece has also become an important state in Sofia's foreign policy. During a February 2001 meeting, Greek Foreign Minister George Papandreou declared that "Greece will always be at Bulgaria's side on its course for integration with the EU and NATO."[48] Actually, Bulgaria has been trying to play a moderating role between its two southern neighbors and thereby serve NATO's interests.[49]

---

[44] Reuters and AP reports (Skopje, 15 May 2000); "NATO: Your Idea Is Welcome," *Standart* (Sofia), 6 March 2001; and "Stoyanov: We Should Support Macedonia," *Standart*, 6 March 2001.

[45] RFE/RL II, 5:47 (8 March 2001), 5:58 (23 March 2001), and 5:68 (6 April 2001).

[46] See RFE/RL II, 5:147 (6 August 2001).

[47] See Nadelina Aneva, "Macedonia Asks Bulgaria for Military Aid," *Standart*, 17 August 2001.

[48] RFE/RL II, 5:28 (9 February 2001).

[49] See interviews with Nikolai Mikov, Ministry of Foreign Affairs (Sofia, 12 November 1999), Ognyan Minchev, Executive Director of the Institute for Regional and International Studies (Sofia, 19 November 1999), and Boyko Todorov, Program Director at Sofia's Center for the Study of Democracy (Austin, TX, 27 February 2001); AP (Sofia), 10 February 2000; and RFE/RL II, 4:30 (11 February 2000).

Bulgaria has developed good contacts with most European NATO members who have repeatedly confirmed that they supported its joining the Alliance. Sofia's relations with the United States have improved immeasurably, especially in the late 1990s. In 1998 U.S. Deputy Secretary of State Strobe Talbott lauded Bulgaria's stabilizing role in the Balkans saying that the country has become a "strong multiethnic democracy that could serve as a model for other Balkan nations."[50] In November 1999 Bill Clinton became the first American president to visit Bulgaria. He announced to a large and jubilant crowd that "we are committed to supporting Bulgaria over the long run economically, politically, and militarily."[51] During a June 2001 visit to Sofia, Doug Bereuter, a U.S. Congressman from Nebraska, said that Bulgaria was a "leader in Southeast Europe" and raised hopes for its early NATO accession.[52]

Bulgaria is no longer the closest ally Moscow has in Europe. Until the fall of the Videnov government in late 1996, Sofia's relations with Moscow had been excellent. Meetings between Russian and Bulgarian leaders rarely included discussion of Bulgaria's possible membership in NATO given that it was a controversial subject – Zhelev supported it while Videnov contended that NATO had to be reformed before Sofia would consider joining.[53] According to some analysts the reason why Bulgaria received a shipment of 100 tanks and 100 armored vehicles from Russia in 1996 – under the Conventional Forces Europe (CFE) Treaty Moscow had the option of destroying these weapons or give them away – was a reward for Sofia's reluctance to apply for NATO membership.[54]

After the UDF government took over in 1997, the Bulgarian-Russian nexus deteriorated. In 1997 Bulgarian Foreign Minister Nadezhda Mihailova described her Russian colleague, Yevgenii Primakov's refusal to meet her "indicative" of Moscow's "unwillingness or inability

[50] DPA (Sofia), 18 March 1998.
[51] See Zhidas Daskalovski, "Clinton's Pep-talk in Sofia," *Central Europe Review*, 1:23 (29 November 1999).
[52] AP and Reuters (Sofia), 1 June 2001.
[53] See, for instance, the report between Russian Prime Minister Viktor Chernomyrdin and Prime Minister Videnov in OMRI DD II, no. 98 (22 May 1995); and Michael Mihalka, "Eastern and Central Europe's Great Divide Over Membership in NATO," *Transition*, 1:14 (11 August 1995): 54.
[54] Reuters (Sofia), 22 July 1996; and OMRI DD II, no. 141 (23 July 1996).

Bulgaria: Progress After Seven Wasted Years

to use ... civilized methods" with other states.[55] Russia has repeatedly expressed its displeasure with Bulgarian aspirations for NATO membership. Sofia, on the other hand, has refused to allow Russian airplanes to fly troops over Bulgaria en route to Kosovo, expelled Russian diplomats and businessmen accused of spying, and unilaterally abolished a 1978 visa free travel agreement with Russia as a result of the EU visa regime. With these actions Bulgaria served notice that it was no longer Russia's "junior partner." In April 2001, Vladimir Titov, Russia's Ambassador to Bulgaria, said that there were differences of opinion but "no rift" between the two countries.[56] In February 2002 Sofia and Moscow settled the latter's long standing debt, $24 million of which would be paid in Russian-made equipment for the Bulgarian army.[57]

Since 1997 Bulgaria has become more active in international, especially regional, organizations in order to alleviate its security concerns and to promote its chances for NATO membership. It joined the Multinational Peace Force in Southeastern Europe in 1998, contributing 5,000 soldiers to its strength. Sofia has been dissatisfied with another organization it has participated in, the Southeast European Stability Pact (SESP). As President Stoyanov told visiting pact coordinator Bodo Hombach, "If Europe wants to see our continent united, it should invest in this pact."[58] Bulgaria is especially interested in pursuing some of the projects considered by the SESP, such as the bridge between Vidin and Calafat on the Danube and railway connection between Bulgaria and Macedonia.[59] Bulgaria has also been active in the Southeastern European Defense Ministerial (SEDM), another formation which includes regular meetings of the region's ministers and deputy ministers of defense. The SEDM has announced its interest in harmonizing national military policies, secured U.S. commitment for

---

[55] RFE/RL II, 1:130 (2 October 1997).
[56] RFE/RL II, 5:69 (9 April 2001). See also Slavka Buzukova and Svetozar Bakhchevanov, "Policy Towards Russia Was Detrimental," *Standart* (Sofia), 24 August 2001.
[57] RFE/RL II, 6:36 (25 February 2002).
[58] "Bulgaria Dissatisfied With Stability Pact," BTA (Sofia), 20 July 2000; and RFE/RL II, 5:13 (19 January 2001).
[59] Margarita Assenova, "Bulgaria: Driving to the West," in Daniel N. Nelson and Ustina Markus, eds., *Central and East European Security Yearbook, 2002* (Dulles, VA: Brassey's, 2002), 288.

192   *The Future of NATO Expansion*

the continuation of the forum, and brought together NATO member
and aspirant states.[60]

Bulgaria's Campaign for NATO Membership

Bulgaria's desire to become a NATO member is based on the fact that
it belongs to a democratic system of values, it is ready to contribute to
common security and to share the risks; and its conviction that NATO
will be the main carrier of collective guarantees for the security of its
members.[61] President Stoyanov said that one reason why Sofia sought
to join the Alliance was because NATO had morals and it "does not
sweep the problems under the carpet, as was the practice within another military machine that counterbalanced NATO a decade ago."[62]
Though Bulgaria is situated in a traditionally volatile region, none of its
vital national interests is immediately threatened by external factors.
Politicians in Sofia appear convinced that Bulgarian participation in
NATO will create a new situation in the security sphere of Southeastern Europe. Prior to leaving for NATO's Madrid Summit in July 1997,
President Stoyanov lamented that previous Bulgarian governments had
wasted years "dithering at Europe's gates" while other former communist countries knew how to choose "the right course" to integration
with Western organizations. He added that membership in NATO "for
us means not only reforms in the army, but [also] democracy, a developed economy, a [high] living standard, free journalists, motivated
young people, and above all, that way of life that has been chosen on
the eve of the twenty-first century."[63]

   As Stoyanov suggested, until 1997 Bulgarian governments did little to convince NATO of their strong interest in membership. In 1996

---

[60] See Nikolay Slatinski and Marina Caparini, "Bulgarian Security and Prospects for
Reform," *NATO Review*, no. 2 (March 1995): 28–32; and "Security and Reconstruction of Southeastern Europe: A Policy Outlook from the Region," (Sofia: IRIS,
1999), 28.
[61] See Valeri Ratchev, "Bulgaria and the Future of European Security," Stephen J. Blank,
ed., *European Security and NATO Enlargement: A View from Central Europe* (Carlisle,
PA: U.S. Army War College, Strategic Studies Institute, 1998), 175–176.
[62] Cited in RFE/RL II, 5:6 (10 January 2001).
[63] BTA (Sofia), 7 July 1997, cited in RFE/RL II, 1:68 (8 July 1997). Stoyanov went farther
when he told American journalist Robert Kaplan that "We have made a civilizational
choice in our desire to join NATO." See Kaplan's *Eastward to Tartary*, 63.

Videnov's government decided not to seek membership in the Alliance in spite of President Zhelev's badgering to "make an unequivocal statement of Bulgaria's desire to join NATO and other European structures."[64] In January 1996, Blagovest Sendov, Chairman of the National Assembly told Russian President Boris Yeltsin that Bulgaria should not become a member of NATO. Subsequently leaders of the UDF and the MRF demanded Sendov's resignation because he expressed his view without the approval of the legislature thereby violating the Constitution (their motion was defeated by a vote of 124 to 92).[65] The BSP justified its opposition to NATO with the prospects of totally changed relations with Russia, involvement in conflicts with which Bulgaria had nothing to do, threats to its non-nuclear status, and having to take on an additional financial burden if Sofia were to join the Alliance.[66] Unlike Romania and Slovenia, Bulgaria was not even mentioned in the communiqué that formally concluded the Alliance's Madrid Summit.

After the UDF government took over the reigns, all major political institutions (president, prime minister, government, and the legislature) unequivocally endorsed the objective of Euro-Atlantic integration.[67] The government assigned the MOD and the Ministry of Foreign Affairs (MFA) the task of developing a national program to prepare for accession. This program, adopted by the cabinet in March 1997, specifies the measures which state institutions should implement in order to achieve NATO membership. Nadezhda Mihailova, the Kostov government's capable foreign minister, assured visiting NATO Secretary-General Javier Solana in 1998 that Bulgaria would "do everything NATO asks in order to prepare for membership in the Alliance."[68] The Kostov government, for instance, agreed to scrap Bulgaria's SS-23, Scud, and Frog missiles which were destroyed in October 2002.

In March 2001 Bulgaria and NATO signed a memorandum giving NATO troops permanent access to Bulgarian territory in order to ease

---

[64] John D. Bell, "Democratization and Political Participation in 'Postcommunist' Bulgaria," 392.

[65] Albert P. Melone, *Creating Parliamentary Government: The Transition to Democracy in Bulgaria* (Columbus: Ohio State University Press, 1998), 208.

[66] See Nansen Behar, "Bulgarian Perception of European Cooperation on Conflict Prevention," *Balkan Forum*, 5:1 (March 1997): 93–94.

[67] See Tsvetkov, "Bulgarian Security Policy," 15–16.

[68] RFE/RL II, 2:65 (3 April 1998).

the resolution of Balkan crises. The opposition BSP had charged, not unreasonably, that the agreement was in large part an electoral ploy to make people believe that it would advance Bulgaria's NATO candidacy.[69] One of the last official trips Prime Minister Kostov took before the 2001 national elections was to Washington in order to, as he said, "get support in the run-up to the elections."[70] He received the blessings of President Bush, Vice-President Cheney, and Secretary of State Powell but they could not help him retain his job.

The Bulgarian government supported NATO's military involvement in the former Yugoslavia even though over 90 percent of Bulgarians opposed it.[71] In fact, Bulgaria – just like Slovakia – also faced the problem of angry young men who wanted to enroll to fight "on the other side" in the name of "Slavic brotherhood." It was reported in March 1999 that 430 such volunteers registered in Bulgaria and some of them were already in Serbia.[72] Even though the government did not permit Russian troops to use its airspace, it did allow Turkish KFOR units on Bulgarian territory for the first time in 121 years on their way to Kosovo. And, as mentioned above, Bulgaria agreed to the "provisional stationing" of NATO troops on its territory for "a longer term, if necessary."[73] NATO leaders from Javier Solana to General Wesley Clark repeatedly expressed their appreciation for Bulgaria's role in the Kosovo crisis. In July 2001 the Bulgarian MOD announced that it "did not rule out" the possibility that arms taken from the Albanian National Liberation Army (UCK) in Macedonia may be destroyed, with United States financial support, in Bulgaria.[74] In September 2002 Sofia quickly granted its airspace to the United States and offered its

---

[69] RFE/RL II, 5:56 (21 March 2001) and 5:63 (30 March 2001).

[70] Reuters (Washington, D.C.), 23 April 2001.

[71] See interview with Evgeni Danilov, Co-Director, Center for Social Practices (Sofia, 12 November 1999); Ivan Krastev, Stefan Popov, and Julia Gurkovska, "2010: The Balkans after Kosovo," *East European Constitutional Review*, 8:3 (Summer 1999): 85; and Gary Dempsey, "Headaches for Neighboring Countries," in Ted Galen Carpenter, ed., *NATO's Empty Victory: A Postmortem on the Balkan War* (Washington, D.C.: Cato Institute, 2000), 64–65.

[72] See Michael Shafir, "The Kosova Crisis and the NATO Hopefuls," RFE/RL II End Note, 3:62 (30 March 1999). The Slovak MOD announced that fighting for another country without official permission was a punishable offense.

[73] AFP (Brussels), 29 March 2001. The National Assembly ratified the agreement with a vote of 202 in favor and 3 abstentions. AP (Sofia), 8 April 2001.

[74] RFE/RL II, 5:128 (10 July 2001).

Bulgaria: Progress After Seven Wasted Years

participation in peacekeeping and other operations in Afghanistan.[75] Sofia has contributed a decontamination facility to the multinational International Security Assistance Force in Kabul. The performance of the Bulgarian contingent has been praised by U.S. commanders.[76]

NATO membership has been quite popular in Bulgaria. During the recent war against Yugoslavia, however, support for joining the Alliance dropped from 60% to barely 50%.[77] By the late fall of 1999 opinion polls suggested that the proportion of those backing NATO membership was back in the 60% range, 20% was against, and 20% was undecided.[78] The government has made a concerted effort to increase public support for NATO. During the Kosovo war ministers went around the country to explain to people the reasons for NATO's actions and the cabinet's stance. Since the early 1990s all UDF members have campaigned on the NATO issue in their constituencies. The raison d'être of the Atlantic Club of Bulgaria, one of the most popular NGOs in the country, is to familiarize the population with NATO and to enhance their support for Bulgarian membership in it.[79] The Club's founder and president, Solomon Pasi, became the Saxecoburggotski cabinet's foreign minister in July 2001. Nonetheless, public support of NATO accession fell to 50% by late July 2002, which analysts attributed to the confusion among the population regarding the scrapping of Bulgaria's stockpile of missiles.[80]

Until 1998 the BSP's position on NATO membership remained overwhelmingly negative. President Zhelev and Prime Minister Videnov often and publicly clashed over the issue.[81] In April 1997, former BSP

---

[75] "Bulgaria Grants Air Space to USA," *Standart*, 26 September 2001; and "Defence Minister, British Consultant Confirm Bulgaria's Involvement in Afghanistan," BTA (Sofia), 11 January 2002.

[76] BTA (Kabul), 21 August 2002.

[77] See Stephen Connors, David G. Gibson, and Mark Rhodes, "Caution and Ambivalence Over Joining NATO," *Transition*, 1:14 (11 August 1995): 42–46; and "NATO and Bulgaria: Brave Gamble," *The Economist*, 29 May 1999, 47; and interview with Captain Kirilov (Warsaw, 13 August 1999).

[78] Interviews with Nikolai Mikov, MFA (Sofia, 12 November 1999); and Dimitar Abadjiev, MP (Sofia, 17 November 1999).

[79] Interview with Solomon Pasi, President of The Atlantic Club of Bulgaria (Sofia, 18 November 1999). See also the MOD's *White Paper*, 93–94.

[80] BTA (Sofia), 2 September 2002.

[81] See, for instance, OMRI DD II, no. 77 (19 April 1995), no. 95 (17 May 1995), and no. 87 (3 May 1996).

196   *The Future of NATO Expansion*

Foreign Minister Georgi Pirinski said that his party opposed joining NATO but was in favor of EU membership.[82] Three years later, however, Georgi Parvanov, the BSP's newly reelected leader stressed his support for Bulgaria's NATO integration. Later that month the Sofia legislature endorsed a government-sponsored resolution backing the cabinet's drive to join the EU and NATO with a vote of 189 to 3.[83]

Bulgarian military diplomacy has traditionally emphasized good relations with Russia. Until the 1990s numerous cooperation agreements were negotiated between the two armies and Sofia was able to secure Moscow's assurances of uninterrupted supply of spare parts and preferential considerations for new purchases of Russian military hardware.[84] After the UDF government took over in 1997, Bulgarian military diplomacy succeeded in developing constructive army-to-army relations with nearly all NATO member states. Particularly valuable are its cooperation agreements and active interaction with neighbors, especially Greece, Turkey, and Macedonia. Bulgarian-Romanian military relations have focused on joining NATO (though it ought to be reiterated that Bulgarian politicians prefer not to be linked to or grouped together with Romania). The two defense ministers agreed to establish a joint peacekeeping unit although the importance of such a venture is likely to be more political than practical.[85] In October 2002 the two armies participated in a joint exercise that aimed to improve the interoperability between their troops.[86]

It was no coincidence that Bulgaria's participation in the PfP "was almost moribund during the two years of Zhan Videnov's government, which favored the development of military cooperation with Russia."[87] After 1997, however, Bulgaria quickly became active in PfP,

---

[82] RFE/RL II, 1:4 (4 April 1997).

[83] RFE/RL II, 4:89 (9 May 2000), 4:103 (29 May 2000); and interview with Boyko Todorov (Austin, TX, 27 February 2001).

[84] See John D. Bell, "Bulgaria's Search for Security," 308; "Military Pact with Russia Planned," BTA (Sofia), 28 October 1991; translated in *FBIS-EEU*, 29 October 1991, 5; OMRI DD II, no. 141 (23 July 1996), no. 42 (22 October 1996), and no. 34 (18 February 1997).

[85] See, for instance, "Military and Security Notes," *RFE/RL Research Report*, 1:37 (18 September 1992), 67; BTA (Sofia), 29 March 2000); and RFE/RL II, 5:19 (29 January 2001).

[86] RFE/RL II, 6:186 (2 October 2002).

[87] Bell, "Bulgaria's Search for Security," 308.

Bulgaria: Progress After Seven Wasted Years

participating in twenty joint exercises in 1998 alone. Since December 1994, Sofia has also pursued – with more intensity, to be sure, after 1997 – the completion of the goals of the Planning and Review Process (PARP). Politicians generally consider PfP as an intermediate stage to full NATO membership. Until 1997, Bulgaria had been rather inactive in international peacekeeping operations but since then it has greatly improved its record in this respect, contributing units to numerous hotspots around the world.[88]

PART III. CIVIL–MILITARY RELATIONS

Depoliticizing the Armed Forces

Dobri Dzhurov, Bulgaria's communist Defense Minister, was instrumental in the overthrow of Todor Zhivkov.[89] The Bulgarian armed forces have been linked to coups and coup attempts in the past and, according to John Bell, constituted "the greatest obstacle to democratic government" in the pre-communist era.[90] In fact, the Sofia government on several occasions found it necessary to publicly deny coup rumors even during the 1990s.[91]

In order to reflect Bulgaria's newly gained full independence, the form of address, oath of allegiance, and uniforms all changed beginning in October 1990.[92] The substantive depoliticization of the army

---

[88] See Simon, "Bulgaria and NATO: 7 Lost Years," 5; *Bulgarian Armed Forces* (Sofia: MOD, 1999), 10–11; Yanakiev Yantsislav, "Bulgarian Soldiers as Peacekeepers: The Viewpoints of The Military and Citizens," *Security Policy: Information Bulletin of the Ministry of Defence of the Republic of Bulgaria*, no. 1 (1999): 39–50; *White Paper*, 23–25.

[89] See, for instance, Bradley R. Gitz, *Armed Forces and Political Power in Eastern Europe* (Westport, CT: Greenwood, 1992), 149.

[90] Bell, "Democratization and Political Participation in 'Postcommunist' Bulgaria," 362; for a contrary view expressed by the hardly impartial General Atanas Semerdzhiev, a former Minister of Interior, see Melone, *Creating Parliamentary Government*, 101–102.

[91] See, for instance, "Army Chief of Staff Denies Coup Rumors," BTA (Sofia), 2 September 1992; "Dimitrov: Coup Rumors Seek to Create Chaos," BTA (Sofia), 3 September 1992; "Military and Security Notes," *RFE/RL Research Report*, 1:37 (18 September 1992): 67; "Bulgarian Chief of Staff Says Military Coup Not Imminent," *Standart* (Sofia), 7 August 1996; and OMRI DD II, no. 152 (7 August 1996).

[92] See " 'Mister' Introduced as Form of Address in Army," *Narodna Armiya*, 18 October 1990, translated in *FBIS-EEU*, 23 October 1990; "Defense Minister Amends Text of Military Oath," *Narodna Armiya*, 29 October 1990 in *FBIS-EEU* 1 November

was more sluggish than in some of the other East European states. Nonetheless, the Central Committee disbanded the communist party's organizations and its propaganda agency in the military in January 1990 and a law on the depoliticization of armed services was passed in October 1990. This law obligated officers to give up their party affiliations. Only 2% refused and they subsequently resigned or were dismissed. Approximately 80% of the officers with ranks up to captain; between 50–60% of the senior officers from major upward; and over 60% of the sergeants and soldiers supported the law for depoliticization.[93] Altogether 6,000 officers and NCOs (4,500 by 1992) left the services although some, especially younger officers with diverse skills, used the law as an excuse to leave in order to abjure their contractual obligations to the military with impunity.[94] According to Dzhurov's successor, Defense Minister Colonel-General Yordan Mutafchiev, as of late 1990 some political officers remained in the military to work and educate others, some had requalified as combat officers, and still others were granted permission to study at higher-level military educational institutions.[95]

Military personnel may not be members of any party or attend political gatherings in uniform. Officers and NCOs cannot be appointed to another government position. Regular military servicemen have the right to run for political office but they are released from the army for the duration of their campaign and, if elected, are considered on unpaid leave for the time of their mandate.[96] The political loyalties of officers apparently no longer matter; already in 1992 the MOD

1990; and "Defense Minister Gives Briefing on Army Changes," *Narodna Armiya*, 1 February 1991, in *FBIS-EEU*, 11 February 1991.

[93] These numbers are from Atanas Semerdzhiev, cited by Melone, *Creating Parliamentary Government*, 90. See also "Party Bodies in Armed Forces Disbanded," BTA (Sofia), 26 January 1990; "Resistance To Army Depolitization Viewed," *Trud* (Sofia), 14 February 1990, in *FBIS-EEU*, 14 February 1990; " 'Weaknesses' in Military Depolitization Noted," *Svoboden Narod* (Sofia) 7 March 1990, in *FBIS-EEU*, 28 March 1990; and, for a summary, Dimitar Dimitrov, "Military Reform and Budgeting for Defence in Bulgaria (1989–2000)," in David Betz and John Löwenhardt, eds., *Army and State in Postcommunist Europe* (London: Frank Cass, 2001), 117–119.

[94] "Defense Minister Announces Army Reform Progress," BTA (Sofia), 5 December 1991; and Bell, "Bulgaria's Search for Security," 306–307.

[95] "Defense Minister on Retraining Political Officers," BTA (Sofia), 13 November 1990, translated in *FBIS-EEU*, 19 November 1990.

[96] Interview with Captain Kirilov (Warsaw, 13 August 1999); and *White Paper*, 47–48.

Bulgaria: Progress After Seven Wasted Years

announced that, for the first time, candidates for military attaché posts were selected by means of competition.[97]

President Zhelev, perhaps more cognizant of the Bulgarian army's history of political involvement than most, continued to stress the ongoing importance of the military's depoliticization. He also denounced the possibility that the National Assembly might politically influence the BAF.[98] In 1994 Bulgaria's first civilian defense minister (DM), Dimitûr Ludzhev, announced that the army's depoliticization was nearly completed though the UDF disagreed and pursued more changes in personnel.[99] Young officers seem to understand more the role of the military in a democratic state and appear to have indigenized democratic principles more thoroughly than older cadres.[100]

Institutional Arrangements

Until the late 1990s one of the problems of Bulgarian civil–military relations was the ambiguous division of responsibilities between political and military institutions regarding the BAF. The most important shortcoming of regulations was the vague legal status of the Chief of the General Staff (CGS). In 1997 the Defense and Armed Forces Law of 1996 was amended and it now clearly subordinates the CGS (who now can only make recommendations) to the defense minister. The Law also requires the DM and his deputies to be civilians and establishes a system for the rotation of senior officer positions every three years.[101] The Bulgarian constitution and laws pertaining to defense divide powers between the president, prime minister and his government, and the legislature over the BAF.[102] This system grants

---

97 "Military and Security Notes," *RFE/RL Research Report*, 1:16 (17 April 1992): 54.
98 "Military Pact with Russia Planned," BTA (Sofia), 28 October 1991.
99 See Dale R. Herspring, "The Process of Change and Democratization in Eastern Europe: The Case of the Military," in John R. Lampe and Daniel N. Nelson, eds., *East European Security Reconsidered* (Washington, D.C.: Woodrow Wilson Center Press, 1993), 58.
100 Interview with Dimitûr Abadjiev (Sofia, 17 November 1999).
101 Plamen Pantev, "The Changing Nature of Civil–Military Relations in Post-Totalitarian Bulgaria," in Andrew Cottey, Timothy Edmunds, and Anthony Forster, eds., *Democratic Control of the Military in Postcommunist Europe: Guarding the Guards* (Houndmills, UK: Palgrave, 2002), 145.
102 This section draws on the *White Paper*, 63–70; and *Membership Action Plan* (Sofia: Government of Bulgaria, 1999), 6–7.

parliament sufficient access to information and could work relatively well.

The commander-in-chief of the BAF is the president who declares war and the conclusion of a peace treaty when the legislature is not in session and appoints and retires senior command personnel. Both long-serving Bulgarian presidents, Zhelyu Zhelev (1990–1996) and Petûr Stoyanov (1996–2001) have played a positive role vis-à-vis the BAF, attempting to ensure and perfect civilian control but staying within the boundaries of their constitutionally outlined prerogatives. Both of them successfully countered tests to their authority, as I shall explain in the next section.

The Consultative Council for National Security, established in 1994 and comprised of representatives from a wide range of ministries and governmental agencies, is headed by the president. The ten-member National Security Council was established in 1998 and is chaired by the prime minister.[103] It plays an important role in safeguarding the national interests and the security of the country. It makes recommendations to the government on matters pertaining to national security. The Interdepartmental Committee on Bulgaria's Integration to NATO, co-chaired by Foreign Minister Pasi and DM Nikolai Svinarov, coordinated the government's efforts to obtain an invitation from the Alliance.

The government is responsible for the direct control of the BAF, bears responsibility for its training, combat and mobilization readiness, the overall conditions in the military and the proper utilization of the defense budget. Needless to say, the government is also accountable for developing appropriate relations with military partners abroad, the satisfaction of treaty obligations, and, most importantly, steering the country toward full Euro-Atlantic integration. Furthermore, the government is charged with the responsibility to prepare an annual report to the National Assembly which evaluates the security challenges for the country.

The DM, a civilian by law, is directly responsible for carrying out state policy regarding the protection of the country, managing all activities in the MOD, ensuring civilian control over the BAF, allocating

---

[103] See Slatinski and Caparini, "Bulgarian Security and Prospects for Reform," 31; RFE/RL II, 2:74 (17 April 1998); BTA (Sofia) 30 September 1998; and *White Paper*, 64.

funds, and conducting personnel policy. For instance, when appointed DM in late 1992, Valentin Aleksandrov said that his chief priority was to keep the army out of day-to-day politics. Aleksandrov moved quickly to replace some of his predecessor's closest aides and managed to undo some of his most controversial measures. As a May 2001 National Assembly report concluded, Aleksandrov's predecessor, Alexander Staliyski, served the communist secret service prior to 1989.[104] Bulgarian defense ministers have often been linked to corruption, either fighting against it or practicing it. Not surprisingly, in one of his first interviews after being appointed, Nikolai Svinarov, the Saxecoburggotski government's DM, suggested that he considered weeding out "financial, economic, and administrative transgressions in the ministry and the army" one of his most important priorities.[105]

The Bulgarian MOD has been comprehensively restructured by 1999. Nonetheless, even after several reductions of personnel it remains an enormous bureaucracy. In 2000 the organizational structures and the MOD's administrative units employed 9,589 people out of the entire armed forces personnel of 99,008 (both figures are planned to be halved by 2004). Since 1997 the MOD has improved its record of integrating civilian and military administrations though the process has yet to be completed. The proportion of civilians is currently 64.8% to be increased to 72.2% by 2004.[106] Although a relatively high number of these civilians are retired military personnel, this is not surprising given the dearth of civilian expertise.

The Chief of the General Staff, the top military officer in the land, is accountable to and shall assist the DM in exercising his authority. The CGS is appointed by the president based on parliamentary recommendation. Bulgaria's 1999–2000 Annual National Plan identified widening the areas of "integration interaction" between the MOD and the GS as one of its objectives.[107] Until 1997 the General Staff and its chief were extremely influential and capable of using legitimate legislative pressures in opposition to the MOD. Since then it has become

---

[104] AP (Sofia), 21 May 2001; and RFE/RL II, 5:97 (22 May 2001).
[105] Bogdana Lazarova, "Bulgaria in NATO within the Current Mandate" (interview with Svinarov), *Standart*, 26 July 2001.
[106] *White Paper*, 45. For a helpful graph of the MOD's structure, see 69–70.
[107] "Annual National Program 1999–2000," of the Membership Action Plan, 5; and interview with Shalamanov (Sofia, 18 November 1999).

more or less integrated into the MOD. The GS is primarily responsible for the management, development, and maintenance of the BAF, the implementation of the activities related to combat readiness and mobilization, and ultimately, guaranteeing the sovereignty of the country.[108]

The National Assembly exercises political guidance over the BAF through the adoption of relevant laws and acts as well as through its control over governmental activities and budget planning. It also has the power to declare war and martial law, conclude peace treaties. The permission to send and use the BFA abroad as well as allow the transit or deployment of foreign troops on Bulgarian territory are also the National Assembly's prerogatives. The legislature's National Security Committee contributes to debates concerning military affairs, supervises the defense-related activities of the executive branch, and monitors the BAF.[109] It was established in November 1991 and is composed of twenty-one MPs reflecting the balance between parliamentary parties. One of the functions of the twenty-three-member Foreign Affairs Committee is to oversee NATO (and other) integration strategies.

The process leading to the legislative approval of the annual defense budget has not been problematic in Bulgaria. It starts with the Ministry of Finance's forecast of the following year's budget according to which the MOD makes its own budget proposal and returns it to the finance ministry. The latter then prepares the integrated final draft budget and sends it to the government which submits it to the National Assembly for consideration. Direct civilian control over defense expenditure is carried out by the National Auditing Chamber as well as the Ministry of Finance. Since 1997 a clear trend of enhanced transparency and publicity regarding defense and security spending have prevailed allowing for more thorough public monitoring and debate on defense-related issues.[110]

---

[108] See the MOD's website, www.md.government.bg/_en_/GST_upr.html
[109] See Slatinski and Caparini, "Bulgarian Security and Prospects for Reform," 31; and Todor Koburov, "National Security Policy: Conceptional Bases, Problems and Prospects," 18.
[110] See Tilcho Ivanov, *Confidence and Security in the Balkans: The Role of Transparency in Defense Budgeting* (Sofia: Institute for Security and International Studies, 1996); "Annual National Program," *Membership Action Plan*, 24–25; and *White Paper*, 56–60.

Shortcomings of Civil–Military Relations

The Bulgarian military has not been involved in domestic political contingencies. The only time a sitting president suggested that the military should be involved in politics resulted in a major scandal. In December 1989, President Petûr Mladenov, who could not make himself heard at a hostile demonstration, had told the defense minister that "the best thing is to let the tanks come."[111] Although no one acted upon Mladenov's suggestion, it was captured on videotape which was made available to the opposition UDF. The ensuing process of denial and cover-up led to his resignation in June 1990 and paved the way for the election of his successor, Zhelyu Zhelev.

One of the MOD's foremost concerns has been the difficulty of generational change between senior and junior officers. In a professional sense, the Bulgarian army was far closer integrated with the Soviet armed forces and more effectively socialized by them than any other in communist Eastern Europe. Among senior officers the bonds to Moscow are not easy to break and spying for Russia is not necessarily viewed as treason. In March 2001 a retired colonel, a former deputy department chief in the MOD's Intelligence Directorate, was arrested outside the entrance to the Russian Embassy in Sofia.[112]

Most contemporary Bulgarian generals were still educated at the Voroshilov General Staff Academy of the Soviet Union and their knowledge of and attitudes toward defense-security affairs have yet to cast off what Deputy Minister of Defense Velizar Shalamanov referred to as the "Voroshilov mentality."[113] As of August 2001, the Chief of the General Staff, Miho Mihov, was a 1988 graduate of Voroshilov; Chief of the Air Force Stefan Ivan Popov was the graduate of two Soviet institutions, the Gagarin Air Force College and the Military College of

---

[111] Bell, "Democratization and Political Participation in 'Postcommunist' Bulgaria," 370–371. See also John D. Bell, "The Radical Right in Bulgaria," in Sabrina P. Ramet, ed., *The Radical Right in Central and Eastern Europe since 1989* (University Park: Pennsylvania State University Press, 1999), 234.

[112] Reuters (Sofia), 10 March 2001; *24 Chasa*, 11 March 2001; and RFE/RL II, 5:49 (12 March 2001).

[113] Interview with Shalamanov, MOD (Sofia, 18 November 1999). For an excellent appraisal of the Voroshilov Academy's role in the career of East European senior officers, see Christopher Jones, *Soviet Influence in Eastern Europe: Political Autonomy and the Warsaw Pact* (New York: Prager, 1981), 219–225.

204 *The Future of NATO Expansion*

the Russian Federation General Staff; and the Chief of the Navy, Vice Admiral Petûr Petrov was a 1982 graduate of the Leningrad Naval War College.[114]

The "old-timers" – who are still well-ensconced both in the General Staff and the MOD – have definitely slowed the pace of military reform in Bulgaria. For this reason, the Ministry of Foreign Affairs, which is partly responsible for Euro-Atlantic integration issues, has found itself in the position of having to push military reform which is not, strictly speaking, its task and which also raises the ire of the military establishment.[115]

Bulgaria does not have an adequate pool of civilian defense experts. Even though DM Georgi Ananiev declared in 1999 that 80% of MOD personnel should be civilians, he could not have been too optimistic considering that the MOD's own 2004 target is 72.2%. Given the shortage of qualified civilians the MOD has been probably better off in any case. Defense ministers and their deputies themselves have possessed remarkably little knowledge about military affairs which has added to tensions between the MOD and the GS. In recent years civilians have been able to take courses on national and international security at the University of World Economy in Sofia and some other colleges but opportunities remain limited.[116] Professional military personnel seem to be more reluctant to give civilian defense experts the benefit of the doubt than elsewhere in Eastern Europe. This has also caused conflicts – and periodic showdowns between civilian and military officials – because respect among officers for the increasingly civilian-staffed MOD has fallen precipitously.[117] To make matters worse, most politicians lack interest let alone specialized knowledge in defense-related issues which impedes truly effective civilian control over the military.

[114] See the Bulgarian MOD's website: www.med.government.bg
[115] Interview with Lubomir Ivanov, Deputy Director, NATO, WEU and Security Issues Directorate, MFA (Sofia, 19 November 1999).
[116] Interview with Shalamanov (18 November 1999).
[117] Engelbrekt, "Bulgaria's Evolving Defense Policy," 48; Nikolay Slatinski and Marina Caparini, "Bulgarian Security and Prospects for Reform," *NATO Review*, no. 2 (March 1995): 31; and interviews with Kalinka Kovatcheva and Capt. Ralitza Mateeva, both NATO Integration Directorate, MOD (Sofia, 18 November 1999).

Another major problem, closely related to the feud between civilians and uniformed personnel, has been the on-going friction between the MOD and the GS. In 1994, this discord developed into a full-blown conflict between DM Valentin Aleksandrov and CGS Lyuben Petrov over the MOD's intention to enforce mandatory retirement at age fifty for professional officers.[118] Petrov (supported by the BSP) claimed that this not only amounted to a purge of the officer corps on political grounds but also endangered the army. Eventually President Zhelev dismissed Petrov, confirming the principle of civilian authority. Civilian oversight was again reaffirmed in 1998 when President Stoyanov fired Major General Angel Marin because he criticized the government in the mass media for its alleged abandonment of the armed forces and described Bulgaria's NATO aspirations as "extremely unhealthy."[119] In March 2002 CGS Miho Mihov tendered his resignation (he retired in June) after he publicly criticized the MOD's plan to reduce the retirement age of military officers. Even after Mihov's departure, differences between the CGS, General Nikola Kolev, and DM Nikolai Svinarov remain on matters relating to cooperation between the GS and the MOD and personnel management.[120]

Relations between the president and prime minister have been contentious when they espoused different political orientations. In 1995, for instance, President Zhelev and Prime Minister Videnov engaged in a verbal battle over the leadership of the armed forces. The government sought to transfer military personnel to and from various units in a way to ensure increased military support for itself. Zhelev accused the BSP government of trying to repoliticize the BAF and usurp his presidential prerogatives as commander-in chief.[121] In July 1996 Videnov reportedly held a secret meeting with top-level military personnel to find out whether they would support him in the case of a military coup.[122]

---

[118] This paragraph draws on Bell, "Bulgaria's Search for Security," 307.

[119] See *Transitions*, 5:4 (April 1998): 15.

[120] RFE/RL II, 6:111 (14 June 2002).

[121] Interviews with Capt. Ognyan Kirilov (Warsaw, 13 August 1999) and Solomon Pasi (Sofia, 18 November 1999).

[122] "Bulgarian Chief of Staff Says Military Coup Not Imminent," *Standart*, 7 August 1996.

PART IV. MILITARY REFORM AND THE STATE OF THE ARMED FORCES

Military Reform

No major structural reforms were implemented in the BAF prior to 1997 owing to the absence of political will and/or of financial resources. For instance there was no appreciable redeployment of troops which still maintained their offensive posture toward the south nor any major reduction in the size of the bloated BAF. Even in the late 1990s disagreements between the legislature (in favor of rapid reform) and the old guard in the MOD and the General Staff had resulted in foot-dragging and inaction.[123] In November 1999 Deputy Defense Minister Velizar Shalamanov admitted to me that "the real physical changes so far have been limited" and reform had mostly affected legal issues, the structure of the MOD and its civilian component.[124] It is important to see that the reform has been driven by politicians – primarily President Stoyanov, Prime Minister Kostov, and his cabinet who had been closely monitoring military reform – rather than by military elites (who were in the driver's seat until 1997 and accomplished little).

Since NATO's 1999 Washington Summit, Bulgarian reform planning and implementation have accelerated. It successfully completed the first cycle of the Membership Action Plan which was endorsed by the North Atlantic Council in the spring of 2000. The time frame for certain military reforms was shortened twice, the target date of previous programs, 2010, was reset to 2004.[125] The new reform program is also more comprehensive and substantial and is guided entirely by NATO criteria. A great deal remains to be done, however, before Bulgaria would even come close to satisfying NATO's admission criteria. In fact, President Stoyanov himself admitted during his July 2001 trip to London that the military will not have achieved full interoperability with NATO in time for the 2002 Prague summit.[126] According

---

[123] Interviews with Commander Craig Kennedy, Naval Attache of the U.S. Embassy (Sofia, 10 November 1999); and Dimitûr Abadjiev (Sofia, 17 November 1999).

[124] Interview with Shalamanov (Sofia, 18 November 1999).

[125] Interviews with Velizar Shalamanov, MOD (Sofia, 18 November 1999) and Lubomir Ivanov, MFA (Sofia, 19 November 1999).

[126] "President Stoyanov Meets Prime Minister Blair in London," BTA (London), 26 July 2001.

Bulgaria: Progress After Seven Wasted Years

to Plamen Pantev, a Bulgarian expert, defense planning continues to suffer from several deficiencies, such as lacking coherence between national security objectives and existing force structures, the absence of long-term thinking, and unrealistic expectations about the availability of financial resources.[127]

The 2001 White Paper of the MOD identifies a number of priorities for military reform.[128] These include the formation of a military-strategic and resource grounded armed forces; the restructuring of the three services according the new principles of subdivision and ensuring their interoperability with NATO forces; the development of the military's management system; the pursuance of a new system of procurement based on united logistics and centralized supply; and restructuring and training Rapid Reaction Forces personnel focusing on Immediate Action Forces. The MOD also intends to make it a priority to use the resources made redundant by restructuring for improving the living conditions of armed forces personnel, combat training, raising interoperability standards, and upgrading certain elements of the air defense system and the communication and information system. Further tasks are the development of a new training system for management agencies and building up an early warning and rapid reaction system for participation in crisis management. Another problem, related to the bloated nature of the officer corps, is the ratio of senior/junior officers (54%/46%) which needs to be reversed, and the relative dearth of non-commissioned officers (NCOs).[129] According to the government's program, 10,000 officers and NCOs would be made redundant by the end of 2002.

Military reform is based on NATO standards because, according to a senior MOD official, they are reasonable standards to maintain and to gain security from and they are relatively simple.[130] Since 1999, a three-stage reform program has been envisioned, the first of which was

---

[127] Pantev, "The Changing Nature of Civil–Military Relations in Post-Totalitarian Bulgaria," 146–147.
[128] See *White Paper*, 20–21.
[129] Jeffrey Simon, "Roadmap to NATO Accession: Preparing for Membership," Institute for National Strategic Studies, National Defense University, Special Report, October 2001, 4. Government experts contend that there are twice as many generals as the BFA needs. See the *White Paper*, 46.
[130] Interview with Col. Valeri Ratchev (Sofia, 13 November 1999).

completed in 2000.[131] In the second stage (2001–2002) the Rapid Reaction Forces are to be formed and all three services and components of the General Staff are to be reorganized. In the third stage (2003–2004) the structural reform of the armed forces is scheduled to be completed. During the second and third stages the reconstruction and modernization of armaments and equipment are expected to continue. It is hoped that as a result of the reform a higher level of professionalism is achieved. By 2004 the Rapid Reaction Forces should be manned to 90% capacity (70% with professional soldiers) and by 2006 the BAF should be made up entirely of professionals. Priority will be given to the establishment of "combat capable units" through improved training and updated equipment. Increasing attention will be devoted to enhancing the motivation of soldiers. The bottom line is to create "conditions for achieving interoperability with NATO forces."[132]

Especially since 1998, NATO has aided Bulgaria's military reform – and particularly its efforts to achieve interoperability – through various assistance programs.[133] Its participation in the Membership Action Plan and the PfP Planning and Review Process has certainly been beneficial for military reform. In 1999 U.S. Defense Secretary William Cohen gave visiting Bulgarian DM Georgi Ananiev a U.S.-developed "action plan" to help guide Bulgarian military reforms. The plan urged Sofia to focus on the training and living conditions of its soldiers; improve logistics, command, control, and communications; and reduce the number of troops to 45,000 from the 100,000 at the time.[134] NATO leaders have repeatedly criticized the pace of Bulgaria's military reform, insisting, for instance, that civilians should not be included in the 45,000-strong army quota and that the BAF should possess at least forty-eight combat aircraft in good working order.[135]

---

[131] This discussion is based on the MOD's 2001 *White Paper*, 41–42.

[132] According to the MOD, by 2004 as much as 38 percent of the defense budget will be allotted to interoperability purposes. See "Annual National Program," *Membership Action Plan*, 9; and Nikolai Lichkov Georgiev, "Standardization Activities in the Ministry of Defense and Tendencies for Their Improvement," *Security Policy: Information Bulletin of the Ministry of Defence of the Republic of Bulgaria*, no. 1 (1999): 24–30.

[133] See, for instance, "NATO To Aid Bulgarian Army Reform," BTA (Sofia), 8 December 1998; and RFE/RL II, 4:74 (13 April 2000).

[134] See AFP (Washington), 20 July 1999; and RFE/RL II, 3:140 (21 July 1999).

[135] See "NATO Insists on BG Army Reinforcement," *Standart*, 26 September 2001; "Bulgarian President, NATO Supreme Commander View Army Reform," *Bulgaria Online*, 7 February 2002; and RFE/RL II, 6:40 (11 March 2002).

Bulgaria: Progress After Seven Wasted Years

While the objectives of military reform appear reasonable on paper, some observers believe that it may be beyond Bulgaria's ability to pay for them.[136] Several components of the program that are psychologically and financially the most difficult to execute – such as the drastic reduction of manpower and the acquisition of modern, NATO compatible armaments – have yet to be accomplished. Col. Valeri Ratchev, one of the Sofia MOD's top experts on NATO integration, publicly admitted already in 1999 that the 2004 target date for the completion of the reform was "probably too optimistic."[137] Former DM Boyko Noev was more confident. In April 2001, discussing a NATO report on Bulgaria's fulfillment of the MAP, he said that "we know what to do, know what our shortcomings are, and how to overcome them." He acknowledged that military reform "is difficult because of its hefty financial costs and the need to lay off valuable military staff."[138] In January 2002 President Parvanov admitted that the "hard part of army reform [was] still ahead" and has since insisted that under his tenure military reform would be regulated by law and would proceed within clearer parameters.[139]

Officers and Soldiers

Officer education has considerably changed since 1989 and especially after 1997. The main problems it has confronted have been the shortage of qualified teaching staff not affected by decades of Soviet/communist political indoctrination, the conservative mindset of much of the officer corps, and the absence of financial resources indispensable for high quality training. Consequently, the reform of the military–educational system is far from complete. The MOD has four undergraduate institutions: the V. Levski Land Forces Academy in Veliko Turnovo, the Panaiot Volov Artillery and Air Defense Academy in Shumen, the Georgi Benkovski Air Force Academy in Dolna Mitropolia, and the

---

[136] See, for instance, Bell, "Bulgaria's Search for Security," 309.
[137] Ratchev's speech at the "NATO: The Choice of the New Generation of Leaders" conference (Sofia, 13 November 1999).
[138] *Monitor* (Sofia), 24 April 2001, cited in RFE/RL II, 5:80 (25 April 2001).
[139] "President Says Hard Part of Army Reform Still Ahead," *Bulgaria Online*, 26 January 2002.

Nikola Vaptsarov Naval Academy in Varna. Prospective reserve officers receive their training at the Hristo Botev Reserve Officer School in Pleven. The G. S. Rakovski Military Academy in Sofia confers master's and doctoral degrees for mid-career officers.[140]

Like other former communist countries Bulgaria also maintained a number of military secondary schools which ensured the supply of prospective officers and NCOs. Owing to the diminished demand for officers several of these institutions have been closed.[141] Developing a cadre of officers capable of working in a multinational environment – with a special emphasis on language training – has been a priority of military education reform. Since 1999 the MOD, with NATO's help, has stressed the training of new faculty for national security studies, established new educational centers for officers, NCOs and civilians, and introduced a new institution, the Command Staff College and Interoperability Center.[142]

Dozens of Bulgarian officers have been trained in the West although, as elsewhere, the opportunity is not always granted to the best prepared candidates. Some of the graduates of foreign academies left the armed forces while others do not always receive positions with responsibilities commensurate with their training. In any case, the higher echelons of the officer corps are still dominated by individuals trained in the Soviet Union. It is difficult to retire them due to their political connections (primarily to the BSP) even though their expertise is "inadequate, antiquated, and might even be dangerous."[143]

Practical training – especially in the air force – has suffered owing to the lack of resources. In Bulgaria, too, the training of pilots has deteriorated mainly because the limited fuel, parts, and resources allow them no more than one-third of the standard annual flying time. Low flight hours may prevent aviators from maintaining their skills let alone to improving them. In addition, several accidents leading to loss of lives and planes have been attributed to lack of experience. In 1996 47 percent of the combat planes were nonoperational and the proportion of

---

[140] See *Bulgarian Armed Forces*, 22–24; and *White Paper*, 74–75.
[141] Ratchev's speech at the NATO conference (Sofia, 13 November 1999).
[142] Interview with Shalamanov (Sofia, 19 November 1999).
[143] Interview with Deputy Defense Minister Shalamanov (Sofia, 18 November 1999).

Bulgaria: Progress After Seven Wasted Years

grounded helicopters was even higher. In the same year, according to CGS Miho Mihov, most pilots could fly only 20 hours.[144]

The prestige of the military profession in Bulgaria has plummeted since the interwar period when it was one of the most sought after careers in the country. In late 1997, for instance, a well-publicized campaign to hire one hundred twenty trainees in a high-technology military field produced only five applicants notwithstanding the high unemployment rates.[145] Although the prospect of eventual NATO membership does make the profession somewhat more appealing, it remains difficult to attract high quality candidates to military academies. In Bulgaria, too, one of the key ambitions of young people is to make money and they know that in the armed forces there is no chance of that. In 1999, for instance, an air force navigator of a MiG-29 earned about $300 per month in contrast to an airline pilot's monthly income of $3,000–5,000.[146]

In 1990, junior officers formed the Georgi Stoikov Rakovski Legion to promote democratization within the armed forces and had written repeatedly to the political leadership expressing their anxiety about the senior officers' symbiotic relationship with the BSP.[147] Both the government and the MOD opposed independent organizations within the armed forces and they outlawed the Legion. Subsequent legislation prohibited trade unions for uniformed military personnel although they are permitted for civilian employees. In 1997 "a group of officers from Sofia" published a letter in newspapers complaining that the MOD was spending large sums on lavish foreign trips and expensive cars for the top brass while at the same time the "hungry, ill-dressed soldiers" were forgotten and wages were not paid.[148]

---

[144] See, for instance, Engelbrekt, "Bulgaria's Evolving Defense Policy," 50; "Bulgarian Air Force May Be Grounded," BTA (Sofia), 17 March 1995; interview with Captain Kirilov (Warsaw, 13 August 1999); and RFE/RL II, 5:164 (29 August 2001).

[145] RFE/RL II, 1:124 (24 September 1997).

[146] Interviews with Kirilov and Abadjiev.

[147] See Duncan M. Perry, "A New Military Lobby," *Report on Eastern Europe*, 1:40 (5 October 1990): 1–4; and Zoltan Barany, "Civil–Military Relations in Comparative Perspective: East-Central and Southeastern Europe," *Political Studies*, 41:3 (December 1993): 607.

[148] OMRI DD II, no. 5 (8 January 1997).

The military, like the state in general, has done a good job in reintegrating ethnic minorities since 1989. In the communist period ethnic Turks and Gypsies were automatically assigned to construction and transportation units so they would not receive weapons training and were prevented from becoming officers. Such discriminatory measures are firmly in the past which is not to say that ethnic minorities show any more enthusiasm for the military career than ethnic Bulgarians. The BAF have also succeeded in opening up the officer and NCO corps to women. Nevertheless, it is hardly surprising that the morale of the officer corps is low given the inadequate budget, poor pay, minimal prestige, and forced reduction of manpower. Owing to the poor labor market officers have little incentive to leave the service and many who do experience difficulties finding employment.[149] At the same time, of all institutions the armed forces have enjoyed the highest level of public confidence in Bulgaria. "The reasons lie in the country's military tradition, the mass character of the army, and the absence, so far, of situations that would put it to a serious test."[150]

Like elsewhere in Eastern Europe the mandatory military service period for Bulgarian men has been repeatedly cut. It was reduced from twenty-four months to eighteen months (for college graduates to one year) in 1990, to twelve months (nine for college graduates) in 1998; and to nine months (six for those with university degrees) in 2000.[151] Alternative service – with a longer time commitment – was introduced in 1991. The obligatory military service is not popular for the same reasons as elsewhere. At the same time, articles in the Bulgarian press frequently complain about the poor health, education, and discipline of conscripts. Finding a sufficient number of draftees may also be a problem in the future considering that Bulgaria, with a current population just below eight million, has one of the lowest birthrates in Europe. During 1992–2000 Bulgaria incurred a net loss of

---

[149] "70% of Former Career Army Servicemen Experience Difficulties," BTA (Sofia), 27 September 2002.

[150] Petûr-Emil Mitev, "Popular Attitudes toward Politics," in Bell, ed., *Bulgaria in Transition*, 55.

[151] See "General Staff Proposes Cut in Military Service," BTA (Sofia), 20 April 1990; "National Assembly Adopts Law on Military Service," BTA (Sofia), 9 August 1990; RFE/RL II, 1:103 (26 August 1997); AP (Sofia), 17 May 2000; and RFE/RL II, 4:96 (18 May 2000).

Bulgaria: Progress After Seven Wasted Years

500,000 citizens while an additional 700,000 people have left the country since 1989.[152]

The State of the Forces

Bulgaria's armed forces are one of the weakest in the region. The communist leader, Todor Zhivkov said that even with Soviet support Bulgaria was incapable of resisting a land attack by NATO spearheaded by the Turkish army.[153] Prime Minister Kostov had joked that his country's contribution to peace in the Balkans was that it could not threaten any of its neighbors; as a Bulgarian commentator summed up eight years of military reform: "God help us if life decides to test our national security system!"[154] Bulgarian military experts openly admit that the combat readiness of the BAF is substandard; according to former CGS Mihov at best 30 percent of army units were combat-capable.[155]

In a February 1999 speech to the army's supreme command officers, Prime Minister Kostov noted that out of a 4.5 million economically active population about 220,000 (i.e., 5 percent) were employed in the security sphere. Even though in per capita GNP terms Bulgaria has been among the last in Europe, it has boasted one of the most bloated military establishments.[156] As noted above, the MOD contends that the size of the armed forces is currently being reduced from 72,000 to 64,000 (the objective is 45,000 military personnel and 5,000 civilians by 2004) although according to other sources the number of active military personnel still stood at nearly 80,000 in 2000.[157] The future aim, of course, is to rely more on professional contract soldiers and less on conscription with the eventual phasing out of the draft altogether but this goal is highly unlikely to be realized by 2006, as planned, in view of Bulgaria's modest resources.

---

[152] *Transitions*, 4:5 (October 1997): 11; and RFE/RL II, 5:71 (11 April 2001).

[153] Bell, "Bulgaria's Search for Security," 306.

[154] Both cited by Bell, "Bulgaria's Search for Security," 309.

[155] See, Slatinski and Caparini, "Bulgarian Security," 30; interviews with Ratchev (Sofia, 18 November 1999) and Todorov (Austin, TX, 27 February 2001); and "President Says Hard Part of Army Reform Still Ahead," *Bulgaria Online*, 26 January 2002.

[156] See *Public Charter for the Reform in the Bulgarian Army, the Military Doctrine, and the Accession of Bulgaria into NATO* (Sofia: K & M Publishing House, 1999), 6–7.

[157] *The Military Balance, 2000–2001* (London: IISS, 2000), 89.

214 *The Future of NATO Expansion*

In GDP percentage terms the Bulgarian defense budget has been quite respectable since 1989; it has exceeded that of the other states in this study (the range has been from the 1990 high of 4.5% to a 1996 low of 2.1%).[158] The reason why the armed forces have been so desperate for funds is because Bulgaria's GDP itself has been very low. In 1999 for instance, Bulgaria's per capita GDP was less than one third of Slovenia's, and less than half of Slovakia's. Bulgaria has been one of the few East European states where the army's fiscal problems approached those of the Russian armed forces. In 1993 an exasperated Defense Minister Valentin Aleksandrov argued that "a country without an army does not need a defense minister. It is absurd to ask the Minister of Defense to cope with a budget of 12.9 billion leva (2.75% of the GDP)."[159] His successor, Dimitûr Pavlov, acknowledged in 1996 that the MOD owed its suppliers more than $10 million, at times had not been able to pay its employees, and would need at least $20 billion over the next ten years to modernize its equipment.[160] Owing to the country's increasing financial stability, defense budgets have steadily increased since 1998 but they are still hopelessly inadequate to support the kind of modernization program Bulgaria needs to pursue. For 2000, the defense budget was officially 2.9% of the GDP, higher than that of any other NATO candidate country, while 3% has been earmarked for 2002.[161]

Bulgarian experts believe that the CFE Treaty has been damaging to Sofia because it exacerbated regional imbalances between Turkey and Greece – that benefit from NATO's assistance in replacing their weapons – on the one hand, and those, like Bulgaria, that are unable to keep pace with them, on the other.[162] Nearly all of the BAF's equipment was acquired before 1989 from the Soviet Union. Its army uses T-55 (1,042) and T-72 (433) tanks in various modifications and its air force relies on MiG-23s (30), MiG-21s (60), and MiG-29s (21).

---

[158] *SIPRI Yearbook,* 2001 data.
[159] Aleksandrov cited in *Bulgarska Armiya,* 22 October 1993; see also Engelbrekt, "Bulgaria's Evolving Defense Policy," 50.
[160] Reuters (Sofia), 3 December 1996; and OMRI DD II, no. 234 (5 December 1996).
[161] RFE/RL II, 4:130 (10 July 2000); and 5:223 (27 November 2001).
[162] See Engelbrekt, "Bulgaria's Evolving Defense Policy," 48; Slatinski and Caparini, "Bulgarian Security," 30; interview with Captain Kirilov; and Tsvetkov, "Bulgarian Security Policy," 28–29.

Bulgaria: Progress After Seven Wasted Years

In 1999 some 60 percent of these airplanes were grounded because of missing spare parts.[163] According to DM Svinarov, in September 2001 only three(!) of the 21 MiG-29s were airworthy as the others lacked spare parts.[164] The Bulgarian navy – with one submarine, one frigate, and seven corvettes – is particularly poorly equipped. All of these weapons are characterized by an inefficient use of fuel which reduces their usefulness for the cash-strapped BAF.[165] Not surprisingly, Bulgaria remains dependent on Russia for the maintenance, especially spare parts, of its arsenal.

In July 2000 DM Noev confirmed reports that Bulgaria planned to purchase an unspecified number of U.S. F-16 fighters in part because of the growing difficulties of maintaining its Soviet-made planes. Prime Minister Kostov quickly overruled him, however, stating that the modernization of the BAF would depend on the economic situation.[166] The new Saxecoburggotski government has repeatedly declared that it would reconsider all previous defense deals. In August 2001 an air force official declared that Bulgaria could not afford to purchase either new or refurbished F-16 fighters. Instead, the government will upgrade 20 MiG-29s using the services of the Russian company, RSK-MiG, that produces the aircraft.[167]

Bulgaria had a relatively vibrant defense industry until 1989, the products of which found buyers among Warsaw Pact members and Third World states. The end of the Cold War wiped out much of this market and some of Sofia's remaining clientele, primarily Libya and Iraq, were blacklisted by the Coordinating Committee for Multilateral Export Controls. In April 2001 the government banned arms exports to nineteen countries, responding to sustained criticism from abroad. By the mid-1990s the Bulgarian defense industry had considerably shrunk losing at least 50 percent of its capacity, a process that has been accompanied by recurrent but rarely successful attempts at privatization and frequent demonstrations by industry workers. On a number of occasions the MOD had to halt the denationalization of defense industrial

---

[163] AP (Sofia), 25 February 1999, citing a report in the Sofia daily *Trud*.
[164] RFE/RL II, 5:175 (14 September 2001).
[165] See *The Bulgarian Armed Forces*, 16–21; and *The Military Balance, 2000–2001*, 89–90.
[166] RFE/RL II, 4:128 (3 July 2000); and "Bulgarian Premier Contradicts Defense Minister," BTA (Sofia), 7 July 2000.
[167] RFE/RL II, 5:164 (29 August 2001); and 6:32 (19 February 2002).

plants owing to large-scale corruption.[168] In 2001 several U.S. arms makers expressed interest in some Bulgarian munitions and small-arms makers but thus far no noteworthy deals have been negotiated.

CONCLUSION

Bulgaria can point to some important achievements twelve years after the end of communism. It was "the least likely to succeed" among the former Warsaw Pact states yet in important ways it has far surpassed its neighbor to the north, Romania. Even though until 1997 Bulgarian governments were unstable, they nonetheless managed to build the foundations of a functioning democracy devoid of authoritarian overtones. This is a tremendous achievement in a country with no democratic traditions and fifty years of servile loyalty to the Soviet Union. Bulgaria has no serious outstanding issues with its neighbors and has conducted a measured yet committed campaign for NATO membership since 1997. The government has supported NATO's activities in the region even at the risk of becoming unpopular. Although the first seven years after the fall of communism were largely lost for economic reform, the UDF government's policies resulted in comparative economic stability, sustained growth, and, in general, giant steps toward the creation of a market economy.

Since 1997 Bulgarian political elites have succeeded in establishing democratic civil–military relations. The armed forces are firmly under the control of civilians even if some problems might remain with the attitudes of the military's "old guard" whose numbers are diminishing due to retirements. At the same time, it is highly questionable whether Bulgaria can be an active contributor to regional security. Sofia, observers suggest, contributes to the security of a volatile region by virtue of its relative stability and by not posing a threat to any of its neighbors might have a point. In all fairness, though, the BAF could scarcely pose a security challenge to anyone as it remains an extremely weak military establishment in need of a great deal of further reform. In the foreseeable future the BAF will not be able to add to NATO's military strength.

---

[168] See, for instance, RFE/RL II, 4:9 (13 January 2000) and 5:27 (8 February 2001); "Military Works Sold Anew," *Standart* (Sofia), 24 August 2001; and "Filchev Investigating Gen. Atanassov," *Standart*, 24 January 2002.

6

Conclusion

I began this book by examining the arguments for and against the first and subsequent rounds of NATO enlargement and then proceeded to scrutinize the four East European states' preparedness for membership in the Alliance. I have two remaining tasks: first, to compare the record of Bulgaria, Romania, Slovakia, and Slovenia with respect to NATO's accession criteria as outlined in Chapter 1; and second, to briefly assess the benefits of potential enlargement scenarios. I strongly support the Alliance's further expansion to Eastern Europe. I am convinced, however, that candidate states should satisfy NATO's conditions of admission *prior* to becoming members.

PREPARATION FOR MEMBERSHIP

In this section I discuss six substantive areas that largely correspond to NATO's accession criteria. I will complement my personal ranking of the four states in each segment with other available ratings.

Democratic Politics and Minority Affairs

When considering the democratic transition and consolidation of Eastern Europe since 1989 it is important to recognize that the Czech Republic, Hungary, Poland, and Slovenia are not the regional norm. Far from it, these are states that have been remarkably successful compared

217

218   *The Future of NATO Expansion*

to the rest of Eastern Europe and particularly when contrasted to the rest of the postcommunist world.[1]

From the perspective of the four countries discussed in this book, Slovenia is clearly head and shoulders above the others with respect to consolidating a democratic polity. I would rank Bulgaria second owing to the fact that even though it had numerous governmental changes that provided ample opportunities for democratic breakdown, there has been no hint of authoritarianism in Bulgarian politics. This is not to say that Bulgaria does not need to battle several major problems, widespread corruption being the most troubling among them. Both of these countries have also pursued relatively enlightened minority policies. This was admittedly easier in Slovenia's case given the comparatively small size of ethnic minorities, the Yugoslav era's legacy of moderate minority policies, and the availability of indispensable resources that allow tangible progress in conflict resolution. Bulgaria did not enjoy any of these advantages but still has managed not only to reverse the shameful persecution of ethnic Turks of the late-communist era, but also to integrate them into political life. Sofia has been much less effective in improving the conditions of its large (nearly 9 percent) Gypsy/Roma minority against whom discrimination does remain a serious social problem.

Democratic consolidation has been far more difficult in Slovakia and Romania. Both states were ruled by populist–authoritarian political elites until 1998 and 1996, respectively, although the fundamentals of democracy – regular elections, multiparty system, etc. – were in place. Since 1998 Slovakia, my third ranked state, has consistently followed a democratic course. It has also improved its minority policies particularly vis-à-vis ethnic Hungarians. Its large Gypsy population, however, continues to suffer from widespread discrimination despite recent governmental efforts. From 1996 to 2000, Romania began the process of consolidating a liberal democracy but the governments

---

[1] On this point, see Valerie Bunce, "The Political Economy of Postsocialism," *Slavic Review*, 58:4 (Winter 1999): 779; and, more broadly, Sorin Antohi and Vladimir Tismaneanu, eds., *Between Past and Future: The Revolutions of 1989 and Their Aftermath* (Budapest: Central European University Press, 2000); and Adrian Karatnycky, Alexander Motyl, and Amanda Schetzer, eds., *Nations in Transit 2001: Civil Society, Democracy, and Markets in East Central Europe and the Newly Independent States* (New York: Freedom House, 2001).

Conclusion

under President Constantinescu at times resorted to ruling by decree and were just as corrupt as their predecessors.

There are four important similarities between Slovakia and Romania. First, both the Dzurinda Administration and the Constantinescu governments used up a great deal of time and energy maintaining their coalitions that could have been spent on more productive endeavors. Second, in both countries the situation of the two large ethnic minorities – the relatively highly mobilized Hungarians and especially that of the increasingly vocal Roma – remain unresolved, although Bratislava has been somewhat more effective in addressing their problems than Bucharest. Third, nationalist-extremist parties are stronger and more popular in these two states than any place else in the former Warsaw Pact, a fact that has troubling implications for the future. Finally, the "old regime" of Ion Iliescu has returned to Romania and Vladimír Mečiar and his party did well in the 2002 Slovak national elections. This is not to say, of course, that after years of being out of power Iliescu and the PSD picked up where they left off. In fact, notwithstanding a host of evident problem areas, Romanian governance has improved since their return to power.

In sum, my ranking is 1. Slovenia, 2. Bulgaria, 3. Slovakia, 4. Romania. It may be instructive to look at some other relevant indices although I do not necessarily agree with all of their data. *The Economist*'s ranking, based on variables like reform progress, stability, and corruption, broadly conforms with my sense of where these states are at the moment regarding their progress toward democratic development.

Looking more squarely at political rights and civil liberties, the Freedom House rankings clearly reflect the "jumps" after more progressive governments took office (see for instance, Romania in 1996–1997 or Slovakia in 1998–1999), though I strongly disagree with the figures suggesting that Bulgarians were better off – even if marginally – under the Videnov – rather than the Kostov-government in terms of their civil liberties.

Market-Driven Economy

No country is more prosperous in contemporary Eastern Europe than Slovenia. This should not suggest, however, that Slovenia has been the most successful in transforming its economy. One might argue that

220   *The Future of NATO Expansion*

TABLE 6.1. *Reform, Stability, and Clean Government*

Country	Reform progress	Stability	Clean government
Bulgaria	3	2	2
Czech Republic	4	3	3
Estonia	5	4	4
Hungary	5	4	4
Latvia	4	3	3
Lithuania	3	2	3
Poland	4	2	3
Romania	1	1	1
Slovakia	3	2	3
Slovenia	5	5	5

Note: Scale: best = 5, worst = 1
Source: "Is Democracy Working?" *The Economist*, 23 June 2001, 46

TABLE 6.2. *Political Rights and Civil Liberties*

Year	Bulgaria	Romania	Slovakia	Slovenia
1989–90	7,7	7,7	–	–
1990–91	3,4	6,5	–	–
1991–92	2,3	5,5	–	2,3
1992–93	2,3	4,4	–	2,2
1993–94	2,2	4,4	3,4	1,2
1994–95	2,2	4,3	2,3	1,2
1995–96	2,2	4,3	2,3	1,2
1996–97	2,3	2,3	2,4	1,2
1997–98	2,3	2,2	2,4	1,2
1998–99	2,3	2,2	2,2	1,2
1999–00	2,3	2,2	1,2	1,2

Note: first digit: political rights, second digit: civil liberties
Scale: best = 1, worst = 7
Source: Freedom House Country Ratings 1999–2000 (www.freedomhouse.org/ratings/index/htm)

the Czech Republic, Estonia, Hungary, Poland, and even Slovakia have done more to restructure their economic systems, but that Slovenia was the one with the head start. The legacies of the past – not just that of communism but even of the more distant past – continue to have a strong effect on the region's economic (as well as political and social) development. Slovenia needs to continue its privatization process and

Conclusion

be more determined to attract foreign investment. I rank Slovakia second in terms of its economic performance. Even under Mečiar, Bratislava pursued economic policies that managed to transform and reorient the Slovak economy. It has become one of the truly vibrant market economies of Eastern Europe.

As for the other two countries, neither of them are functioning market economies at the moment according to the European Union. Having said that, there are substantial differences between them. Bulgaria is considerably farther along the road of economic restructuring than Romania. Since 1997 it has instituted a number of major reforms that have paid dividends – bringing inflation under control via the introduction of a currency board has been perhaps the most important. One can also be confident about the new Bulgarian government's commitment to continued and even accelerated economic reform. Romania's disastrous economic performance has been the result, in large part, of the sustained reluctance of its political elites to embark on substantive market reform. Its economy is by far in the poorest shape among those of the former Warsaw Pact states. At the same time, the first two years of the Nastase government's record does hold out the promise of improved economic performance.

My ranking, then, is 1. Slovenia, 2. Slovakia, 3. Bulgaria, 4. Romania. Recent reports by the Transparency International (TI), the United Nations, and the World Bank provide a more nuanced view of the socio-economic conditions in these states. The World Bank's data profile provides some comparative demographic, social and economic indicators of the four countries. This data suggests the major differences among the four states' varying levels of development. The 2001 Human Development Index of the United Nation's Development Program considers different variables but in the end provides a similar picture. Finally, let us look at corruption, one of the most damaging phenomena that thwarts not only democratic consolidation but also economic development. The Transparency International uses multiple surveys (minimum three per state) to gauge the way people perceive the level of corruption in their countries. TI's 2002 report includes data on 102 countries. Among the former communist states Slovenia received the highest (27th) and Azerbaijan (95th) the lowest ranking. Of the four countries in my study TI ranked Slovenia 27th, Bulgaria 45th–49th, Slovakia 52nd–56th, and Romania 77th–80th, behind Uzbekistan and Russia but slightly ahead of Albania and Kazakhstan.

222 *The Future of NATO Expansion*

TABLE 6.3. *Four-Country Data Profile (2001)*

	Bulgaria	Romania	Slovakia	Slovenia
Population	8,100,000	22,400,000	5,400,000	2,000,000
Surface area in sq km	110,900	238,400	49,010	20,250
Life expectancy at birth	72	70	73	75
Urban population (%)	70	55	58	51
Access to improved water source (% of population)	98	58	84	100
Illiteracy (% of population age 15+)	2	2	n/a	0
GDP (US$ 1991 billions)	10.9	28.8	10.8	12.7
2001	13.6	38.7	20.5	18.8

Source: The World Bank (http://www.worldbank.org/data/countrydata)

TABLE 6.4. *Human Development Index, 2001 (1999 Data, Selected States)*

Rank	Country	GDP per capita (US $)	GDP index	Education index	Human dev. index
1.	Norway	28,433	0.94	0.98	0.939
2.	Australia	24,574	0.92	0.99	0.936
3.	Canada	26,251	0.93	0.98	0.936
6.	U.S.	31,872	0.96	0.98	0.934
14.	U.K.	22,093	0.90	0.99	0.923
29.	**Slovenia**	15,977	0.85	0.94	0.874
33.	Czech Rep.	13,018	0.81	0.89	0.844
35.	**Slovakia**	10,591	0.78	0.91	0.831
36.	Hungary	11,430	0.79	0.93	0.829
38.	Poland	8,450	0.74	0.94	0.828
44.	Estonia	8,355	0.74	0.94	0.812
47.	Lithuania	6,656	0.70	0.93	0.803
50.	Latvia	6,264	0.69	0.93	0.791
55.	Russia	7,473	0.72	0.92	0.775
57.	**Bulgaria**	5,071	0.66	0.90	0.772
58.	**Romania**	6,041	0.68	0.88	0.772
60.	Macedonia	4,651	0.64	0.86	0.766
85.	Albania	3,189	0.58	0.80	0.725

Good Neighborly Relations

None of the four countries face threats to its security by its neighbors, which is not to say that regional relations are entirely harmonious. Slovenia seems to have the fewest problems, although its relations

Conclusion

TABLE 6.5. *The 2002 Corruption Perceptions Index (Selected States)*

Rank	Country	Corruption score	Surveys used	Standard deviation
1	Finland	9.7	8	0.4
7–9	Canada	9.0	10	0.2
10	UK	8.7	11	0.5
16	USA	7.7	12	0.8
27	Slovenia	6.0	9	1.4
29–30	Estonia	5.6	8	0.6
33–35	Hungary	4.9	11	0.5
36–39	Lithuania	4.8	7	1.9
45–49	Bulgaria	4.0	7	0.9
45–49	Poland	4.0	11	1.1
51	Croatia	3.8	4	0.2
52–56	Czech Republic	3.7	10	0.8
52–56	Latvia	3.7	4	0.2
52–56	Slovakia	3.7	8	0.6
68–69	Uzbekistan	2.9	4	1.0
71–76	Russia	2.7	12	1.0
77–80	Romania	2.6	7	0.8
81–84	Albania	2.5	3	0.8
88	Kazakhstan	2.3	4	1.1
93–94	Moldova	2.1	4	0.6
95	Azerbaijan	2.0	4	0.3
102	Bangladesh	1.2	5	0.7

Note: Scale: 10 = least corrupt, 0 = most corrupt
Source: Transparency International: www.gwdg.de/~uwvw/2002Data.html

with Croatia have deteriorated in 2002. The only neighbor with whom Slovakia's contacts have been at times tense is Hungary. Bratislava, like Bucharest, has been unable to resolve its conflict with Budapest with respect to the Hungarian "status law" designed to improve the conditions of Hungarian ethnic minorities abroad. Romania's conflictual relationship with Hungary has often been strained – especially during the presidencies of Ion Iliescu (i.e., prior to 1996 and in 2000–2001) and Bucharest also has found itself at odds with Bulgaria, Moldova, and Ukraine. Bulgaria has been more careful to better its relations with its neighbors. Nonetheless, despite its vastly improved nexus with Turkey, the diplomatic interactions between Sofia and Ankara can still quickly turn delicate. Finally, although Sofia has attempted to devise its policy toward Macedonia with restraint and prudence, one should not

224   *The Future of NATO Expansion*

expect Bulgaria to be unconcerned about the problems of its southwestern neighbor. My ranking – from the perspective of anticipated tranquility – is 1. Slovenia, 2. Bulgaria, 3. Slovakia, 4. Romania.

Campaign and Support for NATO Membership

Of the four countries this book focuses on, two, Slovenia and Romania, have followed unambiguously pro-Western foreign policies throughout the postcommunist era. Slovenia is in the enviable position of having never been dominated by the Soviet Union. The small blemishes on Romanian foreign policy date from 1990–1993 when Iliescu attempted to "reserve his options" and cultivate close relations with Russia. Both Slovakia and Bulgaria put a premium on friendly contacts with Moscow until 1998 and 1996, respectively. Nonetheless, the Russophilia of these states in this period should not be exaggerated; more than anything, it reflected a pragmatic view of Moscow as a source of raw materials (especially energy) and spare parts for Russian/Soviet-made equipment.

The campaigns for NATO membership have been elite-driven because the issue is simply not a priority for most people in the region. Slovenia's pro-NATO campaign has been by far the most guarded of the four, perhaps reflective of the expectation that Ljubljana will do well even without membership in the Alliance. Slovak and Bulgarian elites, while a little more vehement, still tend to observe the rules of diplomacy. Romania's campaign for NATO, often described as "hysterical" and "obsequious," has gone as far as to predict regional conflicts if it was not to be included in the first round. In my view, the more desperate political elites are for success of any sort, the less judicious they are likely to be in their lobbying for membership. My ranking in terms of the sophistication of NATO campaigns: 1. Slovenia, 2. Slovakia, 3. Bulgaria, 4. Romania.

I sought to give some sense of public support for NATO membership in the four countries – citing public opinion polls – and to refresh the reader's memory I reproduce them here, side by side. One might infer from the data in Table 6.6 that the less successful a country has been in the postcommunist transition processes the more it needs NATO and thus, the more supportive its population is of joining the Alliance. Particularly conspicuous is the lack of Slovene and Slovak

Conclusion

TABLE 6.6. *Popular Support for NATO Membership (%)*

	1996	1997	1998	1999	2000	2001	2002
Bulgaria			60	45–50	60		50 (July)
Romania	97	90–95		60–65	92		88 (Oct.)
Slovakia	35	52	58	30		41–52	52 (Oct.)
Slovenia	66	56–62		56	~60		39 (June)

Source: Reproduced from Chapters 2–5

enthusiasm for NATO, which probably results from perceptions that they do not need the Alliance, their preference for neutrality, and lingering misconceptions about NATO. Table 6.6 also clearly illustrates how unpopular NATO's 1999 war against Yugoslavia was among the four aspiring members. Even if one factors in the possible deficiencies of survey methods, the ranking that emerges from this picture depicting public support for NATO membership is pretty clear: 1. Romania, 2. Bulgaria, 3. Slovakia, 4. Slovenia.

Democratic Control of the Military

All four countries have made significant progress toward the creation of balanced and substantive civilian supervision over the armed forces. The armies have been departified and, for the most part, depoliticized. On paper, at least, the armed forces are outside of politics, defense expenditures are determined by the legislature, and no one person – whether president or chief of the general staff – has full control over the military. Problems do remain, however. In Slovakia, for instance, HZDS politicians repeatedly tried to influence the officer corps and tensions persist between the Minster of Defense and the General Staff. Since 1998 however, Slovak civil–military relations have become far more democratic, although personnel policies have yet to be fully reformed. Civilianizing the MOD may have actually gone too far in Slovenia where some ambiguities in national security legislation need to be sorted out.

Thirteen years after the revolution, Romanian elites still approach the issue of the army leadership's responsibility for the bloodshed in 1989 as a partisan matter. Politicians of varying hues have time and again utilized military units in domestic contingencies although, to be sure, the army has been a most reluctant participant. The open veneration for the country's wartime leader Antonescu by high-ranking officers is, at the very least, deeply troubling. Romanian civil–military relations are – according to one of the most knowledgeable experts on the issue writing in early 2001 – in crisis.[2] Bulgaria's relatively highly developed democracy is also reflected in its comparatively well functioning civil–military relations. The most important problem in Sofia has been the lingering influence of communist-era generals and the long-standing, though now abating, feud between the Ministry of Defense and the General Staff.

The pool of independent defense experts essential for robust civilian control is missing in all of these states but Slovenia, although Romania has made far more of an effort in this regard than Bulgaria or Slovakia. Corruption is also a profound problem in the defense sectors of Bulgaria and, to a lesser extent, Romania and Slovakia. With respect to the democratization of civil–military relations, my ranking of the four countries is 1. Slovenia, 2. Slovakia, 3. Bulgaria, 4. Romania.

Military Reform and Expenditure

Although politicians of the candidate countries often state that they are prepared for membership, they have nothing to lose by saying so. As far as military reforms are concerned, none of them were ready by the time of the Prague Summit or will be ready in the near future, something that few politicians, like former Bulgarian President Stoyanov, are willing to openly concede. This is not to say, of course, that little has been done. Slovakia and Slovenia both built armed forces virtually from scratch. Most of the four states to a large extent succeeded in restructuring their armies, establishing a new, NATO-compatible institutional framework for the military establishment, redeploying some of their forces, and revamping military training and education.

All of them need to do more, however, in the areas of force reduction, language training, weapons procurement, interoperability, and standardization. They must take their participation in the Planning and Review Process more seriously and their Annual National Plan reports

---

[2] Larry Watts, "The Crisis in Romanian Civil–Military Relations," *Problems of Post-Communism*, 48:4 (July–August 2001): 14–26.

Conclusion

should be more reflective of achievements than of intentions. The combat readiness of Slovak forces is particularly low and the Bratislava MOD must begin to include joint-service exercises in its training program. The Slovene Army ought to be further restructured and its defense planning needs to be more in line with NATO principles. Romanian military reforms have gone farther than those of the other three states, but financial woes have affected reform implementation more adversely than elsewhere. In particular, further progress is necessary in force restructuring and the formulation of new legislation pertaining to NATO integration.

Bulgaria has accomplished a great deal in reforming its defense sector only when considering how little it had done before 1997. While in Romania military elites have led defense reform efforts and were hindered by political elites, in Bulgaria the opposite has been the case: the Ministry of Foreign Affairs in Sofia has been pushing reform at times in spite of the military leadership. Of the four states Bulgaria is the one with the longest way to go, especially in terms of force reduction, logistics, and training. Put simply, there is no area of defense reform in which it could not use significant improvement. In view of their progress in military reform, my ranking of the four countries is 1. Romania, 2. Slovakia, 3. Slovenia, 4. Bulgaria.

Selected data from the 2000–2001 issue of *The Military Balance*, an annual publication of the London-based International Institute for Strategic Studies, provides a sense of the current status of these armed forces.

The military reforms these states need to implement constitute a heavy financial burden and two of these countries, Bulgaria and Romania, are among the poorest states in Europe. Even though they may spend a sizable proportion of their GNPs on the armed forces, they may not be making tangible progress given the enormous gap between their modest GNPs and the magnitude of requisite resources. Data provided by the Stockholm International Peace Research Institute (SIPRI) show that the four states in this study had, on average, spent at least as large a share of their GDP on defense as the three countries that were invited by NATO in 1997.

The figures in Table 6.8 reveal that all of the four states in my study outspent Hungary in terms of the share of their GDP they devoted to military outlays. Of the four countries, Bulgaria has consistently spent

TABLE 6.7. *Selected Data on Military Personnel and Armaments (2000)*

	Bulgaria	Romania	Slovakia	Slovenia
Total Population	8,231,000	22,500,000	5,400,000	2,020,000
Active armed forces	79,760	207,000	38,600	9,000
Reserves	303,000	470,000	20,000	61,000
Army	42,400	106,000	23,800	9,000
tanks	1,475	1,253	275	46
artillery (ttl)	1,750	1,276	383	36
Navy	5,260	20,800	–	100
submarines	1	1	–	–
frigates	1	6	–	–
Air Force	18,300	43,500	11,500	120
combat aircraft	181	323	84	13
attack helis	43	16	19	8
flying hours	30–40	40	45	–

Source: The Military Balance, 2000–2001 (London: IISS, 2000)

the largest proportion of its GDP on defense, notwithstanding its try-ing budgetary situation. The data also reflect the changing fortunes of the Bulgarian economy as the GDP-share figures bottomed out in 1996. The numbers on Romania illustrate its economic crisis: in 2000 Bucharest spent a little more than one-third the total spent on defense a decade earlier. The two more prosperous states have devoted a smaller and decreasing share of their resources to military purposes. This is especially clear in the Slovene case. Finally, it is noteworthy that of the three new NATO members, only Poland has consistently satisfied the Alliance's suggested military expenditure of 2 percent. Both the Czech Republic and Hungary have steadily increased their defense outlays (both as a share of the GNP and in real terms) since being invited to NATO in 1997. Still, NATO leaders cannot be too pleased about the moderate amount of funds Hungary continues to devote to its defense. In terms of military expenditure, then, my ranking of the four states is 1. Bulgaria, 2. Romania, 3. Slovakia, 4. Slovenia.

While their lack of military preparedness for membership is impos-sible to deny, East European politicians – like Slovak Foreign Minister Eduard Kukan – often respond to criticism by asserting that NATO expansion is, in the final analysis, simply a political decision. There may be more to these assertions than just excuses. As I noted earlier, none of the three states that became members of the Alliance in 1999

TABLE 6.8. *Military Expenditure by Selected East European States (in U.S. $ at constant 1998 prices and exchange rates and as a proportion of Gross Domestic Product)*

	1991	1992	1993	1994	1995	1996	1997	1998	1999	2000	2001
Bulgaria											
million US$	820	618	467	401	395	323	310	330	377	378	361
GDP share %	3.3	3.2	2.8	2.7	2.6	2.4	2.7	2.7	3	3	–
Czech Republic											
million US$	–	–	1148	1077	1015	998	946	1040	1129	1144	1244
GDP share %	–	–	2.3	2.1	1.8	1.7	1.6	1.8	2.0	2.0	–
Hungary											
million US$	964	889	800	678	598	541	515	618	707	731	781
GDP share %	2.2	2.1	1.9	1.6	1.4	1.2	1.1	1.3	1.5	1.5	–
Poland											
million US$	2754	2717	3011	2905	2923	3075	3239	3363	3283	3223	3484
GDP share %	2.3	2.3	2.6	2.3	2.1	2.1	2.1	2.1	2.0	1.9	–
Romania											
million US$	1755	1382	834	981	967	940	1037	827	797	904	888
GDP share %	3.6	3.3	2.1	2.4	2.1	1.9	2.3	2.0	1.9	2.1	–
Slovakia											
million US$	–	–	348	359	462	431	421	398	347	361	394
GDP share %	–	–	2.1	2.1	2.5	2.2	2.0	1.9	1.7	1.8	–
Slovenia											
million US$	–	318	275	270	310	318	303	301	282	252	311
GDP share %	–	2.2	1.8	1.7	1.8	1.7	1.6	1.5	1.4	1.2	–

Source: SIPRI Military Expenditure Database, 2002 (http://first.sipri.org/non_first/result)

The Future of NATO Expansion

TABLE 6.9. *Ranking the Four States*

	Bulgaria	Romania	Slovakia	Slovenia
Democracy/minorities	2	4	3	1
Market economy	3	4	2	1
Good neighbors	2	4	3	1
Campaign for NATO	3	4	2	1
Support for NATO membership	2	1	4	3
Civil-military relations	3	4	2	1
Progress in milititary Reform	4	1	2	3
Defense expenditures	1	2	3	4
Overall score	20	24	21	15

were even close to satisfying the military-related criteria of NATO, and the four newly invited countries surveyed in this study are no different. With respect to their overall preparedness, taking into consideration all the criteria I reviewed above, the ranking is 1. Slovenia, 2. Slovakia, 3. Bulgaria, and 4. Romania. Needless to say, the "overall score" is little more than an exercise in arithmetic as the variables are not comparable – obviously a stable democratic government is infinitely more important than a refined NATO campaign – and assigning precise weights to them would be virtually impossible. Nonetheless, I am confident about the individual-variable rankings and I contend that at present Slovenia is a better candidate for NATO than Slovakia, Slovakia is to be preferred to Bulgaria (despite its minimally lower score in my ranking and owing in part to its position that would allow a contiguous NATO in East-Central Europe), and Bulgaria is considerably ahead of Romania. But, to repeat, it is equally clear that none of them currently satisfy the Alliance's accession criteria.

THE SECOND WAVE OF ENLARGEMENT

As I noted in the Introduction, I doubted the wisdom of the first round of NATO enlargement. Nonetheless, once it did take place, I became a supporter of the Alliance's continued expansion. My arguments are, as noted earlier, that (1) given NATO's promises of further enlargement it has a moral obligation to do so; (2) perpetuating the

Conclusion

current geostrategic situation might create irreversible divisions between East-Central European and Balkan states and, in effect, isolate the latter from Europe; (3) including the four states of my study in NATO would enhance its geostrategic posture, increase its ability to intervene in future Balkan contingencies, and, in all likelihood, promote stability in the region.

At the same time, I believe that as long as aspiring states do not fulfill all of NATO's admission criteria, the Alliance should not have extended invitations to them.[3] Of the nine MAP countries, it would be hard to anticipate that Albania and Macedonia would fulfill NATO's criteria in the foreseeable future. Both countries, but especially Macedonia, face strong challenges to their stability and security, to say nothing of their deficiencies in terms of democratic consolidation and minority policies, economic reform, and other accession criteria. It is not unreasonable to assume that their boundaries will shift in the not-too-distant future. (Many in the region are convinced that Kosovo and northwestern Macedonia, both heavily dominated by ethnic Albanians, will be incorporated into a Greater Albania.)

For a number of reasons this book does not directly deal with the Baltic states all of which also received invitations from the Alliance in October 2002.[4] Nonetheless, I do believe that Estonia, Latvia, and Lithuania have a much stronger claim for membership than Albania and Macedonia partly because they are considerably closer to satisfying membership criteria. Moreover, if any MAP states have faced a long-standing external threat to their security, it is surely the Baltic nations. Not only were they subjugated, devastated, militarily occupied, and

---

[3] See Zoltan Barany, "NATO Expansion, Round Two: Making Matters Worse," *Security Studies*, 11:3 (Spring 2002): 123–157.

[4] On the Baltic states and NATO accession see Peter van Ham, ed., *The Baltic States: Security and Defence after Independence* (Paris: Western European Union, 1995); Olaf F. Knudsen, *Bound To Fail? Regional Security Co-operation in the Baltic Sea Area and Northeast Asia* (Oslo: NUPI, 1996); Ronald D. Asmus and Robert C. Nurick, "NATO Enlargement and the Baltic States," *Survival*, 38:2 (Summer 1996): 121–142; Stephen J. Blank, *NATO Enlargement and the Baltic States: What Can the Great Powers Do?* (Carlisle, PA: U.S. Army War College/SSI, 1997); Žaneta Ozoliņa, "The Regional Dimension in Latvian Security Policy," *Harmonie Paper 8* (Centre of European Security Studies, University of Groningen, August 1999); Yaroslav Bilinsky, *Endgame in NATO's Enlargement: The Baltic States and Ukraine* (Westport, CT: Praeger, 1999); and Jeffrey Tayler, "The Next Threat to NATO," *The Atlantic Monthly*, February 2002, 69–72.

incorporated by the Soviet Union for fifty years but, absurdly, Russian authorities still maintain that the they "voluntarily" joined the USSR in 1941. As Mark Kramer notes, "the whitewashing of Soviet rule in the Baltics is symptomatic ... of Russia's broader failure to distance itself from the Soviet past."[5] For these reasons alone one might sensibly regard these three states, exposed and vulnerable as they are to Russia, as special cases that may merit extraordinary consideration from NATO leaders. My exclusion of the Baltic states in the brief enlargement scenarios below should in no way be taken as an indication that I consider them less worthy than the four states this study has focused on.

I discuss the alternative enlargement scenarios, projected prior to the 2002 NATO Summit, in the order of my preferences. For the sake of avoiding redundancies, I will limit myself to the potential benefits of each scenario, given that I have already examined the individual states' strengths and deficiencies.

1. Invite No One

NATO's "open door" policy should not signify automatic advance to membership. I do not see any compelling reason to bestow full NATO membership on the four states in this study as long as they fail to comply with conditions for membership. The pressure exerted by some of these governments is indicative only of their desperation to accomplish something of import in the eyes of their supporters. The Alliance should not fall for this ploy. Rather, NATO should declare that it will extend membership to them only after they satisfied all membership criteria. In the meantime, Brussels could provide them with further assistance and use the extra time to integrate the three East-Central European members which themselves have yet to satisfy all the conditions of accession. One might argue that it would be unfair to expect the recently invited states to fulfill membership criteria given that the three states that joined NATO in 1999 did not satisfy them either. Still, two wrongs do not make a right and the Alliance should learn from its mistake of prematurely admitting new members.

---

[5] See Mark Kramer, "Why Is Russia Still Peddling This Old Soviet Lie?" *Washington Post*, 10 June 2001. See also Benjamin Smith, "NATO Weighs Baltic Expansion In Face of Russian Opposition," *Wall Street Journal*, 31 May 2001.

Conclusion

2. Slovenia

Extending NATO membership to Slovenia has several arguments recommending it. First, it is clearly the best prepared for membership. Second, given the modest size of both the country and its military establishment and its relative prosperity, it will be comparatively easy to integrate into the Alliance. Third, granting membership to Slovenia would demonstrate to other aspirants that NATO is not just paying lip service to its further expansion. Fourth, there would be no opposition to including Slovenia from Russia. Finally, Slovenia would bridge the geographical gap between Italy and Hungary and allow NATO to encompass a contiguous landmass once again. For the most part though, membership to Slovenia would be a mostly symbolic gesture as Ljubljana could hardly make any direct contribution to NATO capabilities.[6]

3. Slovenia and Slovakia

With the addition of these two states NATO would cover all of East-Central Europe with the exception of the Baltic states and Croatia. Slovakia also promises to be a low-maintenance addition from NATO's perspective, at least relative to the other new invitees. It may not contribute much to either regional security or to NATO capabilities, but at least it is unlikely to be a source of major conflicts.

4. Slovenia, Slovakia and Bulgaria with or without Romania

In my view, the only contributions that either of the two latter states could make in the foreseeable future are their enthusiasm for membership and providing forward-basing options for the Alliance's operations in the Balkans and farther to the east. The second advantage is negated, however, by the fact that both countries voluntarily offered the use of their air space (and, in Bulgaria's case, roads and railway lines) to NATO in the past. On the positive side, too, is the prospect that while Moscow is unlikely to be pleased about the NATO accession of these states (particularly that of Bulgaria), it is also not expected

---

[6] See Roland Dannreuther, "Escaping the Enlargement Trap in NATO-Russia Relations," *Survival*, 41:4 (Winter 1999–2000): 159.

234   *The Future of NATO Expansion*

to show much opposition. Moreover, Romania's inclusion would appease France and cancel its potential opposition to Slovene/Slovak membership.

The leaders of the newly invited countries may figure that if only they could get a membership card from Brussels, their problems would be taken care of. Their incessant lobbying is perfectly understandable but is hardly a sufficient reason to admit them quickly. I strongly disagree with Nicholas Burns who recently said that "All democratic countries have the right to become NATO members."[7] The first round of enlargement has been militarily unsuccessful precisely because the Alliance invited states that were prepared only in political terms. It is clear that NATO's strength has been diluted by its inclusion of Poland, Hungary, and the Czech Republic and, as Jeffrey Simon and Eugene Rumer have noted, the second round of enlargement is unlikely to reverse this trend.[8]

Though the Alliance's invitations to membership are far more subjective than those of the European Union, NATO should not further dilute itself by including states that, at present, do not belong to it. Politicians and military leaders of the four countries in this study openly admit that they will not be able to reform their armed forces according the NATO guidelines for years to come; according to the unusually candid former Slovak defense minister, Jozef Stank, not until 2015.[9] As the lessons of the first wave of expansion show, once states become de facto members of the Alliance, Brussels loses its leverage to compel them to implement promised reforms because NATO does not have an expulsion mechanism. (Incidentally, it has been widely surmised that Hungary would have already been expelled if the Alliance did have such a provision.[10]) What NATO should do is to continue to make all reasonable efforts to assist candidate countries in fulfilling membership conditions. Accepting states that will be assets rather than liabilities and that will be net contributors rather than consumers of

---

[7] "Nicholas Burns: Romania Is a Very Serious Candidate for NATO Membership," *Mediafax* (Bucharest), 21 February 2002.

[8] Eugene Rumer and Jeffrey Simon, "Russia Should Have a Seat at the Table," *Los Angeles Times*, 23 December 2001.

[9] "Army Reshape To Last Until 2015," *Slovak Spectator*, 1–7 October 2001.

[10] Celeste Wallander, "NATO's Price," *Foreign Affairs*, 81:6 (November–December 2002): 5.

Conclusion

security *at the time of accession* will be more rewarding for NATO, its new members, and the cause of European security. NATO has every reason to wait until that time comes.

THE FUTURE OF NATO EXPANSION

NATO is probably the most successful military alliance in the modern age. It brought together and united sixteen nations to contain and defeat European communism. Since that objective has been realized, however, the Alliance has faced a serious existential crisis. Responding to the nagging questions of its organizational identity and purpose can only temporarily be put off by its belated albeit constructive engagement in the Balkans. The Alliance's gradual expansion to integrate increasingly less qualified members is hardly the answer. And yet, that is precisely the direction Brussels has been moving.

Albania, Macedonia, and Croatia – the last became an aspirant member only after the demise of its authoritarian ruler, Franjo Tudjman, in December 1999 – all received encouraging notices at the November 2002 Prague Summit. NATO Secretary-General Robertson has said that it would probably take another five years before Ukraine, a country with enormous political and economic problems to say nothing of its habitual human rights violations, could join the Alliance.[11] Apparently Kyiv's accession already enjoys the active support of six NATO members (including the United States).[12] In Prague Alliance diplomats went out of their way to develop closer ties with Central Asian states – NATO's "new frontier," according to one of them – even though several of them are ruled by regimes that would be unfavorably compared to that of Leonid Brezhnev.[13] These governments have assisted the U.S.-led war in Afghanistan and their strategic location has made them valuable in the "war on terror."

It is a truism that the September 2001 terrorist attacks have changed the world. The fundamental reason for the drastically improved relations between Washington and Moscow or for NATO's "big bang"

---

[11] See "Ukraine Reiterates Bid To Join NATO," UPI (Kyiv), 9 July 2002; and RFE/RL II, 6:127 (10 July 2002).

[12] *Gazèta Wyborcza* (Warsaw), 9 July 2002, cited in RFE/RL II, 6:127 (10 July 2002).

[13] See Paul Ames, "NATO Seeks Ties With Central Asia," AP (Prague), 22 November 2002.

236   *The Future of NATO Expansion*

expansion is not that Vladimir Putin's government suddenly embraced meaningful democracy or that aspiring states quickly satisfied membership criteria but, quite simply, 9/11. The United States and the rest of the western world is facing a new challenge in which American leadership is essential. Our domination of NATO is not unreasonable given that the amount the United States spends on its armed forces annually (about $290 billion in 2002) is more than twice that of the combined military outlays of our European allies ($116 billion). At the same time, Washington has exploited its might by pursuing an increasingly unilateralist foreign policy in which substantive debate is viewed with suspicion.

In the mid-1990s, prior to the first round of enlargement, a great deal of discussion and consultation took place on and between both sides of the Atlantic centering on the wisdom of expansion and the merits and demerits of individual applicants. Such debates have been deafeningly absent the second time around. When President Bush was asked by a Radio Free Europe reporter in Prague what exactly would be the military contribution of the seven new invitees, the President's response was

"First of all, I answer it militarily. I do believe that they can contribute something really important, and that is, they can contribute their love for freedom. These are countries which have lived in totalitarian states. They haven't been free. And now they love freedom, just like America loves freedom."[14]

East Europeans who expended their energy and resources to improve their countries' chances for receiving the coveted invitation from Brussels might suppose that their efforts were wasted. After all, they, like most human beings, have always loved freedom even if they were not fortunate enough to enjoy it. If their "love for freedom" was what counted, they ought to have been invited as founding members in 1949.

Is NATO as a military alliance really dead, as Charles Krauthammer announced after the Prague Summit in a *Washington Post* column? "Afghanistan made clear," Krauthammer argued, "that NATO has no

---

[14] Jeffrey Donovan, "NATO: Transcript of RFE/RL's Exclusive Interview With U.S. President Bush," RFE/RL (Prague, 19 November 2002) available at http://www.rferl.org/nca/features/2002/11/19112002091308.asp.

Conclusion

serious military role to play in any serious conflict."[15] With countries like Bulgaria and Romania poised for full membership in 2004, the question "What is NATO for?" requires a serious response.

If the legislatures of the nineteen member states will ratify the second wave of expansion, NATO will be an Alliance of twenty-six members with decreasing capabilities and declining decision-making powers. It will probably drift into irrelevance and become just another ineffectual and overbureaucratized society like the Organization for Security and Cooperation in Europe except with guns. As Sean Kay surmised, Moscow might well have lifted its objections to NATO's enlargement because Putin and his advisors sensed that it was destined to become precisely "the sort of toothless political institution that Russia hoped for."[16]

It is up to the lawmakers to decide whether NATO is worth saving. If they think it is, they should insist on defining its focus, amending the Washington Treaty by the introduction of an expulsion mechanism, and vote on enlargement based on the actual preparations of the invitees according to the criteria set by the Alliance itself.

[15] Charles Krauthammer, "The Bold Road to NATO Expansion," *Washington Post*, 22 November 2002.
[16] Sean Kay, "Heading Nowhere?" *International Herald Tribune*, 10 May 2002.

References

Newspaper articles are not included; all references are in the footnotes.

Alexiev, Alexander. "Party-Military Relations in Eastern Europe: The Case of Romania," in Roman Kolkowicz and Andrzej Korbonski, eds., *Soldiers, Peasants, and Bureaucrats: Civil-Military Relations in Communist and Modernizing Societies* (London: Allen & Unwin, 1982), 199–231.

American Jewish Committee. *The American Jewish Yearbook* (New York: AJC, 1999).

Andrejevich, Milan. "Slovenia: Politics and the Economy in the Year One," *RFE/RL Research Report*, 1:36 (11 September 1992): 15–23.

Antohi, Sorin, and Vladimir Tismaneanu, eds., *Between Past and Future: The Revolutions of 1989 and Their Aftermath* (Budapest: Central European University Press, 2000).

Antonenko, Oksana. "Russia, NATO, and European Security after Kosovo," *Survival*, 41:4 (Winter 1999–2000): 124–144.

Antonietti, Patrick. "Civil-Military Relations in Slovakia," M.A. Thesis, Department of Politics, Comenius University (Bratislava, 1997).

Arnejčič, Beno. "National Value Orientation of Slovenian Citizens and Their Trust in the Armed Forces," in Erich Reiter, ed., *Österreichisches Jarhbuch Internationale Sicherheitspolitik* (Vienna, 1997), 333–344.

   "Some Aspects of the Accountability of the Slovenian Minister of Defense and Head of the General Staff of the Slovenian Defense Forces," paper presented at the "Democratic Civil-Military Relations Conference" (Ottawa, 26 March 1999).

Asmus, Ronald D., Richard L. Kugler, and F. Stephen Larrabee. "What Will NATO Enlargement Cost?" *Survival*, 38:3 (Autumn 1996): 5–26.

Asmus, Ronald D., and Robert C. Nurick. "NATO Enlargement and the Baltic States," *Survival*, 38:2 (Summer 1996): 121–142.

Assenova, Margarita. "Bulgaria: Driving to the West," in Daniel N. Nelson and Ustina Markus, eds., *Central and East European Security Yearbook, 2002* (Dulles, VA: Brassey's, 2002), 271–297.

Babiuc, Victor. "Reform and the Romanian Armed Forces: Modernization and Interoperability," in Kurt W. Treptow and Mihail E. Ionescu, eds., *Romania and Euro-Atlantic Integration* (Iasi: Center for Romanian Studies, 1999), 120–132.

Bacon, Walter M. Jr. "Romanian Civil-Military Relations after 1989," unpublished manuscript, 1996.

Baer, Josette. "Boxing and Politics in Slovakia: 'Meciarism' – Roots, Theory, Practice," *Democratization*, 8:2 (Summer 2001): 97–116.

Balázs, Imre-József, Andor Horváth, and Lajos Kántor, eds., *Alternatives for Romania* (Cluj: Komp-Press, 1999).

Barany, Zoltan. "Romania and the Warsaw Pact," paper delivered at the "U.S. Air Force Intelligence Conference on Soviet Affairs" (Arlington, VA, 19–22 October 1988).

Soldiers and Politics in Eastern Europe, 1945–90 (New York: St. Martin's, 1993).

"Civil-Military Relations in Comparative Perspective: East-Central and Southeastern Europe," *Political Studies*, 41:3 (December 1993): 594–610.

"Regional Security: Visegrad Four Contemplate Separate Paths," *Transition*, 1:14 (11 August 1995): 56–60.

"Democratic Consolidation and the Military: The East European Experience," *Comparative Politics*, 30:1 (October 1997): 21–44.

"Hungary: Appraising a New NATO Member," *Clausewitz-Studien*, 1 (1999): 1–31.

"Controlling the [Russian] Military: A Partial Success," *Journal of Democracy*, 10:2 (April 1999): 54–67.

"Bulgaria's Royal Elections," *Journal of Democracy*, 13:2 (April 2002): 141–155.

"NATO Expansion, Round Two: Making Matters Worse," *Security Studies*, 11:3 (Spring 2002): 123–157.

Bebler, Anton. "The Armed Conflicts on the Balkans, 1990–1993," *Balkan Forum*, 1:4 (September 1993): 25–48.

"Civil-Military Relations in Slovenia," in Constantine P. Danopoulos and Daniel Zirker, eds., *Civil-Military Relations in the Soviet and Yugoslav Successor States* (Boulder: Westview Press, 1996), 195–212.

"A Double Standard for NATO," *Transitions*, 4:2 (July 1997): 75–79.

"Civil-Military Relations in Slovenia: Temporary Reduction to Irrelevance?" (Ljubljana, 1997), unpublished ms.

"NATO's Enlargement and Slovenia," (Ljubljana, 1999), unpublished ms.

References

Behar, Nansen. "Bulgarian Perception of European Cooperation on Conflict Prevention," *Balkan Forum*, 5:1 (March 1997): 87–94.

Beliakov, N. N., and A. Iu. Moiseev. *Rasshierenie NATO na vostok: k miru ili voine?* (Moscow: Klub "Realisty," 1998).

Bell, John D. "Democratization and Political Participation in 'Postcommunist' Bulgaria," in Karen Dawisha and Bruce Parrott, eds., *Politics, Power, and the Struggle for Democracy in South-East Europe* (New York: Cambridge University Press, 1997), 353–402.

"Bulgaria's Search for Security," in John D. Bell, ed., *Bulgaria in Transition: Politics, Economics, Society, and Culture After Communism* (Boulder, CO: Westview Press, 1998), 305–323.

"The Radical Right in Bulgaria," in Sabrina P. Ramet, ed., *The Radical Right in Central and Eastern Europe since 1989* (University Park: Pennsylvania State University Press, 1999), 233–254.

Bilčík, Vladimír, Martin Bruncko, Alexander Duleba, Pavol Lukáč, and Ivo Samson. "Slovakia's Foreign and Defense Policy," in G. Mesežnikov, M. Kollar, and T. Nicholson, eds., *Slovakia 2001: A Global Report on the State of Society* (Bratislava: Institute for Public Affairs, 2001), 233–296.

Bilinsky, Yaroslav. *Endgame in NATO's Enlargement: The Baltic States and Ukraine* (Westport, CT: Praeger, 1999).

Black, J. L. *Russia Faces NATO Expansion: Bearing Gifts or Bearing Arms?* (Lanham, MD: Rowman & Littlefield, 2000).

Blank, Stephen J. *NATO Enlargement and the Baltic States: What Can the Great Powers Do?* (Carlisle, PA: U.S. Army War College, Strategic Studies Institute, 1997).

"Overview," in Stephen J. Blank, ed., *From Madrid to Brussels: Perspectives on NATO Enlargement* (Carlisle, PA: U.S. Army War College, Strategic Studies Institute, 1997), vii–xii.

"Rhetoric and Reality in NATO Enlargement," in Stephen J. Blank, ed., *European Security and NATO Enlargement: A View from Central Europe* (Carlisle, PA: U.S. Army War College, Strategic Studies Institute, 1998), 5–48.

Threats to Russian Security: The View from Moscow (Carlisle, PA: U.S. Army War College, July 2000).

Brown, Michael E. "The Flawed Logic of NATO Expansion," *Survival*, 37:1 (Spring 1995): 34–52.

"Minimalist NATO: A Wise Alliance Knows When to Retrench," *Foreign Affairs*, 78:3 (May–June 1999): 204–218.

Brzezinski, Zbigniew. "NATO: The Dilemmas of Expansion," *The National Interest*, no. 53 (Fall 1998): 13–18.

Bučar, Bojko. "The International Recognition of Slovenia," in Danica Fink-Hafner and John R. Robbins, eds., *Making a New Nation: The Formation of Slovenia* (Brookfield, VT: Dartmouth, 1997), 31–45.

242   References

Bugajski, Janusz. "Key Elements of Romania's Security Strategy," in Kurt W. Treptow and Mihail E. Ionescu, eds., *Romania and Euro-Atlantic Integration* (Iasi: Center for Romanian Studies, 1999), 47–64.

Bukovetski, Mikhail F. "Transfrontier Cooperation among Countries of Central Europe: The Case of the Carpathian Euroregion," in Vasil Hudák, ed., *Building a New Europe: Transfrontier Cooperation in Central Europe* (Prague: Institute for EastWest Studies, 1996).

Bulgaria, Government. *Membership Action Plan* (Sofia: Government of Bulgaria, 1999).

Public Charter for the Reform in the Bulgarian Army, the Military Doctrine, and the Accession of Bulgaria into NATO (Sofia: K & M Publishing House, 1999).

Bulgaria, Ministry of Defense. *Bulgarian Armed Forces* (Sofia: MOD, 1999).

White Paper on the Defence and Armed Forces of the Republic of Bulgaria (Sofia: MOD, 2001).

Bunce, Valerie. "Regional Cooperation and European Integration: The Visegrad Group," in Peter Katzenstein, ed., *Mitteleuropa: Between Europe and Germany* (Providence, RI: Berghahn Books, 1998), 240–284.

Subversive Institutions: The Design and the Destruction of Socialism and the State (New York: Cambridge University Press, 1999).

"The Political Economy of Postsocialism," *Slavic Review*, 58:4 (Winter 1999): 756–793.

Bútora, Martin, and Zora Bútorová. "Slovakia After the Split," *Journal of Democracy*, 4:2 (April 1993): 71–83.

Bútora, Martin, and František Šebej, eds. *Slovensko v Šedej Zóne? Rozširovanie NATO, zlyhania a perspektívy Slovenska* (Bratislava: Institute for Public Affairs, 1998).

Bútorová, Zora. "Public Reactions to Domestic Political Issues," in Zora Bútorová, ed., *Democracy and Discontent in Slovakia: A Public Opinion Profile of a Country in Transition* (Bratislava: Institute for Public Affairs, 1998), 111–133.

Bútorová, Zora, and Martin Bútora. "Political Parties, Value Orientations, and Slovakia's Road to Independence," in Gordon Wightman, ed., *Party Formation in East-Central Europe* (Aldershot, UK: Edward Elgar, 1995), 107–133.

"Introduction," in Zora Bútorová, ed., *Democracy and Discontent in Slovakia: A Public Opinion Profile of a Country in Transition* (Bratislava: Institute for Public Affairs, 1998), 7–20.

"Slovakia and the World," in Zora Bútorová, ed., *Democracy and Discontent in Slovakia: A Public Opinion Profile of a Country in Transition* (Bratislava: Institute for Public Affairs, 1998), 175–189.

Bútorová, Zora, and Olga Gyárfášová. "Social Climate Three Years After the 1994 Elections," in Zora Bútorová, ed., *Democracy and Discontent in Slovakia: A Public Opinion Profile of a Country in Transition* (Bratislava: Institute for Public Affairs, 1998), 51–67.

References

Bútorová, Zora, Olga Gyárfášová, and Vladimír Krivý. "Parties, Institutions, and Politicians," in Zora Bútorová, ed., *Democracy and Discontent in Slovakia: A Public Opinion Profile of a Country in Transition* (Bratislava: Institute for Public Affairs, 1998), 69–110.

Cambone, Stephen A. "The Strategic Implications of NATO Enlargement," in Stephen J. Blank, ed., *From Madrid to Brussels: Perspectives on NATO Enlargement* (Carlisle, PA: U.S. Army War College, Strategic Studies Institute, 1997), 1–27.

Carpenter, Michael. "Slovakia and the Triumph of Nationalist Populism," *Communist and Post-Communist Studies*, 30:2 (June 1997): 205–220.

Carpenter, Ted Galen, and Barbara Conry. "Introduction," in Ted Galen Carpenter and Barbara Conry, eds., *NATO Enlargement: Illusions and Reality* (Washington, DC: Cato Institute, 1998), 1–14.

Chace, James. "A Strategy to Unite Rather Than Divide Europe," in Ted Galen Carpenter and Barbara Conry, eds., *NATO Enlargement: Illusions and Reality* (Washington, DC: Cato Institute, 1998), 177–185.

Chiriac, Marian. "Deadlocked Romania," *Current History*, 100:644 (March 2001): 124–128.

Clemens, Clay. "The Strategic and Political Consequences of NATO Enlargement," in James Sperling, ed., *Two Tiers or Two Speeds? The European Security Order and the Enlargement of the European Union and NATO* (Manchester, England: University of Manchester Press, 1999), 139–159.

Coenen-Huther, Jacques, ed. *Bulgaria at the Crossroads* (Commack, NY: Nova, 1996).

Connors, Stephen, David G. Gibson, and Mark Rhodes. "Caution and Ambivalence Over Joining NATO," *Transition*, 1:14 (11 Aug 1995): 42–46.

Croft, Stuart. "Enlarging NATO Again," *International Affairs* (U.K.), 78:1 (January 2002): 97–114.

Crowther, William. "'Ceausescuism' and Civil-Military Relations in Romania," *Armed Forces and Society*, 15:2 (Winter 1989): 207–225.

Csergö, Zsuzsa, and James M. Goldgeier. "Hungary's 'Status Law:' A Post-Territorial Approach to Nation-Building?" Presented at the Annual Meeting of the American Association for the Advancement of Slavic Studies (Pittsburgh, PA, 21–24 November 2002).

Cullen, Robert. "Report from Romania: Down with the Tyrant," *The New Yorker*, 2 April 1990, 94–112.

Dannreuther, Roland. "Escaping the Enlargement Trap in NATO-Russia Relations," *Survival*, 41:4 (Winter 1999–2000): 145–164.

Degeratu, Constantin. "Romania: Five Years in Partnership for Peace," *Central European Issues: Romanian Foreign Affairs Review*, 5:1 (1999): 36–46.

Dempsey, Gary. "Headaches for Neighboring Countries," in Ted Galen Carpenter, ed., *NATO's Empty Victory: A Postmortem on the Balkan War* (Washington, D.C.: Cato Institute, 2000), 59–76.

Derdzinski, Joseph. "Ten Years After Independence: Consolidation of Democratic Control of the Slovene Armed Forces," paper presented at the "War

244   *References*

in the Balkans" Conference (Boca Raton, Florida Atlantic University, 23 February 2002).

Diamond, Larry, and Marc F. Plattner. "Introduction," in Larry Diamond and Marc F. Plattner, eds., *Civil-Military Relations and Democracy* (Baltimore: Johns Hopkins University Press, 1996), viii–xxxiv.

Dimitrov, Dimitar. "Military Reform and Budgeting for Defence in Bulgaria (1989–2000)," in David Betz and John Löwenhardt, eds., *Army and State in Postcommunist Europe* (London: Frank Cass, 2001), 113–128.

Donnelly, Chris, and Jeffrey Simon. "Roadmaps to NATO Accession: Preparing for Membership," East European Studies (Woodrow Wilson Center) Meeting Report no. 242 (January 2002), 4 pp.

Drent, Margriet, et al. "Organising National Defences for NATO Membership: The Unexamined Dimension of Aspirants' Readiness for Entry," *Harmonie Paper 15* (Centre of European Security Studies, University of Groningen, October 2001).

Duleba, Alexander. *Slepý pragmatizmus slovenskej východnej politiky* (Bratislava: Štúdie k medzinárodným otázkam, 1996).

Encutescu, Sorin. "Sources of Instability, Risks, and Conflicts on Balkans," in Ivo Samson and Tomáš Strážay, eds., *Risks and Threats in Central Europe for the 21st Century: Impact on Defense Forces* (Bratislava: Friedrich Ebert Stiftung, 1999), 32–37.

Ene, Constantin. "Romania Sets Its Sights on NATO Membership," *NATO Review*, no. 6 (November–December 1997): 8–11.

Engelbrekt, Kjell. "Bulgaria's Evolving Defense Policy," *RFE/RL Research Report*, 3:32 (19 August 1994): 45–51.

European Parliament. "Draft Report on Romania's Membership Application to the European Union and the State of Negotiations" (European Parliament, 23 May 2001), 15 pp.

Eyal, Jonathan. "NATO's Enlargement: Anatomy of a Decision," *International Affairs*, 73:4 (October 1997): 695–720.

Ferfila, Bogomil, and Paul Phillips. *Slovenia: On the Edge of the European Union* (Lanham, MD: University Press of America, 2000).

Fish, M. Steven. "Poscommunist Subversion: Social Science and Democratization in East Europe and Eurasia," *Slavic Review*, 58:4 (Winter 1999): 794–823.

"The End of Meciarism," *East European Constitutional Review*, 8:1/2 (Winter/Spring 1999): 47–55.

Fish, M. Steven and Robin S. Brooks. "Bulgarian Democracy's Organizational Weapon," *East European Constitutional Review*, 9:3 (Summer 2000): 63–71.

Fisher, Sharon. "Tottering in the Aftermath of Elections," *Transition*, 1:4 (29 March 1995): 20–24.

"Prime Minister and President Grapple for Power," *Transition*, 1:11 (30 June 1995): 38–42, 70.

References

"President's Son Hostage in a Political Game," *Transition*, 1:23 (15 December 1995): 51–53.

"Ethnic Hungarians Back Themselves Into a Corner," *Transition*, 1:24 (29 December 1995): 58–63.

"Meciar Retains Control of the Political Scene," *Transition*, 2:16 (9 August 1996): 32–36.

Flanagan, Stephen J. "NATO and Kosovo: Lessons Learned and Prospects for Stability in Southeastern Europe," in Sabina Crisen, ed., *NATO and Europe in the 21st Century* (Washington, D.C.: Woodrow Wilson Center, 2000), 49–54.

Frlec, Boris. "Slovenia's Perspective on Promoting Stability in South-Eastern Europe," *NATO Review*, no. 4 (Winter 1999): 16–19.

Gallagher, Tom. *Romania After Ceausescu* (Edinburgh: Edinburgh University Press, 1995).

"To Be Or Not To Be Balkan: Romania's Quest for Self-Definition," *Daedalus*, 126:3 (Summer 1997): 63–83.

"Ceausescu's Legacy," *The National Interest*, no. 56 (Summer 1999): 107–111.

Garfinkle, Adam. "NATO Enlargement: What's the Rush?" *The National Interest*, No. 46 (Winter 1996/1997): 102–111.

Geipel, Gary L. "The Cost of Enlarging NATO," in James Sperling, ed., *Two Tiers or Two Speeds? The European Security Order and the Enlargement of the European Union and NATO* (Manchester, England: University of Manchester Press, 1999), 160–178.

Georgiev, Nikolai Lichkov. "Standardization Activities in the Ministry of Defense and Tendencies for Their Improvement," *Security Policy: Information Bulletin of the Ministry of Defence of the Republic of Bulgaria*, no. 1 (1999): 24–30.

Gitz, Bradley R. *Armed Forces and Political Power in Eastern Europe* (Westport, CT: Greenwood, 1992).

Glaser, Charles L. "Why NATO Is Still Best: Future Security Arrangements for Europe," *International Security*, 18:1 (Summer 1993): 5–50.

Goldgeier, James M. *Not Whether But When: The U.S. Decision to Enlarge NATO* (Washington, D.C.: Brookings Institution Press, 1999).

Gompert, David C. "NATO Enlargement: Putting the Cost in Perspective," *Strategic Forum*, no. 129 (October 1997): 1–5.

Gow, James. *Legitimacy and the Military: The Yugoslav Crisis* (New York: St. Martin's, 1992).

"Slovenia: Stabilization or Stagnation," *RFE/RL Research Report*, 3:1 (7 January 1994): 135–138.

Gow, James, and Cathie Carmichael. *Slovenia and the Slovenes: A Small State and the New Europe* (Bloomington: Indiana University Press, 2000).

Grabbe, Heather, and Kristy Hughes. "Central and East European Views on EU Enlargement: Political Debates and Public Opinion," in Karen Henderson, ed. *Back to Europe: Central and Eastern Europe and the European Union* (London: UCL Press, 1999), 185–202.

Grayson, George W. *Strange Bedfellows: NATO Marches East* (Lanham, MD: University Press of America, 1999).

Grayston, Neil. "Democratic Control of the Armed Forces of Slovenia: A Progress Report," in Graeme P. Herd, ed., *Civil-Military Relations in Post Cold War Europe* (Camberley, UK: Conflict Studies Research Centre, 2001), 5–13.

Grizold, Anton. "The National Security of Slovenia: The View of Public Opinion," *Balkan Forum* 3:3 (September 1995): 173–206.

———. "Civil-Military Relations in Slovenia," in Anton Bebler, ed., *Civil-Military Relations in Post-Communist States: Central and Eastern Europe in Transition* (Westport, CT: Prager, 1997), 101–109.

———. "The Defence of Slovenia," in Danica Fink-Hafner and John R. Robbins, eds., *Making a New Nation: The Formation of Slovenia* (Brookfield, VT: Dartmouth, 1997), 46–55.

Gyárfášová, Olga. "The Crisis in Kosovo and the Slovak Public: A Lesson on International Politics," *Slovak Foreign Policy Affairs*, 1:2 (Fall 2000): 53–66.

Haerpfer, Christian, Claire Wallace, and Richard Rose, "Public Perceptions of Threats to Security in Post-Communist Europe," *Studies in Public Policy*, no. 293 (Glasgow: University of Strathclyde, 1997).

Harries, Owen, "The Danger of Expansive Realism," *The National Interest*, no. 50 (Winter 1997/98): 3–7.

Heller, Francis H., and John R. Gillingham, eds., *NATO: The Founding of the Atlantic Alliance and the Integration of Europe* (New York: St. Martin's Press, 1992).

Hendrickson, Ryan C. "NATO's Visegrad Allies: The First Test in Kosovo," *Journal of Slavic Military Studies*, 13:2 (June 2000): 25–38.

Herspring, Dale R. "The Process of Change and Democratization in Eastern Europe: The Case of the Military," in John R. Lampe and Daniel N. Nelson, eds., *East European Security Reconsidered* (Washington, DC: Woodrow Wilson Center Press, 1993), 55–74.

———. "After NATO Expansion: The East European Militaries," *Problems of Post-Communism*, 45:1 (January–February 1998): 10–20.

Howard, Michael. "An Unhappy Successful Marriage: Security Means Knowing What to Expect," *Foreign Affairs*, 78:3 (May–June 1999): 164–175.

Hudák, Vasil. "Transfrontier Cooperation in Central Europe," in Vasil Hudák, ed., *Building a New Europe: Transfrontier Cooperation in Central Europe* (Prague: Institute for EastWest Studies, 1996), 1–10.

Huelshoff, Michael. "CEE Financial Reform, European Monetary Union, and Eastern Enlargement," in James Sperling, ed., *Two Tiers or Two Speeds? The European Security Order and the Enlargement of the European Union*

References

and NATO (Manchester, England: University of Manchester Press, 1999), 63–80.

Hunter, Robert E. "Maximizing NATO: A Relevant Alliance Knows How to Reach," *Foreign Affairs*, 78:3 (May–June 1999): 190–203.

"An Expanded Alliance vis à vis the European Union," in Sabina Crisen, ed., *NATO and Europe in the 21st Century* (Washington, D.C.: Woodrow Wilson Center, 2000), 7–14.

Institute for Regional and International Studies. "Security and Reconstruction of Southeastern Europe: A Policy Outlook from the Region" (Sofia: IRIS, 1999).

International Institute for Strategic Studies. *The Military Balance, 2000–2001* (London: IISS, 2000).

Ionescu, Dan. "The President, the Journalists, and the KGB," *Transition*, 1:16 (8 September 1995): 36–39.

"Hammering on NATO's Door," *Transition*, 2:16 (9 August 1996): 37–41.

Ishiyama, John T. "Communist Parties in Transition: Structures, Leaders, and Processes of Democratization in Eastern Europe," *Comparative Politics*, 27:2 (January 1995): 147–166.

Ivanov, Tilcho. *Confidence and Security in the Balkans: The Role of Transparency in Defense Budgeting* (Sofia: Institute for Security and International Studies, 1996).

Ivantyšyn, Michal, Marián Velšic, and Zora Bútorová. "First-time Voters," in Zora Bútorová, ed., *Democracy and Discontent in Slovakia: A Public Opinion Profile of a Country in Transition* (Bratislava: Institute for Public Affairs, 1998), 135–150.

Janos, Andrew C. *Czechoslovakia and Yugoslavia: Ethnic Conflict and the Dissolution of Multinational States* (Berkeley: International and Area Studies, University of California, 1997).

East Central Europe in the Modern World: The Politics of the Borderlands from Pre- to Postcommunism (Stanford, CA: Stanford University Press, 2000).

Janša, Janez. *Premiki. Nastajanje in Obramba Slovenske Države, 1988–1992* (Ljubljana: Založba Mladinska Knjiga, 1992).

Johnson, Bruce Pitcairn. "The Alliance at Fifty: A Conservative Defense of NATO," in Kurt W. Treptow and Mihail E. Ionescu, eds., *Romania and Euro-Atlantic Integration* (Iasi: Center for Romanian Studies, 1999), 11–24.

Jones, Christopher. *Soviet Influence in Eastern Europe: Political Autonomy and the Warsaw Pact* (New York: Praeger, 1981).

"NATO Enlargement: Brussels as the Heir of Moscow," *Problems of Post-Communism*, 45:4 (July–August 1998): 44–55.

Jowitt, Ken. "The Leninist Legacy," in Ivo Banac, ed., *Eastern Europe in Revolution* (Ithaca, NY: Cornell University Press, 1992), 207–224.

Judt, Tony. "Romania: Bottom of the Heap," *The New York Review of Books*, 1 November 2001, 41–45.

Kamp, Karl-Heinz. "NATO Entrapped: Debating the Next Enlargement Round," *Survival*, 40:3 (Autumn 1998): 170–186.

Kanev, Krassimir. "Dynamics of Inter-Ethnic Tensions in Bulgaria and the Balkans," *Balkan Forum*, 4:2 (June 1996): 213–252.

Kaplan, Robert D. *Eastward to Tartary: Travels in the Balkans, the Middle East, and the Caucasus* (New York: Random House, 2000).

Karasimeonov, Georgi. "Differentiation Postponed: Party Pluralism in Bulgaria," in Gordon Wightman, ed., *Party Formation in East-Central Europe* (Aldershot, UK: Edward Elgar, 1995), 154–178.

Karatnycky, Adrian, Alexander Motyl, and Amanda Schetzer, eds. *Nations in Transit 2001: Civil Society, Democracy, and Markets in East Central Europe and the Newly Independent States* (New York: Freedom House, 2001).

Kay, Sean. "What Is a Strategic Partnership? *Problems of Post-Communism*, 47:3 (May–June 2000): 15–24.

Kiss, Yudit. "Sink or Swim? Central European Defense Industry Enterprises in the Aftermath of the Cold War," *Europe-Asia Studies*, 47:5 (1995): 787–812.

"Trapped in Transition: Defence Industry Restructuring in Central Europe," *European Security*, 4:1 (Spring 1995): 56–84.

Kiuranov, Deyan. "Salient Points of Political Behavior in Bulgaria," delivered at the Conference on East European Transitions (Bucharest, August 1994).

Knudsen, Olaf F. *Bound To Fail? Regional Security Co-operation in the Baltic Sea Area and Northeast Asia* (Oslo: NUPI, 1996).

Koburov, Todor. "National Security Policy: Conceptional Bases, Problems and Prospects," *Security Policy: Information Bulletin of the Ministry of Defence of the Republic of Bulgaria*, no. 1 (1999): 15–20.

Kohn, Richard H. "How Democracies Control the Military," *Journal of Democracy*, 8:4 (October 1997): 140–153.

Kolarova, Rumyana. "Bulgaria: Could We Regain What We Already Lost?" *Social Research*, 63:2 (Summer 1996): 543–559.

Komac, Miran, ed. *Protection of Ethnic Communities in the Republic of Slovenia* (Ljubljana: Institute for Ethnic Studies, 1999).

Korba, Matúš. "Civil-Military Relations in Slovakia from the Perspective of NATO Integration," *Slovak Foreign Policy Affairs*, Fall 2001 (2:2): 50–63.

Koulov, Boian. "Political Change and Environmental Policy," in John D. Bell, ed., *Bulgaria in Transition: Politics, Economics, Society, and Culture After Communism* (Boulder, CO: Westview Press, 1998), 143–162.

Krastev, Ivan, Stefan Popov, and Julia Gurkovska, "2010: The Balkans after Kosovo," *East European Constitutional Review*, 8:3 (Summer 1999): 82–90.

Kugler, Richard L. *Enlarging NATO: The Russia Factor* (Santa Monica: RAND, 1995).

"Costs of NATO Enlargement: Moderate and Affordable," *Strategic Forum*, no. 128 (October 1997): 1–6.

References

Kukan, Eduard. "Slovakia and NATO," in Anton A. Bebler, ed., *The Challenge of NATO Enlargement* (Westport, CT: Praeger, 1999), 163–166.

Kupchan, Charles A. "After Pax Americana: Benign Power, Regional Integration, and the Sources of Stable Multipolarity," *International Security*, 23:2 (Fall 1998): 40–79.

ed., *Atlantic Security: Contending Visions* (New York: Council on Foreign Relations, 1998).

"Rethinking Europe," *The National Interest*, no. 56 (Summer 1999): 73–80.

"The Origins and Future of NATO Enlargement," in Robert W. Rauchhaus, ed., *Explaining NATO Enlargement* (London: Frank Cass, 2001), 127–148.

Kurth, James. "The Next NATO: Building an American Commonwealth of Nations," *The National Interest*, no. 65 (Fall 2001): 5–16.

Larrabee, F. Stephen. "The Kosovo Conflict and the Central European Members of NATO: Lessons and Implications," in Sabina Crisen, ed., *NATO and Europe in the 21st Century* (Washington, D.C.: Woodrow Wilson Center, 2000), 32–36.

Lebedev, Alexander. "Source of Instability, Security Risks and Threats in Central Europe on the Eve of the 21st Century," in Ivo Samson and Tomáš Strážay, eds., *Risks and Threats in Central Europe for the 21st Century: Impact on Defense Forces* (Bratislava: Friedrich Ebert Stiftung, 1999), 38–44.

Lefebvre, Stéphane. "Changes in the Romanian Armed Forces," *Jane's Intelligence Review*, 7:1 (January 1995): 8–12.

Leff, Carol Skalnik. *The Czech and Slovak Republics* (Boulder, CO: Westview Press, 1997).

Legvold, Robert. "The Russian Question," in Vladimir Baranovsky, ed., *Russia and Europe: The Emerging Security Agenda* (Oxford: Oxford University Press, 1997).

Lengyel, László. "Economic Traumatology," in Imre-József Balázs, Andor Horváth, and Lajos Kántor, eds., *Alternatives for Romania* (Cluj: Komp-Press, 1999), 72–91.

Lepgold, Joseph. "NATO's Post-Cold War Collective Action Problem," *International Security*, 23:1 (Summer 1998): 78–106.

Leško, Marián. "Príbeh sebadiskvalifikácie favorita," in Martin Bútora and František Šebej, eds., *Slovensko v Šedej Zóne? Rozširovanie NATO, zlyhania a perspektívy Slovenska* (Bratislava: Institute for Public Affairs, 1998), 15–80.

Lieven, Anatol. "A New Iron Curtain," *The Atlantic Monthly* (January 1996).

Light, Margot, Stephen White, and John Löwenhardt. "A Wider Europe: The View from Moscow and Kyiv," *International Affairs*, 76:1 (January 2000): 77–88.

Linden, Ronald H. "After the Revolution: A Foreign Policy of Bounded Change," in Daniel N. Nelson, ed., *Romania after Tyranny* (Boulder, CO: Westview Press, 1992), 203–238.

"Putting on Their Sunday Best: Romania, Hungary, and the Puzzle of Peace," *International Studies Quarterly*, 44:1 (March 2000): 121–146.

Linz, Juan J. and Alfred Stepan. *Problems of Democratic Transition and Consolidation: Southern Europe, South America, and Post-Communist Europe* (Baltimore: Johns Hopkins University Press, 1996).

Lombardi, Ben. "An Overview of Civil-Military Relations in Central and Eastern Europe," *Journal of Slavic Military Studies*, 12:1 (March 1999): 13–33.

MacFarlane, S. Neil. "NATO in Russia's Relations with the West," *Security Dialogue*, 32:3 (September 2001): 281–296.

Malesic, Marjan. "Slovenian Security Policy and NATO," *Harmonie Paper 13* (Centre of European Security Studies, University of Groningen, June 2000), 74 pp.

Mandelbaum, Michael. "Preserving the New Peace: The Case Against NATO Expansion," *Foreign Affairs*, 72:3 (May–June 1995): 9–13.

The Dawn of Peace in Europe (New York: Twentieth Century Fund, 1997).

Marcinčin, Anton, and Miroslav Beblavý, eds. *Economic Policy in Slovakia, 1990–1999* (Bratislava: Centre for Social and Media Analysis and Institute for Economic and Social Reforms, 2000).

Marguš, Jozef. "The Activities of the Army of the Slk Rep in Peace Keeping Operations of the UN and other IOs," in Ivo Samson and Tomáš Strážay, eds., *Risks and Threats in Central Europe for the 21st Century: Impact on Defense Forces* (Bratislava: Friedrich Ebert Stiftung, 1999), 86–90.

Markotich, Stan. "A Balancing Act Between NATO and the EU," *Transition*, 1:23 (15 December 1995): 45–54.

Mastny, Vojtech. "Reassuring NATO: Eastern Europe, Russia, and the Western Alliance," *Forsvarsstudier* (Oslo), no. 5 (1997): 1–105.

Matič, Andrej Auersperger. "Electoral Reform as a Constitutional Dilemma," *East European Constitutional Review*, 9:3 (Summer 2000): 77–81.

McCalla, Robert B. "NATO's Persistence After the Cold War," *International Organization*, 50:3 (Summer 1996): 445–475.

Mearsheimer, John J. "False Promises of International Institutions," *International Security*, 19:3 (Winter 1994): 5–49.

Melone, Albert P. *Creating Parliamentary Government: The Transition to Democracy in Bulgaria* (Columbus: Ohio State University Press, 1998).

Mesežnikov, Grigorij. "Postoje a cinnost politickych stran a hnuti," in Grigorij Mesežnikov and Martin Bútora, eds., *Slovenske referendum: Zrod, priebeh, dosledky* (Bratislava: IVO, 1997), 111–152.

"On Russia's Position in the NATO Enlargement Issue (1992–1997)," in Piotr Dutkiewicz and Robert J. Jackson, eds., *NATO Looks East* (Westport, CT: Praeger, 1998), 99–108.

"The Crisis in Kosovo and Its Impact on the Slovak Domestic Politics," *Slovak Foreign Policy Affairs*, 1:2 (Fall 2000): 31–52.

Mesežnikov, Grigorij, and Martin Bútora, eds. *Slovenske referendum: Zrod, priebeh, dosledky* (Bratislava: IVO, 1997).

References

Michta, Andrew A., ed. *America's New Allies: Poland, Hungary, and the Czech Republic in NATO* (Seattle: University of Washington Press, 1999).

Mihalikova, Silvia. "Political Culture and Civil-Military Relations in Slovakia," *Harmonie Paper 11* (Groningen, Holland: Centre of European Security Studies, University of Groningen, April 2000), 61 pp.

Mihalka, Michael. "Continued Resistance to NATO Expansion," *Transition*, 1:14 (11 August 1995): 36–41.

"Eastern and Central Europe's Great Divide Over Membership in NATO," *Transition*, 1:14 (11 August 1995): 48–55.

Mitev, Petûr-Emil. "Popular Attitudes toward Politics," in John D. Bell, ed., *Bulgaria in Transition: Politics, Economics, Society, and Culture After Communism* (Boulder, CO: Westview Press, 1998), 39–64.

Molnár, Gusztáv. "Romania Has Lost Its Way ...," in Imre-József Balázs, Andor Horváth, and Lajos Kántor, eds., *Alternatives for Romania* (Cluj: Komp-Press, 1999), 121–136.

Moses, Alfred H. "Romania's NATO Bid," *SAIS Review*, 18:1 (Winter–Spring 1998): 137–143.

Mueller, John. *Capitalism, Democracy, and Ralph's Pretty Good Grocery* (Princeton, NJ: Princeton University Press, 1999).

Mungiu-Pippidi, Alina. "The Return of Populism: The 2000 Romanian Elections," *Government and Opposition*, 36:2 (Spring 2001): 230–252.

Mutafchieva, Vera. "The Turk, the Jew, and the Gypsy," in Antonina Zhelyazkova, ed., *Relations of Compatibility and Incompatibility between Christians and Muslims in Bulgaria* (Sofia: International Centre for Minority Studies and Intercultural Relations, 1995), 5–63.

Nelson, Daniel N. "Civil Armies, Civil Societies, and NATO's Enlargement," *Armed Forces & Society*, 25:1 (Fall 1998): 137–160.

Nelson, Daniel N., and Thomas S. Szayna, "NATO's Metamorphosis and Its New Members," *Problems of Post-Communism*, 45:4 (July–August 1998): 32–43.

North Atlantic Treaty Organization. *NATO Handbook* (Brussels: NATO, 1995).

Study on NATO Enlargement (Brussels: NATO, 1995).

"NATO Rationalizes Its Eastward Enlargement," *Transition*, 1:23 (15 December 1995): 19–26 (excerpts from NATO's Study on Enlargement presented on 28 September 1995).

"The Reader's Guide to the NATO Summit in Washington, 23–25 April 1999" (Brussels: NATO Office of Information and Press, 1999).

The Alliance's Strategic Concept (Brussels: NATO, 1999).

Obrman, Jan. "The Czechoslovak Armed Forces: The Reform Continues," *RFE/RL Research Report*, 1:6 (7 February 1992): 46–52.

Odom, William E. "NATO's Expansion: Why the Critics Are Wrong," *The National Interest*, No. 39 (Spring 1995): 38–49.

Ozoliňa, Žaneta. "The Regional Dimension in Latvian Security Policy," *Harmonie Paper 8* (Centre of European Security Studies, University of Groningen, August 1999), 73 pp.

Palacka, Gabriel. *NATO a cena za bezpečnost: Porovnavacia studia o nakladoch prijatia a neprijatia Slovenska do NATO* (Bratislava: IVO, 1997).

Pantev, Plamen. "The Changing Nature of Civil-Military Relations in Post-Totalitarian Bulgaria," in Andrew Cottey, Timothy Edmunds, and Anthony Forster, eds., *Democratic Control of the Military in Postcommunist Europe: Guarding the Guards* (Houndmills, UK: Palgrave, 2002), 140–158.

Pascu, Ioan Mircea. "Defence Plannning in Emerging Democracies: The Case of Romania," in Andrew Cottey, Timothy Edmunds, and Anthony Forster, eds., *Democratic Control of the Military in Postcommunist Europe: Guarding the Guards* (Houndmills, UK: Palgrave, 2002), 129–139.

Perlmutter, Amos. "Political Alternatives to NATO Expansion," in Ted Galen Carpenter and Barbara Conry, eds., *NATO Enlargement: Illusions and Reality* (Washington, D.C.: Cato Institute, 1998), 233–242.

Perlmutter, Amos, and Ted Galen Carpenter. "NATO's Expensive Trip East: The Folly of Enlargement," *Foreign Affairs*, 77:1 (January–February 1998): 2–6.

Perry, Duncan M. "A New Military Lobby," *Report on Eastern Europe*, 1:40 (5 October 1990): 1–4.

Perry, William. "Partnership for Peace Transforming Central, Eastern Europe," *Balkan Forum*, 4:1 (March 1996): 5–15.

Pivarči, Jozef. "Speech of the State Secretary," in Ivo Samson, and Tomáš Strážay, eds., *Risks and Threats in Central Europe for the 21st Century: Impact on Defense Forces* (Bratislava: Friedrich Ebert Stiftung, 1999), 7–9.

Plangu, Ion Mircea. "Defense Planning for 2010," in Kurt W. Treptow and Mihail E. Ionescu, eds., *Romania and Euro-Atlantic Integration* (Iasi: Center for Romanian Studies, 1999), 133–142.

Podoba, Juraj. "Rejecting Green Velvet: Transition, Environment, and Nationalism in Slovakia," *Environmental Politics*, 7:1 (Spring 1998): 129–145.

Poulton, Hugh. *Who Are the Macedonians?* (London: Hurst & Co., 1995).

Pushkov, Alexii K. "Don't Isolate Us: A Russian View of NATO Enlargement," *The National Interest*, no. 47 (Spring 1997): 58–63.

Ramet, Sabrina P. "Democratization in Slovenia – the Second Stage," in Karen Dawisha and Bruce Parrott, eds., *Politics, Power, and the Struggle for Democracy in South-East Europe* (New York: Cambridge University Press, 1997), 189–225.

"The Slovenian Success Story," *Current History*, 97:617 (March 1998): 113–118.

Balkan Babel: The Disintegration of Yugoslavia from the Death of Tito to the War for Kosovo (Boulder, CO: Westview Press, 1999; 3rd. ed.).

References

Ratchev, Valeri. "Combining Political and Military Considerations in Assessing Military Conflicts," *Journal of Slavic Military Studies*, 9:1 (March 1996): 46–54.

"Bulgaria and the Future of European Security," in Stephen J. Blank, ed., *European Security and NATO Enlargement: A View from Central Europe* (Carlisle, PA: U.S. Army War College, Strategic Studies Institute, 1998), 157–183.

Ratesh, Nestor. *Romania: The Entangled Revolution* (Westport: Praeger, 1991).

"Romania: Slamming on the Brakes," *Current History*, 92:577 (November 1993): 390–395.

Rauchhaus, Robert W., ed. *Explaining NATO Enlargement* (London: Frank Cass, 2001).

Reisch, Alfred A. "Central and Eastern Europe's Quest for NATO Membership, *RFE/RL Research Report*, 2:28 (9 July 1993): 32–46.

Reiter, Dan. "Why NATO Enlargement Does Not Spread Democracy," *International Security*, 25:4 (Spring 2001): 41–67.

Remington, Robin Alison. "The Yugoslav Army: Trauma and Transition," in Constantine P. Danopoulos and Daniel Zirker, eds., *Civil-Military Relations in the Soviet and Yugoslav Successor States* (Boulder: Westview Press, 1996), 153–173.

Rizman, Rudolf M. "Radical Right Politics in Slovenia," in Sabrina P. Ramet, *The Radical Right in Central and Eastern Europe since 1989* (University Park: Pennsylvania State University Press, 1999), 147–171.

Robertson, George. "A New Quality in the NATO-Russia Relationship," *International Affairs* (Moscow), 48:1 (2002): 32–37.

Romania, Government. *Two Years of Governance* (Bucharest: The Government of Romania, 1994).

"The Washington Summit and the Continuation of NATO Enlargement: Romania's Expectations and Suggestions" (Bucharest: Government of Romania, March 1999).

"Romania's Strategy of National Security" (Bucharest: Government of Romania, June 1999).

Romania, Ministry of Defense. *Romanian Armed Forces: In the Service of Peace* (Bucharest: MOD, 1997).

Romania, Ministry of Foreign Affairs. *White Book on Romania and NATO* (Bucharest: Ministry of Foreign Affairs, 1997).

Rosapepe, James C. "Romania and NATO; 'Knocking on an Open Door'," *Central European Issues: Romanian Foreign Affairs Review*, 5:1 (1999): 48–57.

Royen, Christoph. "The Role of the EU in Europe's Security After the Year 2000," in Ivo Samson and Tomáš Strážay, eds., *Risks and Threats in Central Europe for the 21st Century: Impact on Defense Forces* (Bratislava: Friedrich Ebert Stiftung, 1999), 55–63.

Ruggie, John Gerald. "Consolidating the European Pillar: The Key to NATO's Future," *Washington Quarterly*, 20:1 (Winter 1997): 109–125.

References

Russell, Theodore E., "NATO Enlargement and Slovakia," in Stephen J. Blank, ed., *From Madrid to Brussels: Perspectives on NATO Enlargement* (Carlisle, PA: U.S. Army War College, Strategic Studies Institute, 1997), 91–97.

Russett, Bruce M., and Allan C. Stam. "Courting Disaster: An Expanded NATO vs. Russia and China," *Political Science Quarterly*, 113:3 (Fall 1998): 361–382.

Samson, Ivo. "Transformation and Structural Change: Slovakia's Postcommunist Security and Military Adjustment to NATO Integration," in Piotr Dutkiewicz and Robert J. Jackson, eds., *NATO Looks East* (Westport, CT: Praeger, 1998), 123–138.

Die Sicherheits- und Aussenpolitik der Slowakei in der ersten Jahren der Selbstständigkeit (Baden-Baden: Nomos Verlag, 2000).

"Slovakia: Toward NATO Indecisively," in Daniel N. Nelson and Ustina Markus, eds., *Central and East European Security Yearbook, 2002* (Dulles, VA: Brassey's, 2002), 145–170.

Sarvaš, Štefan. "One Past, Two Futures?: The NATO Enlargement Debate in the Czech Republic and Slovakia," *Harmonie Paper 4* (Groningen, Holland: Centre of European Security Studies, University of Groningen, January 1999), 65 pp.

"The NATO Enlargement Debate in the Media and Civil-Military Relations in the Czech Republic and Slovakia," *European Security*, 9:1 (Spring 2000): 113–126.

Schmidt, Helmut. "The Transatlantic Alliance in the 21st Century," *NATO Review: 50th Anniversary Edition*, 20–24.

Schulz, Erich, ed. "Neuaufbau und Umstrukturierung der tschechoslowakischen Streitkräfte vor der Teilung," *Osteuropa*, 43:1 (January 1993): A22–A40.

Šedivý, Jiří. "The Puzzle of NATO Enlargement," *Contemporary Security Policy*, 22:2 (August 2001): 1–26.

Selden, Zachary, and John Lis. "NATO's New Members: Net Gain or Net Drain?" *Problems of Post-Communism*, 49:4 (July–August 2002): 3–11.

Serebrian, Oleg. "Romanians between East and West," in Imre-József Balázs, Andor Horváth, and Lajos Kántor, eds., *Alternatives for Romania* (Cluj: Komp-Press, 1999), 167–172.

Severin, Adrian. "Romania Endeavors to Join NATO," in Anton A. Bebler, ed., *The Challenge of NATO Enlargement* (Westport, CT: Praeger, 1999), 159–162.

Shafir, Michael. "Marschall Ion Antonescu: Politik der Rehabilitierung," *Europäische Rundschau*, 22:2 (1994): 55–70.

"Romania's Road to Normalcy," *Journal of Democracy*, 8:2 (January 1997): 144–159.

"The Mind of Romania's Radical Right," in Sabrina P. Ramet, ed., *The Radical Right in Central and Eastern Europe since 1989* (University Park: Pennsylvania State University Press, 1999), 213–232.

Simecka, Martin. "Slovakia's Lonely Independence," *Transitions*, 4:3 (August 1997): 14–21.

Simon, Jeffrey. *Central European Civil-Military Relations and NATO Expansion* (Washington, D.C.: National Defense University, McNair Paper 39, 1995).

"Post-Enlargement NATO: Dangers of 'Failed Suitors' and Need for a Strategy," in Stephen J. Blank, ed., *From Madrid to Brussels: Perspectives on NATO Enlargement* (Carlisle, PA: U.S. Army War College, Strategic Studies Institute, 1997), 29–47.

"Bulgaria and NATO: 7 Lost Years," *Strategic Forum*, no. 142 (May 1998): 1–7.

"Central and East European Security: New National Concepts and Defense Doctrines," *Strategic Forum*, no. 151 (December 1998): 1–6.

"Partnership for Peace: After the Washington Summit and Kosovo," *Strategic Forum*, no. 167 (August 1999): 1–6.

"Transforming the Armed Forces of Central and Eastern Europe," *Strategic Forum*, no. 172 (June 2000): 1–8.

"The Next Round of NATO Enlargement," *Strategic Forum*, no. 176 (October 2000): 1–8.

"NATO's Membership Action Plan (MAP) and Prospects for the Next Round of Enlargement," Woodrow Wilson Center (Washington, D.C.), Occasional Paper No. 58 (November 2000), 24 pp.

"Roadmap to NATO Accession: Preparing for Membership," Institute for National Strategic Studies, National Defense University, Special Report, October 2001, 8 pp.

Slatinski, Nikolay, and Marina Caparini. "Bulgarian Security and Prospects for Reform," *NATO Review*, no. 2 (March 1995): 28–32.

Slovakia, Ministry of Defense. *White Paper on Defense of the Slovak Republic* (Bratislava: Ministry of Defense, 1998).

The Conception of Defence Sector Reform by 2002 (Bratislava: MOD, 1999).

Armáda Slovenskej Republiky 1999 (Bratislava: MOD, 2000).

Slovenia, Ministry of Defense. *Public Opinion, Mass Media, and the Military* (Ljubljana: Ministry of Defense, 1999).

Slovenian Defence Products, 1999–2000 (Ljubljana: MOD, 1999).

Smith, Martin A. "The NATO Factor: A Spanner in the Works of EU and WEU Enlargement?" in Karen Henderson, *Back to Europe: Central and Eastern Europe and the European Union* (London: UCL Press, 1999), 53–67.

Solana, Javier. "NATO and the New Security Architecture," *Balkan Forum* 4:2 (June 1996): 5–12.

Solomon, Gerald B. *The NATO Enlargement Debate, 1990–1997: Blessings of Liberty* (Westport, CT: Praeger, 1998).

Stan, Adrian. "The Euro-Atlantic Structures and Romania," in *Euro-Atlantic Studies* (Centre for Euro-Atlantic Studies, University of Bucharest, 1998), 117–128.

Stan, Lavinia. *Romania in Transition* (Brookfield, VT: Dartmouth, 1997).

Stanchev, Krassen. "Can Economic Reforms Overcome Ethnic Tensions? The Role of Institutions in Bulgaria's Economic Reform," delivered at the Conference on Political and Economic Change in the Balkan States (Sofia, August 1994).

Stefan, Adina. "Romania's Engagement in Subregional Co-operation and the National Strategy for NATO Accession," *Harmonie Paper 10* (Groningen, Holland: Centre of European Security Studies, University of Groningen, December 1999), 55 pp.

Štembera, Milan. "ČSFR-Streitkräfte und Rüstung," *Österreichische Militärische Zeitschrift*, 30:5 (September–October 1992): 390–396.

Švajncer, Janez J. *Obranili Domovino: Teritorialna Obramba Republike Slovenije v Vojni za Svobodno in Samostojno Slovenijo, 1991* (Ljubljana: Viharnik, 1993).

Szayna, Thomas S. "The Military in a Postcommunist Czechoslovakia," Rand Note (N-3412–USDP, 1992), 92 pp.

"Central European Defense Industries and NATO Enlargement," Rand Report (MR-717.0-RC, 1996), 32 pp.

"Slovakia: Trying to Catch Up with Visegrad," in Daniel N. Nelson and Ustina Markus, eds., *East European and Eurasian Security Handbook* (Washington, D.C.: Brassey's 2000), 75–94.

NATO Enlargement, 2000–2015: Determinants and Implications for Defense Planning and Shaping (Santa Monica, CA: Rand, 2001).

"Slovak Civil-Military Relations: A Balance Sheet After Nine Years of Independence," unpublished paper (2002).

Szayna, Thomas S., and James B. Steinberg, *Civil-Military Relations and National Security Thinking in Czechoslovakia* (Santa Monica, CA: RAND, 1992).

Szemerkényi, Réka. "Central European Civil-Military Reform at Risk," *Adelphi Paper 306* (Oxford: Oxford University Press, December 1996).

Tagarev, Petûr. "Kontseptsiata za natsionalna sigurnost i informatsionnoto protivoborstvo," *Informatsiya i sigurnost: Mezhdunaroden zhurnal*, 1:2 (Fall–Winter 1998): 32–42.

Talbott, Strobe. "Why NATO Should Grow," *Balkan Forum*, 3:4 (December 1995): 27–44.

Tang, Helena. *Winners and Losers in EU Integration: Policy Issues for Central and Eastern Europe* (Washington, D.C.: World Bank, 2000).

Tayler, Jeffrey. "The Next Threat to NATO," *The Atlantic Monthly*, February 2002, 69–72.

Tismaneanu, Vladimir. "New Masks, Old Faces," *The New Republic*, 5 February 1990, 17–21.

"Romanian Exceptionalism? Democracy, Ethnocracy, and Uncertain Pluralism in Post-Ceausescu Romania," in Karen Dawisha and Bruce Parrott, eds., *Politics, Power, and the Struggle for Democracy in South-East Europe*, (New York: Cambridge University Press, 1997), 403–451.

References

Tismaneanu, Vladimir, and Dorin Tudoran. "The Bucharest Syndrome," *Journal of Democracy*, 4:1 (January 1993): 41–52.

Trenin, Dmitri. "Russia-NATO Relations: Time To Pick Up the Pieces," *NATO Review*, 48 (Spring–Summer 2000): 19–22.

Troxel, Luan. "Bulgaria: Stable Ground in the Balkans?" *Current History*, 92:577 (November 1993): 386–390.

Tsvetkov, Tsvetan. "Bulgarian Security Policy: Alternatives and Choice," *Harmonie Paper 9* (Centre of European Security Studies, University of Groningen, August 1999), 50 pp.

Ulrich, Marybeth Peterson. "The New Allies: Approaching NATO Political and Military Standards," in Sabina Crisen, ed., *NATO and Europe in the 21st Century* (Washington, D.C.: Woodrow Wilson Center, 2000), 37–48.

United Kingdom, Ministry of Defence. "Review of Parliamentary Oversight of the Romanian Ministry of National Defence and the Democratic Control of Its Armed Forces" (London: Ministry of Defence, February 1997).

"A Strategic Review of the Development of Romanian Security Policy and the Associated Machinery of Government (London: Ministry of Defence, July 1998).

United Nations. *National Human Development Report – Slovakia 1998* (Bratislava: United Nations Development Program, 1998).

Human Development Report 2001 (New York: Oxford University Press for the UN Development Program, 2001).

van Ham, Peter, ed. *The Baltic States: Security and Defence after Independence* (Paris: Western European Union, 1995).

Vasileva, Darina. "Izselnicheskiat vapros i Balgaro-Turskite otnoshenia," in *Aspekti na etnokulturnata situtzia v Bulgaria* (Sofia: Zentar za izsledvane na demokratziata, 1992), 58–67.

Vassilev, Hristo, Lt. Gen. "The Military Strategy of the Republic of Bulgaria," *Security Policy: Information Bulletin of the Ministry of Defence of the Republic of Bulgaria*, no. 1 (1999): 3–14.

Voronkov, Lev. "The Challenges of NATO Enlargement," *Balkan Forum*, 5:2 (June 1997): 5–46.

Walker, Martin. "The European Union and the Eur Secu and Defense Initiative," in Sabina Crisen, ed., *NATO and Europe in the 21st Century* (Washington, D.C.: Woodrow Wilson Center, 2000), 17–22.

Wallander, Celeste. "NATO's Price," *Foreign Affairs*, 81:6 (November–December 2002): 2–8.

Walski, William A. "Comparative Analysis of the Systems of Civilian Control over the Armed Forces in Slovakia and the USA," M.A. Thesis, Department of Politics, Comenius University (Bratislava, 2000).

Waters, Trevor. "Building an Army from Scratch: Slovakia's Uphill Struggle," *Medzinárodné Otázky*, 7:4 (1998): 47–59.

Watts, Larry L. "The Romanian Army in the December Revolution and Beyond," in Daniel N. Nelson, ed., *Romania After Tyranny* (Boulder, CO: Westview, 1992), 95–126.

"The Crisis in Romanian Civil-Military Relations," *Problems of Post-Communism*, 48:4 (July–August 2001): 14–26.

"Democratic Civil Control of the Military in Romania: An Assessment as of October 2001," in Graeme P. Herd, ed., *Civil-Military Relations in Post Cold War Europe* (Camberley, UK: Conflict Studies Research Centre, 2001), 14–42.

Welsh, Helga. "Political Transition Processes in Central and Eastern Europe," *Comparative Politics*, 26:4 (July 1994): 379–394.

Williams, Nicholas. "Partnership for Peace: Permanent Fixture or Declining Asset?" *Survival*, 38:1 (Spring 1996): 98–110.

"The Future of Partnership for Peace," *Balkan Forum* 4:2 (June 1996): 255–283.

Wlachowský, Miroslav. "Foreign Policy," in Martin Bútora and Péter Hunčik, *Global Report on Slovakia: Comprehensive Analyses from 1995 and Trends for 1996* (Bratislava: Sándor Márai Foundation, 1997), 33–53.

Wlachowský, Miroslav, and Alexander Duleba, Pavol Lukáč, and Thomas W. Skladony. "The Foreign Policy of the Slovak Republic," in Martin Bútora and Thomas W. Skladony, *Slovakia 1996–1997: A Global Report on the State of Society* (Bratislava: Institute for Public Affairs, 1998), 81–101.

Wolchik, Sharon. "Democratization and Political Participation in Slovakia," in Karen Dawisha and Bruce Parrott, eds., *The Consolidation of Democracy in East-Central Europe* (New York: Cambridge University Press, 1997), 197–244.

Wyzan, Michael. "A Reluctant Star in the Economic Sphere," *Transition*, 2:25 (13 December 1996): 41–43, 64.

Yanakiev, Yantsislav. "Bulgarian Soldiers as Peacekeepers: The Viewpoints of The Military and Citizens," *Security Policy: Information Bulletin of the Ministry of Defence of the Republic of Bulgaria*, no. 1 (1999): 39–50.

Yost, David S. *NATO Transformed: The Alliance's New Roles in International Security* (Washington, D.C.: United States Institute of Peace Press, 1998).

"The New NATO and Collective Security," *Survival*, 40:2 (Summer 1998): 135–160.

Zloch-Christy, Iliana. *Bulgaria in a Time of Change: Economic and Political Dimensions* (Brookfield, VT: Avebury, 1996).

Index

Action Committee for the
    Democratization of the Army
    (CADA, Romania), 153–154, 167
Afghanistan, 37, 64, 174, 195, 235
Albania, 4, 5, 30, 135, 221, 231, 235
Albright, Madeleine, 104
Aleksandrov, Valentin, 201, 214
Ananiev, Georgi, 204, 208
Andrejčák, Imrich, 55, 72
Antonenko, Oksana, 36
Antonescu, Ion, 131–132, 161–162, 226
Association of Slovak Soldiers, 75, 80
Atlantic Club of Bulgaria, 195
Austria, 59, 60, 64, 89, 96, 98, 100, 101,
    116

Babiuc, Victor, 152, 157, 159–160
Bacon, Walter M., Jr., 144
Badalan, Eugen, 171
Bajuk, Andrej, 92, 96, 111
Balkans, 3, 11, 14, 24, 89, 99, 235
Baltic states, 20, 231–232
    and NATO expansion, 20, 23, 25, 29,
        31, 231–232
    and Russia/Soviet Union, 5
    and Russian minorities, 20, 31
Barnett, Richard, 12
Başescu, Traian, 149
Bay of Piran, 102
Bebler, Anton, 93

Belarus, 19
Belascu, Aron, 133
Bereuter, Doug, 190
Berlusconi, Silvio, 101
Biden, Joseph, 11, 24, 100
Bosnia, 104, 105
Bradley, Bill, 17
Brezhnev, Leonid, 235
Bruncko, Martin, 71
Brzezinski, Zbigniew, 16
Bulgaria, 2, 3, 4, 5, 10, 30, 39, 137, 173,
    175–216
    corruption, 179–180, 201, 211, 216
    defense industry, 215–216
    defense spending, 214
    democracy in, 180–181
    domestic politics, 175–181
    economy, 29, 181–184
    and EU expansion, 180, 183–184, 189
    first round of NATO expansion, 4
    foreign relations, 19, 141–142,
        187–192
    military doctrine, 185–186
    Ministry of Defense, 186, 193–195,
        198–205, 207, 209–210, 213
    NATO membership campaign, 180,
        190–191, 192–197
    preparations for NATO membership,
        29, 195–197, 216, 217–230; Annual
        National Plan, 201; Membership

Index

Bulgaria (*cont.*)
Action Plan, 206, 208, 209;
Partnership for Peace, 187, 196–197,
208; Planning and Review Process,
197, 208
security situation, 3, 184–186
support for membership, 195–196
wars in the former Yugoslavia,
185–186, 194–195
Bulgarian Armed Forces, 185, 197–216
air force, 208, 211
civilian control of, 197–206;
institutional arrangements, 199–202;
problems of, 203–205
conscription, 212–213
depoliticization, 197–199
General Staff, 185, 199–205, 207–208
living standards, 208
military education, 204, 209–210
navy, 215
officers, 198–199, 207, 209–212
reform of, 206–209, 213–214
peacekeeping, 191–192, 194–195
political attitudes, 198–199, 211
and Russian connection, 203–204
size, 207–208, 213
soldiers, 212–213
social organizations, 211
social views of, 211–212
training, 208, 210–211
weapons, 191, 214–215
Burns, Nicholas, 51, 234
Bush, George W., 9, 32, 35, 38, 100, 144,
174, 194, 236–237
Buzatu, Gheorghe, 131

Čapek, Karel, 68
Carmichael, Cathie, 92, 104
Carpenter, Ted Galen, 17, 18, 21, 29
Ceauşescu, Nicolae, 124, 129, 139,
151–152, 157
Central Asia, 235
Chechnya, 21, 37
Cheney, Dick, 194
Chelaru, Mircea, 154, 158, 161
Chernomyrdin, Viktor, 56
China, People's Republic of, 37
Chirac, Jacques, 24, 143

Chitac, Mihai, 152
Chubais, Anatolii, 34
Cioflina, Dumitru, 158, 159
Ciorbea, Victor, 127–128, 134
Clark, Wesley, 194
"clash of civilizations" thesis, 29–30,
32–33
Clinton Administration, 12, 13, 15–16,
17–18, 20, 23
Clinton, Bill, 12, 146
Cmilansky, Jan, 69
Cohen, William, 100, 208
Congressional Budget Office, 12, 17, 18
Conry, Barbara, 21
Constantinescu, Emil, 126, 128, 131, 138,
139–141, 145, 146–147, 152, 157,
159, 164, 168, 171, 173, 219
Conventional Forces Europe (CFE)
Treaty, 86, 170, 190, 214
Council of Europe, 31, 99, 133, 187
Croatia, 96, 97, 101–102, 223, 235
Csáky, Pál, 49, 52
Czech Army, 1, 76
Czech Republic, 1, 9, 15, 18, 52, 54, 60,
66, 89, 217, 220
defense allocations, 1, 228–229
NATO membership, 2, 17–18, 23,
26–27, 28, 234
Czechoslovakia, 4, 10, 45, 54, 68, 72
break-up of, 46–47

Danu, Vasile, 173
Degeratu, Constantin, 145, 158, 159–160
Demirel, Suleyman, 189
Demšar, Drago, 111
Denmark, 25, 143
Department of Defense (U.S.), see
Pentagon
Department of State (U.S.), 23, 51–52
Dnevnik, 111
Drnovšek, Janez, 90, 92, 95, 107
Dzhurov, Dobri, 176, 197
Dzurinda, Mikuláš, 46, 50, 51, 53, 58,
59, 63, 65, 66, 87, 219

Economist, The, 135, 219
Equipment Procurement Strategy
(Romania), 171–172

Index

Estonia, 2, 4, 220
Euro-Atlantic Center (Bucharest), 149
European Commission, 31, 184
European Court of Justice, 31
European Parliament, 31, 53, 96, 131
European Union (EU), 4, 14, 30–31, 187, 221
  integration of new states, 30–31;
    Bulgaria, 180, 183–184, 189;
    Romania, 31, 125, 135, 136, 139,
    141–143; Slovakia, 53–54; Slovenia,
    94–96, 99, 100
  and NATO Expansion, 21, 30–31

Fico, Róbert, 66
Fodor, Lajos, 1
Fontaine, Nicole, 96
France, 24, 44, 98, 143
Freedom House, 47–48
Frlec, Boris, 102
Frunzaverde, Sorin, 157
Funar, Gheorghe, 126, 161

Gaddis, John Lewis, 16
Gajdoš, Jozef, 72, 75–76
Gallagher, Tom, 127–128
Garfinkle, Adam, 39
Garrett, Joseph, 76, 79, 85
Gašparovič, Ivan, 74
Gaulieder, František, 48
Georgi Stoikov Rakovski Legion, 211
Germany, 15, 20, 59, 98
Geoana, Mircea, 140, 173–174
Goldgeier, James, 23
Gorbachev, Mikhail S., 20, 176
Gotsev, Lyuben, 187
Gow, James, 92, 104
Grachev, Pavel, 140
Greece, 3, 11, 19, 184, 189, 223
Grizold, Anton, 97, 98, 111, 113, 116
Gruver, Josef, 188
Guse, Stefan, 152
Gypsies, 47, 60, 127, 132, 181, 212, 218, 219

Habsburg Empire, 89
Haider, Jörg, 101
Hamžik, Pavol, 50, 53

Hart, Gary 17
Havel, Václav, 12, 99, 142
Helms, Jessie, 12
Herspring, Dale R., 153
Hombach, Bodo, 191
Horn, Gyula, 57
Howard, Michael, 25
Hungarian Defense Forces (HDF), 1
Hungarians
  in Romania, 127, 141–142, 149, 219, 223
  in Slovakia, 47, 49, 52, 54, 58–59, 218, 223
Hungary, 1, 3, 9, 10, 15, 18, 22, 23, 24,
    52, 89, 96, 97, 133–134, 137, 217, 220
  defense allocations, 1, 26, 27, 228–229
  foreign relations, 19, 23, 24, 132
  NATO membership, 2, 17–18, 26–28, 234
  preparations for NATO membership, 1, 22
  "status law," 59, 100, 132–133, 142–143
Hunter, Robert, 32, 142
Huntington, Samuel P., 29

Iceland, 143
Iliescu, Ion, 126–127, 128, 130–132, 134,
    136–137, 140, 142, 145, 147, 151,
    152, 154, 156–157, 168, 182, 219, 223
Institute for Research on Life Quality
    (Bucharest), 135
International Monetary Fund (IMF), 4,
    134, 170, 182–183
Ionel, Vasile, 158
Ionescu, Dudu, 138
Iran, 36
Isarescu, Mugur, 127, 128, 135
Italy, 96, 97, 100–101

Janša, Janez, 92–94, 108, 111–114, 182
Jelinčič, Zmago, 107
Jones, Christopher D., 44
Jones, Elizabeth, 51
Jowitt, Ken, 167
Juhász, Ferenc, 27–28

Index

Kačin, Jelko, 103, 111
Kalman, Jozef, 62
Kamp, Karl-Heinz, 38
Kanis, Pavol, 50, 62, 72, 73, 78, 85
Kaplan, Robert, 32
Kay, Sean, 237
Kazakhstan, 221
Kennan, George F., 16
Kipp, Jacob, 44
Kissinger, Henry, 12, 16
Klaus, Václav, 46
Kleiber, Klaus-Peter, 146
Kolev, Nikola, 205
Konrad Adenauer Stiftung, 188
Kosovo, 5, 67
    war in, 5, 27, 28, 64, 87, 146
Kostov, Ivan, 178, 179, 182, 184,
    188–189, 193, 194, 206, 213,
    219
Kováč, Michal, 48–49, 58, 75
Kozlík, Sergej, 54
Kozyrev, Andrei, 34
Kramer, Mark, 232
Krapež, Alojz, 111
Krasnaya Zvezda, 36
Krauthammer, Charles, 236–237
Kravchuk, Leonid, 58
Kučan, Milan, 90–93, 107, 113, 120
Kukan, Eduard, 58, 65, 78, 228

Latvia, 2, 4
Legvold, Robert, 34
Lengyel, László, 133–134
Lithuania, 2, 4
Ludzhev, Dimitûr, 199
Lugar, Richard, 11
Lukanov, Andrei, 176

Macedonia, 4, 5, 30, 184, 186, 188–189,
    223–224, 235
Maior, Gheorghe, 173
Mandelbaum, Michael, 17, 18, 21, 39
Manfred Wörner Association
    (Bucharest), 149
Mareš, Petr, 27
Marin, Angel, 205
Marinček, Lojze, 111
Marino, Adrian, 134, 136

Marshall Antonescu League, 131
Martonyi, János, 59
Mastny, Vojtech, 149
Matlock, Jack, 17
McNamara, Robert S., 17
Mečiar, Vladimír, 24, 45–51, 53, 54–58,
    61–62, 66, 72, 76, 87, 141, 182, 219,
    221
Medgyessy, Péter, 59
Membership Action Plan (MAP), see
    NATO/MAP
Mendelsohn, Jack, 31
Michael I, (former) King of Romania,
    150–151
Migaš, Jozef, 63
Mihai, Lucian, 130
Mihailova, Nadezhda, 190, 193
Mihov, Miho, 203, 205, 211, 213
Mikluš, Marian, 74
Militaru, Nicolae, 153–154, 157
The Military Balance, 169, 227–228
Military Career Guide (Romania), 168
Milošević, Slobodan, 141, 187
Mladenov, Petûr, 176, 203
Mladina, 108
Moldova, 48, 135, 137–138, 140–141,
    223
Montenegro, 105
Moravčik, Jozef, 47, 62
Mueller, John 181
Mutafchiev, Yordan 198

Nastase, Adrian, 130, 132, 133, 135, 136,
    140–141, 147, 149, 157, 165
Nastase, Ilie, 127
The Nation, 12
National Assembly (Bulgaria), 178, 193,
    196, 199–202
National Assembly (Slovenia), 92, 93,
    107, 110
National Association of Romanian
    Soldiers (ANMR), 161, 167
National Council (Slovakia), 49, 55, 70
National Council (Slovenia), 110
National Security Council (Bulgaria),
    200, 202
National Security Council (Slovenia),
    111

Index

NATO (North Atlantic Treaty
Organization)
Membership Action Plan (MAP), 4,
25–26, 63, 226–227; participants, 4
"open door" policy, 3, 32
Planning and Review Process (PARP),
115, 164, 226–227
as "political honor society," 29
Study on NATO Enlargement, 43
NATO accession requirements, 2, 3
military reform, 1
pilot training, 1
"NATO Day" (Romania), 151
NATO expansion 1, 2, 10–44, 230–237
criteria of, 39–44; campaign for
membership, 41, 224–225;
civil-military relations, 41–43,
225–226; defense expenditure,
43–44, 226–228; democracy, 40,
217–219; market economy, 40,
219–222; military reform, 43–44,
226–227, 228; neighborly relations,
40–41, 222–224; support for
membership, 41, 224–225
and European Union, 21, 30–31
extent of, 22–23, 235–237
first round, 1, 2, 3, 12–25; arguments
opposing, 16–22; arguments
supporting, 12–16; and benefits for
NATO, 14; cost of, 13, 17–18;
lessons of, 26–29; military
implications, 21–22; necessity of,
18–19; and potential entanglements,
19–20; and Russia, 15, 20–21, 31;
and security for Eastern Europe, 14;
selection of new members, 23–25;
and spread of democracy, 13–14
postponement of, 38–39
second round, 2, 25–38, 230–235;
arguments opposing, 26–32,
230–235; arguments supporting,
32–33, 230–235; cost of, 31–32;
impact of September 11, 2001, 29,
31, 236–237; necessity of, 32–33; and
"open door" policy, 32; as political
award, 28; options, 232–234;
preparedness of candidates, 29–30,
217–230; and Russia, 31, 33, 34–38

NATO summits
London (1990), 10
Madrid (1997), 25, 32, 38, 62, 104,
146, 172, 173, 192–193
Prague (2002), 2, 9, 26, 29, 37, 65, 67,
151, 206, 235–236
Washington (1999), 2, 25, 104, 206
NATO-Russia Council, 36
NATO-Russia Permanent Joint Council,
10, 20
Necas, Petr, 1
New York Times, The, 16, 52
Nitze, Paul, 12, 17
Noev, Boyko, 209, 215
North Atlantic Cooperation Council,
10
North Atlantic Treaty Organization, see
NATO
Norway, 25

Odom, William, 16
Oglinda TV, 132
"Open Sky" agreements, 18, 150
Orbán, Viktor, 22, 59, 133
Organization for Economic Cooperation
and Development (OECD), 58,
134–135
Organization for Security and
Cooperation in Europe (OSCE), 4,
35, 140, 237

Pantev, Plamen, 207
Papandreou, George, 189
Partnership for Peace (PfP), 10, 11, 39,
61, 226–227
Parvanov, Georgi, 180, 196, 209
Pascas, Vasile, 141–142
Pascu, Ioan Mircea, 137, 147, 157, 161,
168, 173–174, 188
Pasi, Solomon, 189, 195, 200
Paunescu, Adrian, 132
Pavlov, Dimitûr, 214
Pentagon, 13, 18
Perlmutter, Amos, 17, 18, 31
Perry, William, 100, 103
Peterle, Lojze, 91
Petrov, Lyuben, 205
Petrov, Petûr, 204

Pirinski, Georgi, 196
Plangu, Ion-Mircea, 137
Poland, 1, 9, 10, 15, 18, 19, 52, 89, 217, 220
defense allocations, 1, 27, 228–229
NATO membership, 2, 17–18, 23, 26–27, 234
Popescu, Mihai, 162, 166, 170
Popov, Ivan, 203
Powell, Colin, 162, 194
Pravda (Bratislava), 66
Primakov, Yevgenii, 190
Prodi, Romano, 101
Public Against Violence, 46
Putin, Vladimir, 37, 38, 236, 237

Radio Free Europe, 236
Ralston, Joseph, 27
Ramet, Sabrina, 91
Rand Corporation, 13, 17–18
Ratchev, Valeri, 185, 209
Republic of Slovenia Brigade (MORiS), 113
Rice, Condoleezza, 35
Robertson, George, 27, 28, 35, 37, 51, 64, 66, 118, 123, 148, 235
Roma, see Gypsies
Roman, Petre, 152, 159
Romania, 2, 3, 4, 5, 10, 19, 29, 30, 39, 67, 124–174, 187–188
corruption, 128
defense industry, 172
defense spending, 163, 169–170
democracy in, 29, 124–126, 130–131
domestic politics, 125–133
economy, 133–136, 170–171
and EU expansion, 31, 125, 135, 136, 139, 141–143
first round of NATO expansion, 4, 23–24, 139
foreign relations, 19, 139–144
military diplomacy, 150
military doctrine, 138–139
Ministry of Defense, 137–138, 153–164, 168–171
and Most Favored Nation status, 143–144

NATO membership campaign, 144–151
preparations for NATO membership, 29, 172–174, 217–230; Annual National Plan, 164–165; Membership Action Plan, 163; Partnership for Peace, 139, 148; Planning and Review Process, 163–165; Revolution of 1989, 124, 125, 151–153; *Securitate*, 130, 144, 151, 157; security situation, 3, 136–139; support for membership, 149, 165; war in the former Yugoslavia, 138, 146, 166
Romanian armed forces,
in Afghanistan, 144, 150, 174
air force, 166–167
civilian control of, 154–162, 172–173; institutional arrangements, 154–158; problems of, 158–162
conscription, 168–169
depoliticization, 151–154
General Staff, 139, 145, 155, 158–162, 167
internal use of, 158–161
living standards, 167
military education, 157–158, 166
officers, 164, 165–168
reform of, 162–165
peacekeeping, 148
political attitudes, 165–166
size, 162–164, 169
soldiers, 168–169
social organizations, 153–154, 161, 167
social views of, 167–168
training, 166–167
weapons, 170–172
Rosapepe, James, 147, 173
Rühe, Volker, 30
Rumer, Eugene, 234
Rupel, Dimitrij, 95, 123
Russia, 3, 12, 15–16, 19, 31, 33–38, 39, 48, 56–57, 135, 140, 190–191, 215, 221, 224
and NATO enlargement, 15, 20–21, 31, 33, 34–38, 235–237
potential NATO membership, 35–36

Index

Sarvaš, Štefan, 64, 80
Saxecoburggotski, Simeon, 179–180, 183, 188, 195, 201
Schmidt, Helmut, 11
Schlafly, Phyllis, 12
Schssel, Wolfgang, 101
Schuster, Rudolf, 49–50, 58, 63
Sendov, Blagovest, 193
September 11, 2001, 29, 63, 150, 173, 174, 236
Serbia, 5, 19, 105, 137, 141
Serebrian, Oleg, 146
Severin, Adrian, 146
Shafir, Michael, 129
Shalamanov, Velizar, 203, 206
Shaposhnikov, Evgenii, 34
Simeon II, (former) King of Bulgaria, *see* Saxecoburggotski
Šimko, Ivan, 73
Simon, Jeffrey, 55, 97, 116, 234
Šitek, Ján, 61, 72, 75, 76
Slovak armed forces, 67
  air force, 77, 82
  civilian control of, 68; institutional arrangements, 70–74; problems of, 72–73, 74–76
  conscription, 83–84
  depoliticization, 67–69
  General Staff, 70, 72–75
  living standards, 82–83
  lustration of, 69
  military education, 75, 77, 81
  officers, 80–83
  reform of, 76–80
  peacekeeping, 67
  political attitudes, 80
  size, 84–85
  soldiers, 83–84
  social organizations, 75–76, 80
  training, 79–80, 81–82
  weapons, 60, 85–86
Slovakia, 2, 3, 4, 5, 15, 45–88, 89
  corruption, 50
  defense industry, 86–87
  defense spending, 84–85
  domestic politics, 45–52; impact of NATO candidacy on, 50–51
  economy, 52–54

  and EU expansion, 53–54
  first round of NATO expansion, 4, 60–62
  foreign relations, 19, 54–55, 56–61
  military doctrine, 55–56
  Military Intelligence Service, 69
  Ministry of Defense, 69–73, 75–79
  NATO membership campaign, 61–67
  preparations for NATO membership, 32, 79–81, 87–88, 217–230; Annual National Plan, 71; Membership Action Plan, 63, 71, 77, 85; Partnership for Peace, 61, 64
  security situation, 3, 54–56
  support for membership, 64–65
  war in Kosovo, 64, 65, 67, 87
Slovene Army, 108, 115
  civilian control of, 110–112; institutional arrangements, 111–113; problems of, 113–114
  conscription, 120
  depoliticization, 108–109
  General Staff, 111–113
  military education, 109, 112, 118–119
  military exercises, 105–106
  officers, 118–120
  peacekeeping, 105–106
  public views of, 119–120
  reform of, 115–118, 121
  size, 117, 120–121
  soldiers, 120
  Territorial Defense, 108–109, 113
  weapons, 121–122
Slovenia, 2, 3, 4, 5, 52, 89–123, 220
  defense industry, 122
  defense spending, 112, 121
  economy, 95–96
  first round of NATO expansion, 23–24, 98–9, 103
  foreign relations, 98–102, 105–106
  domestic politics, 90–95
  and EU expansion, 94–96, 99, 100
  independence, 90–91
  military doctrine, 97–98
  Ministry of Defense, 104, 110–121
  NATO membership campaign, 94, 102–107

Slovenia (*cont.*)
  preparations for NATO membership,
    31–32, 122–123, 217–230; Annual
    National Plan, 105, 115–116;
    Membership Action Plan, 105, 115;
    Planning and Review Process, 115;
    Partnership for Peace, 103
  security situation, 3, 96–98, 103–104
  support for membership, 106–107
  "Ten-Day War," 90–91, 108
  war in Bosnia, 104
  and Yugoslavia, 90–91, 97–99; and
    Yugoslav Federal Army (JNA),
    108–109, 115
Smer (Slovakia), 51, 66
Sofiansky, Ivan, 182
Solana, Javier, 21–22, 62, 87, 193, 194
Soviet Union, 10, 12, 210
Spiroiu, Nicolae, 157
Stability Pact for Southeastern Europe,
  99, 131, 191–192
Staliyski, Alexander, 201
Stanculescu, Victor, 137, 152, 153, 157
Standard & Poor's, 95
Stank, Jozef, 65, 73, 78, 88, 234
State Defense Council (Slovakia), 70, 71
Stefan, Adina, 160, 170
Stockholm International Peace Research
  Institute, 227, 229
Stoyanov, Petûr, 178, 179–180, 189, 191,
  192, 200, 205, 206, 227
Supreme Council of National Defense
  (Romania), 138–139, 154–157
Šustar, Boris, 94
Svinarov, Nikolai, 200, 201, 205, 215
Switzerland, 116
Syria, 36
Székely, Ervin, 133

Talbott, Strobe, 12, 190
Talpes, Ioan, 130
Tinca, Gheorghe, 145, 157
Tismaneanu, Vladimir, 126
Tito, Josip Broz, 108
Titov, Vladimir, 191
Toth, Ronald, 50
Transparency International, 94, 221–222
Tuchyňa, Pavol, 73

Tudjman, Franjo, 235
Tudor, Corneliu Vadim, 126, 129, 132,
  133, 149, 161, 182
Turkey, 3, 11, 19, 184, 189, 223
Turks in Bulgaria, 176–177, 181, 212,
  218
Turnšek, Tit, 111
Tvrdik, Jaroslav, 27

Ukraine, 58, 60, 67, 137, 140, 235
United Kingdom, 44, 143
United Nations' Human Development
  Index, 52, 221–222
United States
  NATO membership of, 44, 235–237
  relations with Russia, 20–21, 35–37,
    235–237
United States Air Force Academy, 38–39
University of Ljubljana, 112
University of World Economy (Sofia), 204
U.S. Steel, 53
Uzbekistan, 221

Vacaroiu, Nicolae, 127, 138
Vacek, Miroslav, 68
Vaclavik, Milan, 67
Vasile, Radu, 128, 146
Verdet, Ilie, 126
Verheugen, Gnter, 51, 136
Vershbow, Alexander, 37
Videnov, Zhan, 178, 182, 190, 193, 195,
  196, 205, 219
Visegrad Four, see Visegrad Group
Visegrad Group, 15, 47, 53, 57–58, 59,
  61, 64, 66, 145
Voinovich, George, 100
Voroshilov General Staff Academy,
  203–204

Warsaw Pact, 12, 15, 68, 139, 167, 172,
  187, 215
The Washington Post, 174, 236–237
Washington Treaty (1949), 10–11, 25,
  236, 237
Watts, Larry, 170
Die Welt, 130
Western European Union, 187
World Bank, 4, 50

Index

Yugoslavia, 8, 15, 89, 90–91, 98–99, 141, 184–186

Zantovsky, Michael, 1
Zatorsky, Stanislaw, 74

Zeman, Miloš, 1, 28
Zhelev, Zhelyu, 177, 190, 193, 195, 199–200, 203, 205
Zhirinovsky, Vladimir, 34
Zhivkov, Todor, 175–176, 197, 213
Zhuganov, Gennadii, 34

For EU product safety concerns, contact us at Calle de José Abascal, 56–1°,
28003 Madrid, Spain or eugpsr@cambridge.org.

www.ingramcontent.com/pod-product-compliance
Ingram Content Group UK Ltd.
Pitfield, Milton Keynes, MK11 3LW, UK
UKHW011319060825
461487UK00005B/197